THE CONSECRATED URN

An Interpretation of Keats
in Terms of Growth and Form

BY

BERNARD BLACKSTONE

*Byron Professor of English Literature in the
University of Athens*

LONGMANS, GREEN AND CO

LONDON • NEW YORK • TORONTO

LONGMANS, GREEN AND CO LTD
6 & 7 CLIFFORD STREET, LONDON W1

THIBAULT HOUSE, THIBAULT SQUARE, CAPE TOWN
605–611 LONSDALE STREET, MELBOURNE C1
443 LOCKHART ROAD, HONG KONG
ACCRA, AUCKLAND, IBADAN
KINGSTON (JAMAICA), KUALA LUMPUR
LAHORE, NAIROBI, SALISBURY (RHODESIA)

LONGMANS, GREEN AND CO INC
119 WEST 40TH STREET, NEW YORK 18

LONGMANS, GREEN AND CO
20 CRANFIELD ROAD, TORONTO 16

ORIENT LONGMANS PRIVATE LTD
CALCUTTA, BOMBAY, MADRAS
DELHI, HYDERABAD, DACCA

First published 1959

PRINTED IN GREAT BRITAIN BY
SPOTTISWOODE, BALLANTYNE AND CO LTD
LONDON AND COLCHESTER

FOR
BASIL WILLEY

CONTENTS

Earth first proceeds from the intelligible earth which comprehends all the intelligible orders of the gods, and from the intellectual earth which is co-ordinated with heaven. For our earth, being analogous to these, eternally abides, as in the centre of heaven; by which being every way comprehended, it becomes full of generative power and demiurgic perfection. The true earth, therefore, is not this corporeal and gross bulk, but an animal endued with a divine soul and a divine body. For it contains an immaterial and separate intellect, and a divine soul energizing about this intellect, and an ethereal body proximately depending on this soul; and, lastly, this visible bulk, which is on all sides animated and filled with life from its inspiring soul, and through which it generates and nourishes lives of all-various kinds. . . . So that the earth is a divine animal, full of intellectual and animastic essences, and of immaterial powers. . . .

For she not only yields us fruits, and nourishes our bodies through these, but she fills our souls with illuminations from her own divine soul, and through her intellect awakens ours from its oblivious sleep. And thus, through the whole of herself, she becomes the nurse of our whole composition.

Thomas Taylor, Introduction to Timæus (from Proclus)

If you want to understand the invisible, look carefully at the visible.

The Talmud

But men do not understand how to observe the invisible through the visible.

Hippocrates, Regimen, I, xi

Consider the lilies of the field, how they grow.

Matthew, vi, 28

Seercraft is after this fashion. By the visible it gets knowledge of the invisible, by the invisible knowledge of the visible, by the present knowledge of the future, by the dead knowledge of the living. Seercraft herein copies the nature and life of man. A man by union with a woman begets a child; by the visible he gets knowledge of the invisible so that it will be.

Hippocrates, Regimen, I, xii

PREFACE

SIR THOMAS BROWNE apologizes, in the Epistle Dedicatory of *The Garden of Cyrus*, for the oddity of his book. The baroque little treatise which brought Coleridge to the point of seeing 'quincunxes in heaven above, quincunxes in earth below, and quincunxes in the water beneath the earth; quincunxes in deity, quincunxes in the mind of man, quincunxes in bones, in the optic nerves, in roots of trees, in leaves, in petals, in every thing', is indeed no common invention. It spans times, sciences, speculations; ranging 'into extraneous Things, and many Parts of Art and Nature'. Browne defends these excursions, and with them the general plan of his book, on the plea of necessity. It is mid-seventeenth century: for over two hundred years now books have been pouring from the presses of Europe. There are few topics left to discuss: and originality is out of the question. 'The Field of Knowledge hath been so traced, it is hard to spring any thing new.' And so one is driven into eccentricity, into extravagances. 'In this multiplicity of writing, bye and barren Themes are best fitted for invention.' Such themes 'allow excursions, and venially admit of collaterall truths, though at some distance from their principals. Wherein if we sometimes take wide liberty, we are not single, but erre by great example'.

I have taken comfort from Sir Thomas's own great example in writing the following pages. At three centuries' distance from Browne, we may feel even more ruefully than he that the field of knowledge has been traced and re-traced; it is hard indeed, and most of all perhaps in the stony corner that we call literary criticism, to spring anything new. My theme is Keats: not a bye and barren theme in itself, but neither was Browne's theme of gardens: the oddity lay in treating 'so spruce a subject' within the quincuncial framework. The oddity of my own treatment lies in the botanico-physiologico-cosmogonical slant on which I approach, very tentatively, my subject.

Tentatively: since, unlike Browne, I have no professional competence in these fields. Browne disclaims any ambition 'to multiply Vegetable Divisions by Quincuncial and Reticulate Plants; or erect a new Phytology'. Still less do I pretend to erect a phyto-criticism. The idea of this book came to me accidentally; reading D'Arcy Thompson's *Growth and Form* and Agnes Arber's *The Natural Philosophy of Plant Form* at the same time as I was reading Keats for quite another purpose, I was struck by some curious parallels. I remembered that Keats's early training was medical; I remembered the little sketches of plants he had made in the margin of his lecture note-book. I remembered that Browne too was a doctor; and Keats's sketches reminded me of the illustrations to *The Botanic Garden* of another doctor-poet. Darwin's verses and notes led me on to the Mysteries, led me back to Plato and Hesiod. I re-read Bailey's letters in *The Keats Circle*.

I was reading D'Arcy Thompson and Mrs Arber because of a life-long interest in form, and particularly in plant-form; but the reader need fear no botanical profundities in the following chapters. The morphology is of the slenderest. My private interest gave me the direction; once that was taken, I found myself able to use Keats's own terms, almost invariably, to express my ideas about Keats. This is so because Keats's poetry *is* a poetry of growth and form. I am not begging any question here: most readers, I suppose, have felt more or less vaguely the biological, the warmly creative, pulsing, burgeoning and occasionally sticky quality in Keats. Some have been repelled by it. The Arnoldian (and now stereotyped) 'sensuous' barely conceals an antipathy.

Keats would not have become a medical student if he had felt no interest in the structure of the human body. He was not a person to be pushed into studies distasteful to him. To the end he kept up his medical reading for its general usefulness; to the end he toyed with the idea of practising as a doctor. He preferred to be a poet, of course; but he would have made a good doctor. His profound humanism as well as his technical interest in structures, his curious detachment mingled with an unreserved giving of that part of himself that was not detached, mark the true physician. But the greater passion prevailed. Not without some tinge from the lesser —or rather, from the overriding and passionless activity which governed both the lesser and the greater: his 'vast idea', his 'sensation' of the principle of analogy.

His verse moves among resonant hollows, foci of speechful silence. The winds breathe 'Eolian magic from their lucid wombs'; sea-noises in caves are therapeutic; Moneta displays 'In the dark secret chambers of her skull' the agonies of a fallen dynasty. Power dwells in these spaces. And power is gathered up, constantly, into 'the supreme shape' of the urn. As a title for this book two of Keats's own phrases suggested themselves to me; the one I have chosen, and 'The Poetry of Earth', which I have reserved for my Part Two. The second is the diffusive title; the first is the concentrated. Keats's poetry presents a constant pattern: the urn, the artefact, standing in the midst of a floral context; and we can view the pattern in two ways. We can view it as centripetal: the forces of nature—growth—concentrated inwards upon the urn—form; or we can view it as centrifugal: the power of the urn—form— spreading outwards into the processes of nature—growth. An inveterate Platonist, I have preferred the second alternative. The principle precedes the manifestation: we can discuss time in terms of eternity more cogently than eternity in terms of time. But the point comes, of course, at which our distinction is meaningless. Otherwise we have not understood Keats's poetry.

Urns stud Darwin's poetry too. He was a good writer, in his way; it is not Keats's way, and it is not the way of most poets, but there is room in the Pantheon for Darwin. He is in the line of Hesiod, Lucretius, Virgil. He wrote about real things (though in an unreal convention) and he had his own feeling for beauty; agreeing with him or disagreeing, we find ourselves unexpectedly upon new tracks. His verse is always centripetal, the urn-figure arising from the processes of growth: there is no suggestion of a principle. Reading him, Keats must have felt his 'realm of

Flora' somewhat desiccated; but his hollows are there, in caves, calyxes, seed-cases, fruits; and his elementals, posturing as sylphs and salamanders.

Erasmus Darwin looms large in the first part of my book; he may be thought somewhat to disappear from the later parts. Some of the chapter epigraphs keep him in view. But I would like the reader to think of him as a churchyard yew, spreading his wide branches in storm and sunlight over the more remarkable writers who follow him; overshadowing them, dropping an occasional cone, so to speak, into the pools of their verse. Even Blake lives to some extent under his shadow. So does Coleridge (who also fades, though less completely). Much of his thought answers Darwin's: much of it is answered by Keats. I link the three men in terms of wariness, awareness, unawareness: there is thus a progress and a supersession. Plato enters where Coleridge fades out.

A pervading influence is Blake: an influence (better, perhaps, to call him a function) in the complex of Hermetic, neo-Platonist, occultist thought which seized early upon Keats. I have elsewhere argued that Keats had read Blake: in particular, the *Poetical Sketches*. That was five years ago: later reading and thinking have fortified my conviction. I am still not prepared to demonstrate (though I believe) that Keats was acquainted with the Prophetic Books. We are not, in any case, concerned with sources and influences but with affinities: with mental structures which here and there overlap, however wildly they may proliferate in other directions. Darwin, Coleridge, Keats, Blake, were all concerned with analogy; with attacking a cosmic problem. That brings the first two of them together with Keats at the beginning of my book; but the ways in which they tackle the problem differ profoundly from Keats's way, and when they have served their purpose of illustration and contrast, we let them go. Not so with Blake, whose *wholeness* of approach is germane to Keats's from beginning to end. They were whole, too, as men in a way the other Romantics were not. Their friends felt it: Palmer's tribute to Blake, and Bailey's to Keats, witness to something shining from the two men. In a book which I hope will follow this I intend to discuss the

Romantic movement as a disintegration and reintegration, Blake presenting a synthesis which breaks up in Wordsworth, Coleridge, Byron and Shelley to be restored, as far as was permitted, in Keats.

References

The basic texts are indicated as follows:

POEMS: *Keats' Poetical Works*, edited by H. W. Garrod, Oxford University Press, 1939.

LETTERS: *The Letters of John Keats* (4th edition), edited by M. Buxton Forman, Oxford University Press, 1952.

K.C.: *The Keats Circle*, edited by H. E. Rollins, 2 volumes, Harvard University Press, 1948.

Secondary texts:

K.: *Poetry and Prose of William Blake*, edited by Geoffrey Keynes, complete in one volume, The Nonesuch Press, 1927.

Timæus: Thomas Taylor's translation reprinted with a Foreword by R. Catesby Taliaferro in the Bollingen Series, 1944.

Collected Letters: The Collected Letters of S. T. Coleridge, edited by E. L. Griggs, Oxford University Press, 1956.

The references are to pages, except where (in the case of quotations from Keats's letters) I have indicated date and correspondent. In the case of references to the *Timæus*, I have generally added section numbers (in brackets) after the page numbers for the convenience of readers using editions so numbered.

I

THE VAST IDEA

Chapter One

THE BODY OF DIVINE ANALOGY

It has been commonly observed in compliment to the ingenious of our profession, that Apollo was god of verse as well as of physic; and in all ages the most celebrated practitioners of our country were the particular favourites of the muses. Poetry to physic is indeed like the gilding of a pill; it makes the art shine, and covers the severity of the doctor with the agreeableness of the companion.

The Tatler, No. 240.

ADDISON'S arch comment on the relations of poetry and physic belongs to the close of the first decade of the eighteenth century. The names he brings forward later in his essay—Saffold, Lilly, Case—are not impressive; though Lilly has his place in any discussion of Hermetic thought in England. If, however, Addison could have cast his gaze forward to the close of the last decade of the century, he would have noted that the most celebrated practitioner of physic at that time was indeed a man honoured of the muses: the illustrious Dr Erasmus Darwin. Darwin was doctor and poet, physicist and metaphysician. On the title-page of his most considerable work, *Zoonomia; or, the Laws of Organic Life* (1794–6), he sets this epigraph from Virgil:

Principio cœlum, ac terras, camposque liquentes,
Lucentemque globum lunæ, titaniaque astra
Spiritus intus agit, totamque infusa per artus
Mens agitat molem, et magno se corpore miscet.

VIRG. *Æn.* vi

Earth, on whose lap a thousand nations tread,
And Ocean, brooding his prolific bed,
Night's changeful orb, blue pole, and silvery zones,
Where other worlds encircle other suns,
One mind inhabits, one diffusive Soul
Wields the large limbs, and mingles with the whole.

It is a stirring, an imaginative epigraph; I doubt whether anything comparable to it could have adorned the title-page of any treatise on organic life written between Browne and Darwin; and while the contents of *Zoonomia* do not altogether answer to its promise, it is nonetheless symptomatic of a change that was coming over advanced thought at the turn of the century. For more than a century (the *Principia* was published in 1687, and the autumn term of 1684 had witnessed the delivery of the Lucasian lectures *De Motu Corporum*) the endeavour had been towards mechanical explanations of natural phenomena. Such explanations were widely welcomed. Not by everybody, of course; there had been some resistance from the poets, and a handful of divines had expressed their uneasiness; but on the whole things had gone very well for 'the new philosophy'. By 1794, however, it had become the old philosophy—established, orthodox, a trifle dull even in the eyes of its supporters. It was time to look round for something new.

Something new—or something old. Taking his motto from Virgil, Darwin hints, though no more than hints, at the return to a tradition. When we turn the pages, and come across this (Sect. III, i): '*Motion may be defined to be a variation of figure*; for the whole universe may be considered as one thing possessing a certain figure; the motions of any of its parts are a variation of this figure of the whole', we catch our breath in surprise, for he is here reaching forward to *gestalt* and perhaps back to Hermetic philosophy. When he complains, as a physician, of those expert in other sciences, that 'instead of comparing the properties of animated nature with each other, they, idly ingenious, busied themselves in attempting to explain the laws of life by those of mechanism and chemistry; they considered the body as an hydraulic machine, and the fluids as passing through a series of chemical changes, forgetting that animation was its essential characteristic', we are reminded of an earlier physician who found cause to assert the unity and uniqueness of life against the nascent 'mechanism' of his age. But Browne and his followers began their apologies from a religious basis; John Ray vindicated 'The Wisdom of God manifested in the Works of the Creation', meaning by the last phrase, as he is careful to tell us, 'the Works created by God at first, and by him conserv'd to this Day in the same State and Condition in which they were at first made'; William Derham's *Physico-Theology* had for sub-title 'A Demonstration of the Being and Attributes of God from his Works of Creation'. Darwin has no apologetic bias[1] and makes no assumptions about the immutability of the hexemeral creation: on the contrary he is convinced by his own observations and meditations, reinforced by the accumulating evidence of his day, that the universe from distant galaxy to innermost tapeworm is the theatre of incessant change.

In yet other ways, and ways that concern us more nearly in our present enquiry, Browne and Darwin differ *toto cœlo*. The epigraph from Virgil suggests a concern with analogy, with the idea of an Anima Mundi or plastic power, with the notion of a cosmic animal:

> One Mind inhabits, one diffusive Soul
> Wields the large limbs, and mingles with the whole—

and Darwin is indeed concerned with analogy, but in a strictly limited sense. Within the physical sphere he is prepared to speculate; to go, one might say, to grotesque lengths of speculation;[2] but there comes a point where he draws the line—and that point is on the frontiers of the imagination. No losing himself in a mystery or pursuing his reason to an *O altitudo!* Mystery is abhorrent to him, and speculations tainted by its presence impress him, generally, as tedious and absurd.

Such is the case, as we might anticipate, with works of art. Darwin does not disapprove of poetry; is, for that matter, himself a poet. But he has very definite ideas of what should and should not be attempted by poetry. Verse, for him, is not the mysterious product, or vehicle, of a creative agency having access to truths outside the reach of rational knowledge. It is a pleasant mnemonic device, blending the charms of metre, rhythm, imagery, mytho-

---

[1] See Appendix B, I, 1 for a Baconian disavowal of theological intention.

[2] In, for example, listing the possible genesis of insects from the stamens and pistils of flowers.

logical machinery, to convey scientific or moral ideas. It is essentially an *artifice*, detached from the world of reality, and insusceptible of the laws and analogies that obtain in that world. Let us glance at a paragraph from the Preface to *Zoonomia* which immediately follows my last quotation:

> The great CREATOR of all things has infinitely diversified the works of his hands, but has at the same time stamped a certain similitude on the features of nature, that demonstrates to us, that *the whole is one family of one parent*. On this similitude is founded all rational analogy; which, so long as it is concerned in comparing the essential properties of bodies, leads us to many and important discoveries; but when with licentious activity it links together objects, otherwise discordant, by some fanciful similitude, it may indeed collect ornaments for wit and poetry, but philosophy and truth recoil from its combinations.

Darwin is not simply saying here, with Johnson, that incongruous ideas should not be violently yoked together; he is saying that the tracing of analogies outside the field of *the essential properties of bodies* is illegitimate. Wits and poets do it; from which we may know, by implication, what to think of wit and poetry.

What has become, then, of Virgil's *spiritus*? It has, in truth, little part to play in *Zoonomia*. A brief appearance in the first paragraph of Section I, *Of Motion*, and then we meet it no more. 'The whole of nature may be supposed to consist of two essences or substances; one of which may be termed spirit, and the other matter. The former of these possesses the power to commence or produce motion, and the latter to receive or communicate it.' We can list the motions of matter under two categories, primary and secondary. Secondary motions are those given to or received from other matter in motion. Primary motions fall under three heads, 'those belonging to gravitation, to chemistry, and to life': and there may possibly be a fourth (though this has not been sufficiently investigated) comprising the motions of 'the supposed ethereal fluids of magnetism, electricity, heat, and light'.

In his discussion of the motions of life we might expect Darwin to make use of the idea of spirit which adorns his title-page. But no: while carefully distinguishing vital motions from motions in the other two (or three) classes, he proceeds to account for them in terms of irritability, contraction, sensitivity, and stimulus; in short, in the physiological terms which came natural to him as a medical man. We can have no quarrel with him on this account; but it is not quite what was promised. Indeed, in *Zoonomia* he makes no great effort to grapple with the problem of origins; he reserves this theme for *The Temple of Nature* (1803) where, writing verse, he can give free rein to his fancy and indulge in mythological tropes and irrational analogies. Organic life, he there tells us, began beneath the waves 'by spontaneous birth':

> In earth, sea, air, around, below, above,
> Life's subtle woof in Nature's loom is wove;
> Points glued to points a living line extends,
> Touch'd by some goad approach the bending ends;
> Rings join to rings, and irritated tubes
> Clasp with young lips the nutrient globes or cubes;
> And urged by appetencies new select,
> Imbibe, retain, digest, secrete, eject.
> In branching cones the living web expands,
> Lymphatic ducts, and convoluted glands;
> Aortal tubes propel the nascent blood,
> And lengthening veins absorb the refluent flood;
> Leaves, lungs, and gills, the vital ether breathe
> On earth's green surface, or the waves beneath.
> So Life's first powers arrest the winds and floods,
> To bones convert them, or to shells, or woods;
> Stretch the vast beds of argil, lime, and sand,
> And from diminish'd oceans form the land![1]

'Life's first powers' are crass hypostasizations: Darwin would hardly have admitted them into *Zoonomia* or *Phytologia*, but they make a brave show in poetry. So, for that matter, do the gods and heroes of Greek mythology and the elemental spirits of Rosicrucian lore. Tracing the constant process of birth, decay, death and re-birth, Darwin adduces 'the hieroglyphic figure of Adonis' which,

---

[1] *The Temple of Nature*, Canto I, lines 251–68.

he thinks, 'seems to have signified the spirit of animation or life, which was perpetually wooed or courted by organic matter, and which perished and revived alternately':

> So, as the sages of the East record
> In sacred symbol, or unletter'd word;
> Emblem of Life, to change eternal doom'd,
> The beauteous form of fair ADONIS bloom'd.—
> On Syrian hills the graceful Hunter slain
> Dyed with his gushing blood the shuddering plain;
> And, slow-descending to the Elysian shade,
> Awhile with PROSERPINE reluctant stray'd;
> Soon from the yawning grave the bursting clay
> Restor'd the Beauty to delighted day;
> Array'd in youth's resuscitated charms,
> And young DIONE woo'd him to her arms.—
> Pleased for a while the assurgent youth above
> Relights the golden lamp of life and love;
> Ah, soon again to leave the cheerful light,
> And sink alternate to the realms of night.

From the mythological expression we pass directly to the pseudo-scientific statement:

> Hence ere Vitality, as time revolves,
> Leaves the cold organ, and the mass dissolves;
> The Reproductions of the living Ens
> From sires to sons, unknown to sex, commence . . .

And from this, finally, to the concrete illustration:

> So the lone Truffle, lodged beneath the earth,
> Shoots from paternal roots the tuberous birth;
> No stamen-males ascend, and breathe above,
> No seed-born offspring lives by female love. . . .[1]

And this is Darwin's usual mode of developing his theme: first the exposition, in terms of 'powers' and personifications, of a

---

[1] *Ibid.*, Canto II, lines 45–74. For Keats's treatment of the Adonis myth, see *Endymion*, II, 387–587; and below, p. 142.

scientific 'truth'; then the highly artificial mythological expression; then the corollary to the exposition, deducible from the myth; and lastly the individual instance.

It is with the poetry that we shall be most concerned in the following pages; and more particularly with *The Botanic Garden*, Darwin's most influential work. *The Botanic Garden* preceded *Zoonomia* and *Phytologia* in date of publication, though not necessarily of writing.[1] Darwin was prolific, but he was also repetitive; there are few notions in the later works for which we cannot find an expression, and often a better expression, in *The Botanic Garden*. This is not to say that we should neglect the more technical works, or overlook their impact on late eighteenth and early nineteenth century thought. *Phytologia* interested Coleridge, and Wordsworth got the story of his *Goody Blake and Harry Gill* (1798) from the second volume of *Zoonomia*. It is not improbable that Keats, as a medical student, knew the latter work. It is not impossible that his frequent (and sarcastic) allusions to sentimental love owe something to Darwin's discussion of *Erotomania* under Class III (Diseases of Volition), Ordo I, genus II, species 4, as well as to *The Anatomy of Melancholy*.

These are mere probabilities and possibilities. With *The Botanic Garden* we are on firmer ground. When Keats looks forward to meeting Hunt, in October 1816, because 'it is no mean gratification to become acquainted with Men who in their admiration of Poetry do not jumble together Shakspeare and Darwin', it is Darwin's major poem that he has in mind. So too with Coleridge.[2] That omnivorous reader was well versed in Darwin's scientific treatises: there is evidence that he had studied both *Zoonomia*

---

[1] Darwin tells us that most of *Zoonomia* was written above twenty years before its publication in 1794–6; *The Temple of Nature*, which reproduces whole tracts of *The Botanic Garden*, appeared posthumously in 1803; part II of *The Botanic Garden*, *The Loves of the Plants*, was published in 1789, and the first part, *The Economy of Vegetation*, in 1791; *Phytologia* appeared in 1799.

[2] Whose reaction was similar: 'I have met with persons who professed themselves idolatrous admirers of Milton, & yet declared it to be their opinion that Dr. Darwin was as great a poet' (*Collected Letters*, II, 402).

and *Phytologia*. The following passage from *Theory of Life* repeats and supplements Darwin's criticism (quoted above) of his predecessors:

> The sublime discoveries of Newton, and, together with these, his no less fruitful than wonderful application of the higher mathesis to the movements of the celestial bodies, and to the laws of light, gave almost a religious sanction to the corpuscular system and mechanical theory. It became synonymous with philosophy itself. It was the sole portal at which truth was permitted to enter. The human body was treated of as an hydraulic machine, the operations of medicine were solved, and alas! even directed by reference partly to gravitation and the laws of motion, and partly by chemistry, which itself, however, as far as its theory was concerned, was but a branch of mechanics, working exclusively by imaginary wedges, angles and spheres . . . . . In short, from the time of Kepler to that of Newton, and from Newton to Hartley, not only all things in external nature, but the subtlest mysteries of life and organization, and even of the intellect and moral being, were conjured within the magic circle of mathematical formulæ.[1]

Coleridge exaggerates somewhat: the aspiration to a mathematical theory of chemistry, a mathematical or mechanical theory of physiology, was certainly active in the period in question, but the 'philosophers' found difficulty in realizing it; and some of them (names as great as Leibniz and Stahl) even found it repugnant. That does not concern us here. What does concern us is the impact of Darwin on contemporary minds, and in particular on Coleridge's. That impact was ambiguous. Darwin was a doctor, and, in some sense, a vitalist: his 'living Ens' invites the notion of an entelechy. But what does he mean by 'life'? And where does he draw the line between living and dead matter?

Coleridge was alert to these ambiguities. A passage in *The Friend* queries Darwin's doctrine of analogy between the animal and vegetable kingdoms. 'So long back as the first appearance of Dr Darwin's *Phytologia* the writer, then in earliest manhood,

---

[1] Reproduced in Kathleen Coburn's *Inquiring Spirit*, p. 256.

presumed to hazard the opinion, that the physiological botanists were hunting in a false direction, and sought for analogy where they should have looked for antithesis. He [Coleridge] saw, or thought he saw, that the harmony between the vegetable and animal world[s], was not a harmony of resemblance, but of contrast; and that their relation to each other was that of corresponding opposites.'[1] Such passages are evidence of Coleridge's appreciation of and disagreement with Darwin the prose theorist. They introduce, moreover, a theme that will exercise us much in the following pages: that of the contraries. But Coleridge was first and foremost a poet; and it is in his comments on *The Botanic Garden* that we find the personal note most resonant. 'I absolutely nauseate Darwin's poem', he writes to John Thelwall, in a letter of 13 May 1796. Indeed, he had never been an admirer. *Biographia Literaria* tells of his 'frequent amicable disputes concerning Darwin's "BOTANIC GARDEN", which, for some years, was greatly extolled, not only by the *reading* public in general, but even by those, whose genius and natural robustness of understanding enabled them afterwards to act foremost in dissipating these "painted mists" that occasionally rise from the marshes at the foot of Parnassus. During my first Cambridge vacation, I assisted a friend in a contribution for a literary society in Devonshire: and in this I remember to have compared Darwin's work to the Russian palace of ice, glittering, cold, and transitory.' And there is evidence that in term time also the literary club that met in his rooms in Jesus turned their attention to Darwin's verse.[2]

Coleridge, then, was critical; but 'the reading public in general' and the arbiters of taste were enthusiastic. A species of awe

---

[1] Reproduced in Kathleen Coburn's *Inquiring Spirit*, p. 247.

[2] Cf. Christopher Wordsworth's diary for 5 November 1793. Disdain did not, however, deter Coleridge from quarrying in Darwin's poem. He lifts the long footnote on 'LIGHT from plants' in his *Lines at Shurton Bars* verbatim (and without acknowledgement) from the Additional Notes to *The Loves of the Plants*. Lines 42 to 65 of *Happiness* (1791) are a rehash of Darwin's account of the diseases attendant on wine-bibbing in the same poem (Canto III, lines 357–80: and Notes).

breathes in the congratulatory verses by Mr Polwhele prefixed to
The Economy of Vegetation:

> Behold! amid the vegetable bloom,
>   O DARWIN, thy ambrosial rivers flow,
> And suns more pure the fragrant earth illume,
>   As all the vivid plants with passion glow.

Hayley and Cowper chime in: Cowper judiciously, with the
verdict that
> the bard, who'er he be
> And howsoever known
> Who would not twine a wreath for Thee,

is 'unworthy of his own'; Hayley gushingly, with a flirtatious
dialogue between Science and Nature:

> As Nature lovely Science led
>   Thro' all her flow'ry maze,
> The volume she before her spread
>   Of DARWIN's radiant lays.
>
> Coy Science starts—so started Eve
>   At beauties yet unknown:
> 'The figure that you there perceive,
>   (Said Nature) is your own.'
>
> 'My own? It is:—but half so fair
>   I never seem'd till now:
> And here, too, with a soften'd air,
>   Sweet Nature! here art Thou.'

A chorus of praise: and we must ask what it was in Darwin's poem
that evoked the praise; or, to put the question the other way
round, what was the *fin-de-siècle* unease that found relief in *The
Botanic Garden*? The relief, maybe, was spurious, and the unease
finally unallayed; but both were there. I have sometimes wondered if Coleridge is not pointing at Wordsworth in his reference
to 'those, whose genius and natural robustness of understanding
enabled them afterwards to act foremost in dissipating' the Darwinian mists. Was *he*, perhaps, among the *Garden*'s early admirers?

It is not out of the question: *An Evening Walk*, composed while Darwin's poem was in process of publication, has its echoes; and in the Preface to *Lyrical Ballads* Wordsworth toys with the idea that 'The remotest discoveries of the Chemist, the Botanist, or Mineralogist, will be as proper objects of the Poet's art as any upon which it can be employed, if . . .'. But in that *if*, of course, lies the rub: '. . . if the time should ever come when these things shall be familiar to us, and the relations under which they are contemplated by the followers of those respective sciences shall be manifestly and palpably material to us as enjoying and suffering beings.' The Preface was written in 1802, the year of Darwin's death. Wordsworth feels, then, that science has not yet put on a form of flesh and blood, is not yet actual enough to be matter for poetry. But he may not always have felt this. It is quite possible that when *The Economy of Vegetation* first appeared Wordsworth was taken in.

In the 1802 Preface, one may object, Wordsworth is being a little unfair. How is science to become familiar if no one takes the trouble to make it so? And who can do that better than the writer, the poet? Darwin is at least clearing the way for a possible future synthesis. His aim in *Zoonomia* and *The Temple of Nature* was a very respectable one, and one that Wordsworth had much at heart: to rescue the natural order from the trap of mechanism and restore it to life. And this, I think, was at the root of Darwin's appeal for his generation. There was a growing if ill-defined dissatisfaction with the 'universe of death' offered by the followers of Locke and Newton. The late eighteenth century was wearying of the weights and measures, the pulleys and smooth billiard balls, the stones and serpents doing duty for loaves and fishes, the neat theories and diagrams which translated and travestied the complexity and turmoil of events. We feel this unrest not only in the protests of the Blakes and the Smarts and the Clares and the Cowpers—the social outcasts who found a refuge in insanity or vision; it is there too in the more discreet grumblings of Thomson, the mild nostalgia of Mary Tighe, the Gothic fantasies or decorative Celtomania of Gray, Walpole and Mrs Radcliffe.

Darwin's verse deserves a somewhat closer scrutiny than it has received up to now from the historian of ideas. It is by no means neglible as writing; it bears the impress of a powerful if limited mind; it made its mark on Blake, Byron, Wordsworth, Coleridge, Shelley, and Keats. In what follows I shall have space to do little more than indicate some lines of approach which also serve to connect Darwin with Coleridge and Keats. I shall direct my comments mainly to *The Economy of Vegetation*. But our survey will be more than cautionary. There are interesting things in Darwin. He not only sums up, and exaggerates, a point of view; he also offers points of contrast, he opens vistas, he *teases*. He had many defects: timidity was not one of them. It is easy to laugh at the grotesquerie of his diction, but it is by no means certain that the grotesquerie is uncalculated. It may be directed towards an effect: and if that effect is memorableness, the aim is magnificently successful. In Darwin, a rococo imagination clothes a scientific vision in neo-classic garb: the result is of necessity incongruous, but the very incongruity is portentous, 'like the hindquarters of an elephant', and like those formidable masses it can pull its weight. Once acquainted with the lone Truffle, the dread Musquito, the tropic Beetle, or enormous Grampus, we are unlikely to forget them. Impressive individually, they take their places too within a general scheme, as hieroglyphics; hieroglyphics, in the cited instances, of the elements of earth, air, fire, and water, ancient powers that hover above Darwin's scheme and sometimes fuse, sometimes quarrel with Priestley's oxygen and the phlogiston of Stahl.

Yet our final impression is of a divided mind, of gifts obstinately pressed into the wrong service. Biographical data confirm this. We learn of the fluent versifier's congenital stammer, of the intoxicated temperance reformer's swimming a river in full morning dress; Anna Seward has other weaknesses to disclose. But the evidence is already to hand in the poems. Darwin's importance is representative rather than personal; he is a provincial figure in a provincial generation, a divided mind in a divided age. His pontifical manner masks the hesitancies of the bridge-builder, his uneasy classicism emphasizes the encroachments of an industrial civilization; he teeters between two worlds, hoping to keep a foothold in both. Where he is most himself, in his enthusiasm for the springs of life, for the growth of the embryo and the bursting of the seed, we are, alas! least fitted to follow him. For these are specialized subjects. But another specialist, who happened to be a great poet, and gave up specialization for poetry, could and I believe did follow him. Keats is the best comment on Darwin. Conversely, Darwin is the best introduction to Keats. Both were doctors, both wrote poetry, both were fascinated by the processes of birth, growth, fruition, decay, death. There is only one direct reference by Keats to Darwin, and it is, as we have seen, rather a rude one; but rudeness may conceal grudging admiration, and there are excellent reasons why Keats should have admired Darwin. It is, in any case, a fact that we find all Keats's fundamental insights in Darwin in what Blake would have called a petrified form. In other words, Keats is the Los to Darwin's Urizen.

Darwin impresses, to begin with, by the multifariousness of his interests; and perhaps still more by his ability, in *The Botanic Garden*, to weave these into a synthesis. Meeting him in Derby in January 1796, Coleridge observed: 'Dr Darwin possesses, perhaps, a greater range of knowledge than any other man in Europe, and is the most inventive of philosophers. He thinks in a *new* train on all subjects except religion. . . .'[1] He was doctor, botanist, classical scholar, student of ancient mythologies, philosopher, zoologist, amateur of mines and minerals, chemist, meteorologist, astronomer, physicist, and a number of other things as well. His curiosity was inexhaustible. He strikes us as something of a Renaissance figure, out of place in the fustier world into which he was born. He is the last of the virtuosi. Yet he lacked genius, he made no outstanding discovery or theoretic contribution to knowledge. We may say that he tried to do too much, to cover too wide a field; but it is arguable that his polymathy is of the essence, that his impressive-

---

[1] *Collected Letters*, I, 99. A later letter (I, 305) goes even further: 'On the whole, I think, he is the first *literary* character in Europe, and the most original-minded Man.'

ness rests finally on his range and his ability, in Coleridgean phrase, to co-adunate. His real weakness lies elsewhere, in his lack of proportion. His mind is non-hierarchical: it lacks order, and it lacks the gift of discrimination. These are serious defects, and they lead, as we shall see later, to certain outrages upon good taste, human dignity, and reverence.

Darwin is at one and the same time serious and frivolous. He is serious about his subject, frivolous about his treatment. His subject is the Linnæan system of botany: the treatment he gives it is mythological. Here is his 'Proem' to *The Loves of the Plants*:

GENTLE READER,

LO, here a CAMERA OBSCURA is presented to thy view, in which are lights and shades dancing on a whited canvas, and magnified into apparent life!—if thou art perfectly at leisure for such trivial amusement, walk in, and view the wonders of my INCHANTED GARDEN.

Whereas P. OVIDIUS NASO, a great Necromancer in the famous Court of AUGUSTUS CÆSAR, did by art poetic transmute Men, Women, and even Gods and Goddesses, into Trees and Flowers; I have undertaken by similar art to restore some of them to their original animality, after having remained prisoners so long in their respective vegetable mansions; and have here exhibited them before thee. Which thou may'st contemplate as diverse little pictures suspended over the chimney of a Lady's dressing room, *connected only by a slight festoon of ribbons*. And which, though thou may'st not be acquainted with the originals, may amuse thee by the beauty of their persons, their graceful attitudes, or the brilliancy of their dress.

FAREWELL.

The phrase Darwin has italicized for us conveys adequately enough his attitude towards the arts, towards poetry, towards mythology, and towards the theme of transmutation (a major preoccupation of Keats's, as the theme of 'all natural forms identified' in humanity was a major theme of Blake's). The 'Proem' as a whole defines, moreover, the kind of audience for which verse was destined—and often designed—at the close of the century: the predominantly feminine public of the salons and the dressing-rooms. This was the audience to whose judgment Keats hated the idea of submitting himself; it was also the one which (as his publishers pointed out) governed his sales. Darwin is writing for the lady amateur of botany (of the gentle ramble in the park and the album of pressed flowers); for the daughter of the great house and the niece of the cathedral close. Profundities are out of the question: the aim must be to amuse; and, in amusing, to instruct.

'The Muses are young Ladies', he asserts bluffly in the first 'Interlude' of *The Loves of the Plants*. He is replying to 'Bookseller's' query: 'Is then the office of Poetry only to amuse?'

> *Poet.* The Muses are young Ladies; we expect to see them dressed; though not like some modern beauties, with so much gauze and feather, that 'the Lady herself is the least part of her'. There are however didactic pieces of poetry, which are much admired, as the Georgics of Virgil, Mason's English Garden, Hayley's Epistles; nevertheless Science is best delivered in Prose, as its mode of reasoning is from stricter analogies than metaphors or similies.

Why, then, write in verse at all? For the sake of *memorableness*, Darwin replies: empty heads are best filled with tinkling sounds, and if you can contrive it that the sounds mean something— something serious, like the number of stamens in Gloriosa Superba —then you have not written in vain. With a like excuse he draws on Greek mythology and the 'Rosicrucian system' of elemental spirits—the nymphs and salamanders, sylphs and gnomes already exploited by Pope in *The Rape of the Lock*.

> The Rosicrucian doctrine of Gnomes, Sylphs, Nymphs, and Sala-manders, affords proper machinery for a philosophic poem; as it is probable that they were originally the names of hieroglyphic figures of the Elements, or of Genii presiding over their operations. The Fairies of more modern days seem to have been derived from them, and to have inherited their powers.

Very interesting; but unfortunately the Genii of the Elements too, like the Muses, are young Ladies in Darwin's Inchanted Garden; they smile softly, titter, and invite with simpering lips. After Pope and Darwin, the Rosicrucian machinery ceases to be available for a serious poet. It is a pity: there is no knowing what we might have escaped of Rintrahs and Fuzons in Blake's epic if these likeable and manageable creatures had not been so cruelly impounded and set to work at the satiric and scientific treadmills. Even Keats could give them no more than a breath of liberty in his *Song of Four Fairies*.

So too with the figures and episodes of classical mythology. At first glance Darwin is respectful if wrong-headed:

> Many of the important operations of nature were shadowed or allegorized in the heathen mythology, as the first Cupid springing from the Egg of Night, the marriage of Cupid and Psyche, the Rape of Proserpine, the Congress of Jupiter and Juno, the Death and Resuscitation of Adonis, &c. many of which are ingeniously explained in the works of Bacon. . . . The Egyptians were possessed of many discoveries in philosophy and chemistry before the invention of letters; these were then expressed in hieroglyphic paintings of men and animals; which after the discovery of the alphabet were described and animated by the poets, and became first the deities of Egypt, and afterwards of Greece and Rome. Allusions to those fables were therefore thought proper ornaments to a philosophical poem. . . .[1]

I call this wrong-headed, from the point of view which underlies the present book: a view which sees the myth as a verbal or pictorial expression of a reality superior both to the myth and to the phenomenon. This was Blake's view, and I believe it was Keats's. I shall have a good deal to say on the subject later on.

Let us look, meanwhile, at what Darwin actually makes of his gnomes and his sylphs, his heroes and goddesses. In doing so, we shall not be wasting our time. Darwin is a representative figure; by examining his major poem in its salient features we shall be laying a good foundation for our later studies in Coleridge and Keats. All too often we describe the Romantics as 'rebellious' and 'innovating' without any very clear idea of what they were rebellious about, or from what point they began to innovate. The name of Pope is proffered 'with backward mutterings of dissevering power' as the Old Nick of the piece; but the real

---

[1] 'Apology' prefixed to *The Economy of Vegetation*.

2

bêtes noires were much closer at hand: Hayley and Darwin, Beattie and Mason—the dying lights of the Augustan Age. In selecting Darwin from these for closer study, we shall be concentrating on the most vigorous of them and the most interesting in his width of reference. We shall arrive, I think, at a pretty clear idea of what the Romantics were up against in the poetic climate of their time; and, more important, of what they had to 'cast out of themselves', as Blake would put it, before they could become really themselves. Darwin was a big element in the age's climate. The Urizenic 'spectre' which in Shelley took the form of Godwin and in Coleridge the form of Hartley—to mention only two among the major poets—was never without a scaly glint of Darwin in all of them. We shall catch this metallic sheen in Keats's early verses.

In what follows I shall do no more than select from Darwin's epic the passages which seem outstanding, which yield most to analysis, and which bear some relation to what I shall have to say later of Keats's 'vast idea'. *The Botanic Garden* is a work of considerable length, and any detailed discussion would be tedious.

Darwin's professed aim in the poem is 'to inlist Imagination under the banner of Science; and to lead her votaries from the looser analogies, which dress out the imagery of poetry, to the stricter ones, which form the ratiocination of philosophy'. More particularly, he aims at persuading 'the ingenious to cultivate the knowledge of Botany, by introducing them to the vestibule of that delightful science'. This overt purpose may be accepted. But what Keats, and Blake, and a few others, sensed under the suave surface was quite a different design, which Blake might have described, rightly or wrongly, as the attempt to 'depress Mental & prolong Corporeal War'. We may take the charge literally: there occurs in Canto I a passage praising gunpowder because it 'weakens the tyranny of the few over the many'; it makes the puny the equals of the strong:

> Fear's feeble hand directs the fiery darts,
> And Strength and Courage yield to chemic arts.

This, it might be suggested, is the way to extend and prolong war, not to end it. But the point about physical warfare is not the one that I am concerned to make. More important is the attack on 'the minute particulars' that Darwin launches from the outset: the general levelling-down of individualities, the smoothing-out of idiosyncrasies; the 'blindness of the man', as Coleridge protested indignantly, to specific human values. His aim is to reduce the multifarious and difficult-to-manage organization of life to a few simple principles: mental war must be put a stop to, and everyone must agree to accept, if not the quiet ignorance recommended by Locke, then a quiet satisfaction with filaments and fibres, repulsion and attraction as ultimates of knowledge.

That there is no enigma for Darwin is indeed the impression we gain from his Canto I, a section ruled over by the elementals of fire, which purports to celebrate the high theme of the creation and preservation of the universe. The whole thing can be explained, it seems, by gas, from the cosmic explosions which hurled the planets out from chaos, down to the light of the glow-worm. One of Darwin's sublimer passages runs:

> When Air's pure essence joins the vital flood,
> And with phosphoric Acid dyes the blood,
> YOUR VIRGIN TRAINS[1] the transient HEAT dispart,
> And lead the soft combustion round the heart;
> Life's holy lamp with fires successive feed,
> From the crown'd forehead to the prostrate weed,
> From Earth's proud realms to all that swim or sweep
> The yielding ether or tumultuous deep.
> YOU swell the bulb beneath the heaving lawn,
> Brood the live seed, unfold the bursting spawn;
> Nurse with soft lap, and warm with fragrant breath
> The embryon panting in the arms of Death;
> Youth's vivid eye with living light adorn,
> And fire the rising blush of Beauty's golden morn.

---

[1] The Goddess of Botany is addressing the spirits of fire.

> Thus when the Egg of Night, on Chaos hurl'd,[1]
> Burst, and disclosed the cradle of the world;
> First from the gaping shell refulgent sprung
> IMMORTAL LOVE, his bow celestial strung;—
> O'er the wide waste his gaudy wings unfold,
> Beam his soft smiles, and wave his curls of gold;—
> With silver darts He pierced the kindling frame,
> And lit with torch divine the ever-living flame.[2]

We sometimes forget that it was in reply to such accounts of creation as this that Blake was moved to write those Prophetic Books which are so justly accused of violence and over-emphasis. Blake was over-emphatic because he was furious. Was this the stuff accepted by his generation in preference to 'the sublime of the Bible'? Keats, we know, reacted in his own way to the Darwinian onslaught on the rich diversity of being; he too was concerned with the world-view which reduced the 'awful rainbow once in heaven' to a spectrum, so that now

> We know her woof, her texture, she is given
> In the dull catalogue of common things.

That dull catalogue is Darwin's; it is his Nymphs who

> Cling round the aërial bow with prisms bright,
> And pleased untwist the sevenfold threads of light.

And he notes (his comments are as copious as his verses) that 'it was reserved for the immortal Newton to discover that the rays of light consisted of seven combined colours of different refrangibility, which could be separated at pleasure by a wedge of glass'.

The 'Argument of the Second Canto' (a synopsis of its contents in ten divisions) begins thus:

Address to the Gnomes. I. The Earth thrown from a volcano of the Sun; it's atmosphere and ocean; it's journey through the zodiac;

---

[1] Darwin returns to the Creation theme (often with simple repetition of images and phrases) in *The Temple of Nature* (1803). This poem is very largely a versification of *Zoonomia* (1794). No historian of ideas—and especially of associationism and theories of perception in early Romantic thought—can afford to neglect these works.

[2] *Economy of Vegetation*, I, 399–420.

vicissitude of day-light, and of seasons, 11. II. Primeval islands. Paradise, or the golden Age. Venus rising from the sea, 33. III. The first great earthquakes; continents raised from the sea; the Moon thrown from a volcano, has no atmosphere, and is frozen; the earth's diurnal motion retarded; it's axis more inclined; whirls with the moon round a new centre, 67.

Now all these were topics of immediate concern to the new poets; the Romantic Revival was a 'renascence of wonder', and poetry was beginning to reclaim its 'prophetic' function—the right and duty to justify God's ways to man. What does Darwin make of his great argument?

He is not afraid to challenge comparison with Milton. The Creation account in Canto I harks back, in its phrasing, to *Paradise Lost* VII, with a Newtonian identification of God with absolute space:

> Orbs wheel in orbs, round centres centres roll,
> And form, self-balanced, one revolving Whole.
> —Onward they move amid their bright abode,
> Space without bound, THE BOSOM OF THEIR GOD!

The Creation account in Canto II is similar, with a shift of emphasis from fire to earth in accordance with the workings of the Paracelsian machinery. But Darwin's attempt to *explain* the motions of the planets by gravitation and centrifugal force would have struck Milton as impious. We remember Raphael's admonition to the too inquisitive Adam:

> Sollicit not thy thoughts with matters hid,
> Leave them to God above, him serve and feare;
> Of other creatures, as him pleases best,
> Wherever plac't, let him dispose: joy thou
> In what he gives to thee, this Paradise
> And thy fair *Eve*; Heav'n is for thee too high
> To know what passes there; be lowlie wise.

There the humanist speaks. But Darwin is no humanist. No theme is too high or too low for scientific enquiry, in his opinion.

Stick to Paradise? Very well: but Paradise too must be *explained*.
How did the primeval islands arise? How are we to account for
their enjoyment of perpetual Spring? Mr Whitehurst's *Theory of
the Earth*, chap. xvi, will perhaps enlighten us:

> Whence the paradise of the sacred writers, and the golden age of the
> profane ones, seems to have had a real existence. As there can be no
> rainbow, when the heavens are covered with clouds, because the
> sun-beams are then precluded from falling upon the rain-drops
> opposite to the eye of the spectator, the rainbow is a mark of gentle
> or partial showers. Mr. Whitehurst has endeavoured to show that
> the primitive islands were only moistened by nocturnal dews and
> not by showers. . . .

Which goes prettily into verse:

> O'er those blest isles no ice-crown'd mountains tower'd,
> No lighnings darted, and no tempests lower'd;
> Soft fell the vesper-drops, condensed below,
> Or bent in air the rain-refracted bow,
> Sweet breathed the zephyrs, just perceiv'd and lost;
> And brineless billows only kiss'd the coast;
> Round the bright zodiac danced the vernal hours,
> And Peace, the Cherub, dwelt in mortal bowers! [1]

Darwin's prose is clearer than his verse, and it is plain which he
considers the more important. Poetry is the gilding on the pill:
if you can take the pill neat, you may ignore the gilding.

This is not to say that Darwin is a wholly contemptible versifier.
He is not a bore. He has mastered the technique of his craft; he has
assimilated what his Augustan models, and especially Pope, had
to teach him. True, much of his readableness comes from his
absurdity, his 'stuffed owl' side; but much comes too from a
manipulation of metre which, within limits, is extremely skilful.
His stresses are more various than Thomson's, though less so
than Pope's. His lines are not invariably end-stopped, and he has
understood that the couplet gains in resilience if you rhyme verb

---

[1] *Economy of Vegetation*, II, 39–46.

against noun. He is at his best with static descriptions, with decorative picture-painting, as in these lines on the Zodiac:

> Where yet the Bull with diamond-eye adorns
> The Spring's fair forehead, and with golden horns;
> Where yet the Lion climbs the ethereal plain,
> And shakes the Summer from his radiant mane;
> Where Libra lifts her airy arm, and weighs,
> Poised in her silver balance, nights and days;
> With paler lustres where Aquarius burns,
> And showers the still snow from his hoary urns;
> YOUR ardent troops pursued the flying sphere,
> Circling the starry girdle of the year;
> While sweet vicissitudes of day and clime
> Mark'd the new annals of enascent Time.[1]

That is not unimaginative,[2] and any poet might be proud of the fourth line. What is lacking in Darwin's verse is not accomplishment or fervour: it is humility. He is convinced that everything can be explained—a dangerous attitude for a poet. No casements open here on perilous seas: the very billows have been tested for salinity and their exact momentum nicely calculated.

We must be fair, too, to Darwin as a philanthropist—which he undoubtedly was. He belongs to the great liberal tradition of English thought. He may say foolish things about gunpowder, but also says wise things about militarism. He smuggles an eloquent plea for 'the poor fetter'd SLAVE' into his eulogy of Wedgwood ware.[3] He applauds the American Revolution, and his picture of the awakening of liberty in France certainly gave Blake ideas for his descriptions of the rousing of Albion:

> Long had the Giant-form on GALLIA's plains
> Inglorious slept, unconscious of his chains;
> Round his large limbs were wound a thousand strings

---

[1] *Ibid.* II, 21–32.

[2] It strikes me as definitely superior to Keats's Zodiac strophes in *Endymion* IV.

[3] Is it possible that the design for the cameo (with its rubric *Am I not a Man and a Brother* [?]) is by Blake? We know that he engraved *The Fertilization of Egypt* and the illustrations of 'Portland's mystic urn' in this same Part I of *The Botanic Garden*.

By the weak hands of Confessors and Kings;
O'er his closed eyes a triple veil was bound,
And steely rivets lock'd him to the ground;
While stern Bastile with iron-cage inthralls
His folded limbs, and hems in marble walls.
—Touch'd by the patriot-flame, he rent amazed
The flimsy bonds, and round and round him gazed;
Starts up from earth, among the admiring throng
Lifts his Colossal form, and towers along;
High o'er his foes his hundred arms He rears,
Plowshares his swords, and pruning hooks his spears;
Calls to the Good and Brave with voice, that rolls
Like Heaven's own thunder round the echoing poles;
Gives to the winds his banner broad unfurl'd,
And gathers in its shade the living world![1]

That is a sufficiently remarkable passage. It would appeal, we may be sure, to the liberal in Keats, the side of him responsible for the early sonnets to Kosciusko and to Leigh Hunt on his release from prison, and for the outburst against kings in *Endymion*.

Darwin had an agile mind and a great fund of information. We shall not be surprised to find him discoursing on subjects of special interest to both Blake and Keats. The structure of his philosophical epic follows a quaternary pattern, based on the four elements, which is Keats's also in *Endymion*; in this respect indeed, as in so many others, the later poet's work amounts to a challenge, a trial of strength. Among the 'others' I may mention the theme of Egypt. This is a major preoccupation of Darwin's in Cantos II and III. Blake's engraving of *The Fertilization of Egypt*[2] illustrates the stirring couplet on the Monsoon:

High o'er his head the beams of SIRIUS glow,
And, Dog of Nile, ANUBIS barks below.

---

[1] *Economy of Vegetation*, II, 377–94. The long footnote to this passage also influenced Blake, as I have pointed out in my *English Blake* (p. 20, note).

[2] Which suggested to Wordsworth, possibly, his fine simile in *The Prelude*, VI, 614–16:

like the mighty flood of Nile
Poured from her fount of Abyssinian clouds
To fertilize the whole Egyptian plain.

There are moments when Darwin touches a certain grandeur. Canto II gives us this remarkable picture of Cambyses marching his army from Persia to Egypt:

> Slow as they pass'd, the indignant Temples frown'd,
> Low curses muttering from the vaulted ground;
> Low ailes of Cypress waved their deepen'd glooms,
> And quivering spectres grinn'd amid the tombs;
> Prophetic whispers breathed from SPHINX's tongue,
> And MEMNON's lyre with hollow murmurs rung;
> Burst from each pyramid expiring groans,
> And darker shadows stretch'd their lengthen'd cones,
> Day after day their deathful rout They steer,
> Lust in the van, and Rapine in the rear.[1]

This is perhaps less than sublime, but Wordsworth was impressed; a couplet which closes the whole description—

> Grim HORROR shook,—awhile the living hill
> Heaved with convulsive throes,—and all was still!

—is incorporated in his *To Enterprise* (1820); and I am not sure that Keats's 'mountains blue' which

> seem a lifted mound
> Above some giant, pulsing underground

in the *Epistle to John Hamilton Reynolds* (1818) are not derivative from Darwin's 'living hill'.

Darwin gains much of his peculiar effect by the combination in his style of affective with abstract terms. Aldous Huxley employs the same technique in his novels. He likes to describe a single event—let us say, a character's response to bad news—on two planes at the same time. He will give us the ordinary, human terms (the paling of the cheeks, the trembling of lips, the streaming eyes) and with them, *pari passu*, an account in terms of stimulation of the lachrymatory glands and the response of nerve-endings. In this way he achieves detachment, but also a certain

---

[1] *Economy of Vegetation*, II, 445–54.

unreality. He is likely to forfeit his reader's sympathy. Not always, of course. He has his successes—in, for example, *Point Counter Point*, where the episode of the flautist playing Bach's B minor suite, couched initially in terms of columns of air vibrating in accordance with strict Helmholtzian laws, is concluded by the effective 'Through the long sarabande the poet slowly meditated his lovely and consoling certitude'. We pass directly from the field of physics to that of metaphysics.

Darwin's successes are certainly less than fifty per cent. In the following, the emotive terms are ludicrously out of place:

> SYLPHS! YOU, retiring to sequester'd bowers,
> Where oft your PRIESTLEY woos your airy powers,
> On noiseless step or quivering pinion glide,
> As sits the Sage with Science by his side;
> To his charm'd eye in gay undress appear,
> Or pour your secrets on his raptured ear.
> How nitrous Gas from iron ingots driven
> Drinks with red lips the purest breath of heaven;
> How, while Conserva from its tender hair
> Gives in bright bubbles empyrean air,
> The crystal floods phlogistic ores calcine,
> And the pure ETHER marries with the MINE.[1]

But when he is writing from his deepest centre—and he is always so writing when he is on the theme of embryology and germination—he can achieve real *tours de force* of emotive-cerebral synthesis. Here is his diptych of the seed and the crocodile, a point counterpoint of vegetable and animal embryology. Blake read it and learned from it: his 'vegetation' of Urizen (first found in the symbolic book of that name, but repeated in subsequent 'prophecies') is a direct derivation.

> Come, YE SOFT SYLPHS! who sport on Latian land,
> Come, sweet-lip'd Zephyr, and Favonius bland!
> Teach the fine SEED, instinct with life, to shoot
> On Earth's cold bosom its descending root;

---

[1] *Economy of Vegetation*, IV, 177–88.

With Pith elastic stretch its rising stem,
Part the twin Lobes, expand the throbbing Gem;
Clasp in your airy arms the aspiring Plume,
Fan with your balmy breath its kindling bloom,
Each widening scale and bursting film unfold,
Swell the green cup, and tint the flower with gold;
While in bright veins the silvery Sap ascends,
And refluent blood in milky eddies bends;
While, spread in air, the leaves respiring play,
Or drink the golden quintessence of day.
—So from his shell on Delta's shower-less isle
Burst into life the Monster of the Nile;
First in translucent lymph with cobweb-threads
The Brain's fine floating tissue swells, and spreads;
Nerve after nerve the glistening spine descends,
The red Heart dances, the Aorta bends;
Through each new gland the purple current glides,
New Veins meandering drink the refluent tides;
Edge over edge expands the hardening scale,
And sheaths his slimy skin in silver mail.[1]

One cannot deny that a certain grotesque power. The juxta-position of two such emotively contrasted examples of things 'instinct with life' as the 'fine seed' and 'the Monster of the Nile' is a stroke of genius. And what Darwin is saying, in his own way, is really what Blake and Keats were to say: 'Everything that Lives is Holy'.[2]

What Darwin is trying to do, in *The Economy of Vegetation*, is in fact what Blake and Keats also try to do: but his approach is

---

[1] *Ibid.* IV, 421–44. The passage immediately following, on the awakening of the flowers, would seem to have a close connection with Blake's description in *Milton* (K. 527).

[2] Thomas Taylor may have had Darwin in mind in his criticism of 'the moderns' (Introduction to *Timæus*): 'They have just been able to gain a glimpse of the beautiful union of things in the vegetable and animal tribes . . . but this is the very summit of their researches; they are unable to trace the connection of things any further, and rest satisfied in admitting that

The chain continues, but with links unknown'.

confused. He too is searching for a unity, and for a principle of unity. And because his search is an honest one (it is impossible, I think, to read *The Botanic Garden* through without coming to admire and respect its author) he sometimes comes in sight of his goal. But his training is against him. He wants unity without hierarchy, system rather than organization. He is interested, first and foremost, in classifying and explaining phenomena. Natural phenomena have so far proved amenable to explanation by the laws of physics and chemistry. Gravitation has interpreted much: the varieties of motion have been brought under the rule of a single principle. Might not a similar principle be found operative in the realm of organic life? It would not be mechanical, of course —it would be vital. But, we may ask (and here comes the rub with Darwin) what precisely does he mean by 'vital'? Where is the line to be drawn between animate and inanimate? As we read on in *The Economy of Vegetation* and *The Temple of Nature* we begin to suspect that its author is tricking us. What he has given with one hand he is taking away with the other. His notion of life first petrifies, then becomes fluid, and finally gaseous.

Our quarrel with Darwin is not that he chooses to put the latest scientific and technical information and hypotheses into verse. Lucretius and Virgil had done as much; and produced good poetry. What is insidiously cloven-footed, anti-humanist, is his unspoken assumption—which reveals itself in his imagery and episodic material. For consider: if you can bring yourself to talk about the production of nitrous acid in terms of human passion—

> As woos Azotic Gas the virgin Air,
> And veils in crimson clouds the yielding Fair

—there will soon seem to be no reason why you should not talk and think about human passion in terms of nitrous acid.[1] If vital and non-vital are interchangeable, no question of a preference

---

[1] Darwin was by no means the first to arrange such chemical spousals. They were a commonplace with the hermetists, and particularly with the alchemists. The fifteenth-century tract, *Nuptiæ Chymicæ*, is ascribed to Rosenkreutz, the perhaps legendary founder of the Rosicrucians.

can arise.[1] Or rather, there is a preference, and a very natural one, in favour of the simplicity which expression in non-vital terms makes possible. The lowest common denominator has a perennial charm for systematic minds.

Allied to this there is another peril, which Blake expressed thus: 'We become what we behold.' Poring for years on earth-worms, Erasmus Darwin's more famous grandson found, when he came to open a book of verse again, that his appreciation of poetry had shrunk to a worm's capacity. He deplored his loss, but he was never able to do anything about it. The moral is clear. We can only safely and sanely dedicate ourselves to the study of worms if we do so within 'the Body of Divine Analogy': if, with the Cloud in *Thel*, we can make the assertion:

> Every thing that lives
> Lives not alone nor for itself. Fear not, and I will call
> The weak worm from its lowly bed, and thou shalt hear its voice.

The voice of the worm will sound for the spiritual ear only when with the worm we are able to enter the house of 'the matron Clay' and rest quietly there, 'rotting' in Keats's phrase 'like a grain of wheat'. This is what art is about, and mythology; we degrade these things and ourselves when we use them as decoration. Wordsworth has Erasmus Darwin in mind, I believe, when in *The Excursion* he makes the Wanderer 'contrast the dignities of the Imagination with the presumptuous littleness of certain modern Philosophers':

> Oh! there is laughter at their work in heaven!
> Inquire of ancient Wisdom; go, demand
> Of mighty Nature, if 'twas ever meant
> That we should pry far off yet be unraised;
> That we should pore, and dwindle as we pore,
> Viewing all objects unremittingly

---

[1] Coleridge notes his tendency to relapse into mechanistic thinking (*Collected Letters*, II, 695); 'Des Cartes, like Hartley & Darwin, held the possibility of a machine so perfect, & susceptible of Impulses, as to perform many actions of apparent Consciousness without consciousness. . . .' They were right, of course.

In disconnection dead and spiritless;
And still dividing, and dividing still,
Break down all grandeur, still unsatisfied
With the perverse attempt, while littleness
May yet become more little; waging thus
An impious warfare with the very life
Of our own souls!

Inquire of ancient Wisdom! We shall see in the following chapters how Keats responded to this injunction of the poem which he regarded as the greatest of his time.

[*The Botanic Garden* (1789–91)—*Zoonomia* (1794–6)—*Phytologia* (1799)—*The Temple of Nature* (1803)]

Chapter Two

OWLS AND EAGLES

I have read with wonder and delight that passage of Reimarus in which he speaks of the immense multitude of plants, and the curious, regular *choice* of different herbivorous animals with respect to them, and the following pages in which he treats of the pairing of insects and the equally wonderful processes of egg-laying and so forth. All in motion! the sea-fish to the shores and rivers—the land-crab to the seashore! I would fain describe all the creation thus agitated by the one or other of the three instincts—self-preservation, childing, child-preservation. Set this by Darwin's theory of the maternal instinct—O mercy! the blindness of the man! and it is imagination, forsooth! that misled him —too much poetry in his philosophy! this abject deadness of all that sense of the obscure and the indefinite, this superstitious fetish-worship of lazy or fascinated fancy! O this, indeed, deserves to be dwelt on.

s. t. coleridge, 1804 Notebook

AMONG the many regrettables of Coleridge's unfinished or unattempted poems we must count that 'Hymn to Dr Darwin—in the manner of the Orphics' which figures in the 'Gutch Memorandum Book' among the first twenty-five items (including 'Hymns to the Sun, the Moon, and the Elements —six hymns' and an 'Ode to a Moth') of his projected *Works*. We can ill spare it. Composed on one of his good days it would have proved, we may be sure, an effective counterblast to *The Economy of Vegetation*. We lack the Hymn; but we have, scattered about in Coleridge's commonplace books, some indications of what the Hymn might have been.[1] Coleridge was the foremost

---

[1] Coleridge also proposed to examine (in a volume of essays 'Concerning Poetry, & the characteristic Merits of the Poets, our Contemporaries') Darwin's literary theory: 'Of course, Darwin & Wordsworth having given each a defence of *their* mode of Poetry, & a disquisition on the nature & essence of Poetry in general, I shall necessarily be led rather deeper—and these I shall treat of either first or last' (*Collected Letters*, II, 830).

English student of what we now call 'the history of ideas' to question the inevitable rightness of 'progress'. It had occurred to him that a civilization, an age might go astray as an individual goes astray, losing his road in the fog: that history might produce an era of Lost Travellers. With this thought in his mind he looked back over the past and found the fatal crossroads in the seventeenth century.

The theme of the wicked Renaissance—wickedly anti-imaginative, wickedly anti-traditional—is certainly not one of the 'bye and barren Themes' dear, in Sir Thomas Browne's opinion, to the heart of an originality-hunter. It has been traced *ad nauseam* in our own day; and I have had my say about it in a previous book. But I believe we cannot approach Keats profitably—along our present lines—except by way of Coleridge: and what Coleridge had most in common with Keats was his sense of tradition.

A sense of tradition means an apprehension of unity in terms of a principle. The traditionalist surveys the flux from an eminence, and includes the whole in a single glance. The traditional view of the cosmos, in other words, is less that of the Scale of Being than that of the macrocosm-microcosm, in which Man is to Nature as Nature is to God. Yet here again we have to interpret, for it is a feature of all traditional doctrines that their terms are fully invertible; and if the formula just given is true on the plane of manifestation, it is also true, on the plane of understanding or 'Eternity', that Man is the measure of all things and that Nature is his creation just as God is his Principle. It is when he forgets this, and acknowledges God as his judge and Nature as his mother, that he goes astray.

Thus God is rightly worshipped, as both Blake and Keats said, by loving the greatest men best[1]; Nature is correctly perceived ('not with but through the eye') when we know her as the living, richly varied but scattered 'portions of Man's immortal body'. Now this is the hermetic or vitalist point of view which was

---

[1] Keats's 'presidors' (Shakespeare and Spenser) correspond to Blake's 'guardians' or 'angels'. These are the 'tutelary geniuses' (genii) of traditional lore.

abandoned in the seventeenth century[1]—not without a struggle, and not without loss. The non-vitalist view which won the day was magnificently competent to explain natural phenomena in terms of mechanical forces;but it was competent neither to explain man himself nor to satisfy him. The decline of imaginative poetry throughout the eighteenth century implies a drying up of the traditional springs. Writers gave up trying to account for the human condition except in political or social contexts; or else, like Darwin, they traded in incongruities: 'Materialists unwilling to admit the mysterious element of our nature make it all mysterious —nothing mysterious in nerves, eyes, &c., but that nerves think, &c.! Stir up the sediment into the transparent water, and so make all opaque.'[2]

Was there any possibility of return to the integrated life-picture?[3] In the Notebooks we watch Coleridge groping his way:

There is not a new or strange opinion—Truth returned from banishment—a river run underground———fire beneath embers—

Men anxious for this world—Owls that watch all night to catch mice—

Smooth, shining, & deceitful as thin Ice—

Wisdom, Mother of retired Thought,

$$εστι\ τις\ θεος\ ενδον$$
$$πολυν\ εσσαμενοι\ νουν.$$

. . . .

—the prophetic soul
Of the wide world dreaming on things to come.

Shak. sonnets.[4]

---

[1] When 'metaphysic sank and died, and an empirical highly superficial psychology took its place' (Coleridge's 1817 Notebook).

[2] Coleridge, *Anima Poetæ* (from an 1801 Notebook).

[3] A book which has appeared while these pages were going through the press— Mr Owen Barfield's *Saving the Appearances*—has an important bearing on this whole question, and on many particular aspects of Keats's thought. I regret that I have had to confine my references to it to a few footnotes.

[4] *Gutch Memorandum Book.*

Glosses cryptic enough, yet constituting—as we shall find before long—strangely effective keys to our stiffer conundrums. Owls that watch all night to catch mice emblemize the quality I am going to call wariness: a 'note' of the empirical tradition. It is the collector's virtue, or defect; the compulsion to collect, to hoard, to suck dry. There is a real analogy between Erasmus Darwin's *hortus siccus* and cabinet of classified fossils, and the pathetic little heaps of bones and balls of regurgitated fur that garnish the owl's nest. The moment we begin systematizing we begin devitalizing. 'I must create a System or be enslav'd by another Man's', Blake cried with the voice of Los. But he did not create a system: he reanimated a mythology. Living truth cannot be enclosed in a frame. When Blake appealed 'to the Public, from the judgment of those narrow blinking eyes, that have too long governed art in a dark corner', he was appealing from owlish systematization to living experience.

The wary mind begins from a preconception and moves toward a system. The mind that is not wary but aware dips without prejudice into the total process as it flows, submits itself to a pattern which may or may not reveal itself. Minds of this order seek a unity, but are not impatient to grasp it. Coleridge had such a mind. As we study his notebooks, we sense a process unfolding itself, we see a network of sensitive filaments penetrating, exploring the process, but not controlling it. Here he is, sitting in his study at Valetta in 1805, watching the April moon:

In looking at objects of Nature while I am thinking, as at yonder moon dim-glimmering through the dewy window-pane, I seem rather to be seeking, as it were *asking* for, a symbolical language for something within me that already and forever exists, than observing anything new. Even when that latter is the case, yet still I have always an obscure feeling as if that new phenomenon were the dim awaking of a forgotten or hidden truth of my inner nature. It is still interesting as a word—a symbol. It is Λόγος the Creator, and the Evolver!

What we have here is an intuition—call it Platonic, Hermetic, or Berkeleyan as you will—that nature is to be interpreted in terms of man, and not man in terms of nature. Natural forms constitute, taken all together, a symbolic alphabet: the code of a lost wisdom which it is man's task to decipher. Exploring nature, reassembling 'the scatter'd parts of his immortal body', man is elucidating *himself*: the vast work of exegesis glimpsed at the close of *Jerusalem*—

> All Human forms identified, even Tree, Metal, Earth & Stone: all Human Forms identified, living, going forth & returning wearied Into the Planetary lives of Years, Months, Days & Hours

—is a process of self-knowledge.

'The immense difference', Coleridge exclaims again in an 1810 notebook, 'between being glad to find Truth *it*, and to find *it* TRUTH!' The distinction leads to, or depends upon, yet another: on what we may call dynamic as opposed to static understanding. Truth is a matter of being, not simply of knowing. An 1814–1816 notebook offers us an image of the two streams of knowing and being passing unmingled through a lake:

> The lake is formed by the two streams in man and nature as it exists in and for man; and up this lake the philosopher sails on the junction-line of the constituent streams, still pushing upward and sounding as he goes, towards the common fountain-head of both, the mysterious source whose being is knowledge, whose knowledge is being—the adorable I AM IN THAT I AM.

A truth which is vital must also be paradoxical. 'Extremes meet' was Coleridge's favourite adage. In *Aids to Reflection* he goes so far as to assert that truth is, properly speaking, inconceivable: 'For to conceive is a function of the Understanding, which can be exercised only on subjects subordinate thereto. And yet to the forms of the Understanding all truth must be reduced that is to be fixed as an object of reflection, and to be rendered expressible.'[1] This will remind us of Keyserling's remark that no vital truth can be expressed except in profound contrapuntal opposition. Life is a play of contraries: there is no conciliating without first recognizing and accepting them.

---

[1] Coleridge's distinction between the Reason and the Understanding will be familiar to the reader; Blake uses the same terms but in an inverse sense, *i.e.* Coleridge's 'Reason' is Blake's 'Understanding', and *vice versa*.

But Keats found Coleridge impatient. Patient indeed he was in his awareness as opposed to Dr Darwin's wariness. Awareness, which implies impartiality, is noble; but there is yet a third quality— *unawareness*, which Keats had and Coleridge had not, which 'lives in gusto, be it foul or fair', whose symbolism is *le symbolisme qui sait*, and not *le symbolisme qui cherche*. In comparison with this calm power, Coleridge's awareness is fidgety. This is the quality which Coleridge himself noted in the 'little child, who always finds and never seeks'. Keats puts his finger on it in the famous early letter to George and Thomas Keats (December 1817) in which he talks about 'Negative Capability':

> *Negative Capability*, that is when a man is capable of being in un-certainties, Mysteries, doubts, without any irritable reaching after fact and reason—Coleridge, for instance, would let go by a fine isolated verisimilitude caught from the Penetrale[1] of mystery, from being incapable of remaining Content with half-knowledge.[2]

Coleridge was humorously conscious of this compulsion in himself. An 1805 note tells how, although just on the point of going to bed, he was constrained to arrange three pieces of wood on his fire in symmetrical pattern: 'Hence I seem . . . to suspect that this disease of totalizing, of perfecting, may be the bottom impulse of many, many actions, in which it never is brought forward as an avowed or even agnized as a conscious motive.' The disease he came later to attribute, rightly, to the over-reflec-tive cast of his mind: a mind that dealt more easily with thoughts than actions, with concepts than things.[3]

---

[1] Here and elsewhere I see no point in reproducing Keats's grosser lapses of spelling or grammar. Orthography and punctuation remain otherwise untouched.

[2] A letter of nigh two years later (24 September 1819) to George and Georgiana puts it thus: 'The only means of strengthening one's intellect is to make up one's mind about nothing—to let the mind be a thoroughfare for all thoughts. Not a select party.'

[3] 'Partly from ill-health, & partly from an unhealthy & reverie-like vividness of *Thoughts*, & (pardon the pedantry of the phrase) a diminished Impressibility from *Things*, my ideas, wishes & feelings are to a diseased degree disconnected from *motion & action*. . . . I am a Starling self-incaged, & always in the Moult, & my whole Note is, Tomorrow, & tomorrow, & tomorrow . . .' (*Collected Letters*, II, 782).

The theme of unawareness is of great difficulty, and, like truth itself, can be discussed only in terms of 'profound contrapuntal opposition'. Here, symbolism will be our best ally. Symbolism, and that peculiar technique of statement which is non-statement, sense which is nonsense, elaborated by the Taoist and Zen masters for purposes of enlightenment. Rabelais is on the same track, but employs the art of camouflage: his broad, exuberant farce, as Coleridge had the wit to see, masks an all-embracing insight. Rabelais begins from the earth: he pushes the earthy, the coarse, the outrageously physical energies to the point where they explode into spirit. Symbolism begins from spirit and incarnates energy in gross forms. We shall find Keats following all three of these approaches.

Coleridge was by no means an owl; he had, indeed, many aquiline qualities: but these were, as some contemporaries saw, hooded. Shelley's lines in the *Letter to Maria Gisborne* are apt here:

> You will see Coleridge—he who sits obscure
> In the exceeding lustre and the pure
> Intense irradiation of a mind,
> Which, with its own internal lightning blind,
> Flags wearily through darkness and despair—
> A cloud-encircled meteor of the air,
> A hooded eagle among blinking owls.[1]

Mind is stressed; and mind, we feel too often, dominates in Coleridge the totality which, developed in all its powers, might have borne him above the clouds. The senses are at a discount, undeveloped or checked. Mind expands at one moment to embrace the cosmos, forgetting 'the minute particulars'; at another moment it narrows to a concentration on 'little things' displayed by 'glasses': seldom or never are the two seeings fused into 'the

---

[1] Cf. Byron, Dedication to *Don Juan*:

> And Coleridge, too, has lately taken wing,
> But like a hawk encumbered with his hood . . .

Shelley's poem was composed in July, 1820; Byron's first canto, with the Dedication, was finished on 19 September 1818, while Shelley was staying with him in Venice.

double vision'. Yet through the sheer exercise of mind he approaches, at times, excitingly near to the Blakean and what we shall see to be the Keatsian synthesis. Take this extract from an 1806–7 notebook:

> Rest, motion! O ye strange locks of intricate simplicity, who shall find the key? He shall throw wide open the portals of the palace of sensuous or symbolical truth, and the Holy of Holies will be found in the adyta. Rest = enjoyment and death. Motion = enjoyment and life. O the depth of the proverb, 'Extremes meet'!

The equations express an amalgam of error and truth. What meaning can we give to the first? It is difficult to see any sense in which enjoyment is compatible with death. For Coleridge the second was certainly true: it was his case, and his torment, that enjoyment and life were only to be found in motion—the incessant activity of his intellect. Keats's comment is uncannily relevant to this passage in both thought and imagery. Rest, passivity, unawareness: these for Coleridge are *death*: he feels them as enjoyment, a blessed relief from the incessant activity of discursive thought, but it is a guilty enjoyment: 'life' beckons him on to more strenuous, more complex ratiocinations. The identity of rest with death is indeed asserted in some of the most characteristic moments of his poetry: moments of frozen silence, of chained frustration. The glaciers of *Hymn before Sunrise*—torrents frozen to stillness; the icicles of *Frost at Midnight*—arrested eavesdrops; the 'stranger' hanging from the bars, in the same poem—motion inhibited; the becalmed ship in *The Ancient Mariner*: all these image rest under its deathlike aspect.

Coleridge ends his note with the proverb, 'Extremes meet'. It was, we know, a favourite thought: the 1803 notebook offers a number of examples from his reading and observation. They are interesting, but not suggestive: flashes of ingenuity rather than of perception.

1.   The parching Air
Burns frore, and cold performs th' effect of Fire.
Paradise Lost, II, 594.

2. Insects by their smallness, the mammoth by its huge-
ness, terrible . . .

9. The naked savage and the gymnosophist . . . .

This is the kind of thinking appropriate to the construction of
riddles: 'Why is an X like a Y? Because they are both . . .' And
thus, I repeat, not very valuable. Only in the tenth example,
'Nothing and intensest absolute being', do we feel a perception
that can be called metaphysical. We shall find Keats's perception,
though couched in images the most concrete, moving habitually
in this metaphysical realm: Coleridge's *thought* antithesis replaced
by a *felt* synthesis. In particular we shall find the unclouded sky
functioning as 'Nothing and intensest absolute being': the void
which is also the matrix of all manifestation.

[*Notebooks* (1803–17)—*Aids to Reflection* (1825)]

Chapter Three

THE UNWEARIED FORM

There the mighty spirit still coming from within had succeeded in taming the untractable matter and in reducing external form to a symbol of the inward and imaginable beauty. We feel it to this day. We feel it for this reason, because we look at the forms after we have long satisfied all curiosity concerning the mere outline; yet, still we look and feel that these are but symbols. Full worthily have they expressed themselves. Why, having seen their outlines, why, having determined what they appeared to the eye, do we still continue to muse on them, but that there is a divine something corresponding to something within, which no image can exhaust but which we are reminded of when in the South of Europe we look at the deep blue sky? The same unwearied form presents itself, yet still we look on, sinking deeper and deeper, and therein offering homage to the infinity of our souls which no mere form can satisfy.

COLERIDGE on the paintings of Raphael and Michelangelo, in *Philosophical Lectures*, No. V.

OUR concern is with growth and form: processes and patterns; and with Keats as pre-eminently, among the Romantics, the 'maker'. Hence the importance, as we shall come more and more to see, of the plastic in his work; of the consecrated urn standing as image of the finished form, of the bowl of the sky within which the processes of becoming and ceasing-to-be unfold themselves. Both are receptacles; both are symbols of unawareness, of detachment, of the ultimate. Voidness is integral to both. Overwrought with the brede of marble men and maidens, the Urn yet functions essentially as a resonant hollow. The sky seems blue, but it is our atmosphere which provides the colour. In the Mahayana scriptures the void is the common symbol of ultimate Reality; and this 'clear light of the void' is referred to by Coleridge in a number of significant asides. An 1805 note-book remarks that the 'deep sky is, of all visual impressions, the nearest akin to a feeling'. Keats's reaction is simpler, more direct: 'When we look at the Heavens we cannot be proud'. His early work is rich in skyscapes in which the emotions of awe and exultation predominate. The first piece of his own verse that we find quoted, in a letter to George Keats of August 1816, conveys a mood of depression and bewilderment:

> No spherey strains, by me, could e'er be caught
> From the blue Dome, though I to dimness Gaze
> On the far depth . . .

That is an unusual mood for him. Reading poems and letters we note how it is from the sky that inspiration—using the word in the full and literal significance given it by both Blake and Keats—descends. Hence the awe which fills the watcher's mind. Hence too the sense of liberation, of freedom. Exultingly Keats cries, in 'I stood tip-toe . . .',

> There was wide wand'ring for the greediest eye,
> To peer around upon variety;
> Far round the horizon's crystal air to skim,
> And trace the dwindled edgings of its brim

lines in which we feel him clearing a space for plastic action. The joy of escaping from the city is precisely this:

> To one who has been long in city pent,
> 'Tis very sweet to look into the fair
> And open face of heaven—to breathe a prayer
> Full in the smile of the blue firmament.

The prayer is no conventional gesture. There is a 'clear religion of heaven', as we shall find later in *Endymion*; but Keats's prayer is evoked neither by Wordsworth's 'moral intimations of the sky' nor by Coleridge's longing for comfort[1]. It is a prayer of

---

[1] In an 1817 notebook we read: 'We all look up to the blue sky for comfort, but nothing appears there, nothing comforts, nothing answers us, and so we die.' This, of course, is Coleridge in a mood of dejection, and it is unfair to compare Coleridge at his dismallest with Keats at his joyfullest; but one cannot imagine Keats ever thinking in this way. He *finds* comfort in the great elements (see below, p. 49), but does not *seek* it.

praise, not of petition. Keats is asking nothing from the sky, attributing no qualities to it. He is exulting in its clear space, its immensity, its otherness. He is seeing it as the void, and he is feeling it as the illimitable stage of free, untrammelled motion. We glimpse this delight in effortless, silent movement in space in *Sleep and Poetry* where

A pigeon tumbling in clear summer air

images the joy implicit in phase-beauty[1] (in contrast to its sorrow, which has already been frankly recognized); and everywhere we meet with the broad wheeling flight of eagles and sea-birds. He notes on his Scottish tour how the eagles 'move about without the least motion of wings when in an indolent fit', and 'the Hawk balances about the clouds'. It is this purposeless, self-sufficient activity that fascinates him; in an earlier letter (19 February 1818, to Reynolds) we find him reversing the conventional admiration for the busy bee.

Indeed, neither the busy bee nor the wary owl could be Keats's emblem. 'Why should we be owls, when we can be Eagles?' he asks Reynolds again (3 February 1818), commenting on Wordsworth's poetry with its 'palpable design upon us'. 'Why be teased with "nice Eyed wagtails" when we have in sight "The Cherub Contemplation"?' The eagle metaphor is persistent. Is Wordsworth 'an eagle in his nest, or on the wing?' he wonders, in a letter of 3 May. Has he 'an extended vision or a circumscribed grandeur'? Continually the stress falls on freedom and amplitude of flight. Amplitude and calm: the contrast is strong with the fevered images of flight in Shelley—medleys of riven clouds and tempest-driven leaves, sky-borne boats and jagged lightning.

As the eagle is the emblem of airy freedom, so is the swan the lord of Keats's 'undisturbed lakes'. The first paragraph of *Calidore*, and the very early *Imitation of Spenser*,[2] open into lake vistas

---

[1] For my use of this term see below, pp. 341–51.
[2] Both Blake and Keats offer an *Imitation of Spenser* as their apprentice work.

with swans: the collocation of effortless bird with unclouded sky
and crystal lake is significant:

> Young Calidore is paddling o'er the lake;
> His healthful spirit eager and awake
> To feel the beauty of a silent eve,
> Which seem'd full loath this happy world to leave;
> The light dwelt o'er the scene so lingeringly.
> He bares his forehead to the cool blue sky,
> And smiles at the far clearness all around,
> Until his heart is well nigh over wound,
> And turns for calmness to the pleasant green
> Of easy slopes, and shadowy trees that lean
> So elegantly o'er the water's brim
> And show their blossoms trim.
>
> (lines 1–12)

> Now Morning from her orient chamber came,
> And her first footsteps touch'd a verdant hill:
> Crowning its lawny crest with amber flame,
> Silv'ring the untainted gushes of its rill;
> Which, pure from mossy beds, did down distill,
> And after parting beds of simple flowers,
> By many streams a little lake did fill,
> Which round its marge reflected woven bowers,
> And, in its middle space, a sky that never lowers.

> There the kingfisher saw his plumage bright,
> Vieing with fish of brilliant dye below;
> Whose silken fins, and golden scalës light
> Cast upward, through the waves, a ruby glow:
> There saw the swan his neck of arched snow,
> And oar'd himself along with majesty:
> Sparkled his jetty eyes; his feet did show
> Beneath the waves like Afric's ebony
> And on his back a fay reclined voluptuously.
>
> (lines 1–18)

The writing, however unskilful, is spontaneously contrapuntal:
Keats apprehends and conveys a totality linking the elements and
their denizens. The sky is the void, 'universal space' in Keats's

own later phrase, the stainless and unfathomable eternity-infinity from which all manifestations proceed and to which they return. In its immitigable suchness it is for ever set apart from the corrupted currents of this world; the contemplation of it strains and endangers the mind, yet only by that contemplation can the mind come to know itself. This is a paradox implicit—often explicit—in much of Keats; *Endymion* is an attempt at its working-out. Contemplation brings serenity, but a serenity hardly tolerable for the unprepared human spirit.[1] Thus the regular image for the detached state, which is that of the unclouded sky reflected in the unruffled lake, is as regularly broken by Keats with intrusive motions of wings, oars or fins. Young Calidore paddles over the lake, 'eager and awake' to the beauty around him; he contemplates the 'cool blue sky' in its 'far clearness' until 'his heart is well nigh over wound'—strained, that is, almost to breaking point. For relief he turns to the 'pleasant green of easy slopes and shadowy trees'; to the comforting multifariousness of earth. The moment he does so, 'the freaks and dartings of the black-winged swallow' dipping into the lake and disturbing it into 'widening circles' proclaim with admirable cogency the shattering of the contemplative moment.

Sky and lake mingle in their expressive but inexpressible vacuity in many a page of Keats. His mind is essentially fugal: it blends and develops contrasts in a manner alien to the direct melodizing of Wordsworth or Shelley. The immense abstract joy which is the content of the Bachian or Corellian fugue, and which transforms us, during the moments that the disc revolves, into the likeness of itself, is a lonely joy, but also a complex one. It is lonely in its detachment, it is complex in its comprehensive mastery of diverse experience, its reconciling power. It is lonely because it is unsharable, it is complex because it includes so much which means so much to the monads whom, momentarily, it transfigures.[2]

---

[1] The terror of these lonely spaces of the mind is poignantly conveyed in the 1818 *Lines Written in the Highlands*.

[2] The special meaning which the lake image had for Keats helps to explain the anger he felt in June 1818 at (a) the 'disfigurements' of Windermere and

Poetry cannot work with the manifold energies of music. It cannot say more than one thing at the same time, and that it can often say only lamely. But in the subtle manipulation of imagery, in the 'invention' of a master theme susceptible of a variety of treatment, poetry has its own means of achieving a total effect. Keats's master theme is that of space in its three dimensions and its six directions, invisible and indivisible space which reveals its qualities through the visible and limited movements which go on within it, hinting at

> all the secrets of some wondrous thing
> That breathes about us in the vacant air.[1]

This, perhaps, is the key to 'Rest, motion', Coleridge's strange locks. And it is this 'deep eternal theme', as expressed in poetry,[2] with its intensity and richness of imagery,

> More strange, more beautiful, more smooth, more regal
> Than wings of swans, than doves, than dim-seen eagle,

that forms the ground bass to his luxuriant 'divisions'. In poetry, which is itself 'a little Region to wander in' for its lovers,[3] the contraries are reconciled in delight. The attempt at conciliation is to be observed in all Keats's major, and many of his minor, poems. Sky and forest lake-reflected under a fiery sunset fuse the four elements. The sea asserts its power in calm and storm alike:

> It keeps eternal whisperings around
> Desolate shores, and with its mighty swell
> Gluts twice ten thousand caverns, till the spell
> Of Hecate leaves them their old shadowy sound.

(*b*) Wordsworth's political activities. The two things are linked. It was only in the preceding month (3 May, to Reynolds) that he had expressed his deep appreciation of Wordsworth's genius. Now he finds the 'clear lake meddling with itself [To] cloud its pureness with a muddy gloom' (in the words of his sonnet 'How fever'd is that Man who cannot look . . .'). See below, pp. 64–5.

[1] *Sleep and Poetry*, lines 30 and 31.
[2] And not, as the riddle is commonly interpreted, poetry itself. See below, p. 105.
[3] Letter of 8 October 1817 to Benjamin Bailey.

Often 'tis in such gentle temper found,
     That scarcely will the very smallest shell
     Be moved for days from where it sometime fell,
When last the winds of heaven were unbound.

The octet presents the varied glory of the sea; the shell image
anticipates the famous 'But where the dead leaf fell, there did it
rest' of *Hyperion* as an eikon of the immobile serenity, the *sacred*
apathy, as it were, of little fragile things. The sestet immediately
counterpoints this great-small dignity against the human fussiness
and distress:

Oh ye! who have your eye-balls vexed and tired,
     Feast them upon the wideness of the Sea;
Oh ye! whose ears are dinn'd with uproar rude,
     Or fed too much with cloying melody,—
Sit ye near some old cavern's mouth, and brood
Until ye start, as if the sea-nymphs quired!

Nor is the counterpoint merely dramatic: Nature's power is a
healing virtue, to be related, insistently, to man's needs—and,
let us note, to his immediate psycho-somatic imbalance. Nature's
restorative virtues are a commonplace in Wordsworth too, but the
precise therapeutic approach is peculiar to Keats. Therapy attends
upon catharsis: cloying melody gives place to the sea's massively
rich, impersonal rhythms. Within resonant hollows—the poem
moves from cavern to cavern—the healing work is accomplished.

Already, then, in this 1817 sonnet, much of the complexity of
Keats's apprehension of the sea is conveyed.[1] We shall do well to
go a little more closely into his seascapes; the complexity is crucial
for the third book of *Endymion*, and indeed for our whole study
of Keatsian growth and form. His first glimpse of the sea came,
as far as we know, in August of the previous year when he visited
Margate with his brother Tom. Up to this time his verse had

---

[1] The sonnet is touched off, we learn from the April 1817 letter to Reynolds in
which it makes its first appearance, by *Lear*: 'the passage in Lear—"Do you not
hear the sea?" has haunted me intensely'.

contained some two or three references, and those purely conventional. They smack of Tom Moore and Darwin. Though he
rejoices (in a letter of October 1816 to Charles Cowden Clarke)
that in making the acquaintance of Leigh Hunt he is going to
meet a man who in his 'admiration of poetry does not jumble
together Shakespeare and Darwin', we cannot miss the Darwinian
sheen on his 1815 verses *To Some Ladies* and *On Receiving a Curious
Shell . . . from the Same Ladies*. The 'curiosity' of the shell is
Darwin's sentimental-scientific curiosity. The shell is a keepsake,
and so is the poem. Sylphs figure in its 'fretwork': and surely
these are the very accents of the Goddess of Botany addressing an
attendant gnome:

> Hast thou from the caves of Golconda, a gem
>   Pure as the ice-drop that froze on the mountain?
> Bright as the humming-bird's green diadem,
>   When it flutters in sun-beams that shine through a fountain?[1]

Coleridge's comparison of *The Botanic Garden* to 'the Russian
palace of ice, glittering, cold and transitory' is applicable (reading
'parlour' for 'palace') to these most owlish verses.[2]

Margate works a sea-change. We cannot miss the new amplitude of tone in this:

> . . . outspread, is seen
> Ocean's blue mantle streak'd with purple, and green.
> Now 'tis I see a canvass'd ship, and now
> Mark the bright silver curling round her prow.
> I see the lark down-dropping to his nest,
> And the broad winged sea-gull never at rest;
> For when no more he spreads his feathers free
> His breast is dancing on the restless sea.[3]

---

[1] The debt to Tom Moore is plain enough here. Beyer, in *Keats and the Demon
King*, suggests plausible parallels with Wieland's *Oberon*. Darwin's influence is
less precise, perhaps, but more pervasive. And Beattie's *The Minstrel* seems to me
to have closer relations to certain aspects of the early Keats than anything in
Oberon.

[2] The cave and (later) goblet, however, hold deeper resonances.

[3] *To My Brother George* (Margate, August 1816).

Keats's characteristic *grasp* of space is already here, his sense, physical in its immediacy, of the three-dimensioned, six-directioned continuum. Axes and co-ordinates are established through the passage (horizontal) of the ship over the 'outspread' sea, the plummet-flight of the lark (vertical) to its nest, the (oblique) soaring of the sea-gull culminating in a rest-in-motion which effectively conciliates the opposites. The gull begins to take its place as Keats's emblem of effortless mastery on the sea, side by side with those sublime sky and lake *daimons*, the eagle and swan.[1] A 'machinery', the structure of a mythology, vital, manifold and *growing* in contrast to Darwin's Urizenic fabrication, is beginning to organize itself.

There could be no greater contrast to the verses Keats had addressed in 1815 to Ann and Caroline Mathews[2] at Hastings than the letter he sends in September 1817 to two other young ladies, Jane and Marianne Reynolds, who are on holiday at Littlehampton. In April and May of the same year Keats had renewed his contact with the sea on visits to the Isle of Wight and Margate. It was at Carisbrooke that he began *Endymion*, and wrote 'It keeps eternal whisperings ...'. Sea images abound in his letters from both places: sometimes in odd contexts. A sentence in one of Hazlitt's reviews 'appears ... like a Whale's back in the Sea of Prose'. Doubts of his own vocation for poetry he intends 'to whistle ... into the Sea', he tells Leigh Hunt; but a letter sent next day to Haydon is less assured: 'I am "one that gathers Samphire, dreadful trade" —the Cliff of Poesy Towers above me'. The letter to the Reynolds girls, written from Benjamin Bailey's rooms in Magdalen, Oxford, while Keats was deep in the third book of *Endymion*, crystallizes these recent insights. The passage I shall quote is of the first importance for his doctrine of the four elements, to which we must return later. He begins with his impressions of Imogen and Juliet

---

[1] Striking instances may be found in the verse letter to C. C. Clarke (Margate, Sept. 1816) lines 56 and 57; *To the Ladies who saw me Crowned*, lines 6 and 7; *Endymion*, I, lines 453–5.

[2] See above, p. 47.

(reverting to points raised in a previous letter) and then by an odd transition—his mind still insistently linking the sea and Shakespeare —continues:

> Now let us turn to the Sea Shore. Believe me, my dear Jane it is a great Happiness to me that you are in this finest part of the year, winning a little enjoyment from the hard World—in truth the great Elements we know of are no mean Comforters—the open Sky sits upon our senses like a Sapphire Crown—the Air is our Robe of State—the Earth is our throne and the Sea a mighty Minstrell playing before it—able like David's Harp to charm the evil Spirit from such Creatures as I am—able like Ariel's to make such a one as you forget almost the tempest-cares of Life. I have found in the Ocean's Musick—varying (though selfsame) more than the passion of Timotheus, an enjoyment not to be put into words and "though inland far I be"[1] I now hear the voice most audibly while pleasing myself in the Idea of your Sensations.

It can hardly be accident that the reference to David follows immediately upon a series of phrases which transfer to man the vesture of creation which the Psalms reserve for Jehovah. This Blakean identification of humanity with divinity, and of both with 'the four Zoas', marks a significant stride forward in Keats's thinking; I believe contact with the sea, 'the wideness of the sea', no less than study of the *Timæus* and discussion with Bailey, helped him to it. It is plain from the rest of the letter—'don't you think there is something extremely fine after sunset, when there are a few white Clouds about and a few stars blinking—when the waters are ebbing and the Horison a Mystery?'—that the sea has given Keats's perception a new dimension: a suggestion of rich potentialities he could not get from the sky, the lake or the forest. The ebb and flow of the tides, obedient to Keats's moon-goddess; the glimmer of vast surfaces in motion under sunset or starlight: these brought him intimations of strangeness.

---

[1] Cf. the *Immortality Ode*, st. ix. This, and other poems of Wordsworth, he was reading with Bailey at Oxford; the influence of his other reading of this period, and of Bailey's conversation, on the elemental theme of this passage, will be noted later (see below, p. 164, note).

But more suggestive even than these sights, as we see from his letters and verses, was the sea's voice in storm or calm:

> The ocean with its vastness, its blue green,
> Its ships, its rocks, its caves, its hopes, its fears,—
> Its voice mysterious, which whoso hears
> Must think on what will be, and what has been.

That quatrain of his 1816 sonnet *To My Brother George* not only shows us Keats transcending his early models—the language is simple and perspicuous—it shows him too moving from unawareness to awareness, though it will never be the nagging awareness of positive capability. It will be the kind of awareness which is the preparation for a new kind of unawareness: the passage from innocence to experience, from what a Chinese thinker calls 'the no-knowledge of ignorance' to 'the post-gained no-knowledge'.[1] The ocean now has hopes and fears; its voice breaks the spell of the present moment and involves us in time. Blake's humanizing vision 'all Human forms identified' is present.

Sound is stressed again in the April 1817 sonnet already quoted in full; but the phrase 'mighty swell' brings us back to the notion of indolent power which is just as integral for Keats, and which leads him to some of his finest sea effects, his virtuoso anatomies of waves, foam, currents and tides. The sea is presented almost invariably in terms of relationship: its relation to the land as lover and priest, to thalassic beings as 'their native country and own natural home', to rock forms as sculptor and architect. Examples come readily to mind: the famous 'Moving waters at their priest-like task', and in *Sleep and Poetry* the simile:

> as when ocean
> Heaves calmly its broad swelling smoothness o'er
> Its rocky marge, and balances once more
> The patient weeds; that now unshent by foam
> Feel all about their undulating home,

---

[1] This seems to correspond to Barfield's distinction (in *Saving the Appearances*) between 'original participation' and 'final participation'.

(where the Keatsian empathy is patent), and again in *Staffa*, less familiar perhaps:

> 'I am Lycidas', said he,
> 'Fam'd in funeral minstrelsy!
> This was architected thus
> By the great Oceanus!—
> Here his mighty waters play
> Hollow organs all the day;
> Here by turns his dolphins all,
> Finny palmers great and small,
> Come to pay devotion due . . .
> I have been the pontiff priest
> Where the waters never rest,
> Where a fledgy sea-bird choir
> Soars for ever; holy fire
> I have hid from mortal man . . .'

A precisely religious awe is associated for Keats with the sea. This is far indeed from 'the clear religion of heaven': it is something much more complex, richer, less pure, fully human. Coleridge's terms will serve: 'The heaven lifts up my soul, the sight of the ocean seems to widen it.'[1] The sky-vision of unconditioned one-ness is dissipated; we have instead an intuition of populous depths that may well grow ominous. The moment was to come in Keats's life when the sea appalled him and he turned away from it to his early vision of peaceful lake and 'enchanted springs'—a vision associated with Spenser, his earliest 'presidor', as the sea was with Shakespeare. The verse epistle to John Hamilton Reynolds from Teignmouth (25 March 1818) was penned beside his brother Tom's sick-bed (there had been spitting of blood some twelve days before); it opens with a fantasy on Claude's 'Enchanted Castle':

> You know it well enough, where it doth seem
> A mossy place, a Merlin's Hall, a dream.
> You know the clear Lake, and the little Isles,
> The Mountains blue, and cold near neighbour rills.

---

[1] *Anima Poetæ* (1804).

This is clearly 'escapist' from his brother's suffering and from the 'vision of the sea' which had plunged him into 'a sort of Purgatory blind':

> Dear Reynolds, I have a mysterious tale
> And cannot speak it.[1] The first page I read
> Upon a Lampit Rock of green sea weed
> Among the breakers—'Twas a quiet Eve;
> The rocks were silent—the wide sea did weave
> An untumultuous fringe of silver foam
> Along the flat brown sand.

The mysterious tale begins quietly, with one of Keats's characteristic shore-scapes. But he has come far since *To the Sea* and *Sleep and Poetry*: *Endymion* has intervened, with its ocean sojourn[2]; so have the sonnets on Fame and on *Lear*, with their burden of death and self-doubt. Keats has found 'the agony, the strife of human hearts' he had anticipated in 1816, perhaps without guessing how swiftly these things would be upon him. He is no longer able 'to sit upon the shore and a pipe a silly pipe'. His gaze is drawn irresistibly into the depths:

> I was at home,
> And should have been most happy—but I saw
> Too far into the sea; where every maw
> The greater on the less feeds evermore:—
> But I saw too distinct into the core
> Of an eternal fierce destruction,
> And so from Happiness I far was gone.
> Still am I sick of it: and though today
> I've gathered young spring-leaves, and flowers gay
> Of Periwinkle and wild strawberry,
> Still do I that most fierce destruction see,
> The Shark at savage prey—the hawk at pounce,
> The gentle Robin, like a pard or ounce,
> Ravening a worm—

---

[1] The sense of impotence to communicate is new and disturbing to Keats.

[2] Letter of 14 September 1817, to Jane and Marianne Reynolds: 'Endymion and I are at the bottom of the sea.'

the naked vision of Blake that 'life feeds on life', the penetration beneath the surface. Keats will come, in 1818, to the bitter knowledge of the contraries.

[*On Receiving a Curious Shell* (1815)—*To My Brother George* (1816) —*Calidore* (1817)—*Sonnet: It Keeps Eternal Whisperings* (1817) —*On Visting Staffa* (1818)—*To J. H. Reynolds, Esq.* (1818)]

Chapter Four

DILIGENT INDOLENCE

Let go your hold on the Four Elements,
And in the midst of the Eternally Serene allow yourself
to quaff or to peck, as you please.
    YUNG-CHIA TA-SHIH's *Song of Enlightenment*.

I LIKE the title of one of Middleton Murry's books: *The Mystery of Keats*. There *is* a mystery about this man who like Blake was without a mask and like Blake baffled his friends and has consistently baffled his commentators—often without their knowing it. It is very easy to pick out this element or that in Keats's richly diversified personality and weave a satisfyingly coherent account of his mind and its workings around it; it is a little more difficult to discover and to accept a pair of elements which are polar opposites, and to watch Keats's energies weaving their own patterns (elliptical this time, rather than conveniently circular) around the poles.[1] And it is most difficult to renounce thinking in terms of spheres and ellipses altogether and face the fruitful chaos of ideas, sensations, intuitions, half-seeings and blind guesses which did duty in Keats for a philosophy; to watch the chaos heave and bubble and burst into life, into form, into growth leading to further forms, formlessnesses, 'self-creations and self-destroyings'. It is difficult; but it is the only way.

Reading Keats, one is insistently conscious of how little of his central thinking he was able to share with his friends. That may seem paradoxical, in face of the letters. I use the words 'share' and 'central' very deliberately. In the letters we see Keats discussing frankly and copiously a great number of very difficult ideas; but not his central idea. That was hardly for debate, perhaps, even

---

[1] I am using Keats's own metaphor here (see *Letters*, p. 111).

with himself. Of course the letters are very largely (in their 'philosophical' parts) a series of comments, or afterthoughts—attempts to clear up points mooted the day before or even the same night. Leaving aside the long journal-letters to George and Georgiana in America, they are a species of aftermath to discussion, and failing attendance at the discussions we cannot be altogether sure that we have grasped the point. We are given, as it were, a book from which the text is missing, and only the glosses remain. We can never know how far these talks in Hunt's parlour, or Bailey's, or Haydon's penetrated into Keats's 'vast idea'. We cannot know: but I think we can surmise that Keats was never anxious to canvass his 'half-seeings', and in the later years (when his most constructive thinking was done) even less eager than in the old Vale of Health days. All too often he found that 'Conversation is not a search after knowledge, but an endeavour at effect'.[1] He came to learn the limits of understanding, and he was more and more driven in upon himself. 'Think of my Pleasure in Solitude', he writes in October 1818 to George and Georgiana, 'in comparison of my commerce with the world—there I am a child—there they do not know me not even my most intimate acquaintance—I give into their feelings as though I were refraining from irritating a little child—Some think me middling, others silly, others foolish—every one thinks he sees my weak side against my will, when in truth it is with my will—I am content to be thought all this because I have in my own breast so great a resource.' As I read him, I seem to catch an echo of two voices: of Blake's, when he declared with some bitterness, 'I am hid'; and of Browne's, when he confessed, 'I am in the dark to all the world, and my nearest friends behold me but in a cloud'. Both these men, like Keats, were 'very fond of good company'.

Keats's half-seeings were often magnificent, and they are as often conveyed in images of astonishing cogency, 'fine isolated verisimilitudes caught from the Penetrale of mystery'. But because they *are* half-seeings, glimpses, they fit into no complete

---

[1] Letter of 8 March 1819 to B. R. Haydon.

pattern; we find them in contexts that do nothing to elucidate them. For example, the grandest of his sea-similes:

> . . . as when ocean
> Heaves calmly its broad swelling smoothness o'er
> Its rocky marge, and balances once more
> The patient weeds, that now unshent by foam
> Feel all about their undulating home

—a chunk of sheer sensation in which, as you read, you *become* wave and frond—figures in a jejune ensemble of parlour statuary, vases, engravings. We discover its meaning, its concern with an eternal ocean, with human monads that have at last made themselves free from the froth of individual hopes and cares, only as we read on in the verse which follows *Poems 1817*. How far these considerations were present to Keats's mind in late 1816 is a question I cannot hope to answer. His central statement about the elements, again, is made in a letter to Jane and Marianne Reynolds,[1] not the most intelligent of Keats's correspondents. We may surmise that neither Jane nor Marianne would appreciate in the least this remarkable eikon of the Cosmic Man robed in the elemental powers and attentive to the thalassic music. But Keats had little choice of the minds to which he might open his perceptions. Would Hunt or Haydon have been greatly preferable to the Reynolds girls? Coleridge would have understood him; but acquaintance with Coleridge came too late. Shelley would have understood him; but there was some sort of antipathy. Blake would have understood him; but he never, as far as we know, met Blake.[2]

One of the ancillary ideas or problems that Keats did find it possible to discuss with his friends was the question of leisure, or, as he called it, 'indolence'. It is linked, as we shall see later, with

---

[1] See above, p. 49, where the passage is quoted.

[2] The impression he made on Severn—and it persisted for nearly a quarter of a century—is worth noting: 'His was a gigantic mind which would have required another 10 years to mature it.—he seemd a supernatural child in his emotions & speculations . . . he cared not to examine for nature did it for him . . .' (*K.C.*, II, 138).

his other bigger problem of 'abstraction'. Little by little, in the letters and the verse, he is working out his half-seeings into something like a coherent understanding, almost a doctrine, which embraces three terms: indolence, abstraction, silence.

The 'silent workings' of genius within him fascinated Keats at all times. Few poets have been so concerned to *watch*, to turn their attention inwards on the processes of creation. And this implies no turning away of another sort of attention from the world outside. The two can be combined; indeed, each works at its most intense in harmony with the other. The understanding of the identity of the life within and the life without came to him in those moments of detachment when he could 'be still and know'. His verse is full of invitations to be silent, to stop doing whatever one is doing, to let the stream of events flow around and through one as one watches. 'I stood tip-toe upon a little hill . . .': the first line of the first poem in his first published volume leads us into an expectant stillness; we are bidden to 'linger awhile upon some bending planks . . . and watch intently'. 'Stop and consider!' is the watchword of *Sleep and Poetry*, a poem whose very title connects rest and creation. The opening lines of *Hyperion*, again, capture just such a moment of supreme stillness.

Yet even stillness is for Keats a matter of relationship; and it is here that he differs from that other great poet of silence, Wordsworth. Wordsworth gives us the loneliness, the self-sufficiency of silence:

> The silence that is in the starry sky,
> The sleep that is among the lonely hills.

Not so Keats. His silences are companiable: from the human warmth of the sonnet *To My Brothers*:

> Small, busy flames play through the fresh laid coals,
>   And their faint cracklings o'er our silence creep
>   Like whispers of the household gods that keep
> A gentle empire o'er fraternal souls . . .

to the interchange of courtesies between 'silent water' and trees and grass-blades in 'I stood tip-toe . . .', a poem modulating

towards silence through the whole gamut of human-natural
relations:

> The ripples seem right glad to reach those cresses,
> And cool themselves among the em'rald tresses;
> The while they cool themselves, they freshness give,
> And moisture, that the bowery green may live:
> So keeping up an interchange of favours,
> Like good men in the truth of their behaviours.

In *Endymion*, silence itself is humanized, made to breathe and feel;
'obstinate silence', displaced for the moment by a human voice,
comes back

> heavily again,
> Feeling about for its old couch of space
> And airy cradle.

More often Keats presents sound and silence not in opposition,
but as complementary: or, more accurately, in the relation of
manifestation to principle, for silence is the 'ground' of sound
and above all of music. Creative leisure, indolence, is very much a
matter of listening to silence: when we learn to interpret that voice
we have gone a long way towards total understanding; we have
arrived, with Endymion, at the point when

> to his capable ears
> Silence was music from the holy spheres.

More than one of his friends noted Keats's own 'listening look'
when his attention was seized by beauty or strangeness. We could
piece these evidences together, side by side with data from the
poems, to get a fairly complete picture of the silence-indolence-
abstraction triptych; but the synthesis would be tedious, and we
happen to have a better guide in a single document, the letter
which Keats wrote to Reynolds on 19 February 1818. This letter
might almost have been written in reply to Wordsworth's
Gipsies: at least we know that Keats was thinking constantly
and critically about Wordsworth during this month and the
next, and in the previous October he had defended the indolent

gipsies ('they in the visible world had been as picturesque an object as he in the invisible. The Smoke of their fire—their attitudes—their Voices were all in harmony with the Evenings') against the poet's condemnation ('it seems to me that if Wordsworth had thought a little deeper at that Moment he would not have written the Poem at all') while recognizing that the poem is little more than a *jeu d'esprit*.[1] However this may be, the letter to Reynolds remains our most precious prose pointer towards an understanding of this core of Keats's self-knowledge, and we shall do well to study it closely.

There is no preamble. Full of the sense of discovery, of a newly-perceived truth, Keats plunges into his theme:

> My dear Reynolds,
> I had an idea that a Man might pass a very pleasant life in this manner—let him on a certain day read a certain Page of full Poesy or distilled Prose, and let him wander with it, and muse upon it, and reflect upon it, and bring home to it, and prophesy upon it, and dream upon it, until it becomes stale—but when will it do so? Never. When [a] Man has arrived at a certain ripeness in intellect any one grand and spiritual passage serves him as a starting-post towards all "the two-and-thirty Palaces". How happy is such a voyage of conception, what delicious diligent Indolence! A doze upon a sofa does not hinder it, and a nap upon Clover engenders ethereal finger-pointings—the prattle of a child gives it wings, and the converse of middle-age a strength to beat them—a strain of music conducts to "an odd angle of the Isle", and when the leaves whisper it puts a girdle round the earth.

The essence of Keats is here—his 'sphericity', if I may call it so, the supreme bent of his mind for connecting diverse worlds of experience. But what is the discovery that so excites him? His words read easily, and, as with so much of Keats, we may, just as easily, miss or half-catch their meaning. Those who will have their simple Keats at any price will find no difficulties here: he is

---

[1] And even maintaining, as against Hazlitt's 'rightness' in criticizing the poem, that Wordsworth is 'rightest'. For negative capability does not judge (*Letters*, p. 55).

enthusing about poetry, about the luxury of enjoying poetry, about the effect a passage of Spenser or Shakespeare has in starting him off on one of his own flights of imagination. It was a way Keats had, they will say, of initiating his associational 'stream of consciousness'; and that is all.

But that is not quite all. The associationists are right about this particular technique of Keats: it led him to some of his major triumphs and many of his major defeats, and it marks him off in some degree from the other Romantics. But it is a technique Keats has practised from the beginning. There is nothing to get excited about in that—no new discovery. Keats is talking about something else: not about suggestion, but about power. The passage of full poetry or distilled prose starts a man off (if he has reached a certain ripeness in intellect) on a journey towards all 'the two-and-thirty Palaces'. The Buddhist phrase is vital here. For the thirty-two palaces are intellectual mansions, stations of realization in the unending struggle between ignorance and enlightenment.[1] I do not think that Keats used the phrase (wherever he may have found it) carelessly.[2] That is not to say that he uses it accurately. He has a tendency, here and elsewhere, to confuse the noetic and the occult. But he has sensed the power of the 'word'.

The notion of the word as power is very ancient and stems from the doctrine of the primacy of sound in the primitive tradition—a point which we shall return to later. Keats, we know, chanted his own verses (badly, his friends said) and probably chanted other verses, the passages of full poetry that he took with him into the open air, musing and reflecting and prophesying upon them.[3] And as he chanted he felt the verses 'brought home' to him, penetrating, modifying his consciousness, and affecting his perception of

---

[1] Cf. the 'thirty-two marvellous ways of wisdom' of the Kabbala.

[2] A great deal of work yet remains to be done on Keats's reading.

[3] Bailey tells us (*K.C.*, II, 276) how he intoned the 'roundelay' from Chatterton's *Ælla*, adding that the opening line 'Come with acorn cup and thorn' had the greatest charm for him. Readers of this book will see one reason why this should be so. The acorn cup is the smallest of Keats's urns.

the objects around him. The verse acts as a kind of focus, a burning-glass under whose power the 'husk of natural objects' (as he was later to phrase it) is consumed and their 'eternal lineaments' are made manifest. Through the power of the verse he suddenly finds himself able to 'see into the life of things'. It is a peculiarly Keats-ian technique: peculiar, that is, in the Romantic world of poetry. It is not at all peculiar in the world of religion. It is precisely what the great Puritans did with a verse of the Bible; it is precisely what the Indian rishis did with a verse from the Vedas, and if we wish to know what Keats is talking about in this passage of the 1818 letter to Reynolds we cannot do better than turn to the tradition which Keats so constantly, though so surreptitiously, draws upon. Take these words of Professor Zimmer: 'The word *brahman* in the Vedic hymns simply means, in many cases, "this stanza, this verse, this line"'; and further:

> Brahman as the charm, or sacred magic formula, is the crystallized, frozen form (the convenient, handy form, as it were) of the highest divine energy. This energy is perennially latent in man, dormant, yet capable of being stirred to creative wakefulness through concentration. By brooding upon it, hatching it, the wizard priest makes it available to his mind and purpose, bringing it to crystallization in the charm. Not yet so crystallized, in its unprecipitated, liquid or ethereal state, it is the powerful urge and surge that rises from man's unconscious being. Brahman, in other words, is that through which we live and act, the fundamental spontaneity of our nature.[1]

---

[1] I shall refer the reader once again to this passage in chapter v below, where we shall find it of the first importance in the interpretation of Keats's sonnet *The Poet*. It comes from Professor Zimmer's *Philosophies of India* (Routledge and Kegan Paul, London, 1952, pp. 78–9). And this further passage from Keats himself is illuminating: 'A melodious passage in poetry is full of pleasures both sensual and spiritual. The spiritual is felt when the very letters and points of charactered language show like the hieroglyphics of beauty; the mysterious signs of our immortal freemasonry! "A thing to dream of, not to tell." The sensual life of verse springs warm from the lips of Kean and to one learned in Shakespearian hiero-glyphics—learned in the spiritual portion of those lines to which Kean adds a sensual grandeur, his tongue must seem to have robbed the Hybla bees and left them honeyless!' *On Edmund Kean as a Shakespearian Actor* (Keats's 21 Dec. 1817 contribution to *The Champion*).

Keats and Zimmer are talking about the same thing; for to Keats, as to Blake, all great literature is canonical, and Shakespeare is as much a sacred text as Isaiah. Such literature is a source of power as well as inspiration; it can serve the poet as a starting-point for the voyage of spiritual discovery. We note once again the emphasis on the unity of experience in Keats's letter. To the wise man, nothing is a distraction: everything opens out into wisdom, and everything is related in a mutual aid-and-abetting. But the connections cannot be forced or systematized. The child's prattle and the converse of middle age remain themselves, whole and distinct, united only in a greater whole which remains unseen, 'a girdle round the earth', whose meaning is found in the leaves' whisper. There must be no connecting mentally, but simply a living relationship valid for one time and for one place.

And this brings Keats to consider the question of reading. The sacred text, the *mantram*, exists within the canonical *book*: but we cannot use the entire book as a source of power. The *mantram* is a crystallizing out from the book; and we shall often do well to take the crystal and lay the matrix aside.

> Nor will this sparing touch of noble Books be any irreverence to their Writers—for perhaps the honors paid by Man to Man are trifles in comparison to the Benefit done by great Works to the Spirit and pulse of good by their mere passive existence. Memory should not be called knowledge. Many have original minds who do not think it—they are led away by Custom. Now it appears to me that almost any Man may like the spider spin from his own inwards his own airy Citadel—the points of leaves and twigs on which the spider begins her work are few, and she fills the air with a beautiful circuiting. Man should be content with as few points to tip with the fine Web of his Soul, and weave a tapestry empyrean full of symbols for his spiritual eye, of softness for his spiritual touch, of space for his wandering, of distinctness for his luxury.

'Memory should not be called knowledge'—for knowledge is only of the immediate and the new. Note Keats's optimism, again approaching Blake's: men are blinded by custom, fail to realize their own powers, and forfeit their inheritance. The caverned man closes his five windows; but if he chooses to 'step into eternity' the gate is open, and he will find 'space for his wandering'.

The next passage in the letter is one I shall quote later in another context.[1] It is remarkable for the contrapuntal virtuosity with which Keats develops his theme of relationship: 'Minds would leave each other in contrary directions, traverse each other in numberless points, and at last greet each other at the journey's end.' It is followed by a fantasia in praise of 'wise passiveness':

> It has been an old comparison for our urging on—the Beehive; however, it seems to me that we should rather be the flower than the Bee—for it is a false notion that more is gained by receiving than by giving—no, the receiver and the giver are equal in their benefits. The flower, I doubt not, receives a fair guerdon from the Bee—its leaves blush deeper in the next spring—and who shall say between Man and Woman which is the most delighted? Now it is more noble to sit like Jove than to fly like Mercury—let us not therefore go hurrying about and collecting honey, bee-like buzzing here and there impatiently from a knowledge of what is to be aimed at; but let us open our leaves like a flower and be passive and receptive—budding patiently under the eye of Apollo and taking hints from every noble insect that favours us with a visit—sap will be given us for meat and dew for drink . . .

The wise passiveness is wiser than Wordsworth's; it connects more points of the web of being, roots itself deeper and broader, opens itself to wider influences, and eschews preconceptions and expectations. Keats's integral images of flowering, budding and fruiting, of growth proceeding in the plant world under an 'interchange of favours' with the insect world, are developed in a tone of sweet reasonableness impossible to resist. And the reasonableness is carried to the point of laughing deprecation:

> I was led into these thoughts, my dear Reynolds, by the beauty of the morning operating on a sense of Idleness—I have not read any Books—the Morning said I was right—I had no idea but of the morning and the thrush said I was right—seeming to say,

---

[1] See p. 222 below.

O thou whose face hath felt the Winter's wind,
Whose eye has seen the snow-clouds hung in mist,
And the black elm-tops 'mong the freezing stars,
To thee the Spring will be a harvest-time.
O thou, whose only book has been the light
Of supreme darkness which thou feddest on
Night after night when Phœbus was away,
To thee the Spring shall be a triple morn.
O fret not after knowledge—I have none,
And yet my song comes native with the warmth.
O fret not after knowledge—I have none,
And yet the Evening listens. He who saddens
At thought of idleness cannot be idle,
And he's awake who thinks himself asleep.

Now I am sensible all this is a mere sophistication (however it may neighbour to any truths), to excuse my own indolence—so I will not deceive myself that Man should be equal with Jove—but think himself very well off as a sort of scullion-Mercury, or even a humble Bee. It is no matter whether I am right or wrong, either one way or another, if there is sufficient to lift a little time from your shoulders.

Your affectionate friend
John Keats—

We may discount the discounting, though the humour and the humility are pleasing. Keats was writing from his heart. What the morning said and what the thrush said weighed with him. The poem sums up the letter, compressing its paradoxes. 'The light of supreme darkness which thou feddest on' is a phrase welding the two worlds, intellectual and organic, between which Keats's eagle flight moved easily; the main clause belongs to the sphere of the *via negativa*, the relative clause to the sphere of nutrition: the complementary worlds of form and growth.

The sonnet *On Fame*, which comes at the end of his 'soul-making' letter of February–May 1819, shows how, a year later, Keats's thought was still running upon the theme of letting alone, of creative indolence.

How fever'd is that Man who cannot look
    Upon his mortal days with temperate blood
Who vexes all the leaves of his Life's book
    And robs his fair name of its maidenhood
It is as if the rose should pluck herself
    Or the ripe plum finger its misty bloom
As if a clear Lake meddling with itself
    Should cloud its pureness with a muddy gloom
But the rose leaves herself upon the Briar
    For winds to kiss and grateful Bees to feed
And the ripe plum still wears its dim attire
    The undisturbed Lake has crystal space
    Why then should man teasing the world for grace
Spoil his salvation by a fierce miscreed?

The moral of which, plainly, is that man meddles with himself to his own hurt. Nature, more wisely, lets well alone. The 'soul-making' theme is illustrated: man should submit himself passively to the 'world' which acts upon him to give his 'spark of divinity' a 'soul', a personality.[1] The sonnet elaborates Keats's basic ideas of purity, freedom, unawareness, in a cluster of familiar images.

Is this purity, this negative capability, really possible for the poet? Keats's old problem revives. That it is possible for some, who are not poets, he knows. One such person is his sister-in-law, Georgiana, to whom, with her husband, the letter and the poem are addressed. Georgiana had long impressed him by her natural-ness, her spontaneity. A sonnet of December 1816 ('Nymph of the downward smile, and sidelong glance') shows her 'serenely wand'ring in a trance Of sober thought'. In a letter to Bailey of 10 June 1818 he writes:

I like her better and better—she is the most disinterested woman I ever knew—that is to say she goes beyond degree in it. To see an entirely disinterested Girl quite happy is the most pleasant and extraordinary thing in the world—it depends upon a thousand

---

[1] Here Keats's original 'misled' for 'fever'd' in the first line may be judged preferable. The 'fierce miscreed' of the last line is not unconnected with his foregoing strictures on Christianity as a system of moral discrimination and *effort*.

5

Circumstances—on my word 'tis extraordinary. Women must want Imagination and they may thank God for it—and so may we that a delicate being can feel happy without any sense of crime. It puzzles me and I have no sort of Logic to comfort me—I shall think it over.

Keats did think it over. Maybe the antipodal contrast between Georgiana and Coleridge (a famous meeting with whom is described in this 1819 letter) was running through his mind when he wrote the *On Fame* sonnet, and the 'Naiad' who appears in the revised version is no other than his sister-in-law. 'Are there any flowers in bloom you like?' he asks her: and the recital of activities he imagines her engaged in (though conceived in the spirit of nonsense) could have been conceived of none but Georgiana: 'While you are hovering with your dinner in prospect you may do a thousand things—put a hedgehog into Georges hat—pour a little water into his rifle—soak his boots in a pail of water—cut his jacket round into shreds like a roman kilt or the back of my grandmothers stays . . .' Nevertheless, Georgiana puzzles him, and we feel from the letter to Bailey that he did not quite understand her. He was right in pointing to her 'disinterestedness' as the source of her happiness; he was right in saying that she lacked imagination, if by 'imagination' he meant the restless film of images, of speculation, that too often interposes between the perception and the reality; he was wrong in thinking that her state of mind depended on a thousand circumstances; it didn't, it depended on one, her spontaneity.

Georgiana counted for a good deal in Keats's life; she might have counted for a good deal more. I have little doubt that he was in love with her, and that George (quite unknowingly, perhaps) cut him out. She would have made him a wonderful wife. 'There was something original about her,' Henry Stephens wrote twenty-five years after meeting her, '& John seemed to regard her as a being whom he was delighted to honour.'[1] She counted for a good deal too in his poetry, as we shall come to see later. She

---

[1] *K.C.*, II, 212.

incarnated for him 'the magic power of unreflecting love'; she is the Peona, the little sister of *Endymion*, and she is Keats's personal symbol of the sex-relation I call 'biological' or instinctive. She is a figure of warm immediacy in Keats's life, a refuge from abstraction and faery lands forlorn. Let us bear her in mind as, in the next chapter, we trace something of Keats's deep-rooted feeling for community.

[Sonnet: *To My Brothers* (1816)—Letter to J. H. Reynolds (1818)— Sonnet: *On Fame* (1819)]

Chapter Five

THE HUSK OF NATURAL OBJECTS

Ask we what makes one keep and one bestow?
That Pow'r who bids the Ocean ebb and flow,
Bids seed-time, harvest, equal course maintain,
Thro' reconcil'd extremes of drought and rain,
Builds Life on Death, on Change Duration founds,
And gives th' eternal wheels to know their rounds.
ALEXANDER POPE, *Epistle* III.

WE talk of the Romantic Revolt—but the rebels were far from presenting a united front. I picture them to myself as guerrillas, each making a sortie here and there; sometimes jostling and scratching in the darkness. They are dusty, with the dust of the terrain they are struggling to break away from: their boots too are heavy with the local clay. Wordsworth's mud is moral; he belongs in the line of Thomson and Cowper. Coleridge's dust is philosophico-theological; he trails clouds of Berkeley and Butler and Hartley with him to the end. The clay tempering Byron's fire is Popean and mainly satiric (though he appreciated Pope for other things too). Shelley's earthier aspects rest upon Augustan liberalism, Godwin, the Deism of the Enlightenment.

Keats is Augustan too, in his feeling for order, for a community of man and nature rooted in the fruitfulness of the earth and the happiness of society, controlled by the process of the seasons, varied through the transformations of the contraries. The poet he most closely approaches in this respect is Pope. Dr F. R. Leavis has shown, in a memorable essay, how Pope's feeling for Augustan civilization is evoked by ' a profound sense of it as dependent on and harmonious with an ultimate and inclusive order'; and he quotes, in illustration, the lines from the third *Moral Epistle* which I have chosen for my epigraph.

Now this is Keats's inclusive vision too, or at least the core of it. He was to extend the scope of that vision into spheres unexplored by Pope, but it is from Pope that he starts. And no other of the Romantics starts from quite this point. Keats is with Pope and the Augustans not only in his understanding of man in nature, but in his realization—by which I mean a lived understanding—of man in society, and of the unity of all three terms. Wordsworth, Coleridge, Byron, Shelley—they are all true 'Romantics' in their willed or compulsive solitariness, their aggressively exilic life-patterns. Not so Keats. His is a pattern of life rooted in society, in the give and take of common intercourse. 'Men should be in imitation of Spirits "responsive to each others note"', he writes in a letter of 31 August 1819 to John Taylor. For such a life he was fitted by the mildly sceptical, deeply tolerant, undemanding sensibility of his nature. 'Men should bear with each other,' he writes to Benjamin Bailey, 'there lives not the Man who may not be cut up, aye hashed to pieces on his weakest side.' That is the worldly wisdom or common sense of eighteenth-century society, weary of the moral and theological extravagances of the previous age. It made possible the community of men of diverse temperaments and gifts and opinions that we call civilization. It made possible the coffee-house or the club where Johnson and Goldsmith and Gibbon and Boswell and Garrick and Reynolds could all meet together and talk things over, shout at each other sometimes or snarl, but never sulk. Or if they sulked for an hour or a day, they got over it; they didn't split up. Now if we cannot talk of Romantic society splitting up it is because it was never a real unity. It never came together in the first place. Even pairs like Wordsworth and Coleridge, Byron and Shelley, failed in cohesion: the hidden stresses were too great. There was no common ground. Only Keats's cockneyism—which is the relic of the old coffee-house society—stood the strain; only in *his* letters do we catch the accents of Boswell and Addison. And when, from time to time, his circle broke down (Haydon quarrelling with Hunt, for instance) he regarded it quite simply as his job to repair the breach, to bring old friends together again.[1]

The possibilities were more limited, of course, than in the heyday of the Augustan synthesis. There were too many second-rate minds in the circles familiar to Keats. The first-rate ones were ruminating in the Lakes or brooding in the Apennines; and there was no solid background of accepted ideas, no tradition. So we find Keats turning to a more integral cultural pattern, that of the family: and again the distinction from his contemporaries is clear-cut. He is, as they are not, a family man. He is deeply attached to his brothers and his small sister; he welcomes Georgiana as a sister-in-law; he is keenly interested in the child that will be born to the young couple. He is very much at home in the family life of his friends. About the possibility of a family life of his own he is more ambiguous, but the causes of ambiguity—the financial reasons, and the ill-health, and the temperament of the artist—are clear enough. And if he turns to the idea of freedom among the forms and processes of nature, it is even here as one entering a great family, not as one escaping into solitude.

Comparison of Keats's and Wordsworth's 'nature poetry' is favourite examination fodder, and on that level the subject is no longer of interest: the antithesis of bare fields and mountains bare to hush'd cool-rooted flowers fragrant-eyed has lost its power to surprise. Another kind of comparison, in other terms, may yet be fruitful; but we must widen our field. The 'worlds' must be synthesized, and not Keats and Wordsworth only, but Keats and Coleridge, with Darwin in the background, must be brought into play.

Let us glance back at Darwin for a moment. We have seen how glints of his metallic brilliance flash through Keats's early verses. There was an attraction, and I think it was primarily an attraction of subject, not of style: Keats liked Darwin's morphology, his buds and fruits and seed-cases (the illustrations are a pleasing

---

[1] It is notably when his own flame burns low, through illness or disappointment, that his circle shows signs of disintegrating.

feature of *The Botanic Garden*). But the influence, if we can dignify it with that name, could be no more than transitory: the rainbow passage in *Lamia* marks a final rejection. There are ironic asides in poems and letters. Writing to Reynolds from Oxford (21 September 1817) Keats excuses himself from describing the countryside: 'I have not time to elucidate the forms and shapes of the grass and trees; for, rot it! I forgot to bring my mathematical case with me; which unfortunately contained my triangular Prism so that the hues of the grass cannot be dissected for you. . . .' That is good fooling in the manner of *An Island in the Moon*: like Blake's satire, it pillories analysis, dissection, myopia. 'Has Martin met with the Cumberland Beggar or been wondering at the old Leech gatherer', he enquires later in the same letter: 'Has he a turn for fossils? that is, is he capable of sinking up to his Middle in a Morass'—the query brings Wordsworth and Darwin slyly together.

And what of Coleridge? Glasses which little things display fascinated him as they did his friend Poole; he had an intense interest in the structure of organisms, in the chemical properties of matter. It was an interest, we know, that went well beyond the weighing-and-measuring plane, but there is a real sense in which it limited Coleridge. There is a myopia about his nature descriptions, a nigglingness, or else an expansive vagueness. Contours waver; distances are ill-defined. He concentrates on the minutiæ, we suspect, before he has established his view of the whole. Blake would have said that he had begun to look through glasses before he learned to use his eyes:[1] even, that he turned to the microscope for a definition and a clarity that his inadequate use of the unaided eye denied him.

To look at things from a retreat, to see through glass, through

---

[1] Cf. with Blake's 'The Microscope knows not of this nor the Telescope: they alter The ratio of the Spectator's Organs, but leave Objects untouch'd', this from Thomas Taylor: '. . . they boast of ocular conviction through the assistance of the telescope; and what reasoning can invalidate the testimony of the eyes? I answer, that the eyes in this particular are more deceived when assisted by glasses, than when trusting to their own naked power of perceiving' (Introduction to the *Timæus*).

a microscope or a window, was Coleridge's failing; and he was not unaware of it. Coleridge could see, but he could not touch. Even more than Wordsworth's, his sense-perceptions were limited: 'the tyranny of the eye' held him fast. Or, seeing, he remained unmoved—a victim, I suspect, of Wordsworth's doctrine of recollection. He by-passed the immediate response in favour of a 'reconsidered passion'. And about this he is, in his own phrase, complacent.

> Nothing affects me much at the moment it happens. It either stupefies me, and I, perhaps, look at a merry-make and dance-the-hay of flies,[1] or listen entirely to the loud click of the great clock[2], or I am simply indifferent, not without some sense of philosophical self-complacency. For a thing at the moment is but a thing of the moment; it must be taken up into the mind, diffuse itself through the whole multitude of shapes and thoughts, not one of which it leaves untinged, between [not one of]which and it some new thought is not engendered.

This was written in 1799: it is the expression of a mind still thinking in terms of associationism; and Coleridge at a later date would not have regarded his condition with such 'philosophical self-complacency'. I think he would have contemplated it with sorrow. For the whole passage, in its blindness to the supremacy of the moment in-and-out of time, is obtuse: it proclaims the division within himself that he came to analyse with such wry virtuosity, three years later, in the *Dejection Ode*. Unfortunately, when we cease to be complacent about a fact we don't alter the fact. Coleridge remained a divided being.

Let us watch him once again, in the moment of 14 April 1805 (just a year after the *Dejection Ode*) which we have already praised

---

[1] A triviality, Coleridge means; but Blake saw a world of wonder in

> the gorgeous clothed Flies that dance & sport in summer
> Upon the sunny brooks & meadows: every one the dance
> Knows in its intricate mazes of delight artful to weave:
> Each one to sound his instruments of music in the dance,
> To touch each other & recede, to cross & change & return.
>
> (*Milton*, K. 514)

[2] The refuge from actuality in measurement, mechanical repetition.

for its insight and its sympathetic quality, when from his study at
Valetta he saw the moon 'dim-glimmering through the dewy
window-pane'. Our praise must remain, but no longer unqualified.
We have come to appreciate another way of seeing, which functions in unawareness, asking nothing, suggesting nothing. When
we re-read that first phrase of Coleridge's—'In looking at objects
of Nature while I am thinking . . .'—we cannot but remember
another poet whom such contemplation 'teases *out of thought*':
we realize that for Keats Coleridge must be classed with those
'complex minds' that are 'imaginative and at the same time careful
of their fruits',[1] minds which, as Coleridge himself goes on to
declare, 'seem . . . to be seeking, as it were *asking* for, a symbolical
language . . .'. The element of strain, of effort, of interpretation
is present; and, like the dewy window-pane through which
he gazes at the dim-glimmering moon, interposes itself between
Coleridge and the object.[2] Keats, in a similar situation, goes out
in immediate sympathy, picks about the gravel with the sparrow:
careless of everything 'beyond the moment'.

Nor, we note, is there any question with Keats of continuity: no
linking of the new to the old in an attempt at interpretation, at
assimilation. The mind that interprets, assimilates, is afraid. We
fear the new in its unexpectedness and originality, its dangerous
abruptness; we meet it with our old experience, our stock response—and miss its meaning. Coleridge tells us he is 'seeking, as
it were *asking* for, a symbolical language for something within
[him] that already and forever exists, [rather] than observing
anything new'. This is dangerous. It protects the form, but it
inhibits the growth. We feel more secure in this way, of course;
but we cramp ourselves. For the new always presents a challenge,
demands a fresh response; and demands my response, not yours;
and my response of this moment, not the response of the yester-
day's, the stale, me. We have to remain vulnerable, alert, and
sensitive. Response to the new implies a continual dying and rising

---

[1] See below, p. 225.
[2] A later note (1810) plunges deeper into unreality: 'We understand Nature
just as if, at a distance, we looked at the image of a person in a looking-glass. . . .'

again, an amazing humility. We have to learn to act, not to react, not to interpret, but to permit that 'great thing', as Traherne called it, which resides in the instant, to unfold itself within the instant. And not 'bind to ourselves a joy'.

We must not confuse Coleridge's interpretation of the new as the old with Keats's counterpointing of the old with the new. The Keatsian vision is possible only to the mind for which old and new have been, in the creative act, understood and transcended. For such a mind the problem of the One and the Many is non-existent; it is neither monist nor dualist, and the attempt to interpret its findings in terms of existent systems can only be a failure. Hence the elusiveness of Blake, hence the temptation (often succumbed to by his critics) to treat Keats's ideas with less than respect. We can best describe Keats's standpoint as 'non-dualism', in sharp contrast to Coleridge's which is easily recognizable as idealistic dualism. As Shawcross puts it in his introduction to *Biographia Literaria*: 'To him the beautiful in nature was necessarily regarded as symbolical of a spiritual reality, but not co-existent with it, nor yet an essential medium to its fruition. It is at best a reflection by which we are aided to a deeper knowledge of the reality: for, as he writes,

> All that meets the bodily sense I deem
> Symbolical, one mighty alphabet
> To infant minds; and we in this low world
> Placed with our back to bright reality,
> That we might learn with young unwounded ken
> The substance from the shadow.'

This Platonism, already criticized by Blake for its inadequacy to the richness of experience, is one of the two planes (the other might be called sensualism) between which Keats's perception habitually moved, on its own 'broad-belted colure' of intuitive understanding.

For Keats, 'all that meets the bodily sense' is not symbolical but magical. Nature is not a cryptogram but an alembic. The poet is not a philosopher: he is a wizard, whose function it is by virtue of his art to unlock the imprisoned essences of things and make use of them for creative purposes. The goal is transformation. The poet, aided by a talisman (of what kind we shall see shortly), penetrates the creative processes of nature and works in and with them.

This, to me, is the sense of Keats's poetry, taking it as a whole and taking it as sincere. It is a poetry of *magic* to a degree which no other Romantic verse approaches: magic is at its roots and in its flowering. There is nothing conventional, literary, decorative, about Keats's occultism. I shall try to show that it is the core of his perception: that his simplicity, sensuousness and passion are rooted in Hermetic soil.

We have already come upon traces of this. My task in the present chapter will be to link up our past findings, which I purposely left rather vague, with the precisions we shall now encounter. One of these findings, and a crucial one, came in the Reynolds letter. There we found the poet reading a portion, 'a sparing touch', of full poetry or distilled prose; taking it out with him into the open air, wandering with it, prophesying and dreaming upon it. This 'one grand and spiritual passage' served him as a starting point towards all 'the two-and-thirty Palaces'. And we found some help to an understanding of Keats's meaning in the words of an Orientalist who told us how a stanza, a verse, a phrase from the Vedas served the forest-sages of India as a 'charm, or sacred magic formula . . . the convenient handy form of the highest divine energy'.

Side by side with this passage from the 1818 letter I would now like to set Keats's sonnet *The Poet*. This poem, first printed by Miss Amy Lowell in her biography, is not included in de Selincourt's edition. It has received scant courtesy from Keats's commentators.

> At morn, at noon, at Eve, and Middle Night
>   He passes forth into the charmed air,
>   With talisman to call up spirits rare
> From plant, cave, rock, and fountain.—To his sight

The husk[1] of natural objects opens quite
  To the core: and every secret essence there
  Reveals the elements of good and fair;
Making him see, where Learning hath no light.
Sometimes above the gross and palpable things
  Of this diurnal sphere, his spirit flies
  On awful wing; and with its destined skies
Holds premature and mystic communings:
  Till such unearthly intercourses shed
  A visible halo round his mortal head.[2]

Now that is a precise statement of the poetic function: so precise, indeed, and presenting a picture so unlike the accepted one (for we must suppose that Keats is speaking of himself, as he is or as he aspires to be) that it has been largely deprecated or ignored. We shall find, however, that it repays our scrutiny.

We are struck, to begin with, by its dynamism. Coleridge peers through the window-pane, Keats *passes forth* (a phrase we can take both literally and metaphorically) into the charmed air, intent on the exercise of certain powers. He attacks nature at its core, piercing the husk of natural objects, with the aid of a talisman. The four nodal points of the day are selected for the practice of a natural magic which reveals the secret essences of things. He calls up spirits from the forms of earth. He acquires an insight which is superior to book-learning. Such are the statements of the octet.

After this, the affirmations of the sestet seem banal. They may strike us as hyperbole, as bardic nonsense. But they are more than that. They are a precise traditional sequel to the statements of the octet. The octet expresses the functions of the magus within the natural world—the circle of courses, as it is called in Davies's *Celtic Researches*, a book familiar to Keats.[3] The sestet describes his transition (which could come only after his working within the circle of courses) to the realm of forms, the empyrean.

---

[1] Adopting the variant on 'hush' printed (without comment) by Mr E. R. Wasserman in his brilliant discussion of Keats's major poems, *The Finer Tone*.
[2] Dated 1815/16 in the Woodhouse MS.
[3] It is summarized in Appendix A below (see esp. pp. 399–401).

The tradition to which all this belongs is the Hermetic. It is the vitalist world-picture handed down from Plato, the Plato above all of the *Timæus*, to the neo-Platonists, the writers of the *corpus Hermeticum*, the mediæval 'spagyrical philosophers' and alchemists, the sixteenth and seventeenth century occultists; to Robert Fludd, Thomas Vaughan, Sir Thomas Browne, Blake and Thomas Taylor in England; and which runs as a continuous poetic tradition through Henry Vaughan, Milton,[1] Smart, Blake, Coleridge, Yeats. Often flowing underground, it rises again and again in our literature to refresh the roots of poetry.

Where precisely Keats got his hints I am not concerned, at this point, to enquire. We know he read Davies and *The Anatomy of Melancholy*; I shall show later that he was acquainted with the *Timæus* and with other translations of and commentaries on Plato by Thomas Taylor. Burton would put him on the track of Cornelius Agrippa, Paracelsus, the Hermetic writings; it is not unlikely that he followed them up. Sources are not important: what is important for an understanding of Keats is the fact that his mind was of an order to which these sources could appeal. I believe that he conceived his 'vast idea' before he read Burton and Taylor, or talked with Bailey at Oxford on the theme of 'divine analogy'. Nor must we forget that these 'speculations' were very much in the air in the first half of the nineteenth century, fostered by translations from the Vedic scriptures, by such publications as *Asiatic Researches*, by the more home-grown Celtomania.

Of all these 'sources' I shall cite, at this point, only one, the fifteenth-century German Cornelius Agrippa; not because I am convinced that Keats read him, but because he presents his material in a form easily assimilable to Keats's. His *Three Books of Occult Philosophy*[2] describe the operation of the magus in the 'three-fold World, Elementary, Celestiall, and Intellectual'. The first chapter tells *How Magicians Collect vertues from the three-fold World.*

---

[1] The sonnet is, in effect, a reworking of *Il Penseroso*, 85–96, with inversion of Milton's themes in octet and sestet (93–6, octet; 85–92, sestet).

[2] My quotations are from the English version of 1651; the original (1531–3) is in Latin.

Beginning with the 'elementary' (the world of Keats's octet) the magus ascends by degrees through the triple world: an idea which was to exercise Keats greatly in *Endymion*, though his direct sources there were Davies and Taylor. In his second chapter Agrippa tells how by the art of magic one may unite 'the vertues of things through the application of the one to the other, and to their inferior sutable subjects, joyning and knitting them together throughly by the powers, and vertues of the superior bodies'. His third chapter discourses *Of the four Elements, their qualities, and mutuall mixtions.*

> There are four Elements, and originall grounds of all corporeall things, Fire, Earth, Water, Aire, of which all elementated inferiour bodies are compounded; not by way of heaping them up together, but by transmutation, and union. . . .

The whole passage, of which this is only the beginning, is taken almost verbatim from Ovid, *Metamorphoses* XV: the cyclic process it describes corresponds to the ὁδὸς ἄνω κάτω μία καὶ ὡυτή of Heracleitus. Ovid goes back in his turn to *Timæus* 49B. The ideas of mutual penetration, cyclic movement, transmutation, and sensible and ethereal elements, developed in these writings, came to interest Keats increasingly. We shall consider them more closely later.

To return now to the sonnet. How far, it may be asked, granting that the poem is in fact an expression of these archaic attitudes to the world order—how far are we to suppose Keats serious in what he is saying here? Are the statements of the sonnet integral to his thought, or are they mere coruscations of fancy? We know how, in the letters, Keats delighted in playing with an idea, only to drop it later; perhaps the sonnet is just another of these *jeux d'esprit*?

I would answer this question by saying, first, that Keats is always more serious in his poems than in his letters. Leaving aside the farcical verses and the *trivia* which he never intended for publication, I think it is true to say that he does not admit to the 'sanctuary of his working brain'—which is poetry—any 'speculation' that he has not 'proved on his pulses'. He would have thought it wrong to do so. And I would say, in the second place, that if we accept the sonnet as serious, as *meant* in the fullest sense, we shall find it illuminating, and illuminated by, the whole corpus of his writing. Passages that were obscure become clear; passages that have long been hailed as rhetoric, splendid or lush, reveal themselves as subtle thinking. Certain short poems, which have seemed eccentric to the canon, fall into place as integral.

The proof of the pudding, then, will be in the eating. Let us look again at the sonnet and see just what statements it does make. The poet, we are told in the octet, passes forth into the charmed air equipped with a talisman 'to call up spirits rare'. He passes forth at the four nodes of the diurnal round: the notion of fourness, which we shall later have to investigate in some detail, is immediately stressed. He carries a 'talisman', which we have reason to believe (remembering the February 1818 letter) is some 'grand and spiritual' passage of prose or verse: a sort of *mantram*. With the aid of this, he is able to penetrate the 'husk' of natural objects and see into their 'core': he exercises a deep intuition. Finally (in the sestet) we see him leaving the 'elementary' world and visiting in spirit the celestial and intellectual worlds.

Let us put aside for a moment the statements of the sestet (we shall return to them in our study of *Endymion*) and ask ourselves, first, if we have any evidence beside the Reynolds letter for identifying the talisman with a *mantram*, and, second, if we can go a little more deeply into the *purpose* governing the poet-magus's manipulation of the elemental world.

I have already pointed out that Keats, like Blake, held great literature to be, in the fullest sense, inspired and sacred. His commendation of Haydon to the care of heaven 'in the Name of Shakespeare, Raphael and all our Saints' is heartfelt. Shakespeare is the saint of his religion as Raphael is the archangel of Haydon's. Great writing, great painting compose a canon, which radiates power as well as comfort. Shakespeare is his 'presidor', working in and for him. Moreover, Shakespeare works in and through nature. It is a characteristic of Keats, as we have already seen, that he draws no boundary between literature and life. Landor's 'Nature I loved, and next to Nature, Art' would have held no meaning for him. He is at once the least and the most bookish of our poets. The least, for—*vide* the Reynolds letter—he holds no brief for books *as records of past experience*: 'memory is not knowledge'. The most—because, as he says in the same letter, he can use any distilled passage as a key to the two-and-thirty palaces.

We can watch this happening in his letters. If we lack the clue, the transitions are often bewildering. The *mantram* 'Do you not hear the sea?' from *Lear* is simple enough in its operation; it 'haunts him intensely', opens up to him the being of the Channel before his eyes, and we have the miracle of 'It keeps eternal Whisperings . . .'. But what are we to make of this, from the Reynolds sisters letter: 'Which is the best of Shakspeare's Plays? *I mean in what mood and with what accompaniment do you like the Sea best?*[1] It is very fine in the morning when the Sun

> Opening on Neptune with fair blessed beams
> Turns into yellow gold his salt Sea Streams . . .'?

A little earlier he has given us his great eikon of the four elements. 'The Sea is a Robe of State', he tells us there. But the robe of state is a cloth of gold: the Shakespeare couplet casts its radiancy back upon the eikon. This is the way, giving and receiving, that Keats's perception works. The verse opens vistas into the actuality.

This brings us to our second question. And here we at once find ourselves in deeper waters. What is the poet aiming at in his intercourse with the elements? We are tempted to reply, Understanding: the insight into connectedness made possible by the *mantram*, the sacred formula, working upon the phenomena. But that is only the first step. 'The greater is behind.' For, with Keats, the poetic experience is emphatically *poesis*, a making. And this is what it has in common with nature: rather, this is what identifies it with nature. *Art is nature working in man at its highest intensity.* Not *ut pictura poesis*: neither poetry nor nature is a picture. Each

---

[1] My italics. This is perhaps the clearest example in Keats of the synthesis remarked on in note 2, p. 86, below.

is an *opus*, an *operatio*, a working. A working and a making.[1] Keats
does not invite you, as Wordsworth or Coleridge or Shelley does,
to look at a scene; he invites you to participate in a process.
'Linger awhile', he suggests, and 'watch intently'. As you watch
you will be drawn into the working. 'Stop and consider!' he
urges in another poem: stop what you are doing so busily, and
look around you. It is the workings of nature we are to watch.
Minnows weaving to and fro in the stream; goldfinches fluttering;
'the leap of buds into ripe flowers'. The mind co-operates; and
not the mind only, for the body has its share in the dance. A breeze
blows and

> The eyelids with the passing coolness play,
> Like rose leaves with the drip of summer rains.[2]

They are interesting, these minnows of 'I Stood Tiptoe...', linking up with the 'poor patient oyster' of *Endymion* III as expressions of Keats's feeling for the cold, silent creatures of Nature:
the 'Manifestations of that beauteous life Diffus'd unseen throughout eternal space'[3] which are not usually considered beauteous,
though to Blake's eyes and Browne's these little engines too had
their own fearful symmetry. And I think when Keats said at the
last that he had loved the principle of beauty in all things this was,
at least in part, what he meant. It is easy to love cats and dogs,
deer and eagles; because we can humanize these manifestations
of life, by domestication or fabulizing, we can use them in con-
structing a cozy Micky Mouse world in which we feel at home.
It is not so easy with the minnow or the oyster, the Earwig arm'd,
the tender Maggot: even the lucky golden Spinner may evoke
more squirms than gratitude.[4] You can't bring them in to the
human circle just by looking at them and stroking them and

---

[1] Note the profound comment jotted on a flyleaf of Keats's copy of Milton:
'... there was working in him as it were that same sort of thing as operates in the
great world to the end of a Prophecy's being accomplished . . .'. This casual
remark sums up Blake's *Milton*.

[2] Sonnet, 'After dark vapours have oppress'd our plains' (1817).

[3] *Hyperion*, I, 317, 318.

[4] The last three examples are from Blake, *Milton*, Book I.

6

teaching them tricks: you have to go out to them and wriggle with them, meet them on their own terms or not at all. It is usually not at all. Their world—earthy, crumbly, slimy, cold—is not our world. They live, to begin with, on a different scale of magnitudes; we cannot compress our ways of thinking and feeling to the point of empathy, any more than, at the opposite end of the scale, we can feel at home in the interstellar spaces. Our only guide is analogy, and analogy means the vital interconnection of the three worlds. In this sense, Keats is indeed a poet of nature (to pick up the original thread of this chapter) in his synthesizing faculty; for 'nature governs the whole world by her powers, by her summit comprehending the heavens, but through these ruling over the fluctuating empire of generation, and everywhere weaving together partial natures in amicable conjunction with wholes'.[1]

Keats is the poet of *lived* analogy. He not only observes nature in her ruling and her weaving: he participates, consciously, in the Great Work. Here we may find it difficult to follow him, though it was not so difficult in the early nineteenth century, and would not have been difficult at all for the seventeenth. Phrases like 'all the mighty world Of eye, and ear—both what they half create, And what perceive', and 'in our life alone does Nature live', and 'I live not in myself, but I become Portion of that around me, and to me High mountains are a feeling . . .': these phrases in Wordsworth, Coleridge and Byron bespeak a common vitalism.[2]

---

[1] Thomas Taylor, Introduction to *Timæus*.

[2] A major obstacle to the understanding of our older literature lies in the very rapid change undergone by the 'climate of ideas'. We *think* we are understanding Milton and Pope and Blake and Keats when we are following the words and grasping the connections of thought; we are not aware that our whole way of thinking has been so rapidly transformed in the last hundred years that the *content* of the older writers' thought eludes us, as the true colours elude the eyes of a colour-blind man. Thus much of what these writers offered as simple doctrine comes to us as simple metaphor; the impact of their thought is deadened; depth is lost, and we are left with the decorative surfaces. Hence the immense importance of the 'historian of ideas' in English studies; but his work will be useless, or positively detrimental, unless he has so acclimatized himself to the period he is interpreting that he can bring its way of thinking to life in whole and in parts;

Blake and Keats expounded this vitalism with an intensity unparalleled in their age; they set it at the centre of their thought and their work; they lived by it. It is present in Blake in a much more aggressive guise than in Keats. We have learned to accept Blake; not to read him, perhaps, but to accept him as a rather formidable fact which can't be ignored or explained away: a great but difficult, obscure, incoherent thinker, writer, painter. Now we don't want to think of Keats like that. He is an anthology poet: we know him: he belongs to us. He is not difficult, we are sure. If there are obscurities, phrases or even paragraphs which defy our comprehension, then it is Keats's fault, not ours. He has been led astray by his rhymes, his raptures, by his inaptitude for abstract thinking, his technical immaturity. He is writing hastily, and it would be a waste of time to linger over every phrase: let us pass on to what matters: his gusto, his pure, weighted passages of natural description, his magically evocative atmosphere, his *curiosa felicitas*, the dramatic intensity of *St Agnes' Eve* and the first *Hyperion*.

It won't do, of course. If we are to set Keats among our major poets, we have to take him seriously, the whole of him; and when we come across something we don't understand, we have to worry out the meaning. And is it so very difficult? I think not. It is nowhere near so difficult, because nowhere near so complex, as Blake's meaning. Granted that we find and accept the clue, the talisman—and Keats almost pushes it into our grasp—the unravelling of the golden ball is virtually automatic. That is not to say that our appreciation of Keats's poetry as poetry becomes automatic—very far from it; but we no longer have to struggle with the basic structure, the foundation on which the poetry is built. We have learned to find our way about.

The concept of fourness, of the quaternion, will play no small part in the exposition of Keats's poetry (in particular *Endymion*)

---

and this means, I think, more specialization, more life-long 'soaking', than we are likely to get in our universities at present. On the subject of our changing 'representations' of the outside world, and our ways of thinking about them, see Barfield, *op. cit., passim.*

which follows. It will be our compass-card, as it was Keats's. Indeed, it will bear the same relation to our theme that the quincunx bears to Browne's in *The Garden of Cyrus*. But note: there is nothing idiosyncratic about Keats's preoccupation with 'the adorable Tetractys'. It is a postulate of Romantic perception and hence of Romantic expression. 'The adorable Tetractys' is Coleridge's phrase, borrowed from Pythagoras; Blake inverts it, and we have 'the Human Fourfold', a datum of the psyche. Dramatized, it emerges as Blake's Zoas, the four 'faces' of Albion, or as Shelley's four-visaged charioteer in *The Triumph of Life*. Zoa, life: the emphasis is insistently biotic. And this (it is the argument of my book) was Keats's preoccupation. If we can appreciate Blake's and Jung's belief in the quaternary structure of the psyche, in the metaphysical reality of the four elements, in the importance as concepts of the four seasons, the four directions, the four ages: then we shall see nothing strange in the fact that a poet as instinctive as Keats should find himself very much at home with the quaternion. And let us remember another thing: Keats and Blake, above their contemporaries, were striving desperately to orientate themselves, to get their bearings in a world in which they felt themselves Lost Travellers. And to this end a compass is not a luxury but a necessity. North, South, East and West are notions that cannot be avoided; and from the four cardinal points it is an inevitable step to the seasons, the ages and the elements.

The concept of fourness is the compass card, the guide to an horizontal orientation. But Blake and Keats are not living in a two-dimensional universe. There is also up-and-down: the four points in the three worlds. In earlier chapters we have seen Keats's preoccupation with *space*, his 'plotting' of its voidness through the manifestations, the movements which come to birth within it. 'Whence then', enquired Shao Chih, 'comes the vitality of all things between the four points of the compass, between heaven above and earth beneath?' T'ai Kung Tiao's answer is relevant: 'The Positive and Negative principles influence, act upon, and regulate each other. The four seasons alternate with, give birth to, and destroy one another. Hence, loves and hates, and courses rejected and courses adopted. Hence, too, the intercourse of the sexes.'[1] This is a Chinese way of expressing the unity of the cosmos, but it is very close to Keats's way. Space is not simply the locus of objects but the field of principles: more significantly, the sphere in which objects 'expand' into meanings which reveal the principles. The meanings are revealed by the functioning-in-relationship of the objects. There is very little idea of cause-and-effect in Keats, and there is very little idea of cause-and-effect in classical Chinese metaphysics. Objects, events, are related not in a sequence but in a synchronicity. 'That beauteous life Diffus'd unseen throughout eternal space' is a pattern which gives its meaning to the event. The relation is not with what goes before or comes after, but with all that is happening, that is *in esse*, at the moment. This being so, we can understand why it is that Keats cannot arrive at a conclusion by 'consecutive' (*i.e.* discursive) reasoning, and also how it is that the doctrine of correspondences has so great an attraction for him. 'Stop and consider!' he says. *Stop*: arrest your movement in time; *consider*, exercise consideration, that 'togetherness with the stars' which alone can grant a glimpse of the total meaning.

Our understanding of a poet as many-sided and as many-layered as Keats depends, more perhaps than we are willing to admit, on an understanding of the 'climate' in which he functioned and in particular of the elements in that climate which have disappeared from ours. The early nineteenth century was a curious period: an age tensing itself for the great spring forwards into the technical era, yet nostalgic, to a degree, for the warmer, more comforting world-view of the past. In the poets this world-view has a brief and beautiful reflorescence. We have to attend to the features of this view with some care if we are really to penetrate the heart of Keats's mystery. We can apply to the study of poetry these wise words of Mrs Arber, written in another connection:

Much is lost if we attend only to the currents which have led straight on to what we are pleased to regard as the enlightened conceptions

---

[1] *Chuang Tzŭ*, trans. by H. A. Giles, ch. xxv.

of our own period. If we look carefully at hypotheses discarded in the past, we find that, like dormant buds, they are sometimes capable of initiating new branches of thought, after the vitality of the main trunk, which once over-shadowed them, has become exhausted.[1]

Keats's own 'branched thoughts, new grown with pleasant pain' are not seldom the late shoots of dormant buds from the stock of Agrippa and Burton and Browne.

All this bears upon our enquiry: the nature of the poetic act for Keats. We have seen that it is a working, and a synchronicity. There is no 'recollection'. He watches the flower, and as he watches he is the flower and he grows with it; he experiences that bliss. For Keats the workings of nature and the workings of the poetic mind and the workings of the human fourfold are one indivisible process.[2] Put like that, it seems a thing one might say of any good poet. But it is true of Keats in a sense in which it is not true of, say, Wordsworth. Wordsworth views the phenomenon and he is moved and exalted and carried away by what he sees; he returns to himself, and he broods and secretes; and in due course he recollects and reconstructs. But he is not inside the process, and the experience and the experiencer and the poem are not dynamically one. We can hardly imagine, indeed, what the Keatsian experience could have been like. We can understand far more easily what the Wordsworthian experience was like because, at our humble level, it is our experience. It is what Keats called it, 'the egotistical sublime'. It is an immensely powerful and valuable

---

[1] Agnes Arber, *The Mind and the Eye*.

[2] When he writes 'In the calm grandeur of a sober line We see the waving of the mountain pine' there is no suggestion that the line is about pines or mountains: what he means is that the same energy that displays itself in nature as the waving pine, displays itself in verse as the sober line. A different energy, he goes on to say (though of course participating in the one Energy), manifests itself indifferently as a hawthorn glade or a beautifully 'staid' tale. In the *Psyche* ode the transference is complete: 'branched thoughts, new grown with pleasant pain, Instead of pines shall murmur in the wind'. In 'God of the meridian' we have the still more synæsthetic 'My bowl is the sky And I drink at my eye'; a few lines later 'branching thoughts' are suffused with sunshine. All this is a matter of 'divine analogy'.

searchlight directed into the night of being; it illuminates, but the light is imposed upon the darkness.[1] The Wordsworthian vision is searching, violent, possessive. But the poet of Keats's order is continually 'going out' of himself into other existences, as he explains in the famous letter of 27 October 1818 to Richard Woodhouse: 'he is continually informing and filling some other Body'.

Already we are in a sphere where it is difficult to follow Keats. But we have to take one step further still. Living with the life of non-human things, the poet is also the magus; participating in the process, he is able in some measure to direct its course. There is an interchange. There is a pulsation, as Keats called it, in the Great Animal which is the cosmos, a systole and diastole[2]; and with that pulse the poet must integrate himself. Man is nature's consciousness of herself; he is the instrument of her self-knowing. But he is more than that: he is the middle term between the upper and the lower worlds: he is the bridge and the reconciler. And he is still more: working within the rhythms of nature, he is the universal alchemist who brings to fruition the Great Work in and through his art.

There is a strange passage in *Endymion* which suggests that human love is indispensable to the processes of nature; we shall turn to this passage later.[3] There is a sentence, again, in a letter to Haydon of 10–11 May 1817—the same letter which ends 'So now in the Name of Shakespeare Raphael and all our Saints . . .' —which runs:

I know no one but you who can be fully sensible of the turmoil and anxiety, the sacrifice of all what is called comfort the readiness to Measure time by what is done and to die in 6 hours could plans be brought to conclusions—the looking upon the Sun the Moon the Stars, the Earth and its contents as materials to form greater things— that is to say ethereal things—but here I am talking like a Madman greater things than our Creator himself made!!

---

[1] 'His Genius is explorative of those dark Passages' (*Letters*, 143).
[2] *Epistle to J. H. Reynolds*, 39–40.   [3] See below, p. 131.

And that is the nearest, I think, that he ever got in a letter to the expression of his 'vast idea'. Haydon might be fully sensible of the self-sacrifice inherent in the life of an artist: but could he follow Keats in his central 'speculation'? We must return a negative answer: Haydon would have thought the 'Madman' and the double exclamation mark fully justified.

The 'passing forth' of the magus is accomplished, Agrippa tells us,[1] by virtue of the elemental affinity of the human soul with the features of its environment. For the soul 'answers to the Earth by Sense, to the Water by Imagination, to the Air by Reason, to the Heaven by the Intellect, and the Soul goes out into a Harmony of them, according as these are tempered in a mortall body'. The motion of souls out from themselves and into other existences takes place in a medium which is not itself elemental. 'Now they conceive such a *medium* to be the spirit of the World, *viz.* that which we call the quintessence: because it is not from the four Elements, but a certain first thing, having its being above, and besides them . . .This spirit is after the same manner in the body of the world, as ours in the body of man.'[2]

We can see, now, that the purpose of the poet's passing forth is nothing less than the evocation of 'spirits' (indeed this is explicitly stated by Keats): those hypostasized expressions of the *Anima Mundi* which exist in plant, cave, rock and fountain. They are evoked with a view to using them 'to form greater things—that is to say ethereal things . . . greater things than our Creator himself made'. This is, of course, the *magnum opus* of the alchemists; the intervention in, with a view to expediting, the cosmic process whereby every natural form is striving to pass from matter to spirit.[3]

But before we can manipulate we must understand. In a frag-

---

[1] *Op. cit.*, Book II, ch. xxi.   [2] *Ibid.*, Book I, ch. xiv.

[3] 'What is the object of research of the philosophers?' the adept is asked in Paracelsus' *Short Catechism of Alchemy*; and he replies, correctly: 'Proficiency in the art of perfecting what nature has left imperfect, and the attainment of the treasure of the philosopher's stone.'

ment dated 1818 Keats makes another attempt to define the poet
in terms of universal sympathy:

> Where's the Poet? show him! show him,
> Muses nine! that I may know him!
> 'Tis the man who with a man
>   Is an equal, be he King,
> Or poorest of the beggar-clan,
>   Or any other wondrous thing
> A man may be 'twixt ape and Plato;[1]
> 'Tis the man who with a bird,
> Wren or Eagle, finds his way to
> All its instincts; he hath heard
> The Lion's roaring, and can tell
>   What his horny throat expresseth,
> And to him the Tiger's yell
>   Comes articulate and presseth
> On his ear like mother-tongue . . .

This may remind us of certain of the *Proverbs of Hell*: 'The
wrath of the lion is the wisdom of God. . . . The tygers of wrath are
wiser than the horses of instruction. . . . When thou seest an Eagle,
thou seest a portion of Genius; lift up thy head.'[2] Keats is one
with Blake too in his perception that energy is eternal delight.[3] 'I
affirm, Sir, that Poetry, that the imagination, generally speaking,
delights in power, in strong excitement, as well as in truth, in
good, in right, whereas pure reason and the moral sense approve
only of the true and good', he quotes approvingly from Hazlitt.

---

[1] This is Keats's first reference to Plato, and follows close upon his month with
Bailey at Oxford (see below, pp. 161–6).

[2] It is worth noting that the lion and the eagle are both *solary* creatures, em-
perors of their respective elements.

[3] Another of Blake's great sayings, 'Fire delights in its Form', comes to mind
when we read this note on Keats by Woodhouse: 'He has affirmed that he can
conceive of a billiard Ball that it may have a sense of delight from its own round-
ness, smoothness, volubility & the rapidity of its motion' (*K.C.*, I, 59). And compare with Keats's 'All our passions are, in their sublime, creative of . . . beauty'
Blake's 'Violent Passions emit the Real, Good & Perfect Tones' (Reynolds's
Discourses *Marginalia*).

Or again, in his own characteristically concrete illustration from a letter-entry of 19 March 1819 to his brother and sister-in-law:

> May there not be superior beings amused with any graceful, though instinctive attitude my mind may fall into, as I am entertained with the alertness of a Stoat or the anxiety of a Deer? Though a quarrel in the Streets is a thing to be hated, the energies displayed in it are fine; the commonest Man shows a grace in his quarrel. . . . This is the very thing in which consists poetry. . . .

Keats's sympathy with natural forms, his alert attention to the life-patterns of animals, is indeed akin to Blake's in its impartiality and non-sentimentality. Blake's pæan to

> The Flea, Louse, Bug, the Tape-Worm, all the Armies of Disease,
> Visible or invisible to the slothful vegetating Man,

(the man, that is, who is *not* poet or magus, who does not pass out of his selfhood in the motion of sympathy)

> The slow Slug, the Grasshopper that sings & laughs & drinks,

is paralleled by Keats's sonnet on the grasshopper and the cricket, by his admiration for Shakespeare's snail,[1] by his empathy with the minnows enjoying the stream's pressure. Most of all, perhaps, by his genial portrait of Mrs Reynolds's cat. The sonnet, which I am tempted to quote in full, evokes a vivid picture of poet and cat enjoying Mrs Reynolds's fireside together in complete companionship.

> Cat! who hast pass'd thy grand climacteric,
>   How many mice and rats hast in thy days
>   Destroy'd—How many tit bits stolen? Gaze
> With those bright languid segments green, and prick
> Those velvet ears—but pr'ythee do not stick
>   Thy latent talons in me—and upraise
>   Thy gentle mew—and tell me all thy frays
> Of fish and mice, and rats and tender chick.

---

[1] *Venus and Adonis*, 1033–8, quoted in the letter of 22 November 1817 to Reynolds. Shakespeare's image remained with him to emerge in the 'trembling delicate and snail-horn perception of beauty' of the 10 April 1818 letter to Haydon.

Nay, look not down, nor lick thy dainty wrists—
  For all the wheezy asthma,—and for all
Thy tail's tip is nick'd off—and though the fists
  Of many a maid have given thee many a maul,
Still is that fur as soft as when the lists
  In youth thou enter'dst on glass-bottled wall.

Note how the whole thing *moves*. It is a film, not a photograph. The cat is moving as Keats talks to it, moving in space; Keats's mind is moving, in time, through the stages of a feline life-pattern; retracing an existence from 'grand climacteric' to youth, linking episode to episode not by a process of abstract memory but by the present evidences of what we shall come to know as 'phase-beauty'. Nothing could be further from the maudlin sentiment of Coleridge's lines *To a Young Ass* or the moral exaltation of Wordsworth's *Fidelity*.

[Sonnet: *The Poet* (1815/16)—*Where's the Poet?* (1818)—Sonnet: *To Mrs Reynolds's Cat* (1818)]

II

THE POETRY OF EARTH

Chapter Six

THE DOWER OF SPANNING WISDOM

The Source of Nature whose Course is Eternal, the holy Quaternion, is
the first Cause, not only of the Being of all things, but of their Well-
being likewise, having sown and diffus'd thro' all the Universe the
Good that is innate and natural to it, as an incorruptible and intelligent
Light.

HIEROCLES, *Commentary on the Golden
Verses of Pythagoras.*

OUR progress up to the present chapter has been far from
chronological. I have given myself leave to cast about
here and there in the poems and letters in an attempt
to establish principles of interpretation which may serve us well,
I hope, in what follows. But from now on we can steer a steadier
course. And we shall find it possible to keep more closely to the
texts: to direct our attention now rather more upon the poems
than the letters, although the letters will continue to provide
valuable ballast for our voyage through the poems.

I have presented my thesis that Keats is a traditional, indeed a
'hermetic' writer; that he was alive to certain considerations that
exercised other minds in his age, notably Blake and Thomas
Taylor, to a less extent Coleridge.[1] We shall find the more
definite expressions of these 'speculations' crystallizing out in the
early period of Keats's writing: in the *Poems 1817* and *Endymion,*
and in some of the miscellaneous verse that can be attributed
certainly or dubiously to this period. They are none the less active

---

[1] 'Metaphysics and poetry and "facts of mind", that is, accounts of all the
strange phantasms that ever possessed "your philosophy"; dreamers, from Thoth
the Egyptian to Taylor the English pagan, are my darling studies. In short, I
seldom read except to amuse myself . . .' (Letter of 19 November 1796 to John
Thelwall). The tone of the passage, and the final sentence, make comment
unnecessary.

in the later verse, but they are less intrusive: they have been assimilated into the texture of thought and technique, moulding and enriching, marshalling and directing creative energies.

The temptation to be neat should generally, I think, be resisted; above all, when we are considering the work of a poet such as Keats. Impulsiveness, spontaneity, cannot be systematized. And Keats's life was too short to provide much scope for the evolutionist, the dealer in influences and developments. What is 'mature work', what is *juvenilia*? 'O chestnut tree, great-rooted blossomer, Are you the root, the blossom, or the bole?' There are few pointers for the apologist. We must take or leave what Keats has written. But that means taking seriously, or rejecting, all that Keats has written. I don't mean that we have to be solemn about verses that Keats obviously meant as fun: yet even these we must accept, recognize as facets of the whole. An alert impartiality is, indeed, our best 'talisman' to an understanding of Keats. I think that he, like Blake, 'developed' little in the course of his creative life; though he gained, perhaps more than Blake, in worldly wisdom: his extremes were not so extreme. But he was, in the last resort, as intransigent about the holiness of the heart's affections; he had achieved his master vision early, and he stuck to it.

It is this master vision, what Keats calls his 'vast idea', that we have now to consider. He uses the phrase for the first time (and indeed the last) in *Sleep and Poetry*:

> What though I am not wealthy in the dower
> Of spanning wisdom; though I do not know
> The shiftings of the mighty winds that blow
> Hither and thither all the changing thoughts
> Of man: though no great minist'ring reason sorts
> Out the dark mysteries of human souls
> To clear conceiving: yet there ever rolls
> A vast idea before me, and I glean
> Therefrom my liberty; thence too I've seen
> The end and aim of Poesy.

That is definite enough; though we may not be clear what it is definite about. Our difficulty arises, in part, from the want of evidence. In discussing Keats, we must employ the technique of the palæontologist: he, from the few bones extant of all that once existed, recreates the structure that was; we, from the few bones that exist of all that might have been, create the potential structure. There is room for speculation. To my mind, the 'vast idea' links up with the findings of *The Poet*, envisaging a 'possible sublimity' not detached from sensuous perception, embracing the contraries.

We have taken the 'talisman' of our sonnet to be a *mantram*, a verbal charm. This in general I think it is; but we need not confine ourselves to this reading. We learn from Agrippa that a man may contain within himself his own talisman; for man's nature, 'seeing it is the compleatest image of the whole universe, containing in itself the whole heavenly harmony, will without all doubt abundantly afford us the Seals, and Characters of all the Stars, and Celestiall influences, and those as the more efficacious, which are less differing from the Celestiall nature'.[1] We gather (and the impression is confirmed by Gaffarel)[2] that the most efficient magus is he who carries his 'seal' within himself; and that this seal is related intimately to the stars.

Now as we read through Keats's earliest volume of poems—those of 1817—we find a group of three ideas constantly recurring. We have already noted the insistence in these poems on the *receptacle*, the inverted bowl of the unclouded sky with its connotation of the void. We have appreciated Keats's vision of the void in its two complementary aspects: as the immitigably other, as eternity; and as the matrix of forms, that which itself remains void yet in which there is a coming-to-be. We can now look at the nexus of ideas which links these two conceptions: the triad of spirits, stars and immortality. In a poet who confessedly weaves his verses into a flowery band to bind him to the earth we may find it a little odd that his eyes are so obstinately fixed on the sky. We shall not meet with this star-gazing in the young Wordsworth or even in the young Coleridge.

---

[1] *Op. cit.*, Book I, ch. xxxiii.　　[2] In *Curiosités Inouyes* (1637).

Poems 1817 includes two lengthy pieces which have been much admired for their delicate and sympathetic nature descriptions. Each of these poems contains a long passage of non-descriptive verse which has generally been felt to break the unity of the whole. They are passages which I, for one, have heartily wished away. They have made me feel uncomfortable, with the irritation of incomprehension. Their effect is that of the Petrine episode in *Lycidas*—something alien and unassimilated. They are not the only parts of *Sleep and Poetry* and 'I stood tip-toe ...' which invite criticism, of course; but the elements of cockney archness and bad taste have been readily accounted for. 'The influence of Leigh Hunt' remains a convenient waste-paper basket for any bits of Keats we may want to scrap.

The Huntian basket won't serve for the doctrinal passages in *Poems 1817*. They are not passing indiscretions: they are culminations deliberately led up to and away from. If to us they appear intrusive it is because we have failed, as in the case of *Lycidas*, to grasp the whole process of the poem. The connections of thought baffle us. For this, Keats must bear his share of the blame: his technique is not yet adequate to his vision.

The first 112 lines of 'I stood tip-toe . . .' provide a series of glimpses into the existence, the life from moment to moment, of living, growing things—glimpses in which the element of relationship is subtly stressed. This, as we have seen, is Keats's common 'method'—the snapshot technique of the 15 April letter.[1] In the letter, Keats is on the move: he has no time to note the relationships among and within his glimpses. In the poem he can 'linger awhile', watching the growth 'Of buds into ripe flowers'. Yet the glimpses remain glimpses; Keats does not, as Wordsworth does, create large landscapes and connect them with the quiet of the sky. Keats's relationships are within the moment and for the moment only. We feel they are passing, growing and changing as we watch them. The sky is there, sensed as the void; and the places of nestling green for poets made are there too, delighted in for their warm immediacy. There is no attempt at a synthesis.

---

[1] See below, p. 206.

There is no synthesis, that is to say, consciously meant and presented as such by the poet. He does not marshal his detail, dispose it and connect it in subservience to a whole. We are presented, in this poem, with the detached observation only. Yet these observations, as they follow one another, do in fact compose a synthesis. It is one on which the poet passes no comment. It arises directly from the eye. It is organic, pursuing a natural line of growth. Let us watch it as it develops in the poem.

The first paragraph clears a space for growth; the eye sweeps round the horizon from the summit of the 'little hill', revelling in its freedom, touching here and there on clouds, leaves, woodlands, streams. It descends to the vegetable kingdom in the two short paragraphs which follow, penetrating to 'aged roots', expanding to the 'summer thrones' of wind-luxuriating woodbines. This seems straightforward enough: but Keats's forest pictures are never entirely simple. Strange forces move about his 'woodland alleys'. His 'old oak forests' belong to the domain of magic; and their curiously mixed population of fauns, Druid priests and buried lovers cannot be enclosed within the simple dimensions of rhetoric or history.

At line 47 (the fourth paragraph) the poem modulates into a major key. As a 'solary' flower the marigold is sacred to Apollo, and Apollo is the god of verse. The connections are swiftly, lightly made. Personal aspirations, as in *Lycidas*, are stimulated by the god's appearance:

> So haply, when I rove in some far vale,
> His mighty voice may come upon the gale.

The short paragraph which follows serves to link the animal with the vegetable kingdom through the butterfly-mimicking sweet-peas, 'on tip-toe for a flight', stretching out their 'taper fingers'. The theme of metamorphosis, an important one for Keats, is lightly touched upon. From line 61 onwards we find ourselves back in the minor: in the world of fishes, doves and finches. Keats has moved down from the hill to the banks of a stream. As we watch with him the linked motions of minnows 'wrestling

with their own sweet delight' and goldfinches 'in a wanton freak'
skimming the surface, connecting the worlds of earth, air and
water, we too are drawn into the process, sharing its delight.

But human voices wake us and we drown. With line 93 the
human world intrudes, and the human world in its direst guise for
Keats's poetry. 'The shadow of a living woman' falling across
Keats's page, Garrod has all too truly said, is the shadow of disaster.
The intrusion here is gratuitous; it adds nothing to the poem. The
maiden smiles and disappears. But the mood of the poem has
changed. Herself inoperative, the maiden has acted as a catalyst:
existing in full daylight, she nevertheless effects (through the
Keatsian love-moon nexus) the transition to the night sky. We
modulate by way of a tuft of evening primroses and the flitting
of moths into

> the moon lifting her silver rim
> Above a cloud, and with a gradual swim
> Coming into the blue with all her light.

And we have left the sphere of detached, impersonal observation
(objective we cannot call it, for in Keats's empathy the objective-
subjective distinction vanishes) for the sphere of 'lovely dreams'.
Immediately the poem forfeits its assurance and becomes troubled.

We know that Keats's original name for the poem we are discussing was 'Endymion', and we know how much of himself
and his problems he wove into the later and longer poem of that
name. 'I stood tiptoe upon a little hill' is an attempt which is
manifestly incomplete. What I believe happened is that Keats saw
the possibilities of using the Endymion theme in a much more
ambitious poem than originally planned, and of packing into it the
insights he had so far gained into his 'vast idea'. He began work
on this in Spring 1817. But he saw there were good things in his
original lines and he left them as they stood. Probably he was
conscious, too, of the incongruity of tone between the first
hundred or so lines and those that follow.

We have seen that the poem falls into two parts. The first gives
an impressionistic series of glimpses into nature in her 'minute

particulars'. The second part is a rhapsody on the moon as the queen and inspirer of poets; it includes certain not entirely congruous episodic material. We are taken on brief excursions into mythology on themes Keats was later to treat at greater length: Cupid and Psyche, Pan and Syrinx, Narcissus and Echo. The method is recognizably that of the later *Endymion*, with its interpolated 'masques'. Neither in 'I stood tip-toe...' nor in *Endymion* is the technique wholly successful. But that does not concern us here. What is interesting is the intense seriousness with which Keats approaches the Endymion legend, and the values which it clearly holds for him. It is, he says,

> That sweetest of all songs, that ever new,
> That aye refreshing, pure deliciousness,
> Coming ever to bless
> The wanderer by moonlight—to him bringing
> Shapes from the invisible world, unearthly singing
> From out the middle air, from flowery nests,
> And from the pillowy silkiness that rests[1]
> Full in the speculation of the stars.

The poet who first sang such a story must have 'burst our mortal bars' (the wording is close to the 'fragile bar' of *Endymion* I, 360), must have passed into some 'wondrous region'. In short, must have been of the order of the magus as well as the poet. There is a clear contrast between the natural objects of the first half of the poem, firmly set in their places of nestling green, and the 'shapes from the invisible world' of this later section.[2]

In its last thirty-two lines 'I stood tip-toe...' passes somewhat

---

[1] Darwin's line 'Eve's silken couch with gorgeous tints adorn' follows immediately (*Economy of Vegetation*, I, 119) on the passage

> Cling round the aerial bow with prisms bright,
> And pleas'd untwist the sevenfold threads of light,

which Keats had in mind in the 'cold philosophy' diatribe of *Lamia* and in a letter quoted above (p. 71); a note to the same passage distinguishes the lower from the higher regions of the atmosphere.

[2] A contrast which is precisely that of octet and sestet in *The Poet* (see above, p. 75).

bewilderingly to the glories of Endymion's bridal night.[1] It is in these lines that Keats first gives direct expression to one of his key ideas: the healing function of myth, of beauty, of planetary influences. There are strong traces of his early medical training. The imagery of disease and health is prominent in his verse; the 'sweet dreams, and health, and quiet breathing' which open the later *Endymion* bring this earlier one to a close. On Endymion's marriage night heavenly influences rain down upon the earth:

> The breezes were ethereal, and pure,
> And crept through half closed lattices to cure
> The languid sick: it cool'd their fever'd sleep,
> And soothed them into slumbers full and deep.
> Soon they awoke clear eyed; nor burnt with thirsting,
> Nor with hot fingers, nor with temples bursting:
> And springing up, they met the wond'ring sight
> Of their dear friends, nigh foolish with delight;
> Who feel their arms, and breasts, and kiss and stare,
> And on their placid foreheads part the hair.

'Ethereal' is an important word for Keats: it means precisely the opposite of 'material', and what Keats is saying here is that the breezes are supernatural: the air of which they are composed belongs to the category not of the impure but of the pure elements, of which Agrippa writes: 'Of the first Order are the pure Elements, which are neither compounded nor changed, nor admit of mixtion, but are incorruptible, and not of which, but through which the vertues of all naturall things are brought forth into act.'

In April 1819 Keats wrote a poem on the four elements (later called *Song of Four Fairies*) which is so relevant to our present considerations that I shall anticipate by quoting it at this point. The fairies are the Rosicrucian salamander, sylph, gnome and nymph, familiar to us from *The Botanic Garden*; Keats gives the last three the names of Zephyr, Dusketha and Breama. In accordance

---

[1] Which do not, incidentally, figure in the later poem, though some hint of the wedding's *therapeutic* function is given in Book IV, lines 829–34. The first mention of 'Cynthia's bridal night' comes in the sonnet *To My Brother George* (of August 1816) which celebrates the wonders of sun, ocean and air.

with Hermetic doctrine he makes Fire and Air the active or masculine elements, and Earth and Water the passive or feminine. The poem, which invites a Purcellian setting as a miniature masque, opens with a chorus:

Salamander.	Happy, happy glowing fire!
Zephyr.	Fragrant air! delicious light!
Dusketha.	Let me to my glooms retire!
Breama.	I to green-weed rivers bright!
Salamander.	Happy, happy glowing fire!

Dazzling bowers of soft retire,
Ever let my nourish'd wing,
Like a bat's still wandering,
Faintly fan your fiery spaces,
Spirit sole in deadly places.
In unhaunted roar and blaze,
Open eyes that never daze,
Let me see the myriad shapes
Of men, and beasts, and fish, and apes,
Portray'd in many a fiery den,
And wrought by spumy bitumen,
On the deep intenser roof,
Arched every way aloof,
Let me breathe upon their skies,
And anger their live tapestries;
Free from cold, and every care,
Of chilly rain, and shivering air.

What Keats emphasizes here, with Agrippa,[1] is the austere purity of the element—'Spirit *sole* in deadly places'—together with its 'irascible' quality—Agrippa's 'revenge'—and its action on 'the myriad shapes'. 'Fire delights in its Form'; the aphorism is Blake's and Keats's poem is the comment on it.

---

[1] *Op. cit.*, Book I, ch. v, *Of the wonderfull Natures of Fire, and Earth*. The passage is too long to quote. Both *Poimandres* and *Timæus* show creation as taking place in fire. The expression 'nourish'd wing' is explained by the Hermetic doctrine that the superior elements (fire and air) are 'nourished' by exhalations from the inferior elements (earth and water). Thus in *Sleep and Poetry* we read of the myrtle that '*feeds* A silent space with ever sprouting green' (251-2). The doctrine is found, too, in Heracleitus and *Paradise Lost*, V.

In accordance with the hermetic disposition of the elements in pairs (Agrippa's chapter VI of Book I) Keats arranges a marriage between Salamander and Dusketha, and another between Zephyr and Breama. Zephyr cries:

> Gentle Breama! by the first
> Violet young nature nurst,
> I will bathe myself with thee,
> So you sometimes follow me
> To my home, far, far, in west
> Beyond the nimble-wheeled quest
> Of the golden-presenc'd sun:
> Come with me, o'er tops of trees,
> To my fragrant palaces,
> Where they ever floating are
> Beneath the cherish of a star . . .
> Clouds of stored summer rains
> Thou shalt taste, before the stains
> Of the mountain soil they take,
> And too unlucent for thee make.
> I love thee, crystal Fairy, true![1]

Again the emphasis is on 'soleness', the purity of the uncompounded elements. Breama will taste the cloud-rain in its freshness before mixture with gross earth. Similarly, in his account of the bridal of Earth and Fire, Keats makes use of the idea of the 'central fire' referred to by Agrippa (and by Berkeley in sections 166–230 of his *Siris*):

> Adder-eyed Dusketha, speak,
> Shall we leave these, and go seek
> In the earth's wide entrails old
> Couches warm as their's are cold?

It is Salamander who speaks; and Dusketha replies exultingly:

> By thee, Sprite, will I be guided!
> I care not for cold or heat;
> Frost and flame, or sparks, or sleet,
> To my essence are the same;—
> But I honour more the flame.

---

[1] The next line (63) should I think be given to Breama.

Sprite of Fire, I follow thee
Wheresoever it may be,
To the torrid spouts and fountains,
Underneath earth-quaked mountains;
Or, at thy supreme desire,
Touch the very pulse of fire
With my bare unlidded eyes.[1]

The poem, which recalls *Il Penseroso* in its metre and its exploitation of Hermetic lore, has been unaccountably neglected or scorned by Keats's commentators. It is not great poetry, but it is charming and sincere; and Keats gets inside the skin of these delicate creatures as he got inside the skin of Mrs Reynolds's cat. A striking effect of verisimilitude is produced less by description than by modifications of rhythm, of sentence structure, of dialogue tone: the metrical shifts in the concluding lines are particularly effective. And it is not a mere *tour de force*. Keats is writing of beings quite real to him; at the same time he is releasing the powers that Erasmus Darwin had imprisoned in *The Botanic Garden*. He is demonstrating, with some virtuosity, how poetry *could* be written about the Rosicrucian elementals.[2]

The second long poem in the 1817 volume is *Sleep and Poetry*. Here the themes that were broached in 'I stood tip-toe . . .' (to be drawn together in stricter counterpoint in the four-part *Fairies' Song*) find a new exposition. *Sleep and Poetry* is cast in the form of a

---

[1] Cf. *Timæus*, 116 (31): '. . . hence the Divinity, beginning to fabricate, composed the body of the universe from fire and earth.' A Chinese text declares: 'When the abysmal and the fire mix, the holy fruit is born.' The birth of the holy fruit is celebrated in Keats's Nativity Ode (see below, p. 374) which is written in the same metre. Fire is basic in Keats's thinking on creativity. At Margate, in 1817, he is 'in continual burning of thought'. Calling on the 'begetters of our deep eternal theme' to aid him (in the *Lear* sonnet), he pleads:

But when I am consumed with the Fire
Give me new Phoenix-wings to fly at my desire.

The emphasis is constantly on direct, fearless experiencing, the penetration into essence. See also below, p. 106, note 1.

[2] I wonder why Mr Robert Gittings (in *John Keats: The Living Year*), calls the poem 'unfinished'.

riddle with appended clues; or, more exactly, there are two riddles of which the answer to the first is given.[1] We are asked in the first ten lines what it is that is gentler than a wind in summer, more soothing than the humming of a bee, and so on. The answer is, Sleep—which is then suitably apostrophized. But all this simply leads up to the second riddle. What is higher beyond thought than Sleep?

> Fresher than berries of a mountain tree?
> More strange, more beautiful, more smooth, more regal,
> Than wings of swans, than doves, than dim-seen eagle?
> What is it? And to what shall I compare it?
> It has a glory, and nought else can share it:
> The thought thereof is awful, sweet, and holy,
> Chacing away all worldliness and folly;
> Coming sometimes like fearful claps of thunder,
> Or the low rumblings earth's regions under;
> And sometimes like a gentle whispering
> Of all the secrets of some wond'rous thing
> That breathes about us in the vacant air . . .

These are remarkable terms. The thing Keats is talking about (it is not poetry, as the symmetry of the title would demand, but what he later calls a 'vast idea') is incomparable. It is superior to the richest symbols of the visible world; it possesses an unsharable glory. Meditation upon it is 'awful, sweet, and holy' and has the power to dispel worldly thoughts. It comes sometimes, like the Wordsworthian theophany, with fearless visiting, with soft alarm, or with severer intervention. I have not hesitated to paraphrase here, for we all are too ready to pass over such statements as vague generalities. No—Keats is very much in earnest, and it is important that we grasp what he has to say. He will not dogmatize, or insult his reader by over-definition:

> No one who once the glorious sun has seen,
> And all the clouds, and felt his bosom clean
> For his great Maker's presence, but must know
> What 'tis I mean, and feel his being glow.

---

[1] A love of riddling marks Keats's poetry, often in combination with the Celtic theme of metamorphosis.

In what follows he still refuses to define, but he gives us a series of 'ethereal finger-pointings' to the wondrous thing. I have called them clues to the riddle; but the clues are themselves disguised. Unlike Wordsworth, Keats does not 'speak out'. It is partly that he is too modest, too unsure of himself and of his findings; but it is also that he refuses to write the kind of poetry that 'has a palpable design on us'. Moreover, he seems to have believed that there is an esoteric knowledge, which must not be divulged. He has resolved, if granted the status of a poet, to

> Write on my tablets all that was permitted,
> All that was for our human senses fitted.
> Then the events of this wide world I'd seize
> Like a strong giant, and my spirit teaze
> Till at its shoulders it should proudly see
> Wings to find out an immortality.[1]

The vision of the charioteer which follows should not be overlooked or dismissed as baroque extravagance. It is a vision of Apollo: and Apollo is to be the 'golden theme' that will run through Keats's verse from now on. The chariot is traditional,[2] interpreting supremacy, creative power (in *Paradise Lost* the demiurge drives out into chaos in such a vehicle): and Apollo is originally the poet: 'Knowledge enormous makes a god of me.' He is the type of every true poet who becomes deified through participation in gnosis, entering into the 'images', as Blake puts it, 'on the fiery chariot of contemplative thought'. For in the same

---

[1] The wings are more than decorative: they convey a young man's eagle mind. The wish to seize, to manipulate and mould the stuff of the material universe is spagyric. The implications of the first two lines are tremendous. Here again Keats is with Blake. The limits of our universe are imposed by our senses. If these were more numerous, we should apprehend more; if they were keener, we should apprehend more clearly; if they were flexible, we should, at will, apprehend either unity or diversity. (Cf. the 'capable ears' of Endymion: below, p. 172).

[2] We may compare Plato's chariot with its winged steeds (as in Keats's vision) in the *Phædrus*, or the chariot in which Krishna addresses Arjuna, or from which Beatrice addresses Dante. The sixth chapter of Zechariah, which Keats recommends his schoolgirl sister to study for its Messianic significance (letter of 31 March 1819) opens with a vision of four chariots.

chariot that he drives up to heaven he also descends from heaven to liberate the energies imprisoned in gross matter.[1]

Keats's charioteer does four things. He descends from heaven; he 'talks To the trees and mountains'; he summons a host of spirits; and he writes something down. Once again, recognizably, we are in the world of *The Poet*. This descent of the hero into matter as demiurge and saviour reproduces a most ancient pattern of which Milton's picture is a late example. In Hermetic doctrine creation is not a unique act isolated in time, but a continual process. We find this in *Timæus*; we find it most clearly in Treatise XI of the *Corpus Hermeticum*. There is an eternal descent, an eternal awakening, an eternal ascent of that which is awakened. Hermes is instructed by Nous that

> God is the source of all things, Eternity is the essence, and the cosmos is the matter. The power of God is Eternity, and the work of Eternity is the cosmos, which never has had a beginning, but is for ever coming into being by the power of Eternity. Consequently nothing that is in the cosmos will ever perish[2] (for Eternity is imperishable) nor can it be destroyed, for the cosmos is surrounded by Eternity.

The minor verse Keats was writing about this time—most of it quite negligible technically—together with some allusions in his letters, will clinch our conviction of the very early and great importance the symbol of Apollo had for him. 'I hope Apollo is not angered at my having made a Mockery at him at Hunt's', he writes,[3] in reference to his wearing a laurel wreath while taking wine with Hunt one summer evening. He is serious: Woodhouse notes that 'he mentioned the circumstances afterward to one or two of his friends, expressing his sense of the impropriety of what he had done; and his intention of recording it, by some apologetic verses suited to the occasion'. These verses

---

[1] Those ascents and descents, however motivated, are a commonplace of Keats's poetry, and express one aspect of his feeling for relationship. They link the worlds. The chariots themselves may be seen as mobile super-urns enclosing divinities.

[2] A profoundly Blakean doctrine.

[3] *Letters*, 52.

were the *Ode to Apollo*, of which only the final strophe need be
quoted:

> The Pleiades were up,
>   Watching the silent air;
> The seeds and roots in Earth
>   Were swelling for summer fare;
> The Ocean, its neighbour,
> Was at his old labour,
> When, who—who did dare
> To tie for a moment thy plant round his brow,
>   And grin and look proudly,
>   And blaspheme so loudly,
> And live for that honour, to stoop to thee now?
>   O Delphic Apollo!

A negligible event celebrated in negligible rhyme—but clearly it
had its importance for Keats. And that importance could only
exist if Apollo was a reality for him. The short, panting clauses
of the February 1818 'God of the Meridian' carry the same
note of awe.

Keats's vision of Apollo in *Sleep and Poetry* is followed by a
well-known passage of literary judgment in which England's past
poetic glories are set against the work of the Augustan 'school of
dolts'.[1] Behind the overt literary references we sense deeper
vitalist-mechanist evaluations. Before the 'schism' the all was
revealed to man.

> From the clear space of ether, to the small
> Breath of new buds unfolding.

We may remember Blake's 'The narrow bud opens her beauties
to the sun', and 'Whatever grows from its pure bud or breathes
a fragrant soul'. This last image is given by Blake (in *Vala*) as an
example of contracted vision in juxtaposition with 'The Elemental
Planets & the orbs of eccentric fire' as images of expanded vision.
Keats makes precisely the same contrast. He has a 'copiousness

---

[1] Britain as the land of Apollo is a major theme of Davis's *Celtic Researches*. See
below, Appendix A, pp. 397-401.

of glance' which can take in the minute and the gigantic with
equal ease, and connect them in a valid synthesis.

It is only with the next paragraph—'Could all this be forgotten?'
—that Keats turns to an indictment of the eighteenth-century
poets. Men were thought wise who could not understand the
creative power of Apollo, who were divorced from a living and
growing nature, who could do no more than translate their own
imperceptions into a devitalized rhetoric. But this unfortunate
period is over. The spirits of the great poets have inspired a new
race of bards. Though not, as yet, to a perfect balance of strength
with sweetness and light. Much of the new verse is harsh and
clumsy (he is perhaps thinking of Wordsworth and Byron here):

> . . . in clear truth the themes
> Are ugly clubs, the Poets Polyphemes
> Disturbing the grand sea.

And in the famous lines that follow he gives us his own definition
of poetry as 'a drainless shower of light—the supreme of power
—might half slumb'ring on its own right arm': a synthesis of
richness and effortless ease often emphasized in his letters.

In the following paragraph—lines 270 to 312—he defends himself from the charge of presumption. It is true that he has not yet
attained the insight of the magus: but he is approaching it. The
passage is important for our theme and must be quoted at length:[1]

> What though I am not wealthy in the dower
> Of spanning wisdom; though I do not know
> The shiftings of the mighty winds that blow
> Hither and thither all the changing thoughts
> Of man: though no great minist'ring reason sorts
> Out the dark mysteries of human souls
> To clear conceiving: yet there ever rolls
> A vast idea before me, and I glean
> Therefrom my liberty; thence too I've seen
> The end and aim of Poesy. 'Tis clear
> As any thing most true; as that the year

---

[1] The first ten lines with their mention of the 'vast idea', have already been
cited (p. 95 above).

Is made of the four seasons—manifest
As a large cross, some old cathedral's crest
Lifted to the white clouds. Therefore should I
Be but the essence of deformity,
A coward, did my very eye-lids wink
At speaking out what I have dared to think.
Ah! rather let me like a madman run
Over some precipice; let the hot sun
Melt my Dedalian wings, and drive me down
Convuls'd and headlong! Stay! an inward frown
Of conscience bids me be more calm awhile.
An ocean dim, sprinkled with many an isle,
Spreads awfully before me. How much toil!
How many days! what desperate turmoil!
Ere I can have explored its widenesses.
Ah, what a task! upon my bended knees,
I could unsay those—no, impossible,
Impossible!

The tone has turned a little shrill towards the close: we could spare the exclamations and the aposiopesis. But Keats's sincerity is patent. Note that he is not talking primarily of poetry, but of noesis: the 'vast idea' that eludes him and yet from which he 'gleans his liberty'. The vast idea comes first; only in the second place—'thence too'—does poetry come in. Poetry is the medium of the idea. Keats might almost say with Dante:

> O voi che avete gl' intelletti sani,
> Mirate la dottrina che s' asconde
> Sotto il velame degli versi strani.

Under the 'strange verses' of this section of *Sleep and Poetry* (which Keats does in fact call 'this strange assay') the elements of a revelation are hidden. But Keats does not quite know what the revelation is. It is a half-seeing. He is going to spend the rest of his short life trying to grasp and to express the vast idea in its fullness.

Meantime we must examine the clues that Keats gives us. He speaks of 'spanning wisdom': wisdom pontifical, bridge-building. But bridges between what? If our conclusions up to the present have any validity, we can answer this question. The wisdom of the poet-magus is all-embracing: it spans earth and heaven and hell, the three worlds of which Diana is Queen,[1] the four elements, the kingdoms of minerals, plants, animals, and men—the material and the ethereal. It is his task to restore a vanished, or reveal a hidden unity. He knows (our second clue) 'the shiftings of the mighty winds that blow Hither and thither all the changing thoughts Of man'. These are not physical winds: they are the 'ethereal' breathings of the *anima mundi* at work in the creation towards an end in which the transfigured man can participate. It is this participation, I believe, which Keats intuited as his 'vast idea'. And the third clue, of the 'great minist'ring reason' that ordinates and makes apprehensible the 'dark mysteries of human souls', points us to no less a power than the *Nous* of Hermes, the Demiurge of Plato, which stands above the *anima mundi* and governs all things.

We are offered yet a fourth clue in the paired similes which illustrate the clearness of the end and aim of Poesy. He cannot mistake the purpose of poetry, he says: it is as clear as anything *most true*. And then, as examples of things most true, he gives us two quaternary symbols: the four seasons of the year, and the cross over some old cathedral. These examples are not chosen at random. They lie at the very root of Keats's thinking.

The theme of the quaternary is, of course, Pythagorean and Hermetic. The four humours, Keats would have read in his Burton, 'have some analogy with the four elements, and to the four ages in man . . .'[2] It would be interesting, though scarcely possible, to trace the growth of the quaternary idea in Keats's mind, and to explore its ramifications. But we haven't the materials. We shall, however, return to the point later in our discussion of *Endymion*.

Before we go on to study his longest poem, I would like to say something about Keats's use of the word 'ethereal', which from

---

[1] As Keats recognizes in the final couplet of the 1818 sonnet *To Homer*.

[2] *Anatomy*, Pt. I, Sec. 2, Mem. i, Subsec. 2. Cf. Keats's sonnet *The Human Seasons*.

now on will be even more prominent in his verse than it has been. It is indeed a key word for Keats. Its antonym is 'material'; the distinction is very like that drawn between the 'subtle' and the 'gross' bodies in Hindu metaphysics. The alchemical process, in the Great Work, distils the ethereal from the material substance. Keats plays with this notion in a variety of contexts, some jocose, some serious. In a letter of 26 March 1818 to James Rice we find a peculiarly enlightening whimsy about Milton. Keats is writing from Rice's 'favourite Devon' (no favourite with Keats, because of the incessant rain):

> I have heard that Milton ere he wrote His answer to Salmasius came into these parts, and for one whole Month, rolled himself, for three whole hours in a certain meadow hard by us—where the mark of his nose at equidistances is still shown. The exhibitor of said Meadow further saith that after these rollings, not a nettle sprang up in all the seven acres for seven years and that from said time a new sort of plant was made from the white thorn, of a thornless nature very much used by the Bucks of the present day to rap their Boots withall. This account made me very naturally suppose that the nettles and thorns etherealized by the Scholars rotatory motion and garner'd in his head thence flew after a new fermentation against the luckless Salmasius and occasioned his well known and unhappy end.[1]

This is nonsense, in Rabelais' milder vein; but it is revealing nonsense. The idea behind it is serious, and we have met it before. It is an application of the doctrine of correspondences. Milton the Puritan poet is deflated; Milton the tower-dwelling magus of *Il Penseroso* enjoys a farcical apotheosis. We may remember the equally Rabelaisian 'intripled turn' performed by Blake under the Lambeth poplar trees, 'when Klopstock' like Salmasius 'England defied' and was duly punished by sympathetic magic.

Magic is possible, through the law of correspondences, because universal space is pervaded by ether. And ether, in Keats's view, is the spiritual substance in which all subtle bodies live and move and have their being. The process of nature, participated in by

---

[1] Keats at this time was 'feasting upon' Milton (see Letter of 27 April 1818 to Reynolds).

man the magus as an under-agent of what in *Endymion* Keats will call the 'throned seats unscalable', is continuously transmuting gross into subtle bodies. There is no hard and fast division between spiritual and material. An everlasting interchange goes on between them. Intellect itself is not individual: it exists in the ether as a kind of reservoir to be drawn upon by individual minds. Really great minds form a species of Cartesian vortices in the ether: having their being in 'a dizzy void', they draw intellect into themselves. The store is not inexhaustible: and 'very likely a certain portion of intellect was spun forth [at the Creation] into the thin Air for the Brains of Man to prey on', he tells Rice.[1] The greater minds, such as Milton's, suck an excess of this intellect into themselves and leave precious little for anyone else; hence the dearth of first-rate verse since Milton. The eighteenth-century 'desert' is accounted for.

All this leads us back to Agrippa and Burton[2] and their speculations on the medium in which mind and elements act and react upon one another. 'The innumerable compositions and decompositions which take place between the intellect and its thousand materials before it arrives at that trembling delicate and snail-horn perception of Beauty' are carried out in this medium, he tells Haydon in a letter of 8 April 1818. Note that the systole and diastole operate in the intellect as well as in the materials. If we now read the Scottish tour letter of June 1818[3] we shall understand how mountains and lakes are also manifestations of the great Power, like mighty poets; and how the task of the poet is to quintessentialize the mountain-intellect into poetic form for the benefit of mankind.

In a letter of 22 November 1817 to Bailey, Keats advances a 'truth'—note that he does not call it a 'speculation' or a surmise—which has 'pressed upon' him lately and increased his humility.

---

[1] Conversely, 'the worldly elements. . . . prey on his nature' (Letter to George Keats, April 1819).
[2] And beyond them to *Timæus*. See too Appendix C, 3.
[3] To Tom Keats. See below, p. 210.

Men of Genius are great as certain ethereal Chemicals operating on the Mass of neutral intellect—but they have not any individuality, any determined Character—

For a long time I took 'the mass of neutral intellect' to be a rather clumsy equivalent for 'people of ordinary intelligence': the men and women who are not poets, not artists. Men of genius raise the man in the street to the level of their own perception of beauty and truth. Closer scrutiny shows that this was not Keats's meaning. In writing 'the mass of neutral intellect' he is being scrupulously exact and he means the same as the 'grand materials' of the later letter; he means the intellect of mountains, clouds, rivers, stars, the sun and moon (we remember the still earlier letter to Haydon). This intellect is neutral and non-acting until it is 'harvested' and made available to mankind.

Keats goes a step further (and a big step) in his thinking on this very subtle question, when in the 'soul-making' letter of April 1819 to George and Georgiana, he distinguishes the 'three grand materials' which act upon one another to produce 'identities'. 'Intellect' has now become 'Intelligence', 'ether' has become the 'Elemental space'; the 'human Heart' works upon Intelligence in the Elemental space, forming the 'atoms of divinity' into individual souls each capable of its proper bliss. We see that the old theory has been expanded to elucidate quite another and more fundamental creation. Here once again we catch the voice of *Timæus*, or rather of the Introduction to *Timæus*, in which Taylor paraphrasing Proclus tells how 'partial souls' are introduced into the 'spacious receptacle' of 'the mundane animal' (the cosmos), and ' become mundane through the luciform vehicles with which they are connected. . . . For we are endued with an intellect subsisting in energy, and a rational soul proceeding from the same father and vivific goddess as were the causes of the intellect and soul of the universe. . . .' [1]

---

[1] In the *Timæus* itself we read: 'it [is] impossible for intellect to accede to any being, without the intervention of soul. Hence, as the result of this reasoning, placing intellect in soul and soul in body [the Divinity] fabricated the universe. . . .' (p. 115).

It is not my purpose to go into Keats's theology here. Let us note simply how an understanding of the inter-workings of genius and neutral intellect (to return to the phraseology of the 1817 letter) sheds light on the mystery of the *mantram*, the talisman. The passage of full poetry or distilled prose is magical, instinct with power, because it has drawn its original energy from natural forces. It is a concentrated form of cosmic 'intellect', and it is able to react upon cosmic forms. It may also release the imprisoned energies in man. The dead revive in the third book of *Endymion* when the virtue inherent in the scroll is applied to them. In *The Cap and Bells* the magician gives the king 'an old and legend-leaved book' to take with him as a 'potent charm' on his quest. He is merely to lay it on Bertha's table, and it will work of its own power. Such, for Keats, is the force of the stored-up *word*. We shall come later to see how it is not only in books that the word is 'garnered'. Resonant hollows, natural and artificial, have similar power to teach and to transmute.

[*I stood Tip-toe* (1816)—*Sleep and Poetry* (1816)—*Song of Four Fairies* (1819)]

Chapter Seven

A SYMBOL OF IMMENSITY

The land is too pure to admit the sordid and the base. The road which conducts to it is too intricate to be discovered by the unskilful and stupid, and the journey is too long and laborious to be accomplished by the effeminate and the timid, by the slave of passion and the dupe of opinion, by the lover of sense and the despiser of truth. The dangers and difficulties in the undertaking, are such as can be sustained by none but the most hardy and accomplished adventurers; and he who begins the journey without the strength of Hercules, or the wisdom and patience of Ulysses, must be destroyed by the wild beasts of the forest, or perish in the storms of the ocean; must suffer transmutation into a beast, through the magic power of Circe, or be exiled for life by the detaining charms of Calypso; and in short must descend into Hades, and wander in its darkness, without emerging from thence to bright regions of the morning; or be ruined by the deadly melody of the Syren's song. . . . . .

THOMAS TAYLOR, Introduction to *Parmenides*.

WE saw how, in the sonnet on Mrs Reynolds's cat, structure and rhythm functioned in such a way that we were able to move about with Keats in a temporal pattern within the poem. We find ourselves able to do this on a much bigger scale in *Endymion*. Keats himself described the work as 'a little Region to wander in' for the lovers of poetry—a space in which 'they may pick and choose, and in which the images are so numerous that many are forgotten and found new in a second Reading: which may be food for a Week's stroll in the Summer'.[1] I shall take permission from these words to treat *Endymion*, in the comments that follow, less as a consecutive narrative than as a storehouse of ideas and images.

Keats, in mid-April 1817, found the country round Southampton 'most delightful . . . some open Down but for the most part

[1] *Letters*, 52.

thickly wooded'. He had left London to be by himself and write *Endymion*. His next stage was Carisbrooke, with a flying visit to Shanklin: 'a most beautiful place—sloping wood and meadow ground reaches round the Chine, which is a cleft between the Cliffs of the depth of nearly 300 feet at least. This cleft is filled with trees . . .'. But May 10th finds him at Margate: 'this treeless affair', he complains. 'I fancied that I . . . could contrive to do without trees', he writes to Leigh Hunt. He could not do without trees, because the presence of growing things was a necessity for him in springtime, and because *Endymion* itself is a forest poem. A great charm of Oxford for him that autumn lay in its 'plenty of Trees thank God'. The chine at Shanklin passed nostalgically into Book II of *Endymion*, which he wrote in the 'dark city', as the 'wooded cleft', the 'solitary glen' looking out to 'the blue of ocean'. *Endymion* is all trees. It begins and ends, and develops its main action, within 'a mighty forest'. Even in the 'deep, deep underworld' of Book II a myrtle wood springs up with magic speed. But trees are always magical for Keats: they whisper secrets, they shelter, instruct and console.[1]

The setting of the action within a *selva oscura*, together with mention (Book I, 76) of the wolf and the leopard (two of the three beasts encountered by Dante at the beginning of his adventures), help to establish the pilgrimage pattern of the poem. This will not concern us in our present enquiry, except in so far as the pilgrimage pattern is also an initiation pattern, penetrated with ideas of growth, fruition, metamorphosis and rebirth. The pilgrimage in *Endymion* is basically of this kind; it is a progress through the elements, and its purpose is transformation. The poem, then, is metaphysical; but Keats has not mastered his metaphysics. He is working them out, personally, within the poem: a way of writing poetry which may be engaging in a sonnet or ode, but which does not make for good narrative writing. Too much of *Endymion* is experiment, laboratory work, detritus even: Keats

---

[1] After death the 'Bards of Passion and of Mirth' commune not only with the spheres of Sun and Moon but also with 'the Whisper of heaven's trees'. Cf. too 'the prosperous woods' of *Lamia*, and Appendix A, pp. 401–3.

knew it to be so, and there is little to add to his own strictures on the poem in Prefaces and letters.

Our concern in this section will be with the process in *Endymion*, not with the doctrine, though doctrine there is, in however inchoate a form. The process of the poem itself, and of Keats within the poem, and the images of growth and fruition which reinforce these processes: through a study of these we may find openings into the more poised, more achieved world of the great Odes and the romances. That is the expectation, the forward glance; a backward glance from *Endymion* may lead us into closer understanding of the prentice work of 1817, and particularly into understanding of the 'vast idea'. The forward glance is Keats's in his præludium:

> And now at once, adventuresome, I send
> My herald thought into a wilderness:
> There let its trumpet blow, and quickly dress
> My uncertain path with green, that I may speed
> Easily onward, thorough flowers and weed.   [I, 58–62]

With his usual frankness, he lets us into the spirit in which he undertakes the poem. It is 'with full happiness' that he will 'trace the story of Endymion':

> The very music of the name has gone
> Into my being, and each pleasant scene
> Is growing fresh before me as the green
> Of our own valleys.   [36–9]

He is identifying himself to the fullest possible extent with the story: and it is a process, not a picture. There is an integration going on with the flow of life. He is not looking back at something he has heard or read or thought or even experienced himself: he is living *now*, and his living is his writing. 'Now . . . now', he says—

> I will begin
> Now while I cannot hear the city's din;
> Now while the early budders are just new
> And run in mazes of the youngest hue
> About old forests . . .   [39–43]

We feel the excitement there, the anticipation, the dawning discovery, the eagerness to be off. We are in the moment, the now; but we are also blending the old with the new, we are separating and rejecting nothing; and we are integrating ourselves with the larger processes, the sap rising and the budding of trees and the progress of the seasons:

> And, as the year
> Grows lush in juicy stalks, I'll smoothly steer
> My little boat . . .

We see that he won't keep it static: there is no sitting down to write:

> . . . I'll smoothly steer
> My little boat, for many quiet hours,
> With streams that deepen freshly into bowers.
> Many and many a verse I hope to write,
> Before the daisies, vermeil rimm'd and white,
> Hide in deep herbage; and ere yet the bees
> Hum about globes of clover and sweet peas,
> I must be near the middle of my story.
> O may no wintry season, bare and hoary,
> See it half-finish'd; but let Autumn bold,
> With universal tinge of sober gold,
> Be all about me when I make an end.
> And now at once, adventuresome, I send
> My herald thought into a wilderness. . . .   [45–59]

Keats has invited us to wander about in *Endymion* for the sake of its images. By 'images' he may have meant its ancillary similes, metaphors, personifications; these are interesting, but they are dependent upon broader patterns which will engage us more profitably. There is a sense in which *Endymion*, on all counts a symbolical poem (though there is little agreement as to what it is symbolical of), is one great image: the eikon of transformation. Looked at more closely, the poem opens itself to us as a double image, embracing the Yin and the Yang, the feminine and the masculine components of totality. And this, in a major product

of Keats's deeply sincere and intuitive mind, was to be expected:
the problem in the poem, indeed, is the conciliation of these
contraries.

In this attempt Keats does not succeed. The two image-structures never really fuse. Or, let us say, they fuse at the beginning
of the poem, in the only section which we feel as completely
satisfactory: the feast of Pan. And this is because in Pan and his
worship the masculine and feminine are united elementally; the
'one' embraces the 'many' on the ground of unconscious being,
existence unquestioning of itself. This is 'innocence'. But the point
of the poem is that 'innocence' must give place to 'experience',
being must become conscious of itself, break its existential felicity,
separate into Yin and Yang, leave 'the circle of courses', and seek
a new unity on the plane of 'spirit'. The enterprise is fundament-
ally 'heroic'. These ideas are expressed by Keats clearly enough
in the long address by Endymion to Peona in Book I. Clearly,
but not very satisfactorily, for reasons we shall see in a
moment.

The action of *Endymion* is set within a pastoral community
existing on the slopes of Mount Latmos in the Golden Age, itself
the first Age of a cosmic cycle, or Great Year. We have no means
of knowing how Keats conceived of the Great Year: hardly, I
should think, with any precision. 'This planet's sphering time',
he calls it in Book II.[1] The cyclic conception is pervasive in *Endymion* and *Hyperion*, and indeed in much Romantic poetry. Byron's
Darkness gives a powerful picture of the close of a Great Year, and
there are frequent references in Shelley. We must set our smaller
patterns of growth and form against this all-embracing pattern if
we are to feel the range of Keats's thought in his later poems, where
he explores time as in the earlier ones he had surveyed space (the
Shakespearian *mantrams* 'In the dark backward and abysm of time'

---

[1] His main ideas in this connection all seem to me to come from Plato, and particularly from *Timæus* and *Cratylus* which I believe he read and discussed with
Bailey at Oxford. I suggest that much of the first two books was rewritten after
his Oxford visit. *Aeneid*, VI, 745, *perfecto temporis orbe*, is perhaps the original of
Keats's 'when this planet's sphering time was done'.

and 'Shall, for that vast of Night that they may work' haunt
him from his Carisbrooke days). But we begin with the smaller
patterns, with immediate processes of nutrition, growth,
fruiting:

> Upon the sides of Latmos was outspread
> A mighty forest; for the moist earth fed
> So plenteously all weed-hidden roots
> Into o'er-hanging boughs, and precious fruits.   [63–6]

Paths wind 'through palmy fern, and rushes fenny'

> To a wide lawn, whence one could only see
> Stems thronging all around between the swell
> Of turf and slanting branches. . . .   [82–4]

Motions centre upon a stillness. Mid-point in 'the sacred sward'
stands a marble altar, decked with flowers. It is morning.

> Man's voice was on the mountains; and the mass
> Of nature's lives and wonders puls'd tenfold
> To feel this sun-rise and its glories old.   [104–6]

These are 'the silent workings of the dawn', a process completed,
not interrupted, by the 'joyful cries' of 'a troop of little children',
and later by the ritual prayers and hymns of the Pan festival. Man
is, as ever, integrated with nature. For Keats, as for Blake, 'Where
Man is not, Nature is barren'. And this integration is the purpose
of the festival itself. The preservation of the Golden Age, the
prosperity of the community within the Golden Age, depend
intimately on worship—the kind of worship Keats speaks about
most pointedly in *Psyche*.

With respect to the complete cycle, the Golden Age is transient.
But with respect to the life of the tribe, it is something eminently
stable. The function of the shepherd-king, within the ritual context, is to preserve the Golden Age; to ensure that no elements
of decay, of evil, invade the life of the community. He must
strive at all times, and especially at the great nodal festivals of

spring, summer, autumn and winter,[1] to integrate the clan's life with the elemental powers. Endymion's task is unequivocally stated:

> To nurse the golden age 'mong shepherd clans.[2]

He is shown as the pastoral prince, who is also the vegetation king; and on him, under Pan, depends the common welfare. He is mentioned together with Pan in the address prefaced by the 'venerable priest' to the great chorus:

> we have had
> Great bounty from Endymion our lord.

A picture which is precisely the antithesis (consciously so, I think) to Titania's in *Midsummer Night's Dream* is painted in this speech: man and nature are functioning well together, there is no friction, and all will continue to go well so long as the clan's vows are not 'wanting to our great god Pan'. The spring festival calls for a renewal of these vows.

The 'sacred fire' is now kindled on the altar, wine is poured out upon the sward; and the chorus lifts its voice in the famous hymn. In five powerful strophes, the god is hailed as forest-dweller, sitting 'in desolate places'; as lord of nature, receiving the first fruits, and wandering 'through sunny meadows'; as king of the satyrs, directing their services to man; as the cosmic magus,

> Dread opener of the mysterious doors
> Leading to universal knowledge;

and finally as the earth-element itself in its pure or 'ethereal' state,

> the unimaginable lodge
> For solitary thinkings; such as dodge

---

[1] Cf. the 'passing-forth' of the poet-magus in Keats's sonnet at the four points of the day. *Endymion* is in one sense a simple expansion of *The Poet*.

[2] Book II, 895. As these are *mountain* shepherds, we may assume that the present cycle is one following upon destruction by flood, not by fire (as Keats would learn from *Timæus*). It is significant that the 'unfooted plains' are inhabited only by wild beasts.

Conception to the very bourne of heaven,[1]
Then leave the naked brain.

Thus, under the dome of heaven,

That spreads so clear o'er our solemnity,

honour is done to Pan in his multiple aspects. Rich embroidery of flowering and fruit is woven around idyllic human activity:

the birth, life, death
Of unseen flowers in heavy peacefulness;

'dank moisture' breeding 'the pipy hemlock to strange overgrowth'; 'broad-leaved fig-trees' foredooming their 'ripen'd fruitage', and

yellow-girted bees
Their golden honeycombs

(where again the future is anticipated in the instant).

The final strophes modulate from this warm, sleepy naturalism into the realm of the forms. Pan is the 'dread opener of the doors leading to universal knowledge'. But note: as such he cannot be worshipped by the shepherds; not, even, by Endymion. This is carefully stressed in what follows; and with reason, for we are at a crux of the poem. In all traditional pilgrimages the pilgrim must come to realize, at the completion of his quest, that his travails have been strictly unnecessary, that he is back where he has always been, and that simple ignorance has been his only bar to enjoyment of the supreme good. Endymion is redeemed at the conclusion of the poem when, in complete despair, he challenges the right of heaven to divide the heavenly from the earthly beauty: the moment he does so, Diana and the Indian maid are found to be one; the division has been made only by his own 'meddling intellect'.

Endymion is not listening to the hymn. He is worrying, and

---

[1] The phrase is repeated in *Letters*, 95, in a context deprecating Wordsworth's 'egotistical' philosophy. We remember that it was Keats's reading of the Hymn to Pan which Wordsworth greeted with his 'A pretty piece of paganism!'

worry is closing his mind to the here and now. He will seek the higher life which seems to be beckoning to him not in the multiple energies of Pan or Apollo but in the reflected splendours of Diana the moon-goddess. When the hymn is completed, he joins the circle of elders who are telling 'strange histories',

> potent to send
> A young mind from its bodily tenement.

Each auditor anticipates his separate, personal felicity in the world to come. Endymion adds nothing to their speculations; but 'a cankering venom' at his heart plunges him into an isolation deeper than any they can know. He has lost contact with reality.

It is at this moment that the element earth, which he has forgotten, and indeed is beginning to despise, puts forth a flower: the girl Peona. I offer this expression not as a preciosity but as the most accurate account I can give of the event. Peona, Endymion's sister, is the embodiment of earthly, uncomprehending love and loyalty. She incarnates the maternal, the limited, the unspeculative. She is, therefore, in one sense, Endymion's greatest enemy on the journey he is about to undertake. In Peona Keats dramatizes the 'homely nurse' of Wordsworth's great *Ode*, though it is the glories he *is to know* from which Peona tries to distract her brother's attention. She

> breathes a sister's sorrow to persuade
> A yielding up, a cradling on her care.[1]

She takes him in 'a little shallop' to 'a bowery island' where

> Under her favourite bower's quiet shade,
> On her own couch, new made of flower leaves

he falls asleep. The water, the island, the bower compose the sphere of unconscious felicity which Endymion must relinquish for a life of struggle. He sleeps, and wakes refreshed. We under-

---

[1] The peony is a flower that plays an important part in Hermetic astro-botany. It is under the protection of the moon, and the human organ with which it is associated is the lungs. Erasmus Darwin, in a footnote to line 7 of Canto III of *The Loves of the Plants*, tells us that 'even at this day bits of dried root of Peony are . . . sold under the name of Anodyne necklaces, and tied round the necks of children'.

stand that the factors of the unconscious life are not in themselves
'bad' or even insufficient: they are insufficient for Endymion,
now, because he finds them so. This is the point reached by Keats
himself in *Sleep and Poetry*:

> Yes, I must pass them for a nobler life.

In fact, Keats did not pass them; he came, or was coming, to identify them with the nobler life when death took him. If he had
passed them, we would have lost *St Agnes, Isabella, Autumn*; we
would have gained an inferior Wordsworth or Matthew Arnold
and lost the inimitable poet of earth.

It is unfortunate that Keats's most considerable cuts in *Endymion*
are made in Book I and relate to the person and actions of Peona.
As she exists in the published version she is a somewhat shadowy
figure, and her function is by no means clear. My reading of her
part in the narrative depends to some extent on these omitted
passages.[1] Peona's sprinkling of water from 'a dark well' upon
Endymion, her giving him wine, and offering him an 'amulet'
to smell, are particularly noteworthy actions; singing and lute-
playing are all that remain in the final version of these charms oı
the senses. The music acts on Endymion as a 'deep intoxication'
and he is led by Peona's sympathy to tell her of the causes of his
discontent.

This brings us to the familiar legend. In what form it was
familiar to Keats we need not enquire.[2] He had delighted in the
tale from early days, and we remember that 'I stood tip-toe . . .'
is a fragment of a projected *Endymion*. Nor need we trace in any
detail the course of the narrative as Keats presents it to us, though
some sort of summary is essential if only in view of Keats's own
dire confusions. The three visions of an unknown goddess which
Endymion now describes to Peona—visions which have delighted,
distracted, and unbalanced him—are ill-conceived: in Keats's
own epithet, 'mawkish'. We feel personal stresses warping his

---

[1] For which the reader is referred to the Garrod edition, notably in the footnotes to pp. 76–86.

[2] The Notes in de Selincourt's edition (pp. 414–17) give the main references.

workmanship: there is an uneasiness quite absent from the atmosphere of the Pan festival. Peona's comment, with its typical fruition image, is most apposite:

> 'Is this the cause?
> This all? Yet it is wonderful—exceeding—
> And yet a shallow dream, for ever breeding
> Tempestuous Weather in that very Soul
> That should be twice content, twice smooth, twice whole,
> As is a double Peach.'[1]

The visions of the goddess *are* shallow dreams; and Peona cannot conceive of reality except in terms of physical wholeness. The two image structures which, I have suggested, clash in the poem and give it its peculiar air of unreality, are neatly contrasted here as dream and fruit. From her point of view, Peona is right in preferring the fruit; from his point of view, Endymion is right in following the dream. But we must look a little more closely at the dilemma here.

Endymion, like all writing genuinely rooted in tradition, assumes a correlation between the macrocosm and the microcosm. The cyclic process of the four ages is mirrored in the physical and spiritual life of man. If Endymion's function is 'to nurse the golden age 'mongst shepherd clans' it is because the Golden Age offers the best possibilities to its inhabitants for a realization superior to itself. Similarly childhood in the microcosm is the period 'of which is the kingdom of heaven'.[2] But in the world and in man the cycle is always the circle, the wheel of becoming, St James's τροχὸς τῆς γενέσεως[3] from which there is no release except through 'realization'.

In all tradition the conditions for such liberation are immutable.

---

[1] Again using a cancelled passage (*Poems*, p. 86).

[2] The microcosmic parallel of 'to nurse the golden age' is given by Coleridge: 'To carry on the feelings of childhood into the powers of manhood, to combine the child's sense of wonder and novelty with the appearances which every day for perhaps forty years has rendered familiar . . .' *The Friend*, Essay XV.

[3] The General Epistle of James, iii. 6.

The initial impulse comes from a higher power.[1] The road to liberation leads through the elements. The postulant must effectively identify himself, at every stage, with the element at whose centre he stands. He must place himself between the contraries and reconcile them in himself. There must be an acceptance and an integration. Only in this way can he free himself from 'the hateful siege of contraries'[2] and enter into possession of the higher states. In so doing, a reciprocal process unfolds itself. The postulant, passing through the elements and identifying himself with them, not only achieves his own liberation but also draws the elements up with him into the higher states. This is, basically, the Christian doctrine of the redemption of the fallen cosmos, of the creation groaning in travail 'until now'.[3] Microcosmically, the realization of the eternal now redeems 'the weak and beggarly elements'[4] of the body. The hint is given quite clearly in the Hymn to Pan, where the god is described not only as the 'dread opener of the mysterious doors Leading to universal knowledge' but also as the 'leaven That spreading in this dull and clodded earth, Gives it a touch ethereal—a new birth'.

All this, I believe, was in Keats's mind as he wrote *Endymion*. It is a working out of his original 'vast idea': the idea which had come to him before he met Bailey. But I do not know how much of the original Book I was revised by him after the meeting with Bailey. The month at Oxford certainly amplified and deepened his 'half-seeings', while confusing their expression; and I think he began, half-way through, to get tired of his legend. The Endymion story is not too happy a vehicle—especially on its dream-eroticism side—for the theme of transformation. It is an intensely *interesting* vehicle, from our point of view; the moon is the goddess of phases, of *deceptively* transmuting agencies; and where she is the goddess of energies, as Plato presents her,[5] it is of energies

---

[1] Keats envisaged both Endymion and Peona as 'overshadowed by a Supernatural Power' (*Letters*, 86).

[2] *Paradise Lost*, IX, 121–2: quoted by Keats in *Letters*, 215.

[3] Romans viii. 22.   [4] Galatians iv. 9.

[5] And as in *Endymion*, III. See below, pp. 150–3.

wholly physical and partly sinister. That is to say, she is emphatically the arbitress of growth, and as emphatically the enemy of forms. As an inspirer to the goal of transformation, she was a dangerous choice for Keats.

It is thus doubly ironic that the moon should be the ruler of Endymion's destiny. His need is *growth*, and Diana is the arbitress of growth; yet, through his misconception of her nature, he is propelled through a series of *forms* of so visionary a character that, as he himself sees, they afford him no possibility of striking root:

> '. . . where soil is men grow,
> Whether to weeds or flowers; but for me,
> There is no depth to strike in.'   [II, 159–61]

A rolling stone gathers no moss. It is only when he returns to the forest that Endymion solves his paradox. The two clashing image-structures run through the poem as pilgrimage pattern and fruition pattern respectively: they touch, but never coalesce.

We feel the same confusion in the long and interesting speech in which Endymion explains his philosophy to his sister: a speech which, he says in a letter of 30 January 1818 to his publisher,

> must I think have appeared to you, who are a consequitive Man, as a thing almost of mere words—but I assure you that when I wrote it it was a regular stepping of the Imagination towards a Truth. My having written that Argument will perhaps be of the greatest Service to me of any thing I ever did. It sets before me at once the gradations of Happiness even like a kind of Pleasure Thermometer—and is my first Step towards the chief attempt in the Drama—the playing of different Natures with Joy and Sorrow.

A passage of such importance to Keats *as he was writing the poem* will amply repay our scrutiny. It occupies lines 769 to 857, running on into the account of the hero's second theophany.

Endymion begins with a comparison of what is with what was. His original ambition was for earthly glory; a worthy ambition in itself, but now it is superseded; a 'higher hope' has come to him, too great and majestic to leave room for regret at the shattering of lesser hopes. He has left 'the circle of courses' for 'the circle of happiness'.[1] The circle of courses, Davies explains, comprehends 'the material creation, and the condition of humanity'. The circle of happiness is that 'which man would ultimately attain'. But there is a third circle, 'the circle of space, which none but God alone can pervade'. It is this circle that Keats refers to in the words 'till we shine Full alchemiz'd, and free of space'.[2] Endymion will not be content with the circle of happiness, which 'becks Our ready minds to fellowship divine, A fellowship with esssence, till . . .' There must be the final apotheosis.

Keats believes with Blake, with the Pythagoreans, and I think with the Druids, that man can attain divinity in this life on condition of losing his self hood. Davies obscures the issue rather in saying that the circle of space is that which God alone can pervade. For man too attains to this circle when, abandoning his illusory selfhood and attaining, or rather recognizing, what Blake would call his identity, he fulfils the conditions for 'deification'.[3] Note that Keats's expression 'free of space' does not mean 'free from space', but 'given the freedom of space', as we talk of the freedom of a city. We shall find other uses in Keats of this idiom with reference to the lower elements.

Endymion now expands his account of these three 'circles' —which correspond, macrocosmically, with the 'triple world' of earth, atmosphere, and heaven, and, microcosmically, with the

---

[1] These phrases are Davies's in *Celtic Researches*; to attempt to link Davies's thought with Blake's at this point would mean too long a discursion, and I must refer the reader to Appendix A.

[2] The exclamation 'Behold The clear religion of heaven!' refers to the lines which precede (777–80), and not to those which follow, as certain of Keats's commentators have assumed in their efforts to prove him a non-metaphysical poet.

[3] I cannot agree with Mr Wasserman (in *The Finer Tone*) that 'the realm of pure immortality . . . in Keats's theology, can never be the home of man either in this life or in the next'. In support of his thesis of the 'mystic oxymoron' Mr Wasserman advances a very forced interpretation of the concluding '—but no more' in the Hymn to Pan (*Endymion*, I, 302), a phrase which is surely a mere interjection in the sense 'Let us now bring our praises to an end'. He leans heavily on this misreading in his subsequent discussion of five of Keats's more important poems.

scheme of body, soul and spirit. He presents first the circle of courses, the realm of Flora and old Pan:

> 'Fold
> A rose-leaf round thy finger's taperness,
> And soothe thy lips: hist! when the airy stress
> Of music's kiss impregnates the free winds,
> And with a sympathetic touch unbinds
> Eolian magic from their lucid wombs.'   [781–6]

Already, in the last two lines, we are passing (through the 'sympathetic touch') out of the first into the second circle. Old songs awaken in spots where Apollo's foot has trod. And if we can feel these things,

> '. . . that moment have we stept
> Into a sort of oneness, and our state
> Is like a floating spirit's.'

This is not yet the circle of happiness: it is only 'a sort of oneness' (depending on reminiscence) that we have stepped into, and our state is only 'like' a spirit's.

> 'But there are
> Richer entanglements, enthralments far
> More self-destroying, leading, by degrees,
> To the chief intensity: the crown of these
> Is made of love and friendship, and sits high
> Upon the forehead of humanity.'   [795–802]

The delight in Flora and old Pan, in listening to the wind, in the Orphean music, was a solitary delight. Keats has already made this clear in the lines of *Sleep and Poetry* to which the final 'humanity' here refers us back. It is in preparation for a 'clear conceiving' of 'the dark mysteries of human souls' that the 'vast idea' rolls before him: 'and I glean Therefrom my liberty'. Once again we find our clue in Davies. He tells us in the 'three circles' passage that it is when a man by 'pure virtue and fortitude' achieves 'a just balance' of his nature, that he attains 'the *point of liberty*' (Davies's italics) whence he passes into the circle of happiness.

Keats interprets this point of liberty, quite correctly, as the point of freedom from the solitary selfhood and the tasting of the joys and responsibilities of friendship, love, and human understanding.

Love, indeed, is the highest point that happiness can attain:

> '. . . its influence,
> Thrown in our eyes, genders a novel sense,
> At which we start and fret; till in the end,
> Melting into its radiance, we blend,
> Mingle, and so become a part of it,—
> Nor with aught else can our souls interknit
> So wingedly: when we combine therewith,
> Life's self is nourish'd by its proper pith,
> And we are nurtured like a pelican brood.'   [807-15]

The nourishment is so delicious that men who might have made the world ring with their praises 'have been content to let occasion die', sleeping in love's elysium. Now Endymion can understand this, even if he cannot himself accept such a complete domination by earthly love. For who knows what, in this universe of mystical correspondences, may be the relationship between the fecundity of Nature and human passion? Keats's statement is curiously precise:

> ' Just so may love, although 'tis understood
> The mere commingling of passionate breath,
> Produce more than our searching witnesseth:
> What I know not: but who, of men, can tell
> That flowers would bloom, or that green fruit would swell
> To melting pulp, that fish would have bright mail,
> The earth its dower of river, wood, and vale,
> The meadows runnels, runnels pebble-stones,
> The seed its harvest, or the lute its tones,
> Tones ravishment, or ravishment its sweet,
> If human souls did never kiss and greet?'   [832-42]

Keats is advancing a theory the direct primitive expression of which is the setting up of the bridal bed in the cornfield. Enriched once more with his basic images of fruition and nurture, it breaks into the 'thin element' of the passage's Platonic aspirations with a warm glow of occultism. The two currents in *Endymion* again separate out. Is the hero content to root himself in this earthly love? No: he must go on to further speculation, quitting the circle of happiness for the circle of space:

> ' Now, if this earthly love has power to make
> Men's being mortal, immortal; to shake
> Ambition from their memories, and brim
> Their measure of content; what merest whim,
> Seems all this poor endeavour after fame,
> To one, who keeps within his stedfast aim
> A love immortal, an immortal too.'[1]   [843–9]

Thus Endymion approaches an understanding, circles it, and shoots off on his destined course. The rest of the poem will be concerned with his pilgrimage through the elements.

[*Endymion*, Book I (*c*. 20 April 1817—*c*. 1 June 1817)]

---

[1] This last line hardly makes sense; the substitution of *he* for *an* would be a slight improvement.

Chapter Eight

THE SPARRY HOLLOWS

High at the head a branching olive grows,
And crowns the pointed cliffs with shady boughs.
A cavern pleasant, though involv'd in night,
Beneath it lies, the Naiades' delight.
Where bowls and urns, of workmanship divine,
And massy beams in native marble shine;
On which the Nymphs amazing webs display,
Of purple hue, and exquisite array.
The busy bees, within the urns secure
Honey delicious, and like nectar pure.
Perpetual waters thro the grotto glide,
A lofty gate unfolds on either side;
That to the north is pervious by mankind:
The sacred south t' immortals is consign'd.[1]
                Odyssey, XIII, in Porphyry: *The Cave
                of the Nymphs.*

ENDYMION is a poem magical, alchemical, occultist. It is a
formidable attempt by a mind which is far from having
mastered its materials to work out a synthesis of experience:
a synthesis which will benefit the poet rather than his readers.
It falls apart because it is a medley of incongruous elements: a
deeply sensed, patiently observed pattern of growth in nature
and man; an intensely desired but hardly experienced climax of
romantic love; a dimly discerned possibility of spiritual love, with
its apex in liberation. All these are elements of the 'vast idea',
but their interconnexions are hidden from Keats. He must explore
them as best he can. Half-way through his pilgrimage he will come
to see, and acknowledge, how little he is prepared for it. 'He had
no trick to hide his defects', as Bailey notes.[2]

He constructs the poem with some care. There is an initiation

---

[1] See Appendix C below.   [2] *K.C.*, II, 293.

through the elements;[1] at each stage the aspirant confronts a new ordeal,[2] advancing 'by degrees' to the point of liberty; contraries are reconciled within the elements and the aspirant himself. Keats develops this scheme, tentatively, within the framework of his four books: thus Book I deals (patchily) with Fire, Book II with Earth, Book III with Water, and Book IV with Air.[3] The first book is patchy because fire is not an element within which Endymion can conveniently journey; we have to rest content with the representative images of the altar-flame and the rising sun ('Apollo's upward fire') and the promise of *Hyperion*. Throughout, the quaternary—the theme of fourness—is firmly stressed. The frame is myth.

There are, I think, four possible views of myth, all of which have been held at various times. There is what we may call the *narrative* view: mythology gives us an account in imaginative terms of events in the past history of the race which have come to seem peculiarly significant. Great heroes, lawgivers and rulers are apotheosized into gods or demigods. There is the *allegorical* view: myths and legends are an expression in imaginative terms of the goings-on of the universe, of the natural forms and forces it contains and of their relations. There is the *psychological* view: mythology provides us with an exteriorization of events in the psyche. There is the *analogical* view: myth is a valid representation in symbolical form of eternal verities; it may indeed be the best way of mediating these verities (inexpressible in direct terms) to man. On the natural plane, the structure and forms of the universe are in like manner a representation of the 'intelligible world', the world of 'ideas'.

These view-points may be useful instruments for the understanding of a poem; but there are obvious dangers in handling them. These dangers are particularly great in respect of the third

---

[1] Which, as Apuleius asserts, was an important feature of the Isis cult. That Keats had some knowledge of Apuleius is clear from his letter of April 1819 to George and Georgiana Keats: he almost certainly owed the knowledge to Bailey.

[2] The temptations in the four books are, respectively, sensual content, selfishness, fear, despair.

[3] And, to some extent, with Fire in the empyreal region above the Moon.

and fourth views, which have much in common.The macrocosm-microcosm analogy itself suggests that it is 'in the brain of man and in his circling nerves' that the great archetypes live and move and have their being. Blake, whose phrase I have borrowed, presents a synthesis which is metaphysics-psychology-politics-sociology. He could do this because he had a firm grasp of the metaphysics, the 'body of Divine Analogy': yet not even he escapes confusion. When we turn to later 'psychological' commentators on and expounders of myth it is usually to find that the body of divine analogy has been dissolved in a whirl of complexes and appetencies. The Principle has been forgotten; only the manifestations remain.

I have hitherto kept clear of any attempt at 'psychological explanations' of Keats's mind and art. The dangers latent in all such enterprises are patent; and starv'd lips in the gloam with horrid warning gapèd wide have not, of recent years, been lacking. The attempt to interpret art in terms of psychological theory must necessarily fail because it ignores the hierarchical disposition of things; the high dream cannot be explained through the low dream and in great art we are dealing with states of experience which are, literally, God-given. If art is the freeing of the mind from emotion, as Mr Eliot has said, it is also the freeing of the mind from the personal image, from the enclosing structure of reactions and conditionings, from the habit-energies of accumulated past experiences inadequately responded to. It is a creation, in so far as it is valid, of the new from the new: a process of discovery outgoing the frontiers of the individual consciousness.

That is art at its greatest; and at its greatest we can apply to it no other criteria but its own. We can respond to it only in its own terms—as Keats, for instance, responded to the passages of full poetry or distilled prose which served him as guides to the two-and-thirty palaces. Then we cease to 'explain' the poem, to ourselves or to others: we are drawn into the poem and live with it, for the moment, its own intense and peculiar life. But not all art is great, though it may be profoundly interesting. The artist, from time to time, fails in the realization of his poem or his picture; and we may wish to know just why he fails. Such a wish is not altogether illegitimate, if an understanding of the artist's failures helps us to an appreciation of his successes. In the case of Keats, and particularly when we are reading *Endymion*, we are as pervasively conscious of defeat and deficiency as we are of solid achievement. The poet's own Preface and letters point with touching candour to these things: and to the reasons for them. He discerned a flaw within himself which he calls sometimes morbidity, sometimes lack of experience, and in the Preface ' a space of life between [the boy and the man] in which the soul is in a ferment, the character undecided, the way of life uncertain, the ambition thick-sighted'. We shall find occasion, at the close of our survey of *Endymion*, to probe a little deeper into this flaw in Keats's make-up; for the moment let us be content to call it immaturity, incompleteness. In himself, in his 'inner region', Keats was the most complete (after Blake) of the Romantics. He has an all-roundness that astonishes us as we read his letters and ponder the multiple meanings of his verse. But this 'sphericity' was not obvious to himself. For it to become clear, a great deal of rubbish had to be cleared away; and Keats knew this, though he didn't know how to distinguish with absolute accuracy between the rubbish and the jewel.

When Jung writes in his *Modern Man in Search of a Soul*: 'A perception of the significance of fourness, of the totality of the psychic structure, means illumination of the "inner region": this recognition is a first step, a necessary station on the road of inner development', we are struck by the applicability of this to the poetry of Keats. Fourness has already come to seem a kind of compass card in plotting the Keatsian universe. But we have to be on our guard here. The Jungian archetypes, the Jungian 'collective unconscious', have become a fashion in criticism; it is all too easy to accept them as counters which will replace the rigours of constructive critical thinking. We are tempted to substitute psychology for metaphysics as our basis. Illegitimately, for the most penetrating psychological interpretation is like an image in a mirror, correct in every detail except that the right and left sides are reversed. Moreover, there are few psychologists capable of giving a steady picture; Jung himself betrays a serious obliquity whenever he comes to speak of the traditional doctrines. But this *caveat* does not mean that we should refuse what help the psychologists can give us in revealing the principles common to the sciences and the arts alike. Our caution must be in the interpretation. Provided that we always bear in mind the axiom that the truths which the poet embodies in his art, and the art itself, are given from above and are principially altogether independent of the contingent and individual sphere (are indeed precisely the way out of that sphere into a realm closed to the investigations of the psychologist) we may receive much aid from an intelligent and imaginative analysis of the psyche.

Thus, in considering the way in which Keats reproduces many of the root ideas of the traditional doctrine (which had become so largely forgotten in his day) we shall be saved from positing far-fetched 'influences' and improbable 'sources' (though we should not shut our eyes to the clues which come to hand) if we can accept such a statement as this from C. G. Jung: 'The most sensible way of explaining such parallelism is by resorting to the hypothesis of the collective unconscious—of a universal similitude or identity of the basic structure of the human psyche. It seems likely that the collective unconscious contains a number of patterns, "archetypes", common to the whole of humanity. We must suppose that, under similar conditions, they function in the same way regardless of place and time, and that they produce the same ideas regardless of tradition.' This is the *psychological* expression of a truth which is far more completely, accurately, and beautifully conveyed by the doctrine of the Supreme Identity. (Jung's last phrase, '. . . regardless of tradition', suggests that he does not understand what tradition is.) But the psychological statement has its value too: especially for those who cannot grasp or accept the traditional doctrine. It is only when Jung assumes, as he sometimes does, that the psychological statement is an ultimate, and not a mere analogy on the human plane, that his approach arouses misgivings.

The 'incoherence' of *Endymion* may be explained by the fact that Keats was living every episode of his poem as he wrote it. Not thus is great art produced—the art of a Virgil or a Milton. But vital art, not yet great, is produced in this way. In spite of the definite quaternary structure imposed on the poem we do not grasp it as a whole; the wealth of episodic detail is too great. For Keats as he wrote it, however, the episodes were as important as the structure. They mirrored the stages, the adventures, the risks of his own spiritual journey. They represented the progressive fishings-up of the elements of the 'unconscious' which were in conflict and which needed, in Jung's terms, to be reconciled with the conscious mind if 'transformation' were to be achieved.

And here Jung's words are again apposite: 'The experiencing of the unconscious is a personal secret communicable only to the very few, and that with difficulty. It isolates the individual to whom it happens. But isolation effects a compensatory animation of the psychic atmosphere, and this is uncanny. The figures that appear are feminine, whereby the feminine nature of the unconscious is pointed out. They are fairies or beguiling sirens and lamias who infatuate the lonely traveller and lead him astray.' With *Fairy's Song*, *Song of Four Fairies*, *La Belle Dame Sans Merci*, and *Lamia* in mind, we can appreciate the relevance to our theme of that last sentence. For there are evil transformations as well as good ones. The road to liberation is beset with perils. We know from his letters how isolated Keats felt himself at this early period of his quest; and how inevitable the isolation seemed, as well. The traveller was in danger of becoming lost indeed. For these figures of lamias and sirens are no cardboard bogies. They represent real perils: for Keats, possibilities of temporary and partial integration on the lower 'psychic' level, phantoms of delight beckoning the pilgrim to a bower of bliss.

These considerations help to explain much that is obscure in Keats's poetry.[1] They cast light on the stern rebuke administered

---

[1] What is valuable in Jung, of a metaphysical order, is to be found in his sources, as Jung would be the first to admit: but he was pointed to the sources by his findings in deep analysis. Nothing of this order in Jung will come as a surprise to a student of the Hermetica, of Boehme, of Blake, but his methodology is valuable. Anyone who doubts the correspondence of the archetypes to the

by Moneta in the second *Hyperion*, and on Keats's dissatisfaction
with both the first *Hyperion* and with *Endymion*. For in the last
analysis Endymion's quest of the moon-goddess is not a journey
to the highest goal. The moon is a deity of phases: Keats's danger
is that of a still further disintegration. We feel this in the con-
flicting values of the poem: erotic phantasies succeed efforts at
self-abnegation, metaphysical insights clash with earth-bound satis-
factions and dissatisfactions. In fact, the presentation of the journey
as the quest for a companion, though inevitable for Keats (as for
Shelley) at this stage, cannot be an ultimate.

These conjectures of mine are borne out by the penetrating
humility of the Preface to *Endymion*: 'The imagination of a boy is
healthy, and the mature imagination of a man is healthy; but there
is a space of life between, in which the soul is in a ferment, the
character undecided, the ambition thick-sighted. . . .' There was
simply no possibility of Keats's reviewers' understanding this. One
of Jung's books is called *Modern Man in Search of a Soul*: Keats
might be called the first modern man, that is to say the first modern
incarnation of that very ancient man who had been buried for so
long under the neo-classical debris.

It is time to plunge with Endymion into the underworld. We
meet him early in Book II, still lovelorn; he wanders 'through
wilderness, and woods of mossed oaks'; led by a magic butterfly,[1]
he comes to a fountain by a cavern's mouth, and is warned by a
naiad that he

> must wander far
> In other regions, past the scanty bar
> To mortal steps

---

persons of Keats's narrative may read pp. 123–53 of J. Jacobi's authoritative *The
Psychology of C. G. Jung* (5th edition, Routledge, 1951), which not only makes
possible precise identifications (the Shadow is clearly Peona, the Anima is Cynthia,
the Magna Mater is Cybele, the Old Man is Glaucus, the Self is the integration
attained in the Cave of Quietude) but even presents the archetypes in the same
order of appearance (with the allowable transposition of the third and fourth).

[1] The butterfly is born from a flower's centre, a fancy reminiscent perhaps of
Erasmus Darwin (see above, p. 4). On its wings are 'character'd strange things':
Endymion reads the hieroglyphics, as later (III, 761–5) he deciphers a mystic shell.

before he can rest in the enjoyment of his love. In the soliloquy that follows, Endymion ruefully compares the happiness of those who are content within the circle of courses with his own misery. A voice from the cave urges him to

> '. . . descend where alleys bend
> Into the sparry hollows of the world!
> . . . He ne'er is crown'd
> With immortality, who fears to follow
> Where airy voices lead: so through the hollow
> The silent mysteries of earth, descend !'   [II, 202-14]

Echoes from *Æneid* VI reverberate in the caves of this second book,[1] which owes a good deal, too, to his knowledge of the Eleusinian mysteries.[2] The account of the hero's wanderings which follows reproduces the stages of the postulant's progress. What he has undergone up to now corresponds to the Lesser Mysteries; what he is about to undergo, to the Greater. Here, too, is the promise of immortality held out by the mystery cults to their devotees. It is a promise which has to be 'proved on the pulses'; and while we cannot be certain what the final revelation at Eleusis or Samothrace may have been, it was clearly in the nature of a sacrament or 'showing' won through a series of purgations and ordeals. And this is what we find, rather clumsily worked out, in *Endymion*. Book II stresses what may be called a 'purgation through wonder': the hero is distracted from his own misery into impersonal astonishment at the marvels revealed to him, and thus begins that process of self-naughting which is essential for his final victory. From time to time he comes back to himself,[3] and to a sense of dereliction and dismay, a kind of 'dark night'; and the ordeal or temptation in this second book is precisely that of fixation in selfish gloom, as the ordeal of the first book was that of acquiescence in Peona's blandishments. Invocations to the goddess

---

[1] Keats's familiarity with Virgil is often overlooked. We are told that he made a complete translation of the *Æneid*, and there are many echoes of the *Georgics* in Book I of *Endymion*. For the possible influence of Porphyry see Appendix C.

[2] 'The silent mysteries of earth' are precisely the Eleusinian σιωπή.

[3] 'The journey homeward to habitual self' of line 276.

save him from these temptations, and further visions restore to
him his sense of wonder: the process is repeated again and again
at ever higher levels.

When Endymion enters the cave he embarks on an adventure
which is, at first, 'far too strange and wonderful for sadness'. His
appetite to 'dive into the deepest' is sharpened 'by degrees'. The
inner region unfolds itself as a world of contraries, neither dark
nor bright, but 'mingled up'. The prince moves 'through a vast
antre' (the 'antrum immane' of *Æneid* VI, 11) along winding
passages and across a ridge

> that o'er the vast beneath
> Towers like an ocean-cliff, and whence he seeth
> A hundred waterfalls, whose voices come
> But as the murmuring surge.[1]   [240–3]

Amazed, he sees in the distance 'an orbed diamond', gleaming
'like the sun Uprisen over chaos'.[2]

> While astonishment
> With deep-drawn sighs was quieting, he went
> Into a marble gallery, passing through
> A mimic temple, so complete and true
> In sacred custom, that he well nigh fear'd
> To search it inwards; whence far off appear'd,
> Through a long pillar'd vista, a fair shrine,
> And, just beyond, on light tiptoe divine,
> A quiver'd Dian.   [254–62]

The contraries are now presented in architectural, plastic form:
the vast amorphousness of caverns gives place suddenly to the
precise and lucid beauty of a Greek temple. And how eloquent of
Keats's feeling for tradition, for ancient piety, is that 'complete
and true In sacred custom'—a phrase none of his contemporaries
could have written.

---

[1] Echoes of *Lear* and *Othello* enter Keats's verse here.

[2] Cf. *Manfred*, I, i, in which 'a star is seen at the darker end of the gallery,
beckoning the hero on to communion with the elemental spirits'. Keats knew
and quotes from *Manfred*. See below, pp. 189–202. Cf. also *Vathek*, (Everyman
edn., p. 270).

Foremost among the wonders presented to the journeying
Endymion is a masque of Adonis, a vision of death and rebirth
whose relevance is immediately apparent. For here is the love
of an immortal for a mortal; the descent of the mortal into the
under-world; his rising again into the upper air and to the thrones
of the gods—outlines as much of Endymion's as of Adonis' story.
The description of the Bower of Adonis is Ovidian rather than
Virgilian in quality; there is effeminacy in this vignette of the
sleeping youth glimpsed in a prospect of flowers:

> Sideways his face repos'd
> On one white arm, and tenderly unclos'd,
> By tenderest pressure, a faint damask mouth
> To slumbery pout; just as the morning south
> Disparts a dew-lipp'd rose. Above his head,
> Four lily stalks did their white honours wed
> To make a coronal. . . .   [403–9]

Endymion is regaled with wine, pears, cream, plums, and manna:
a strange repast anticipating the feast prepared by Porphyro for
Madeline. While he feasts, a Cupid tells him the Adonis story.
Finally Venus descends in her dove-drawn chariot, accompanied
by Eros; she assures Endymion that she knows all his grief, and
that he is loved by an immortal. One day he will be blest:

> 'So still obey the guiding hand that fends
> Thee safely through these wonders for sweet ends.'

Cheered by these words, Endymion continues his journey

> Through caves, and palaces of mottled ore,
> Gold dome, and crystal wall, and turquois floor,
> Black polish'd porticos of awful shade,
> And, at the last, a diamond balustrade . . .   [574–97]

to find a new and more austere vision awaiting him in 'deepest
gloom':

> Forth from a rugged arch, in the dusk below,
> Came mother Cybele! alone—alone—
> In sombre chariot; dark foldings thrown

About her majesty, and front death-pale,
With turrets crown'd. Four maned lions hale
The sluggish wheels . . .   [639–44]

This is a powerful picture, and Keats stresses its uniqueness. For
Cybele, the Great Mother, is the ultimate vision in the chthonic
world, the supreme dispenser of the mysteries. She represents the
nadir of Endymion's descent. And because she is the ultimate,
she is also the inexplicable. The hero catches the merest glimpse of
her before she disappears. There is no communication, no comment. For only action counts now. Hence the poem continues
immediately:

Wherefore delay,
Young traveller, in such a mournful place?
Art thou wayworn, or canst not further trace
The diamond path?[1]   [649–52]

Keats's continued emphasis on *diamond* is curious. All through
the preceding descriptions, indeed, his imagery has been relent-
lessly mineral —gold dome, crystal wall, turquois floor, diamond
balustrade—and the 'diamond path' serves to sum up and clinch
this impression. The diamond path is the path to the diamond
(as we speak of the London road)[2]: it is also the path through the
diamond, for Endymion is, without knowing it, already inside
the haven that he seeks so eagerly. The answer to the narrator's
question: 'Wherefore delay . . .?' comes pat, with a kind of
liturgical repetition:

He was indeed wayworn;
Abrupt, in middle air, his way was lost.   [655–6]

---

[1] The sequence of thought in Virgil is similar: 'Hence came the Mother whose
cult-name Cybele is that of her other mountain haunt . . . hence came the faithful
silence of her mysteries, and yoked lions passed under their Mistress' chariot.
Come then, and let us follow where the gods' bidding leads' (*Æneid*, III, 111–14:
translation from R. W. Cruttwell, *Virgil's Mind at Work*). Keats increases Virgil's
and Ovid's two lions to four.

[2] Remembering the 'orbed diamond' that beckoned him from afar at his
entrance into the underworld (see above, p. 141).

For his search is ended, without his knowing it; he is in the exact centre of the diamond (which remains invisible); and no further progress along the diamond path is possible. For this reason the silken cord[1] is tossed 'into his grasping hands' and he swings off upon it into the void, alighting in a nest of flowers.

And thus the progress upward through the four kingdoms —mineral, vegetable, animal, human—begins. Flower scenes, flower images dominate the remainder of this second book. After a love-episode with his unknown goddess (which calls for no comment) Endymion arrives at the outlet of the mineral world. Here he pauses to reflect on the course of his past life: his youth, his enthronement as shepherd-king, his loves, his ambitions and achievements, and finally his recent adventures in the underworld.

> 'And now', thought he,
> 'How long must I remain in jeopardy
> Of blank amazements that amaze no more:
> Now I have tasted her sweet soul to the core
> All other depths are shallow: essences,
> Once spiritual, are like muddy lees,
> Meant but to fertilize my earthly root,
> And make my branches lift a golden fruit
> Into the bloom of heaven: other light,
> Though it be quick and sharp enough to blight
> The Olympian eagle's vision, is dark,
> Dark as the parentage of chaos.'   [901–12]

I have said that the love-episode with Diana calls for no comment (in the sense that it reproduces the 'mawkish' pattern of previous theophanies, leading this time to consummation); Endymion's words are themselves the comment on it. For him it has been a crucial experience (though Keats signally fails to convey this to us); it has lifted him above his former preoccupations, transforming his vision of reality. 'Essences' he had once thought 'spiritual' are now revealed as earthly: and this earthliness, this mineral kingdom, falls into its place as nourisher of the 'earthly root' (mineral becoming vegetable) which in its turn is the basis for

---

[1] Following a cancelled reading (*Poems,* 116).

the glory of the fruit-laden branches. This image of the earth-nourished root directing energy upwards into the golden fruit is richly suggestive and perfectly traditional.[1] In the epithet *golden* alchemical significances are evident: a proportion of the muddy lees of earth has been transmuted into the noble metal.

Let us note that there is no question of repudiating the muddy lees which remain untransmuted; they are there at the base, at the root, as an essential element in the total process. For as long as the cycle lasts the earth element, the *materia prima*, will send its energies coursing through the living structure; for as long as the cycle lasts the structure will break down continually into the *materia prima*. A steady concern with the roots is a 'note' of Keats's poetry that none of his contemporaries reproduces. None of them sinks down, as he does, below the surface of the earth, below branches and fruit and flowers, to live this earthly life of loam and moisture. We find it suggested first in 'I stood tip-toe . . .', where he paints a 'bush of May flowers with the bees about them':

> And let long grass grow round the roots to keep them
> Moist, cool and green; and shade the violets
> That they may bind the moss in leafy nets.   [32–4]

In this embryo 'Endymion' the earthiness is still unstressed; Keats is too enchanted with the lightness and brightness of the upper world to spare more than a glance for the roots; but who else would have spared a glance?[2] In the later *Endymion* there is

---

[1] Cf. *Timæus*, 220 (90) '. . . the most principal and excellent species of the soul . . . resides in the very summit of the body, elevating us from earth to an alliance with the heavens; as we are not terrestrial plants, but blossoms of heaven.' The fruit is the vegetable correspondence of the sun. Hermetic correspondences through the four kingdoms are as follows: *Prototype:* the Sun (*i.e.* the spiritual sun of which the physical sun is itself a symbol); *mineral correspondence:* the Diamond; *vegetable correspondence:* the Golden Fruit; *animal correspondence:* the Lion or Eagle; *human correspondence:* the King-magus (who has attained the 'diamond body'). Here too we have the system of 'nourishment' through the four elements: earth (soil) nourishes water (sap), which nourishes air (the flower), which nourishes fire (the fruit). I discuss the passage further in the last chapter.

[2] Only, perhaps, Erasmus Darwin. Cf. the 'root-inwove morass' of *The Economy of Vegetation*, II, 116, with Keats's 'moist earth'. See below, pp. 363–6.

development: we pass downwards from the bright world to bring within the circle of understanding the darker, grosser elements. Hampstead's laburnum-shaded gardens and hazel copses green are exchanged for the glooms and mysteries of the 'mighty forest', where

> the moist earth fed
> So plenteously all weed-hidden roots
> Into o'erhanging boughs, and precious fruits.   [I, 64–6]

The weighted movement of this contrasts unambiguously with the light, airy rhythm of the earlier verses. The whole triple process is held in the field of awareness.

[*Endymion*, Book II (*c.* early June—31 August 1817)]

Chapter Nine

THE DEEP, DEEP WATER-WORLD

NYMPHS! YOU adorn, in glossy volutes roll'd,
The gaudy conch with azure, green, and gold.
YOU round Echinus ray his arrowy mail,
Give the keel'd Nautilus his oar and sail;
Firm to his rock with silver cord suspend
The anchor'd Pinna, and his Cancer-friend;
With worm-like beard his toothless lips array,
And teach the unwieldy Sturgeon to betray.
Ambush'd in weeds, or sepulchred in sands,
In dread repose He waits the scaly bands,
Waves in red spires the living lures, and draws
The unwary plunderers to his circling jaws,
Eyes with grim joy the twinkling shoals beset,
And clasps the quick inextricable net.
YOU chase the warrior Shark, and cumberous Whale,
And guard the Mermaid in her briny vale;
Feed the live petals of her insect-flowers,
Her shell-wrack gardens, and her sea-fan bowers;
With ores and gems adorn her coral cell,
And drop a pearl in every gaping shell.
ERASMUS DARWIN, *The Economy of Vegetation.*

WE have come gradually to understand that Endymion's road to self-integration is by way of a journey envisaging the reconciliation of the opposites. It is no easy road. At the outset of his journey he is metaphysically 'innocent': unaware of the double-faced character of all mortal things. He moves in an unreal world of black and white: of pure pleasure, sheer pain, unmitigated evil and good, all seen in strict opposition. He has to learn his lesson by hard experience.

In his travels through the earth element he discovers, slowly but surely, that an ambivalent meaning attaches to the objects and events that present themselves to him. The 'diamond path' is the track through a mineral kingdom which at first sight seems the quintessence of the antivital: the dark, hard, inhospitable kingdom of the grave. Yet the diamond, as Jung points out, is the pure crystalline form of the carbon which with its fourfold valency is the basis of organic life. It is the diamond path which leads to the centre of what Buddhism calls the diamond body, the pure achievement of wholeness.[1] Once this is won, the scene changes abruptly: the earth element is left behind, and a new field of trial and experience opens before the neophyte: the deep, deep water-world.

Thus the hero passes into the element which of all four is the most ambivalent, which exhibits in its extremest form the theme of creation, growth and destruction. The sea, which produces the forms of life as from an inexhaustible womb, is quick to overwhelm them. Teeming with life, prolific and benign, she is also remorseless and cruel as the grave. What is more, she is peculiarly subject to the moon-goddess: her beauty is the beauty of phases. She exhibits every characteristic of the triform deity.

The paragraph from Darwin that I have placed at the head of this chapter well conveys the ambiguous character of the sea. The power that 'guards the Mermaid in her briny vale' and 'feeds the live petals of her insect-flowers' also 'teaches the unwieldy Sturgeon to betray'. The 'warrior Shark', a few lines later, anticipates Keats's 'Shark at savage prey' in the 1818 *Epistle to J. H. Reynolds*.

When Endymion enters the water-world he not only experiences but also inevitably takes on its elemental powers. This is implicit in the legend of Glaucus. There is a transmutation from the earth-hero into the water-hero, from Arthur into Lancelot du Lake. Inevitably, too, his encounters will now be with beings exhibiting a pre-eminently double or ambiguous character: with zoophytes, with monsters, with forms rich in the pathetic or sinister aspects of 'phase-beauty'. For the water-world is governed by the triple-formed Diana. Her sway, most dramatically evident

---

[1] It may be worth remarking that the earth's centre, in the *Republic*, is a diamond.

in the ebb and flow of tides, reaches down to the hardly differenti-
ated existence of the 'poor patient oyster'.

> The mighty deeps,
> The monstrous sea is thine—the myriad sea!
> O Moon! far-spooming Ocean bows to thee,
> And Tellus feels his forehead's cumbrous load. [III, 68–71]

The sea is 'monstrous' and 'myriad' because it is the theatre of 'an
eternal fierce destruction' as well as of an exaggerated coming-to-
be. Keats faces the latter aspect in *Endymion*; but neither in that
poem, nor in the Reynolds *Epistle*, does he feel able to face the
problem of cruelty.[1]

The 'preface' to the third book has met with little applause from
Keats's commentators. It sticks out like the doctrinal passages in
Sleep and Poetry, already discussed: and it is as integral, in a sense,
as they are. In a real sense: for the theme of kingship with which it
deals is a main theme of *Endymion*. Thematically it is relevant;
tonally, technically, it is a mistake: it breaks, as the critics saw,
the flow and the atmosphere of the poem. The first one-and-
twenty lines are weak: they indict modern kings in terms rich
with growth-and-fruition imagery, but the imagery hardly fits the
tone, which is querulous or too high-pitched. From this unfortunate skirmish with earthly monarchs Keats passes on to his
antithesis:

> Are then regalities all gilded masks?
> No, there are throned seats unscalable
> But by a patient wing, a constant spell,
> Or by ethereal things that, unconfin'd,

---

[1] Erasmus Darwin points out, in a note to lines 277–8 of Canto I, that of the
three sources of nourishment of animal bodies (mother's milk, seeds or eggs, and
the bodies of living animals and plants) the third is 'a less perfect part of the
economy of nature than those before mentioned, as contributing less to the sum
of general happiness'. The idea horrified Keats; for relief he turns to the aspect of
co-operation in nature, to what Sir Charles Sherrington calls 'the fairy-like visiting acquaintance between the planet's population of insects and its population of
flowers'.

> Can make a ladder of the eternal wind,
> And poize about in cloudy thunder-tents
> To watch the abysm-birth of elements.
> Aye, 'bove the withering of old-lipp'd Fate
> A thousand Powers keep religious state,
> In water, fiery realm, and airy bourne;
> And, silent as a consecrated urn,
> Hold sphery sessions for a season due.   [22–33]

What are these powers? They are precisely the celestial gods of *Timæus*, who reign above the circle of courses and are superior to Destiny ('old-lipp'd Fate'): these are the rulers of the ethereal elements. Under their sway the gross elements are born out of the abyss[1] and commence their revolutions in the lower world. The celestial gods must not be confused, Plato tells us, with the traditional gods: Saturn, Rhea, Oceanus, and the rest. These latter are the manifested equivalents of the celestial deities. Hence, Keats goes on to lament:

> . . . few of these far majesties, ah, few!
> Have bared their operations to this globe—
> Few, who with gorgeous pageantry enrobe
> Our piece of heaven—whose benevolence
> Shakes hands with our own Ceres; every sense
> Filling with spiritual sweets to plenitude,
> As bees gorge full their cells.   [34–40]

This is the Keats whose aspiration is out from the circle of courses and the circle of happiness into the circle of space. 'Our own Ceres' is the mundane Ceres, the manifested goddess: for, as Taylor points out in a footnote to the *Cratylus*[2], 'The first subsistence of Ceres is among the intellectual gods, where, considered as united with Saturn, she was called by ancient theologists Rhea, and as pro-

---

[1] Cf. *Timæus*, 172–3 (52D–53). But the whole of this part of *Timæus* (from 44D to 61) is vital for an understanding of Keats in this connection. Compare too the lament of Saturn in lines 106–16 of Book I of *Hyperion*, where Saturn is speaking in his 'ethereal' character.

[2] On p. 50 of the 1793 edition which was on Bailey's shelves and which Keats most probably read. See below, pp. 161–6.

ducing Jupiter, Ceres. She is therefore of a vivific nature and consequently produces and distributes. But the character of distribution particularly belongs to her, according to her mundane subsistence; since she is the divinity of the planet Saturn, and it is the province of Saturn to distribute all things intellectually.'[1]

Ceres is mentioned by Keats in parenthesis, as it were; his main concern is with a more exalted deity, who yet condescends to our human world, and not to our human world only, but to our whole circle of courses, human, animal, vegetable and mineral. This is 'Apollo's sister', Diana. The moon is the enchantress of the sublunary world.

> Thou dost bless every where, with silver lip
> Kissing dead things to life. The sleeping kine,
> Couched in thy brightness, dream of fields divine:
> Innumerable mountains rise, and rise,
> Ambitious for the hallowing of thine eyes;
> And yet thy benediction passeth not
> One obscure hiding-place, one little spot
> Where pleasure may be sent: the nested wren
> Has thy fair face within its tranquil ken,
> And from beneath a sheltering ivy leaf
> Takes glimpses of thee; thou art a relief
> To the poor patient oyster, where it sleeps
> Within its pearly house.—The mighty deeps,
> The monstrous sea is thine. . . .   [56–69]

It is a remarkable vision of nature in all its complexity responding to lunar influence.[2] And here we have the 'biological' Diana, the

---

[1] From the *Hyperion* passage referred to in note one opposite, the line 'Of peaceful sway above man's harvesting' comes particularly to mind here.

[2] Taylor, quoting Proclus on *Timæus*, notes: 'Diana, who presides over all the generation in nature, and leads into light physical reasons, supernally extends as far as to subterranean natures.' This is a later note: the 1793 version has (footnote to *Cratylus*, p. 61): 'Diana first subsists in the supermundane vivific triad . . . this goddess, according to her mundane subsistence, is, as is well known, the divinity of the moon; from whence, says Proclus (in Plat. Polit., p. 353), she benignantly leads into light the reasons of nature.' Keats seems indebted in the whole of this prayer to Lucius's invocation of the moon in *The Golden Ass*: 'Queen of heaven, whether thou art pure and nourishing Ceres, the original parent of fruits . . . or

mistress of growth amorphous and polymorphous: what has she
to do with the Diana who is 'that completest form of all completeness', the romantic goddess of the silver bow?We may well ask.
Keats will expend all his efforts in *Endymion* to reconcile the two;
but with small success.

For here, once again, we witness the clash of the two strains
already noted in the poem. Where Keats is presenting those large
'abstractions', which are his 'only life' because they are not
abstractions to him but verities proved on his pulses, he is superb.
Where, on the other hand, the 'love interest' of the story, and
his own compulsions, lead him into erotic and sentimental phantasies, he is quite deplorable. This was a rift in his sensibility that
bothered him his life through. We have already seen how hard
he struggled against the 'cloying treacle'. He struggled in the
tangled courses of his life, and he struggled in the complex
currents of his poetry. *Endymion* is the measure of his defeat: yet
it is, also, the earnest of his triumph.

The rift shows widest and deepest in Book III. We are at a loss
to reconcile a Cynthia who 'pines for one as sorrowful', whose
'cheek is pale for one whose cheek is pale', with the 'regality'
whose pure light

> fathoms eddies, and runs wild about
> O'erwhelming water-courses; scaring out
> The thorny sharks from hiding holes, and fright'ning
> Their savage eyes with unaccustomed lightning.　　[87–90]

This is the objective vision. All the more, for this, do we feel the
incongruity between Diana and Cynthia. We can accept the moon
as the triform Hecate, austerely impartial in her benison to every

---

whether thou art celestial Venus, who, in the first origin of things, didst associate
the different sexes . . . or whether thou art the sister of Phoebus . . . or whether
thou art Proserpine, terrific by nocturnal howlings . . . with that female light of
thine, illuminating every city, and with moist fires nourishing the joyful seeds of
plants . . . grant me rest and peace, after the endurance of so many cruel misfortunes . . .' (Thomas Taylor's translation, 1822. Keats may have drawn on the
original Latin text, or on some other translation, perhaps Adlington's). It will be
noted that Apuleius here identifies Ceres with Diana.

manifestation of life[1]; we cannot accept her, at the same time, as
the lovelorn maiden. Keats is asking too much of his readers.

But as 'poor Cynthia' she is presented in the lines that follow.
She sends a beam down 'to the deep, deep water-world, To find
Endymion'. He is comforted, and pursues his submarine journey,
marvelling at the wonders of the deep, 'the superannuations of
sunk realms'.[2] Even here the urn is central:

> gold vase emboss'd
> With long-forgotten story, and wherein
> No reveller had ever dipp'd a chin
> But those of Saturn's vintage; mouldering scrolls
> Writ in the tongue of heaven, by those souls
> Who first were on the earth. . . .   [126–131]

The emphasis is insistently on wisdom: lore committed to words,
or moulded into form. Keats is leading up to his cathartic vision
of the Old Man. It follows swiftly. As Endymion, overcome with
awe at the sight of these wonders, lifts his thoughts up to the
moon-goddess who has been his comfort since childhood, he
glimpses in the distance a seated figure:

> He saw far in the concave green of the sea
> An old man sitting calm and peacefully.
> Upon a weeded rock this old man sat,[3]
> And his white hair was awful, and a mat
> Of weeds were cold beneath his cold thin feet.   [191–5]

This is the third of the great archetypal figures of *Endymion*. And,
like all archetypes, he is ambivalent. Peona, the emanation or

---

[1] A passage from D'Arcy Thompson's *Growth and Form* is worth setting against
the *Timæus* and the *Cratylus*: 'More curious and still more obscure is the moon's
influence on growth, as on the growth and ripening of the eggs of oysters, sea-
urchins and crabs. Belief in such lunar influence is as old as Egypt; it is confirmed
and justified, in certain cases, nowadays, but the way in which the influence is
exerted is quite unknown.'

[2] *The Fall of Hyperion*, I, 68.

[3] Cf. the 'lampit rock of green sea weed' of the *Epistle to Reynolds*. There is a
sense in which the Old Man is Keats himself. Again, he may owe something to
Wordsworth's Leech-gatherer, referred to by Keats in a letter of this same
September to Reynolds (*Letters*, 47. See above, p. 71).

'anima' of Endymion in Book I, exemplified Blake's dictum: 'Corporeal friends are spiritual enemies'. Cybele, in Book II, the Magna Mater Deorum, is the source of life and death; her chariot is drawn by beasts of prey, her priests emasculate themselves. Here, in Keats's third book, the wise old man will shortly reveal himself as the young fool. For the moment he is unambiguously majestic. His mantle is enwrought with figures dim of ocean-forms

> with every shape
> That skims, or dives, or sleeps.   [203–4]

He epitomizes the sea's multiplicity. And, precisely because he does so, Endymion fears him. The 'ordeal' of this third book will achieve the mastery of fear by compassion.

The old man is reading in a book. He looks up, and sees Endymion. Rising, he hails the newcomer 'in a voice of solemn joy' as his deliverer, as the restorer of his lost youth. 'Thou art the man!' Endymion is not unnaturally alarmed at this: is the old man a ghoul, and will he regain his youth by feeding upon Endymion after the fashion of Blake's 'Mental Traveller'? He shrinks back; and then, recovering his courage, challenges the stranger to do his worst. The old man weeps at this misunderstanding and Endymion's heart is softened. He has already, in listening to the woes of Alpheus and Arethusa, at the close of the second book, learned to feel for others' sorrows. Now he is called upon to act.

The old man tells his story. His name is Glaucus, and he was once a fisher-boy, 'a lonely youth on desert shores'. Loving the sea, he began 'to feel distemper'd longings':

> to desire
> The utmost privilege that ocean's sire
> Could grant in benediction: to be free
> Of all his kingdom.[1]   [375–8]

He plunges into the sea, and finds that he is able to breathe within its depths. This gives him a wonderful sense of freedom, 'forgetful

---

[1] As in Book I, line 780 (quoted above, p. 129), the meaning is 'to enjoy the freedom of'; cf. later in this Book III, line 467: 'free of haunts umbrageous'.

utterly of self-intent'; but he soon falls into the slavery of love for
the nymph Scylla, who repulses him. He calls on Circe for aid,
falls into her power, and discovers her sinister aspect too late. She
condemns him to a thousand-year sojourn at the bottom of the
sea, at the end of which period he will die. He is compelled to
accept this doom, and finds, floating in the sea, the corpse of
Scylla:

> Cold, O cold indeed
> Were her fair limbs, and like a common weed
> The sea-swell took her hair. [623–5]

Pitying, he places the body in a niche within a submarine 'fabric
crystalline'. He himself grows suddenly old. For a 'cruel, cruel
space' of time he remains, despairing, in his sea-prison. But one
day there is a great storm. A ship is wrecked, and its crew drowned.
The bodies float down past him through the water; from the hand
of an old man he takes a scroll and a slender wand; reading the
scroll, he finds a prophecy relating to himself. The prophecy first
describes his plight, and then goes on to a promise:

> *If he utterly*
> *Scans all the depth of magic, and expounds*
> *The meanings of all motions, shapes and sounds;*
> *If he explores all forms and substances*
> *Straight homeward to their symbol-essences;*
> *He shall not die.* [696–701]

Moreover, he will be enabled to deliver all other drowned lovers
from death; in this pious work he will be assisted by

> *A youth, by heavenly power lov'd and led*

who will appear in due course of time. Endymion is the youth;
the hour foretold by the prophecy is here.

The words of the prophecy are remarkable, and will again
recall to us the statements of *The Poet*. Keats's concern with magic
is unremitting; we cannot dismiss it as a passing or minor extravagance. The Glaucus episode is central in Book III, and clearly
embodies strong personal fears and convictions of Keats's own.
With the descent into the waters the crucial phase of initiation has

begun. The first stage reached its climax, as we saw, when the hero's way was lost in reaching the very centre of the earth-element, of the hard unwavering mineral kingdom. Making the leap of faith, he swung off on the divine cord into the unknown. He has learned what 'earth' has to teach him, and is ready for new purgations.

The element of water is, we have seen, the peculiar seat of deity in its creative and its destructive aspects: the forms of life arise from the primal waters and are reabsorbed into them. As Keats might have read in a footnote on p. 43 of the 1793 Taylor transla-tion,[1] 'Ocean, according to Proclus, in Tim. lib. 4, is the cause of all secondary natures, of all motion, whether intellectual, animastic (ψυχικὴ) or natural'. It is pre-eminently the sphere of transforma-tions: gross earthly forms entering it suffer a sea-change into something rich and strange. To plunge into water is baptism; that is, initiation *par excellence*. It is on the face of the waters, at time's genesis, that the Divine Breath moves, thereby fecundating the Egg of Night. But for man to enter—or re-enter—the watery element is dangerous. It is an immersion in the unconscious life, whose 'freedom' we achieve only at our peril. 'I plung'd for life or death.'[2] We may be captured, overwhelmed, destroyed by the primitive forces, the very 'fishy' playmates, that will accost us there. So long as Glaucus was content to stroll the sea-shore, a happy solitary, he was safe: dolphins sported before him, monsters displayed their green and golden mail for his delight.[3] But the moment he sought closer acquaintance with the depths his happi-ness and freedom were in jeopardy. He fell under the domination of one of the passions, the sea-forms, by which he had been hither-to untroubled. Love presents itself as overwhelming physical desire:

> 'My passion grew
> The more, the more I saw her dainty hue
> Gleam delicately through the azure clear.'   [407–9]

---

[1] See below, p. 165.   [2] *Endymion*, III, 380.
[3] The analogy with 'th'unwieldy Elephant' and 'Serpent sly' gambolling before the unfallen Adam (in *P.L.*, IV) is noteworthy.

And to gain possession of Scylla, he is constrained to resort to the powers of evil. He 'bows a tranced vassal' to Circe, 'this arbitrary queen of sense'. It is not long before 'specious heaven is changed to real hell'.[1]

The meaning of this parable for Endymion is plain. He now accepts the role of deliverer. But once again the limitations of Keats's chosen 'action' become apparent. It is not active enough. The part of the hero in the Endymion legend is essentially passive: he is 'led', 'guided', 'destined', but of his own strength and will initiates and performs nothing. Endymion has reached a stage in his quest when we expect him to confront and overcome some great peril. The testing is vital for his own development. Instead we are entertained with a conjuring act. Endymion, robed in the magic cloak, undoes 'a tangled thread and winds it to a clue', reads from a magic shell a message invisible to the old man, and breaks the wand against a pedestal; finally he scatters fragments of the torn scroll first on Glaucus (who regains his youth) and then on the thousands of dead lovers (who are restored to life). Among these is Scylla. All is done to the accompaniment of strange music.

> Delicious symphonies, like airy flowers,
> Budded, and swell'd and and, full-blown, shed full showers
> Of light, soft, unseen leaves of sounds divine.   [798–800]

The musical image (linked here very strikingly with Keats's most intimate symbols of growth and flowering) leads on, as so often in his verse, to an architectural consummation. The great multitude troops over the sea floor to the palace of Neptune. Keats outdoes himself in describing the structure: here spatial values are conveyed in rich quaternary images:

> Far as the mariner on highest mast
> Can see all round upon the calmed vast,
> So wide was Neptune's hall: and as the blue
> Doth vault the waters, so the waters drew

---

[1] Keats deviates from his Ovidian original, where Glaucus *repulses* Circe's proffer of love. It is essential to Keats's theme that Glaucus should surrender his will to the enchantress.

Their doming curtains, high, magnificent,
Aw'd from the throne aloof . . .
                              . . . there did spring
From natural west, and east, and south, and north,
A light as of four sunsets, blazing forth
A gold-green zenith 'bove the Sea-God's head.
Of lucid depth the floor, and far outspread
As breezeless lake, on which the slim canoe
Of feather'd Indian darts about, as through
The delicatest air: air verily,
But for the portraiture of clouds and sky:
This palace floor breath-air,—but for the amaze
Of deep-seen wonders motionless,—and blaze
Of the dome pomp, reflected in extremes,
Globing a golden sphere.   [866–886]

It is a brilliant passage, combining as it does Keats's basic delight in the freedom of movement in space with his equally basic feeling for unity. The masque of Neptune occupies the same position in this third book of *Endymion* as the vision of Cybele did in the second book. It crowns the achievement of a new stage in the journey of self-transcendence. There are strong points of contrast with the Cybele vision. That was secret, shut-in, dark, with ominous overtones (the 'mystery' aspect of initiation). This, on the contrary, is public, bright, spacious (baptism is performed *coram populo*). The gathering at Neptune's palace is, despite its size, very much of a family affair. Endymion's progress is steadily from solitude to society.

'Cybele' we can label the contracted vision, 'Neptune' the expanded, in Blake's use of these words. Or, in Keats's own terms, the one looks to the roots, the other to the leaves and flowers. From the one to the other there is a natural progression; nor could the other exist without the one. 'One' and 'other', indeed, in a more than grammatical sense[1]; and multiplicity in unity is a concept lying

---

[1] It was while Keats was working on this Book III, in all probability, that his companion Bailey was pondering 'Plato upon *one & other*' in *Parmenides*, *Sophist* or *Timæus* (see *K.C.*, I, 9) and in all probability discussing the problem with Keats.

behind Book III and this passage in particular. The cardinal points —'natural west, and east, and south, and north'—serve both to 'adunate' and to fling open: and the conciliating image of the cross is there, with its vigilant figure suspended:

> Far as the mariner on highest mast
> Can see all round upon the calmed vast . . .

It is almost the only simile in the whole poem to present a human figure in a human situation; and that it should come at this point is significant.

Not only the quaternion of the cardinal points, but that of the four elements too is subtly woven into the Neptune-vision. In the remote and purified world of the waters, as in the superlunary realm of ether invoked at the beginning of this third book, the elements are undifferentiated and we are privileged to view them as they unite and separate and unite again—'the abysm-birth of elements'. For this is Thales' world of the universal waters, from which all things rise and to which they shall finally return. Here water arches over water in simulation of the sky, sub-aqueous sunsets gleam above the sea-god's head, living beings inbreathe a kind of marine air, and 'a golden sphere' is the apotheosis of our common earth.

I have called this conclusion of Book III a pageant: and one may note that not only this section but others, and indeed the poem as a whole, exhibit many features of the masque. This may help us to see a little further into that curious remark of Keats to Taylor 'It [the 'Wherein lies Happiness' speech] set before me at once the gradations of Happiness even like a kind of Pleasure Thermometer —and is my first step towards the chief attempt in the Drama— the playing of different Natures with Joy and Sorrow.'[1] There is no doubt that in writing the poem Keats owed a good deal to *Comus*; and not least in this third book. The mixture of lyrical description, dramatic action, interspersed songs and dances, and the 'playing of different Natures with Joy and Sorrow', are

---

[1] Letter of 30 January 1818. See above, pp. 128–32.

peculiarly Miltonic. Set tableaux abound: we have the feast of Pan in Book I, the Garden of Adonis in Book II, and the Palace of Neptune in this third book, to be followed by the starry threshold of Jove's court in Book IV.

The pageant ends with feast, dancing and song. A Hymn to Neptune, Venus and Cupid parallels but hardly rivals the earlier Hymn to Pan. Endymion witnesses a procession of Oceanus, Doris, Nereus, Amphion, Amphitrite, and Thetis; he faints, 'far strayed from mortality', and is conveyed by Nereids to 'a crystal bower'. In his sleep he hears words of encouragement from his divine mistress. When he wakes,

> a placid lake
> Came quiet to his eyes; and forest green,
> Cooler than all the wonders he had seen,
> Lull'd with its simple song his fluttering breast.
> How happy once again in grassy nest!   [1029–33]

Endymion is back again in the familiar forest world.

[*Endymion*, Book III (4 September—26 September 1817)]

Chapter Ten

HEAVEN'S AIRY DOME

As the sun quadruply divides the three worlds, *viz.* the empyrean, the æthereal, and the material, on account of the communion of the zodiac with each; so he again divides the zodiac into twelve powers of gods, and each of these into three others: so that thirty-six are produced in the whole. Hence a triple benefit of the Graces is conferred on us from those circles. Which the god quadruply dividing, produces, though this division, a quadripartite beauty and elegance of seasons and times.

THOMAS TAYLOR, Introduction to *Cratylus*.

A SERIES of letters from Benjamin Bailey to John Taylor, Keats's friend and publisher, written between February and May 1818, tells the story of his more recent 'speculations'. They are engaging, enthusiastic letters. They reveal a mind and personality neither brilliant nor profound, but genuine, idealistic and warm-hearted. They help us to understand the influence that Bailey undoubtedly had on Keats in those weeks of 4 September–4 October 1817 when the third book of *Endymion* was in the making. During this period Keats was staying with Bailey in the latter's rooms at Magdalen, Oxford. The importance of the association, brief as it was, has been underestimated. As we read these letters we can understand why Keats said of Bailey in January, 1818: 'He is one of the noblest men alive at the present day . . . that sort of probity and disinterestedness[1] which such men as Bailey possess, does hold and grasp the tip-top of any spiritual honors that can be paid to anything in this world.' It is high

---

[1] We find Keats using the word 'disinterested' only twice before: once in reference to Bailey, and again in praise of his impulsive and generous sister-in-law Georgiana. See above, p. 65. Later (*Letters*, 315), he says he can think of only two persons who 'have had hearts completely disinterested—Socrates and Jesus—'.

praise. Bailey thought as highly of Keats, and of his poetry. Of *Endymion* he writes: 'Nothing but the finest poetry can now touch me, but that *does* touch me in the most secret springs, the "resting-places calm & deep" of my soul.'[1] And thirty years later he pays this tribute to its author: 'The errors of Keats's character—and they were as transparent as a weed in a pure and lucent stream of water,—resulted from his education; rather from his want of education. But like the Thames waters, when taken out to sea, he had the rare quality of purifying himself. . . . Socially, he was the most loveable creature, in the proper sense of that word, as distinguished from *amiable*, I think I ever knew as a man. And he had abundantly more of the *poetical character*, a hundred times told, than I ever knew in any individual.'

Bailey was reading for Anglican orders: the 'errors' he discerned in Keats would be moral and doctrinal—would consist, rather, in the tenuity of Keats's moral and doctrinal convictions. No doubt he tried to influence Keats; no doubt Keats put his attempts gently but firmly aside. There would be endless discussions.[2] Bailey was a fervent Wordsworthian and Miltonist; he was also a lover of Plato, and here he was able to give a new direction to Keats's thinking. The two friends understood and valued each other. Bailey's perception of Keats's power to 'purify himself . . . when taken out to sea' shows an acute interest, and implies communion of thought. As we read these early 1818 letters of Bailey to Taylor, we shall not be surprised to find that his 'greatest speculations' were Keats's speculations too.

We may glance first at the letter of 18 May; it is not the earliest, but it provides a useful catalogue of these speculations, which may be amplified and elucidated from earlier and later letters. After telling Taylor that he has invited Keats to revisit Oxford, and that

---

[1] *K.C.*, I, 19.

[2] And others were looked forward to. 'I hope I shall soon see you,' Keats writes in May 1818 in anticipation of an imminent visit, 'for we must have many new thoughts and feelings to analyse, and to discover whether a little more knowledge has not made us more ignorant' (*Letters*, 147).

he has 'promised to assist him in his Greek'[1] if he will come, he goes on to speak of his own writing. He is preparing a series of essays on the following subjects: (i) Moral Principles, (ii) the relative state[s] of man and woman, (iii) an enquiry into 'What is Power?', and (iv) the Unity of Nature. The first two essays, indeed, are already written; and he hopes to have the lot completed by the end of the month. They are to be followed by others on 'The Insufficiency of Language', 'Considerations previous to reading an author', a rewritten 'first essay on *Paradise Regained*', another on 'the moral beauty of Poetry', and a concluding paper devoted to Keats's poems. For these essays he has 'abundance of matter'; which, he says, 'makes it more difficult to throw my speculations into form than if I had infinitely less. . . . I am convinced writing a large volume upon one subject is much less difficult than treating several subjects, especially if they be deep & elemental truths, in the form of separate essays.'

Now all these topics have some relevance to what Keats was thinking and writing, just about this time. 'The relative state[s] of man and woman' was to take up a good deal of space in his letters; and it is to be one of the themes of *Lamia*. 'The insufficiency of language' as it exists nowadays will be contrasted with 'that large utterance of the early gods' in *Hyperion*; the same poem will discuss in its own terms the question 'What is power?' But it is above all the theme of 'The Unity of Nature' that will interest us. Can it be that Bailey was preoccupied with that same 'vast idea' of cosmic analogy which had 'rolled before' Keats at the outset of his poetic career, and which was still spurring him on to ever-fresh efforts of comprehension and expression?

Bailey's letters demonstrate that this was indeed so. In the pursuit of these august speculations the Oxford theological student is in accord with Keats and Coleridge and Blake and Thomas

---

[1] We find Keats proposing to 'learn Greek, and very likely Italian', in a letter of April 1818 to Reynolds from Teignmouth; there are other reports of his Greek studies, but in September he writes quite definitely, to George: 'I do not think of venturing upon Greek' (*Letters*, 424).

Taylor—and, on another plane, with Erasmus Darwin. He expresses himself quite precisely on the subject in an earlier letter (22 February):

> Indeed I find I have an odd and useless sort of mind. I have brooded over my pregnant thoughts, and nursed their offspring. I have, to *my own* perception, done this with much *regularity*. My *first* perceptions[1] have become more strong by the greater maturity of time and thought and knowledge. As far as my weak mortal eye-sight will carry me I have seen, from my first glances, an analogy, conformity, & unity in all things; or, to speak more intelligibly perhaps, the two last are perceptible *by* analogy. I have thought that this principle is the governing one of the universe, and that I have equally perceived it in nature, external & internal—in the minds of men as reflected through the best authors—and (as far as we can glimpse) in the eternal mind—of which everything that exists, it seems to my apprehension, is but the image of the Decree—the word, the Logos.[2] Now all this (which were I to indulge myself I could write on to the end of time almost)—all this, I say, *to me is clear as noonday*. But, I dare say, I have not made my notions more clear to you than at best a sort of dusky twilight.

Now 'all this' is plainly from Plato—'whom I can sufficiently follow to fill my mind with his fine abstractions without deluding me with his errors'. Bailey continues, in terms strangely reminiscent of Book II of *Endymion*:

> I dig for diamonds, and take 'the wings of the morning'[3] to adore the Goddess of Truth which I burn after like a man in a fever. The more prudent hands sow & reap, & spin & weave; and I am laughed at. . . . Plato had 'the vision and the faculty divine'. He looked into the 'adyta', the 'penetralia', the inmost recesses of truth. . . .[4]

---

[1] An echo from the *Immortality Ode*. The two friends read the Ode together: it was, significantly, the most 'metaphysical' section (strophe ix, with its 'obstinate questionings') which most excited Keats (*K.C.*, II, 275).

[2] Cf. Coleridge's note quoted above, p. 34.

[3] It is worth remembering that the psalm (cxxxix) continues '. . . and dwell in the uttermost parts of the sea, even there shall thy hand lead me . . .'.

[4] Was 'penetralia' a favourite word of Bailey's? If so, Keats may have picked it up (see the December 1817 letter quoted above, p. 36).

He is wiser than Aristotle, who 'could not miss of the unity & eternity of the godhead with his vast intellectual energy . . . but it was for Plato to see the non-eternity of matter, which the other could not comprehend, but held the eternity of what is but a feeble echo or prototype of the Divine Intelligence'. Bailey ends by asking Taylor to send him certain dialogues of Plato that he is in need of. 'I have but a patch-work collection of his works— Greek & English. I have Taylor's Translation of 4 dialogues—and 2 little volumes *from the French London 1749* of a few dialogues.' The two little volumes are the French translation by Dacier[1]; the four dialogues were the *Cratylus, Parmenides, Phædo,* and *Timæus* in Thomas Taylor's translation of 1793. No book exercised a profounder influence on Keats's mind.[2]

There is no direct evidence that Keats read Plato in Taylor's translation. The indirect evidence is, to my mind, overwhelming. His verse and his letters take on a quite new, a much more precise metaphysical flavour after the Oxford interlude. His ambition now is to

grow high-rife
With Old Philosophy
And mad with glimpses at futurity![3]

Yet so integral to Keats's 'vast idea' are the speculations Platonized for him in Bailey's chambers that there is no firm line to be drawn between his early and his later theorizing. We might be tempted to link Keats's concern with the spiritual influence of the great dead to a footnote like this from the *Cratylus:* '. . . the souls of truly worthy men, after their departure from the present life . . .

---

[1] Whose translation of the Golden Verses of Pythagoras, with the Life by Hierocles, may also have been on Bailey's shelves, and may have enriched Keats's understanding of the 'adorable tetractys'.

[2] The books he asked to be read to him as he lay dying were the works of Jeremy Taylor, 'Madame Dacier's Plato' and *The Pilgrim's Progress.* (Jeremy Taylor was another of Bailey's favourite authors.)

[3] Letter of 23 January 1818 to Bailey. Note the '*Old* Philosophy' (Platonism) and the 'glimpses at futurity' (occultism). In Letter 22 we find a strong interest in a 'metaphysical' poet—Katherine Philips—whose vocabulary ('to element', 'active souls', 'sense' and 'intelligence') touched Keats's at this time.

are the benevolent guardians of mankind.' But his trust in Shake-speare the 'Presidor' long antedates his reading in Plato. Again, this Taylorian comment on a paragraph in the *Phædo*:

> Heroes from the last order of souls which are the perpetual attendants of the gods . . . are characterized by a venerable and elevated magnanimity; and, as they are wholly of a reductorial nature, they are the progeny of Love, through whom they revolve about the first beauty in harmonic measures, and with ineffable delight . . .

may stand as a gloss on lines 171–7 of *Sleep and Poetry*:

> Here her altar shone,
> E'en in this isle; and who could paragon
> The fervid choir that lifted up a noise
> Of harmony, to where it aye will poise
> Its mighty self of convoluting sound,
> Huge as a planet, and like that roll round,
> Eternally around a dizzy void?[1]

But the reverence for great men is a bardic commonplace, and as germane to Blake's thought as to Keats's. The true worship of the Holy Ghost, in Blake's view, was to reverence his workings in the human mind (*i.e.* in art) and 'to love the greatest men best'. He is with Keats too in his mystical patriotism: 'All things begin and end in Albion's ancient Druid rocky shore.' Both men, above the other Romantics, extol Albion as the seat of primitive art and wisdom.

Book IV of *Endymion* begins with a long exordium expanding the thesis of *Sleep and Poetry* and enthusiastically affirming the power and originality of the English Muse. It must be quoted at length.

> Muse of my native land! loftiest Muse!
> O first-born on the mountains! by the hues

---

[1] The likeness here is more striking, with its unusual image. It is of course not out of the question that Keats had read Plato before his Oxford visit. A footnote to *The Minstrel* refers to the *Timæus*, and Beattie was one of Keats's early favourites. If he followed it up, he would be led to Taylor's 1793 translation, and there he would find the other dialogues too. There is room for a closer study of Taylor's influence on the Romantic poets than I can attempt here.

Of heaven on the spiritual air begot:
Long didst thou sit alone in northern grot,
While yet our England was a wolfish den;
Before our forests heard the talk of men;
Before the first of Druids was a child;—
Long didst thou sit amid our regions wild
Rapt in a deep prophetic solitude.
There came an eastern voice of solemn mood:—
Yet wast thou patient. Then sang forth the Nine,
Apollo's garland:—yet didst thou divine
Such home-bred glory, that they cry'd in vain,
'Come hither, Sister of the Island!' Plain
Spake fair Ausonia; and once more she spake
A higher summons:—still didst thou betake
Thee to thy native hopes. O thou hast won
A full accomplishment! The thing is done,
Which undone, these our latter days had risen
On barren souls. Great Muse, thou know'st what prison
Of flesh and bone curbs, and confines, and frets
Our spirit's wings: despondency besets
Our pillows; and the fresh tomorrow-morn
Seems to give out its light in very scorn
Of our dull, uninspired, snail-paced lives.[1]

This majestic personification of the English Muse holds much of
the flavour of Blake's Seasons in *Poetical Sketches*, something even
of the patience of his waiting Albion outstretched on the rock of
ages. There are early-Blakean phrases and rhythms:

> . . . amid our regions wild
> . . . Despondency besets
> Our pillows.

Whether Keats had read *Poetical Sketches*[2] or not, we are recognizably present here in Blake's fresh morning world of vision and

---

[1] Compare these last six lines with the well-known exordium to Book I
(especially lines 6–13). The change of tone is eloquent of the many vexations
which have come in the intervening seven months. Platonism is a refuge.

[2] As I suggested in a paper published in *The Cambridge Journal* for December
1925 (Vol. VI, No. 3).

unlimited potentialities. The English Muse is a spiritual entity, very much alive for Keats, as were his Rosicrucian elementals. She is a being who exists before there are men to interpret her in ode and epic and tragedy. She is 'first-born on the mountains'; she is (in an even more remarkable phrase) 'by the hues of heaven on the spiritual air begot'.[1] Appointed guardian over the sacred island which was to be the birthplace of Latona, she steadfastly rejects invitations from Palestine and Greece and Italy. In the end her faith is vindicated—first by the glories of Elizabethan poetry (Keats's earlier verse provides elucidation here) and now, in Keats's own day, by the beginnings of a new Renaissance. So much seems clear. What is not so clear is the place of this manifesto in *Endymion*. Why should Keats have written it as an introduction to his fourth and last book? Is it not out of place? We could have accepted it happily enough at the beginning of the whole poem, as a general manifesto of Keats's faith in English letters: as it stands, we expect it to have some special reference to the events or ideas of Book IV. And this we do not find.

---

[1] A remarkable and a difficult phrase. To get some light on it I have had to go rather far afield. 'Spiritual air' we are already familiar with: it is ether, the repository of 'intellect'. But what of the 'hues of heaven'? That they are principially superior to the 'spiritual air' is plain: they are the begetters, the masculine powers. As such we may well identify them with the thousand powers keeping their state in *Endymion*, III, 30; who, as *Timæus* showed us, are no other than the celestial gods (see above, p. 150). But why does Keats call them 'hues', colours? The only light I can find on this comes from the Vedas. In a creation narrative which parallels some central paragraphs of the *Timæus*, we read how 'All was *tamas* [obscurity]; It [the supreme Brahma, *i.e.* Keats's "heaven"] commanded a change, and *tamas* took on the hue of *rajas* [intermediate between obscurity and luminosity]; and *rajas*, having received a fresh command, put on the nature of *sattwa*'. Sattwa is defined by Guénon (*Le Symbolisme de la Croix*, from which I take my quotations) as 'conformity to the pure essence of Being, which is identical with the light of Knowledge, symbolized by the luminosity of the celestial spheres that represent the superior states of being'. And a note adds: 'The word *varna*, which properly means 'colour' ('hue'), and, by generalization, 'quality', is employed analogically to designate the nature or the essence of a principle or of a being.' Keats seems to be using the word 'hues' in this energetic sense here: they are the active principles by which a manifestation is 'begotten' on the ether. Note the singular 'Heaven, Hues and Prototypes' (parodying Acts ii, 9–11) of the 10 May 1817 letter to Leigh Hunt: he is already at work on *Endymion*, and his mind is already pondering principles and manifestations.

I think there are two explanations. The first, and the most important, is 'psychological': Keats is returning to 'the Mothers' after his sojourn, throughout Book III, in an emphatically masculine world.[1] We should not minimize this aspect of Keats. He felt a deep content in the maternal depths of femininity; a repose which contrasts sharply with the agitation wrought in him by the desirous, romantic, 'jealous' (to use the Blakean word) side of the man-woman relationship. We feel this in his appreciation of Georgiana, of 'Charmian',[2] and of Isabella Jones; we can feel it in his delight in creating the great maternal archetypes of Meg Merrilies, Moneta, Autumn: Book IV is to be the theatre of the triumph of Peona, of the reconciliation of the Yin and the Yang. The English Muse, in her serene, immobile poise, is a superb janitress to the action which follows. Dwelling alone in northern grot, 'rapt in a deep prophetic solitude', surrounded by wolf-infested forests untrodden of men, she is majestic in her listening patience. She constitutes a focus, a spiritual centre upon which converge 'voices' from east, south-east and south. Though she is not charmed away from her native land, these voices are far from unavailing: they are received into her consciousness and harmonize there, and in the fulness of time lend their riches to English poetry.[3]

Thus Keats is saying (and this brings me to my second 'explanation'): 'While I appear to be dealing with a legend which belongs to Greek poetry and Greek mythology, I am in fact treating of universal truths in English verse: between the great literatures there are no frontiers. The English muse sits on terms of equality with the Nine; from the beginning she has participated in the universal mythos.'[4] This point of view was doubly important for Keats as giving him a sense of 'belonging' at a period in his life when he felt an increasing dissatisfaction with his surroundings and, still more, with his own achievements. He needed

---

[1] A sojourn actual as well as imaginative, in that he had spent the month with Bailey at Oxford.

[2] See Letter of October 1818 to George and Georgiana Keats.

[3] The idea of interchange is already present in lines 359–63 of Book II.

[4] In this interposition of 'doctrinal' with narrative material *Endymion* resembles *The Excursion* more than any other contemporary 'long poem'.

consolation: and he goes for consolation to the English Muse. She participates in the universal mythos; and he, as an English poet, reflects this participation. This is a perennial theme in Keats; his assumption of the laurel crown (for which he felt such immediate and genuine remorse) was one expression of it; we come across a great many more in his letters. I have spoken often enough of the deep sense of tradition in which, among his contemporaries, only Blake surpasses or even approaches him. He has been concerned with the same theme—the participation of the individual poet in the great myth—in an earlier book of *Endymion*. I will ask the reader to turn back with me now to a consideration of a passage in Book II which is crucial for Keats's thought but which could not profitably have been discussed earlier—which, indeed, seems to me to have been an interpolation, an afterthought, in the context in which it stands, and which has much more relevance to our present enquiry. It is an undramatic, non-narrative disquisition[1] on the genesis of myth, and it follows (quite incongruously) the most lamentable of Endymion's love-passages with his goddess. In these lines Keats not only attempts to 'place' the individual writer in relation to the whole tradition (an important theme) but also discusses the nature of myth itself, and discusses it in opposition to a theory of its nature held by Wordsworth and formerly by himself. Here is the paragraph:

> Ye who have yearn'd
> With too much passion, will here stay and pity,
> For the mere sake of truth; as 'tis a ditty
> Not of these days, but long ago 'twas told
> By a cavern wind unto a forest old;
> And then the forest told it in a dream
> To a sleeping lake, whose cool and level gleam
> A poet caught as he was journeying
> To Phœbus' shrine; and in it he did fling
> His weary limbs, bathing an hour's space,
> And, after straight, in that inspired place

---

[1] All this has connections with the 'Hyperborean' thesis of Davies's *Celtic Researches* (Appendix A, pp. 396–401.)

He sang the story up into the air,
Giving it universal freedom. There
Has it been ever sounding for those ears
Whose tips are glowing hot. The legend cheers
Yon centinel stars; and he who listens to it
Must surely be self-doom'd or he will rue it:
For quenchless burnings come upon the heart,
Made fiercer by a fear lest any part
Should be engulphed in the eddying wind.
As much as here is penn'd doth always find
A resting place, thus much comes clear, and plain;
Anon the strange voice is upon the wane—
And 'tis but echo'd from departing sound,
That the fair visitant at last unwound
Her gentle limbs, and left the youth asleep.—
Thus the tradition of the gusty deep.[1]   [II, 727–53]

Now what is Keats doing here? He is interrupting the course of his story to make a pronouncement on the nature of the story itself—on this particular myth and, by implication, on myth in general. Why Keats should choose this point for his very important statement is uncertain. His hero has passed a crisis, yes: but the crisis seems to have no particular relation to the pronouncement. I strongly suspect that Keats inserted this passage in his revision of the poem; that its terms were very much in his mind as a result of his discussions, with Bailey, of the fourth book of *The Excursion*, and as a result also of his reading in Taylor's Introduction to *Timæus* of 'certain superficial moderns' who 'frame hypotheses concerning the ancient theology so ridiculous, that they deserve to be considered in no other light than the ravings of a madman, or the undisciplined conceptions of a child'. Feeling this to be true, Keats felt bound to register his protest against Wordsworth's 'associational' account of myth. It no longer satisfied him.

I have elsewhere suggested that the temple 'complete and true

---

[1] This report of the genesis of the Endymion legend is expanded from the more tentative account in lines 181–204 of 'I Stood Tiptoe . . .'. The 'sleeping lake' comes from the account of the Narcissus legend in the preceding paragraph of the same poem.

In sacred custom' of the second book of *Endymion* is identical with the 'fane In some untrodden region of my mind' of the *Ode to Psyche*. We can hardly imagine Shelley, Wordsworth, or even Coleridge using the epithet 'sacred' in such a context. In these matters, as in so many others, Keats counterbalances the excesses of his contemporaries. He was a searcher for tradition; he was an affirmer, against Shelley, of the sanctity of custom; against Coleridge, he asserted the validity of wisdom flowing from remote and unorthodox fountains.[1]

These 'againsts' must not, of course, be taken literally; Keats was not against anything, not even the dogmatism of Wordsworth which he was unable to accept—for Wordsworth too has a right to his own vision. Keats agreed with Blake that 'everything that lives is holy'. Holy, sacred—the words recur in his poems and letters. 'The holiness of the heart's affections', the 'sacred fire' on Pan's altar, Endymion's awe when

> to his capable ears
> Silence was music from the holy spheres,   [II, 674–5]

the 'sacred seasons' which in *Hyperion* 'must not be disturbed'; and, again in the *Ode to Psyche*, the ancient days

> When holy were the haunted forest boughs,
> Holy the air, the water, and the fire.[2]

Those days are gone, he mourns: the primeval days of holiness or wholeness when man, integrated to his environment, worshipped without formulæ. We can see, in reading Keats, that it is the natural order that is 'holy' for him; not the mechanical world-order of Newton and Locke, but the totality seen, as with Blake,

---

[1] Coleridge too we find, in *A Tombless Epitaph*,
> Piercing the long-neglected holy cave,
> The haunt obscure of old Philosophy,

but for him its wisdom is a dead wisdom.

[2] Note that Diana's shame for her yielding to love is not merely personal—she also grieves for the maiming of the divine order:
> . . . my crystalline dominion
> Half lost, and all old hymns made nullity

> (*Endymion*, II, 693–4).

'not with but through the eye', accepted in its minute particulars, yet cognisant, in Keats's own phrase, of 'the abysm-birth of elements'. Keats is thus a prime exponent of the urge which drove the Romantics to return, as best they could, to a pre-scientific view of the universe. To return—that is, with Keats, personally and non-argumentatively to find there *his* living reality. Not, like Blake or Wordsworth, to argue the matter out, to condemn and chide (though that needed doing too), but to realize in his own being the basic unity of life: its 'holiness'.

I need not stress this point: it is evident enough from the Letters alone, and may now be regarded as a critical commonplace. But our concern is with Keats's poetry, and some may feel that the Letters have been exploited more than enough. It is chiefly from the poems that I shall illustrate, in what follows, my contention that Keats was through and through a traditionalist; yet not in any sense that would have made sense to his contemporaries. There are traditions and traditions: some of them more radically opposed to the unity-of-all-things than any simple individualism could be. For there is an *ecclesia* of Urizen as well as of Los. Keats was concerned to get back behind all human traditions to the primitive doctrine literally handed down, in the first ages of the world, not from man to man, but from God to Man. This to him, we may say quite certainly, was the meaning of Greek myth. He was not aware, as Blake and Coleridge were, of the degree to which the rationalizing spirit of the Greeks had distorted the Everlasting Gospel; he was more aware than Blake was that the Greek mythology (as distinguished from Greek philosophy) had preserved precious fragments of the truth. And he knew far better than Wordsworth how myth arose.

Wordsworth has often been praised for the account he gives in Book IV of *The Excursion* of the origin of myth. Keats himself admired it, I believe, at the time he was writing 'I stood tip-toe . . .'. He discussed it with Bailey at Oxford, and later he came to see it for what it was: a 'sinewy-necked'[1] wriggle of the rationalist

---

[1] Blake's expressive epithet for the composite Bacon-Newton-Locke.

Cerberus. Let us look at this celebrated passage. The Wanderer is speaking:

'Once more to distant ages of the world.
Let us revert, and place before our thoughts
The face which rural solitude might wear
To the unenlightened swains of pagan Greece.
—In that fair clime, the lonely herdsman, stretched
On the soft grass through half a summer's day,
With music lulled his indolent repose:
And, in some fit of weariness, if he,   .
When his own breath was silent, chanced to hear
A distant strain, far sweeter than the sounds
Which his poor skill could make, his fancy fetched,
Even from the blazing chariot of the sun,
A beardless Youth, who touched a golden lute,
And filled the illumined groves with ravishment.
The nightly hunter, lifting a bright eye
Up towards the crescent moon, with grateful heart,
Called on the lovely wanderer who bestowed
That timely light, to share his joyous sport:
And hence, a beaming Goddess with her Nymphs,
Across the lawn and through the darksome grove,
Not unaccompanied with tuneful notes
By echo multiplied from rock or cave,
Swept in the storm of chase, as moon and stars
Glance rapidly along the clouded heaven,
When winds are blowing strong. The traveller slaked
His thirst from rill or gushing fount, and thanked
The Naiad. Sunbeams, upon distant hills
Gliding apace, with shadows in their train,
Might, with small help from fancy, be transformed
Into fleet Oreads sporting visibly.
The Zephyrs fanning, as they passed, their wings,
Lacked not, for love, fair objects whom they wooed
With gentle whisper. Withered boughs grotesque,
Stripped of their leaves and twigs by hoary age,
From depth of shaggy covert peeping forth
In the low vale, or on steep mountain-side,

And, sometimes, intermixed with stirring horns
Of the live deer, or goat's depending beard—
These were the lurking Satyrs, a wild brood
Of gamesome Deities; or Pan himself
The simple shepherd's awe-inspiring God!'

To Keats's reading of the Hymn to Pan in *Endymion* Wordsworth had responded with 'A pretty piece of paganism!' We know from his Letters Keats's opinion of these lines from *The Excursion*: it might be summarized as 'a pompous piece of rationalism'. Indeed, it is difficult to see how this account of the origin of myth is any advance on the spirit of *The Economy of Vegetation*. In diction it is a mass of eighteenth-century clichés; in theme, it takes each of Keats's sanctities in turn and proceeds to deflower them. The tone is patronizing to the ancients. 'Those bewildered Pagans of old time', as the Wanderer later styles them, in 'indolent repose' (like the poor Gipsies), aided by fancy (not imagination) saw things that were not there. That is all there is to it.

Not thus did the ancients, not thus did Blake and Keats view the world within a world which is myth. Blake would have seen the unenlightened swain of ancient times (though not, perhaps, of ancient Greece) as a being endowed not with a more hair-triggered fancy, but with more 'enlarged and numerous senses' than modern man. He would be capable, then, of perceptions impossible today: the spiritual entities that throng the mountains and groves and the atmosphere would put on shape for him. All the senses were involved. Pythagoras is traditionally reported to have been the last man to hear the music of the spheres: and we remember that Endymion too had this power:

to his capable ears
Silence was music from the holy spheres.[1]

It is not necessary for us to share these beliefs with Blake and Keats but bear them in mind we must if we are to understand the deeper resonances of their verse.

---

[1] Cf. J. Evola, *La Dottrina del Risveglio* (Bari, 1943): 'The man who is really capable of perceiving and of grasping the "divine sounds" is then also capable of pronouncing the word which is power, the Mantra. . . .'

Now Wordsworth's account of myth is simply this: that 'un-enlightened' human fancy, working on natural appearances, gives rise to illusions. These illusions are not unbeneficent, for they exteriorize the moral sense and lead men to a love of Nature:

> Diverting evil purposes, remorse
> Awakening, chastening an intemperate grief
> Or pride of heart abating: and, whene'er
> For less important ends these phantoms move,
> Who would forbid them, if their presence serve—
> On thinly-peopled mountains and wild heaths,
> Filling a space, else vacant—to exalt
> The forms of Nature, and enlarge her powers.

Passing over without comment the really extraordinary consideration that Wordsworth puts between parentheses, let us ask ourselves if we find anything here but a smug mixture of moralizing and sentiment. This is versified anthropology, and it is dull versification: Erasmus Darwin did the same kind of thing much better.[1] And it takes the heart out of ancient legend as effectively as Newton's prism took the magic out of the rainbow. More effectively, indeed; for to wiser and calmer thought than was Keats's when he wrote *Lamia* the prism adds without superseding: the artist's vision of the phenomenon exists in its own right side by side with that of the 'philosopher'.

Let us return, now, to the Keatsian statement on the nature of myth. It is not altogether easy to understand: or let us say, rather,

---

[1] Here Owen Barfield, *op. cit.*, is particularly relevant. Of the ancients living at 'a time when man—not only as a body, but also as a soul—was a part of nature in a way which we today, of course, find it difficult to conceive' (p. 123), he writes: 'it is only by reconstructing in imagination, and not just in theory, the nature of the representations they confronted that we can hope really to understand the mode of their thinking' (p. 87). And he is ready 'to affirm categorically that, for the nineteenth-century fantasy of early man first gazing, with his mind *tabula rasa* at natural phenomena like ours, then seeking to explain them with thoughts like ours, and then by a process of inference "peopling" them with the "aery phantoms" of mythology, there just is not any single shred of evidence whatever' (p. 42). We note that Barfield's key words, 'peopling' and 'phantoms', are also Wordsworth's.

that it yields layers of meaning. Keats is telling us here, through the symbolism of the elements, about the vital importance of tradition and the living forms in which tradition is handed down to us.

He begins with the assertion that the ditty (the legend, in the present case, of Endymion) is not of these days. It is archaic. It was told long ago by a cavern wind unto a forest old. But where, we may ask, did the cavern get the story from? Even this question, though it may seem at first sight like asking what song the Syrens sang, will not baffle us. If we have been paying attention to Keats's narrative, we shall remember the moment in Book II when the Naiad, who as a butterfly has led Endymion to the cavern's mouth, leaves him with these words:

> 'Farewell!
> I have a ditty for my hollow cell.'   [II, 129, 130]

And her ditty is precisely what she knows of the story of Endymion himself. I shall have more to say later about the function of resonant hollows in Keats's verse (and particularly about urns): let us note in the meantime that such hollows store up the treasures of legend for future ages, under the guidance of spiritual beings. This idea of *storing* is peculiarly germane to Keats's mind. The cave stores the legendary nourishment as the bee stores honey.[1] And when the destined moment of time dawns, the element of air (the natural medium of sound) confides the sacred message to the element of earth (the forest old). In *The Fall of Hyperion* too the wind 'blows legend-laden through the trees' (a line that Keats quotes with special satisfaction in his letter of 21 September 1819 to Woodhouse). We may link all this up, I think, with Taliesin's whispering trees in *Celtic Researches*.

From earth the legend is passed on to water: in a dream the forest tells the ditty to a sleeping lake. Now a lake is Keats's favourite symbol for the receptive unconsciousness—the mirror which reflects the pure eternity-infinity—so that, if we are interpreting the whole process microcosmically, we have arrived at

---

[1] See Appendix C.

the point where the legend has been conveyed by word of mouth (the cavern wind) through the ear (the forest old) and has penetrated the mind (the sleeping lake). Returning to the macrocosmic plane, we next find the poet bathing in the lake (microcosmically, sinking down into full passive receptivity) before journeying on to Phoebus' shrine (the abode of the fourth element, fire). 'In that inspired place' (Blake's burning fire of thought) he sings it back 'up into the air', thus 'giving it universal freedom'. Universal freedom—for two reasons: first, because the cycle is now completed, from air to air, from sound to sound through the four elements: and second, because the doctrine as couched in the poet's inspired words is now available to begin its beneficent work in the hearts of all those who, hearing, can feel its power.

What that beneficent work may be can only be hinted at here. The object of myth is always and everywhere realization, enlightenment and transformation: never, as Wordsworth would have it, moral improvement and amusement: whatever myth is traditional, orthodox and therefore integral must contribute to this end. This point is implicit in Keats's poem, which if it is about anything is about initiation and deliverance. The confusion in the poem stems from Keats's unsureness of what 'deliverance' was to mean for him. Dante knew the goal before he set out for it: that was the advantage of writing within a living tradition. Keats didn't know: hence his flounderings and sillinesses. Hence, too, the extreme interest of his poem for the curious reader—the reader, that is, who reads less for the rich savour of completeness than the tart tang of promise, whose interest in 'possible sublimity' complements his satisfaction in achievement. One can combine both interests, of course, but not always in the same poem.

We have no difficulty, at any rate, in grasping the importance that Keats attaches to the correct transmission of the legend. He uses expressions which may seem exaggerated. The legend 'cheers yon centinel stars'; its significance is not merely human, it links macrocosm and microcosm. It is so precious that men fear lest it be mutilated or lost. This fear is groundless: the Tradition cannot be destroyed, 'as much as here is penn'd' will always be available: the suggestion being (and we have met with it before in Keats) that behind the doctrine expressed in words or imagery lie reaches of significance quite unfathomable, inexhaustible.[1] Thus Keats carries the function and origin of mythology well away from the Wordsworthian sphere into a field of transcendant, noetic perception.[2]

But the myth was not working out very well for Keats. He was getting tired of *Endymion*. The Oxford interlude had brought him new thoughts, and new thoughts cried out for new forms. He wanted to finish with what he was doing and move on to something fresh. The fourth book of the poem is more perfunctory in treatment than the other three. He takes a good deal of trouble over his exordium on the English Muse; he is proud of it, and he quotes it in its entirety in a letter of 17 October 1817 to Bailey; but there are many traces of haste in its sequel. The action opens abruptly, with a woman's voice, an unknown voice raised in lament for exile:[3]

> 'Ah woe is me! that I should fondly part
> From my dear native land! . . .'   [IV, 30–31]

It is a young Indian girl, as Endymion discovers when he has made his way through the underwood into a clearing where she lies 'panting in the forest grass'. She is dark, warm, sensuous, eager for love. And the prince at once falls in love with her, with the comic haste of the enchanted lovers in *A Midsummer Night's Dream*. The episode here is not intended to be comic; it is so because

---

[1] Cf. *Sleep and Poetry* (76–80), where Keats retires to 'an enchanted grot' or to a green hill 'fearful from its loveliness' to

> Write on my tablets all that was permitted,
> All that was for our human senses fitted.

[2] It is noteworthy that this was the first of the three passages adduced by Shelley, in his letter to the Editor of the *Quarterly*, as giving promise of Keats's attainment of 'ultimate excellence'. The third passage is the description of the aged Glaucus quoted in part above, p. 153.

[3] Not, as de Selincourt would have it (*The Poems of John Keats*, notes to *Endymion*, p. 443), for 'her lost lover'. It is some lines further that she begins to sigh with longing for a *possible* lover.

Keats has failed to prepare us for it, and also because we have had such a surfeit of love-episodes already that a fresh series of them strikes us, inevitably, as ridiculous.

Endymion falls in love with the strange girl to his own amazement and dismay. He hears her voicing a doctrine of the interrelations of nature and human love which he himself has proposed in his early speech to Peona.[1] 'There's not a breath', she maintains,

> 'Will mingle kindly with the meadow air,
> Till it has panted round, and stolen a share
> Of passion from the heart!'   [83–5]

Endymion may be delighted to find his own theories thus repeated, but the reader is struck by the deepening unreality of the situation. It is hard enough to accord a willing suspension of disbelief to the Indian maid's presence in this lonely spot, to her fervid appeals for a lover, and to Endymion's prompt response; but it is harder still to accept her excursions into metaphysics. And all the more so since she is clearly intended by Keats to incarnate the principle of simple human love. At this point *Endymion* touches its nadir of implausibility.

Endymion declares his love, but shamefacedly; he is not happy about it. He feels himself a traitor to his celestial mistress. The girl professes to be astonished. Is there anything wrong in the enjoyment of simple human happiness? Like Peona, she enforces her spell with music. She sings the 'Sorrow song' which expresses lyrically the dominant theme of man's interlinking with nature; Endymion listens entranced.[2] Next she sings of Bacchus and his crew; of his triumphal progress through the East, and of how she left her Indian home to follow him. In brilliance this ode rivals the Hymn to Pan; it presents a series of Titianesque pictures clearly and dramatically realized.[3] And behind the pictures Keats's characteristic perception is active. 'Out of the blue' of space, the remote

---

[1] See above, p. 131.

[2] Its flow is hypnotic; and each stanza brings a different human 'intensity'—of health, of anger, of grief, of joy—into relationship with a different aspect of Nature.

[3] The dynamism of these, in contrast to the preceding Sorrow Song, is contrapuntal to Endymion's own passive acceptance of fate.

quietude of mountains, comes the manifestation into the green
and red world of events:

> 'And as I sat, over the light blue hills
> There came a noise of revellers: the rills
> Into the wide stream came of purple hue—
>   'Twas Bacchus and his crew!
> The earnest trumpet spake, and silver thrills
> From kissing cymbals made a merry din—
>   'Twas Bacchus and his kin!
> Like to a moving vintage down they came,
> Crown'd with green leaves, and faces all on flame;
> All madly dancing through the pleasant valley,
>   To scare thee, Melancholy!'   [193–203]

'All I can do is by plump contrasts'[1]: Keats's words are
amply borne out here. The contrast is emotional and technical.
Endymion's own melancholy is confronted with the recollected
'madness' of delight of Bacchus and his crew; and the dynamism
of this brilliant aria balances the static power of the Hymn to
Pan in the earlier festival. Pan's own satyrs are lured out of their
'forest haunts' by the odour of wine:

> 'For wine we follow Bacchus through the earth;
> Great god of breathless cups and chirping mirth.' [235–6]

Bacchus is a cosmopolitan deity set sharply against the rustic
reticences of the wood-god. His power is immediate, violent and
transient; Pan's is subtler, deeper, more lasting.

In the strophes that follow, Keats conveys the unimpeded
rhythms of natural life, its multifariousness, its irresistible attraction. The Indian maid embodies this attraction for Endymion.
But as he prepares to embrace her, a warning voice echoes through
the forest: '*Woe, Woe to that Endymion! Where is he?*' The dire
question which greeted Adam at his fall now sounds for the shepherd-prince. Following the voice, Mercury himself appears; he
swoops down, just touches the ground with his wand, and soars
skyward again. Immediately two jet-black steeds rise from the

---

[1] Quoted below, p. 293.

turf: Endymion and his love mount, and are carried through the air. The final stage of the hero's wanderings has begun.

The final stage and, for the reader, the most tedious! Keats is getting bored with his fable; indeed, he confesses as much in his letters. He is anxious now to press on to the end, complete his set number of lines and begin something new. And of course the quality of the writing suffers. I described the first three books as masque-like; the fourth is more in the nature of a pantomime, and a pantomime none too skilfully staged. Ropes and pulleys are hardly disguised in these aerial flights and descents, these appearances and disappearances of gods and goddesses. Endymion and his new love are carried up to heaven; they fall asleep, wake and sleep again. Waking, Endymion is confronted by Diana: 'His heart leapt up as to its rightful throne'—but the girl is sleeping by his side, and she is so beautiful that 'he [cannot] help but kiss her'. Diana weeps, and fades; the maid awakes and smiles. All is statement; the descriptive detail of the first three books, which in its warm or terrifying immediacy made us overlook the improbabilities of the action, is here necessarily absent: the reaches of upper air afford no scope for natural imagery.

Torn between his two loves, Endymion touches the point of despair.

> 'What is this soul then? Whence
> Came it? It does not seem my own, and I
> Have no self-passion or identity.
> Some fearful end must be; where, where is it?
> By Nemesis! I see my spirit flit
> Alone about the dark . . .'   [475–80]

Rousing the twin steeds, he rides 'direct towards the Galaxy'. For a while he holds 'converse soft and strange' with his beloved; but as the moon rises from behind a cloud, the girl begins to fade away and finally disappears. Endymion is left alone. And abruptly Keats abandons the pantomimic for the allegorical mode: a shift which in its suddenness is likely to mystify the reader. We meet many of these transpositions in the course of *Endymion*, and to them the poem owes no small part of its obscurity. I have already suggested

a similarity of structure with *The Excursion* in *Endymion's*
alternation of narrative and 'doctrinal' matter: it is one of these
'speculative' passages, following the crudely realized air-voyagings,
which now confronts us.

We have seen Endymion reduced to despair; it is when despair
is at its keenest (*i.e.* on the disappearance of the Indian maid) that
he suddenly finds himself in 'the Cave of Quietude'—a state, not a
place as the purlieus of Olympus or the stretches of the Galaxy
are places, and a state which perhaps balances the 'den of discontent' of Book I (lines 928-9) though its significance is more
richly developed. And this significance is so important for Keats's
total doctrine of liberation that the passage must have our closest
attention. I shall quote it almost in full.

> There lies a den,
> Beyond the seeming confines of the space
> Made for the soul to wander in and trace
> Its own existence, of remotest glooms.   [512-15]

Already, a year before the 'soul-making' letter, Keats is venturing
upon its central speculation. The space made for the soul to wander
in is the cosmos, the circle of courses; the 'den' of which he speaks
lies 'beyond' this space. It is a state of despair, and no one living
escapes it:

> . . . the man is yet to come
> Who hath not journey'd in this native hell.   [522-3]

We see that the 'den' is not the Cave (as Keats's commentators
have taken it to be): it is a region in which we wander, and other
'dark regions are around it'. But at the centre of the 'den' there is
an extraordinary calm. Here the soul may rest. It first experiences
the horror of the den, and this is painful indeed—

> But few have ever felt how calm and well
> Sleep may be had in that deep den of all.
> There anguish does not sting; nor pleasure pall;
> Woe-hurricanes beat ever at the gate,
> Yet all within is still and desolate.   [524-8]

This is obscure, yet not impenetrably so. Keats is trying to say something of importance, but he is saying it rather clumsily. We may paraphrase the first two lines as 'Few have experienced the calm sleep to be had in the ultimate depths of that den'—that is, in what in a moment he will call 'the Cave of Quietude'. The Cave lies at the centre of the den. The den is the condition of despair into which the soul is thrust by anguish greater than it can bear. When this anguish reaches its climax, and the soul accepts it, ceases to fight against it without seeking to run away from it, but rather takes refuge in the centre of the anguish itself: then there is a dialectical reversal, an 'enantiodromia'. *There* 'anguish does not sting, nor pleasure pall'. This is the 'point of no return' beyond the pairs of opposites. Endymion has now reached this central point, as in Book II he reached the centre of the diamond, and in Book III the profoundest depth of the sea. It is a state which is won *suddenly*, unconsciously: it cannot be gained by effort:

> Enter none
> Who strive therefor: on the sudden it is won.
> Just when the sufferer begins to burn,
> Then it is free to him . . .   [531–4]

(again in the sense of achieving the 'freedom' of a city: he instals himself boldly as a denizen of his own despair)

> . . . and from an urn,
> Still fed with melting ice, he takes a draught—
> Young Semele such richness never quaft
> In her maternal longing! Happy gloom!
> Dark Paradise! where pale becomes the bloom
> Of health by due; where silence dreariest
> Is most articulate; where hopes infest. . . .   [534–40]

(The urn, we note, is again central, or initiatory, as it will be in *The Fall of Hyperion*.) This is a state beyond desire, beyond hope (for hope, as Mr Eliot puts it, may be hope for the wrong thing, and in the Cave of Quietude there is no anxious searching after comfort or assurance); a state in which anything can be its own

contrary. In this depth the whole can be salvaged from the complete wreck of the partial:

> O happy spirit-home! O wondrous soul!
> Pregnant with such a den to save the whole
> In thine own depth.   [543-5]

And thus the depth is in the soul itself; the soul retreats into its own
abyss—of loneliness, fear, or sorrow—and finds there a strange
new happiness.

> Hail, gentle Carian!
> For, never since thy griefs and woes began,
> Hast thou felt so content: a grievous feud
> Hath led thee to this Cave of Quietude.   [545-8]

Nothing in *Endymion*, indeed nothing in the whole of Keats's
writing, impresses me as this passage does with the sense of his
extraordinary insight. He has come, at twenty-three, to an understanding which few men reach at twice those years. He has tasted
the quality of the peace that passes all understanding, the peace
which lies in full acceptance of *what is*: he has understood the
secret of the joy that is beyond happiness. From such an understanding there is nothing that cannot be anticipated. We reap its
first-fruits, but its first-fruits only, in the Odes.

Immured in his Cave of Quietude, the prince is borne through
the Galaxy, deaf to the music of the heavenly hosts as they chant
his prothalamion. These delicate verses are the most Spenserian in
Endymion; and we may take them as Keats's gesture of farewell to
Spenser: from now on he will own another 'Presidor'. We welcome the hymn as bringing earthly warmth and flowering, for
the first time, into the regions of 'the frozen purity of air' through
which we have been passing in Book IV; but soon we are back in
the beloved forest world itself. Endymion is carried down by
his steed to 'the green head of a misty hill'; and here he finds his
Indian maid waiting for him.[1] He embraces her, and in so doing

---

[1] The 'Ah, me!' of line 622 is certainly a sigh from the maiden and should have
its own inverted commas.

renounces his quest. Henceforth he will be content with simple
human happiness:

> 'Behold upon this happy earth we are;
> Let us aye love each other; let us fare
> On forest-fruits and never, never go
> Among the abodes of mortals here below,
> Or be by phantoms duped. O destiny!
> Into a labyrinth now my soul would fly,
> But with thy beauty will I deaden it.'   [625–31]

'Let us love, and eat forest-fruits': the collocation is eminently
Keatsian, whether we take the forest fruits as real or symbolical.
Love and feasting go regularly together in his climaxes, and
in these banquets fruit from Kali's wish-fulfilling tree is never
absent. For with the fruit, the consummation of the total process
of the plant, the richness and dynamism of earth pass into the
processes of human love; just as, at seeding-time, the *conscious*
ecstasy of human love penetrates the vegetable cycle. This give-
and-take we have already come to see as a master principle of
Keats's thought.

But Endymion has not yet attained his 'abode of rest'. In every
phrase we feel the tension of the opposites. 'I will be content with
earthly happiness', he cries; but the protestation is hollow.

> 'I have clung
> To nothing, lov'd a nothing, nothing seen
> Or felt but a great dream! O I have been
> Presumptuous against love, against the sky,
> Against all elements, against the tie
> Of mortals each to each, against the blooms
> Of flowers, rush of rivers, and the tombs
> Of heroes gone!'[1]   [636–43]

He has sinned against his own glory, rejecting 'his natural sphere'.
He now bids farewell to the 'great dream', and welcomes the

---

[1] Cf. *The Anatomy of Melancholy*, III, I, iii, 2, where those who do not feel
natural love are said 'to be unworthy of that air they breathe, and of the four
elements'. Endymion's 'nothing . . . but a great dream' admits the truth of
Peona's charge in Book I (see above, p. 126).

simple fruition of his 'Indian bliss'. Now in a sense this marks Endymion's supreme defeat, the nadir of his cosmic wanderings in search of truth; yet, by virtue of an enantiodromia carried over from the Cave of Quietude, it is also the moment of his triumph. For in the Cave he has come to understand that victory is the fruit of acceptance, and that it is not through our striving that we reach the goal, though our striving is essential to bring us to its threshold. Endymion has done his utmost, or what seems his utmost: but there is one trial more—and it is his sweet Indian maid who will expose him to it. From her, who seems the embodiment of gentle, meek, obedient, unreflecting love, he meets with rejection.

'I may not be thy love', she announces. While Endymion reposed in the Cave of Quietude, she received this command from on high. And the prince is in despair again: he has forfeited both his divine and his human destiny, and finds himself doomed to a life of loneliness. At this point Peona makes her second appearance. She greets her long-lost brother with delight; urges him to be happy with his Indian maid, and prattles on about the good times they will have together. But Endymion has accepted his unanticipated doom: 'A hermit young, I'll live in mossy cave.'[1] Peona will visit him from time to time and bear his counsels to the clan:

> 'Through me the shepherd realm shall prosper well;
> For to thy tongue will I all health confide.
> And, for my sake, let this young maid abide
> With thee as a dear sister. Thou alone,
> Peona, mayst return to me.'   [863–7]

The maid in her turn vows to become one 'of Dian's sisterhood'. There is to be one last meeting of the three; the time, that same evening; the place, the grove behind Diana's temple.

And so the stage is set for the final scene of this strange eventful

---

[1] Prophetic of Keats's own case two years later: 'I am becoming accustom'd to the privations of the pleasures of sense. In the midst of the world I live like a Hermit. I have forgot how to lay plans for enjoyment of any Pleasure . . .' (*Letters*, 399).

history. For the rest of the day Endymion remains sorrowing, motionless as a corpse; when evening falls, he makes his way slowly to the sacred grove. He will say farewell, and die.

> 'Night will strew
> On the damp grass myriads of lingering leaves,
> And with them shall I die; nor much it grieves
> To die, when summer dies on the cold sward.
> Why, I have been a butterfly, a lord
> Of flowers, garlands, love-knots, silly posies,
> Groves, meadows, melodies, and arbour roses;
> My Kingdom's at its death, and just it is
> That I should die with it: so in all this
> We miscall grief, bale, sorrow, heartbreak, woe,
> What is there to plain of? By Titan's foe
> I am but rightly serv'd.'   [933–44]

And in so saying Endymion is, from the standpoint of the Circle of Courses, fully justified. He has failed, palpably, to free himself from 'mortality's harsh net'; he has not broken the circle; he remains the shepherd-prince who is also the vegetation-king and who must die with the dying of the year. In this sense, the year is his 'kingdom', and we may remember that Keats had planned the writing of the poem to extend from spring to autumn.[1]

But Endymion bears too great a mind for defeat. As he enters the precincts of Diana's grove, he rebels against the verdict of death. He is *not* a king of the butterflies—he is consciously a spiritual being:

> 'I did wed
> Myself to things of light from infancy;
> And thus to be cast out, thus lorn to die,
> Is sure enough to make a mortal man
> Grow impious.'   [957–61]

At the last moment, then, 'in sort of deathful glee', Endymion asserts himself (a thing he has not done throughout the poem).

---

[1] See above, p. 119.

When the two maidens appear, he no longer acquiesces in his fate:
instead, he appeals to heaven for a sign:

> 'Sister, I would have command,
> If it were heaven's will, on our sad fate.'   [975–6]

And his prayer is heard. The 'dark-eyed stranger' is transfigured
and reveals herself in all her glory as the goddess:

> . . . into her face there came
> Light, as reflected from a silver flame:
> Her long black hair swell'd ampler, in display
> Full golden; in her eyes a brighter day
> Dawn'd blue and full of love.   [982–6]

It is the climax; but we are not permitted to dwell on it. Keats
hurries on to his conclusion. Hero and heroine embrace, and at
once vanish. Peona is left alone to return

> Home through the gloomy wood in wonderment.

The final cadence of *Endymion* brings echoes of the two
Paradises. And indeed Milton has been a pervasive presence in the
poem. So, too, have Spenser and Wordsworth. The main Shake-
spearean contribution is from *A Midsummer Night's Dream*. On
the structural side, quarries as far apart as Fletcher (in *The Faithful
Shepherdess*) and Shelley (in *Alastor*) have supplied basic material;
on the philosophical side, we have the stimulus (mainly in revision) of the *Timæus*. Wieland's *Oberon*, as an American critic has
demonstrated, is responsible for some episode sequences. Finally,
there is the persistent contagion of Hunt to be noted and deplored.

One further 'influence' has not, as far as I know, been acknowledged. Byron's *Manfred* was published on 16 June 1817, when Keats
(in all probability) was about half-way through his Book II. We
know Keats read *Manfred*, though we don't know exactly when.[1]
He quotes from it, not quite accurately, in a letter of 3 May 1818,
to J. H. Reynolds: 'Until we are sick, we understand not;—in

---

[1] No letters survive for the period 10 June to 5 September.

fine, as Byron says, "Knowledge is Sorrow"; and I go on to say that "Sorrow is Wisdom"—and further for aught we can know for certainty "Wisdom is folly"!' This is a pendant to the famous enquiry into the Miltonic and the Wordsworthian vision ('And here I have nothing but surmises, from an uncertainty whether Miltons apparently less anxiety for Humanity proceeds from his seeing further or no than Wordsworth . . .'), and a preface to the even more famous comparison of life to the 'large Mansion of Many Apartments'. That Byron is central in the discussion—as an oracle, perhaps, rather than a disputant—is noteworthy. Byron is brought in to support one of Keats's most vital 'speculations': the relationship between knowledge, sorrow, and wisdom.

Now this had been a prime theme of *Endymion*. Keats himself pointed to the Sorrow Song as the core of his meaning: the 'interassimilation' between the natural and the human worlds. There is more than a suggestion of this theme in *Manfred*, to which we shall return in a moment. Meanwhile let us note that *knowledge* is in equal or even superior degree an *Endymion* theme; more than that, it is dominant in *Hyperion*: Oceanus' plea for the acceptance of *what is* admits 'the pain of truth' ('Knowledge is Sorrow') and Apollo's final cry is 'Knowledge enormous makes a God of me'. The cross-currents between Byron and Keats are interesting here. Keats's idealistic metaphysics may seem far enough removed from Byron's scepticism, but both revolve around a common centre. Keats read *Manfred*, I imagine, in midstream of writing *Endymion*, and felt its impact. I think it stimulated, if it did not positively arouse, his dramatic ambitions: the sorrow-happiness idea is the context for the first mention we have (letter to John Taylor of 30 January 1818) of his aspirations 'towards the chief attempt in the Drama'. We should not forget that *Manfred* was Byron's first dramatic poem. Keats could not know that Byron had no thought of seeing it staged.

It is interesting to survey Keats's wavering reactions to the phenomenon of Byron. A sonnet to the poet, dated December 1814, has rightly been called 'feeble' by de Selincourt. It has little interest apart from its identification of Byron as the poet of *sorrow*; and in 1817 he is still this for Keats. 'Byron! how sweetly sad thy melody': the sonnet is an embroidery on its opening line. It is perhaps fortunate that Byron had no opportunity of reading this poem, which addresses him as a dying swan, delightful through his 'O'ershading sorrow' and griefs dressed 'With a bright halo, shining beamily'.

> Still warble, dying swan! still tell the tale,
> The enchanting tale, the tale of pleasing woe.

Sorrow and Byron are connected, significantly, with the moon; indeed Byron is, before his final metamorphosis into a swan, the moon itself.

How long this enthusiasm for Byron persisted we cannot know: it was still alive in his medical student days,[1] but the friendship with Haydon and Hunt (dating from late 1816) was likely to damp it. One of the 'ugly Polyphemes' in *Sleep and Poetry* may well be Byron. But *Manfred* clearly relit the flame. For in *Manfred* Keats saw Byron tackling, in his own defiant, extravagant way, aspects of the 'vast idea' which had most deeply concerned him in *Endymion*. We have noted the occult resonances of that poem. Here is what Byron has to say, in a letter of 15 February 1817 to John Murray announcing the completion of his drama: '. . . it is in three acts, but of a very wild, metaphysical, and inexplicable kind. Almost all the persons . . . are Spirits of the earth and air, or the waters[2]; the scene is in the Alps; the hero a kind of magician [who] wanders about invoking these Spirits. . . .' The Poet in Keats's sonnet of that title, written a year or two before, is of Manfred's clan: the play could not fail to interest Keats if for this reason alone. And let us not forget that there was an element in Byron's earlier verse—in particular in *Childe Harold*—an element of self-losing, of merging, which Keats could appreciate as he could not appreciate (while respecting) Wordsworth's egotistical

---

[1] *K.C.*, II, 209.
[2] Precisely Keats's elements in *Endymion*; the element of fire being deferred, as we have seen, to *Hyperion*.

sublime. Byron claimed a power[1] of going out of himself into the natural forms surrounding him in his travels which compares with Keats's own 'continually informing and filling some other body.' In contrast to Wordsworth, of whom Shelley wrote:

> He had a mind which was somehow
> At once circumference and centre
> Of all he might or feel or know;
> Nothing went ever out, although
> Something did ever enter:

we have in *Childe Harold* the longing 'to mingle with the universe', and the fulfilment of that longing:

> I live not in myself, but I become
> Portion of that around me; and to me
> High mountains are a feeling, but the hum
> Of human cities torture . . .

This is Byronic, not Wordsworthian. Whether it is identical with the Keatsian empathy is another question. What is unquestionable is that Keats would feel its attraction.

I shall attempt no detailed comparison of *Manfred* and *Endymion*. The two poems breathe different atmospheres: the Platonic idealism of the one has no affinity with the remorse-stricken despair of the other. Still less am I tempted to assess them in terms of 'sincerity' or 'high seriousness'. But on the technical plane, the plane of 'machinery' and imagery, there are interesting parallels to be drawn. Keats would at once identify Manfred with Byron, as he identified himself with Endymion. Endymion is a magus, Manfred is a magus: both are poets. Both seek command over the elements (Endymion's task, we remember, was to explore, with Glaucus, 'all forms and substances Straight homeward to

---

[1] And on occasion deplored its absence: '. . . the recollections of bitterness . . . have preyed upon me here [in the Alps]; and neither the music of the Shepherd, the crashing of the Avalanche, nor the torrent, the mountain, the Glacier, the Forest, nor the Cloud, have . . . enabled me to lose my own wretched identity in the majesty, and the power, and the Glory, around, above, and beneath me' (Journal, 29 September 1816).

their symbol-essences'). The first scene of *Manfred* shows the hero
invoking the 'spirits of the unbounded Universe':

> Ye, who do compass earth about, and dwell
> In subtler essence—ye, to whom the tops
> Of mountains inaccessible are haunts,
> And earth's and ocean's caves familiar things—
> I call upon ye by the written charm
> Which gives me power upon you—[1]

And the first spirit rises as 'a star is seen at the darker end of the
gallery', an appearance which reminds us of the 'orbed diamond'
which Endymion sees 'far away' before entering 'a marble
gallery' in the underworld. The spirit speaks in rhythms and
images that bring Keats's *Song of Four Fairies* irresistibly to mind:

> Mortal! to thy bidding bow'd,
> From my mansion in the cloud,
> Which the breath of twilight builds,
> And the summer's sunset gilds
> With the azure and vermilion,
> Which is mix'd for my pavilion. . . .[2]

The spirits have no favourable message for Manfred; his defiance
of them foreshadows Endymion's defiance, in the closing scene
of the poem, of the destiny which seems to label him 'King of the
butterflies'. Here is Byron (still Act I, sc. 1):

> The mind, the spirit, the Promethean spark,
> The lightning of my being, is as bright,
> Pervading, and far darting as your own,
> And shall not yield to yours, though coop'd in clay!

So too Endymion swears by

> the Promethean clay by thief endued

that he did wed himself 'to things of light from infancy',

> 'And thus to be cast out, thus lorn to die,
> Is sure enough to make a mortal man
> Grow impious.'

---

[1] Byron's 'talisman', like Keats's is *written*.
[2] Cf. especially lines 45 to 60 of Keats's poem.

The defiance here is amply Byronic. It is, in fact, hardly consistent with the personality of Endymion as it has unfolded itself through the course of the poem, and the *invraisemblance* reinforces the admitted unsatisfactoriness of the poem's conclusion. The Promethean note is, indeed, quite irrelevant to Keats's poem and can originate only in a recollection of Byron's. The whole point of *Endymion* is a won, a disciplined acceptance, achieved through sorrow and knowledge.

Manfred's desire to see the spirits face to face has no place in *Endymion*, nor do the spirits themselves speak. But the manifestation of 'a beautiful female figure' as the physical embodiment of the elements, and Manfred's reaction, recall the successive theophanies of Keats's poem:

> *Manfred:* Oh God! if it be thus, and *thou*
>   Art not a madness and a mockery,
>   I yet might be most happy. I will clasp thee,
>   And we again will be—　　[*The figure vanishes.*
>   My heart is crush'd!
>   [*Manfred falls senseless.*

Diana's appearances and disappearances, Endymion's ecstasies and swoonings, are curtly adumbrated here. The incantation which follows likewise telescopes Keatsian preoccupations in *Endymion*. I italicize these.

> *When the moon is on the wave,*
>   And the glow-worm in the grass,
> And the meteor on the grave,
>   And the wisp on the morass;
> When the falling stars are shooting,
> And the answer'd owls are hooting,
> *And the silent leaves are still*
> *In the shadow of the hill,*
> Shall my soul be upon thine,
> *With a power and with a sign.*

Indications inconclusive in themselves, but relevant, in the total context, to my conviction of the pervasive presence of *Manfred* in

Endymion. Compare too, for its connection with the Song of Sorrow theme, this later strophe from the incantation:

> From thine own smile I snatch'd the snake,
> For there it coil'd as in a brake;
> From thy own lip I drew the charm
> Which gave all these their chiefest harm;
> In proving every poison known,
> I found the strongest was thine own.[1]

Here sorrow has given place to hate. The later address to the Witch of the Alps (II, 1) is nearer to Keats's correspondence;

> . . . the hues of youth
> Carnation'd like a sleeping infant's cheek,
> Rock'd by the beating of her mother's heart,
> Or the rose tints, which summer's twilight leaves
> Upon the lofty glacier's virgin snow,
> The blush of earth embracing with her heaven,—
> Tinge thy celestial aspect. . . .

Manfred's confession to the Witch of the Alps includes many features of Endymion's confession to Peona. For him, as for the shepherd prince, earthly ambitions are eclipsed by a thirst for the knowledge which brings supernatural power:

> From my youth upwards
> My spirit walk'd not with the souls of men,
> Nor look'd upon the earth with human eyes;
> The thirst of their ambition was not mine,
> The aim of their existence was not mine. . . .

---

[1] This, and the lines which follow, contributed to *Lamia*, in particular the picture of the 'palpitating snake, Bright, and cirque-couchant in a dusty brake'. Byron's lines themselves ('By thy cold breast and serpent smile, By thy unfathom'd gulfs of guile . . .') connect Coleridge and Keats. That Hazlitt saw the connection is I think evident from the page of his *Liber Amoris* (publ. 1823) headed 'Written in a Blank Leaf of *Endymion*'. It consists of two sentences of which I quote the second: '—But by her dove's eyes and serpent shape, I think she does not hate me; by her smooth forehead and her crested hair, I own I love her; by her soft looks, and queen-like grace (which men might fall down and worship), I swear to live and die for her!' It is curious that Hazlitt's love-affair should seem to mimic, in so many of its features, Keats's passion for Fanny Brawne; and that throughout its course memories of *Endymion*, *Lamia*, and *Manfred* should have possessed his mind.

He delights in 'The difficult air of the iced mountain's top, Where the birds dare not build', just as Endymion has known

> the chilly sheen
> Of icy pinnacles, and [dipp'd his] arms
> Into the deadening ether that still charms
> Their marble being. . . .[1]

Note how Byron's terms are assimilated, transformed, not simply reproduced. They are deeply felt. Keats could not but respond, and respond personally, in his own 'sensations', to Manfred's or Byron's delight in the energies of nature fused with man's:

> . . . to plunge
> Into the torrent, and to roll along
> On the swift whirl of the new breaking wave
> Of river-stream, or ocean, in their flow.
> In these my early strength exulted; or
> To follow through the night the moving moon . . .
> Or to look, list'ning, on the scattered leaves,
> While Autumn winds were at their evening song.
> These were my pastimes, and to be alone. . . .

These are not Keats's terms. They are Byron's: taut, masculine, completely assured as the terms of *Endymion* are not assured; but the preoccupations are Keats's. So too is the fusion. Byron's 'going out' is realized in dynamic gesture: Keats's is more receptive, thoughtful. It is noticeable that where he attempts to develop the hints derived from *Manfred* he fails. For instance, a brief satiric speech by Nemesis on kingship closes Act II, scene 3; Keats extends this into the long diatribe which opens his third book. Both passages have been condemned by the critics as out of place, and we can apply *a fortiori* to Keats's lines Jeffrey's strictures on Byron's: 'We cannot be persuaded that satirical and political allusions are

---

[1] Scene III of *Manfred* is set on 'The Summit of the Jungfrau Mountain': the First Destiny describes 'The glassy ocean of the mountain ice . . . a dead whirlpool's image: And this most steep fantastic pinnacle . . .'. Keats's 'icy pinnacles' are more at home here than on the summit of Latmos.

at all compatible with the feelings and impressions which it was
here his business to maintain.'

The quest theme of *Endymion* is strongly paralleled in Byron's
Act II, scene 4. Compelled by Nemesis, the spirit of Astarte appears.
Manfred's comment again suggests the natural-human interchange
of the Sorrow Song:

> Can this be death? there's bloom upon her cheek;
> But now I see it is no living hue
> But a strange hectic—like the unnatural red
> Which Autumn plants upon the perish'd leaf.

Manfred has sought her throughout the world:

> I cannot rest.
> I know not what I ask, nor what I seek:

(and this is precisely Endymion's case)

> For I have call'd on thee in the still night,
> Startled the slumbering birds from the hush'd boughs

(just as, in a similar state of anguish, 'an innocent bird Before
[Endymion's] heedless footstep stirr'd'[1])

> And woke the mountain wolves, and made the caves
> Acquainted with thy vainly echoed name . . .
> I have outwatch'd the stars,
> And gazed o'er heaven in vain in search of thee.
> Speak to me! I have wander'd o'er the earth,
> And never found thy likeness. . . .

The total situation, with its background of crime and remorse, is
of course far from Endymion's; but we see that it has aspects
which could not fail to interest Keats as he read *Manfred* and wrote
his poem.

These are the main points of resemblance. Less important ones,
perhaps, are the lines which praise the moon for her transmuting

---

[1] '. . . to entice', Endymion thinks, 'My stumbling down some monstrous
precipice'. Manfred too contemplates suicide by this means; and the idea is found
in Virgil's eighth Eclogue (59–60). Cf. *Sleep and Poetry*, 301, 302 (above, p. 110).

power (in Act III, scene 4) and which may be compared with
Endymion, III, lines 52 to 60; the picture of the 'star condemn'd'
(in Act I, scene 1) which may have suggested 'when our planet's
sphering time is done' in Book II, line 251; and Manfred's line, 'It
hath enlarged my thoughts with a new sense' (in Act III, scene 1)
which is close to Endymion's 'genders a novel sense' in Book I
line 808. Verbal and situational echoes are in fact few: what
interested Keats were salient aspects of the plot: the theme of
wandering, Manfred's magical powers over the elements, the
emphasis upon his 'self-losing' within natural forms, and the
correlation of knowledge and sorrow. It would be interesting
to know just when Keats read *Manfred*: perhaps with Bailey at
Oxford; and not impossibly the Byronic sublime was balanced
against the Wordsworthian and the Miltonic in those long discussions in Magdalen on September evenings in 1817. The May
1818 letter seems to suggest it; earlier, in February letters to
Reynolds and to his brothers, we find him eagerly awaiting the
publication of the fourth Canto of *Childe Harold*. And the earliest
reference is the most significant of all. It comes in his first letter
to Bailey following the month at Oxford. Keats has got back to
Hampstead to find 'every body at Loggerheads': Hunt, Haydon,
Horace Smith, all quarrelling with one another. 'I am quite
disgusted with literary Men—and will never know another except
Wordsworth—no not even Byron.'

It is a far cry from this to the final burst of indignation over
Don Juan as reported by Severn: 'How horrible an example of
human nature is this man, who has no pleasure left him but to
gloat over and jeer, at the most awful incidents of life. . . .'[1]

---

[1] Footnote to Keats's letter of 24 October 1820, written from on board the
Maria Crowther. A fortnight earlier we find Byron writing to John Murray in
disgust at 'Johnny Keats's *p-ss a bed* poetry . . . ' He wants to read no more: 'No
more Keats, I entreat:—flay him alive; if some of you don't, I must skin him myself:
there is no bearing the drivelling idiotism of the Mankin.' Previous outbursts
had been frequent, largely provoked by Keats's supposed attack on Pope. On
hearing of Keats's death Byron expressed, sincerely I think, his regret, and
acknowledged the greatness of *Hyperion*.

Whatever credit this remark does to the goodness of Keats's heart, it is naïve: it has understood Byron's richly antithetical technique as little as the reviewers of 1917 grasped the clashing moods of Eliot's *Prufrock*. But the words are reported only; and if they derive from Keats, it is a sick Keats. They may be genuine enough: indeed, we can follow in the letters the steady process of dethronization from October 1817 to October 1820. And what is interesting is to guess at the reasons for this depreciation. They are not as simple as they might seem.

An obvious reason, as Mr Robert Gittings has noted in his fascinating *John Keats: The Living Year*, was jealousy. Byron's poems sell: his own don't. Byron is a lord, handsome, rich, famous: Keats is unknown. Mild fun is poked at 'superfine rich or noble poets—ut Byron', in a letter of 21 September 1818: but Keats includes himself in the satire: 'common ut egomet'. In the next month he quotes a verse of Hunt's, with approbation, as Byron's:

> I am free from Men of Pleasure's cares,
> By dint of feelings far more deep than theirs.[1]

In December Byron is acknowledged as one of the 'three literary Kings' of 'our Time'; a slight touch of spleen is evident here, and spreads in the long journal-letter of February–April 1819 to George and Georgiana Keats. 'There is a Poem from Rogers dead born—and another Satire is expected from Byron call'd Don Giovanni.' A little later he is discussing literary sales. 'I was surprised to hear from Taylor the amount of Murray the Booksellers last sale—what think you of £25,000? He sold 4000 copies of Lord Byron.' Poor Keats! what news has he to give of his own sales? We turn the page, and are not surprised to read that 'Lord Byron cuts a figure—but he is not figurative'. Two months later, in the same letter, he tells the story of Reynolds's brilliant parody of *Peter Bell*, and adds: 'It would be just as well to trounce Lord Byron in the same manner. I am still at a stand in versifying —I cannot do it yet with any pleasure. . . .'

---

[1] To George and Georgiana Keats (*Letters*, 233).

In February 1818 it had been a great compliment to Reynolds's letter that it 'gave [Keats] more pleasure than will the 4th Book of Childe Harold.'[1] Those were early days: the fate of *Endymion* had not yet been decided by the *Quarterly* reviewers. How different is his reception of *Don Juan* in September 1819! His obtuse guardian Abbey laughs at his delusions that he is a poet but reads him some passages 'from Don Juan (Lord Byron's latest flash poem) and particularly against literary ambition'. Poets are fools, of course; but Lord Byron makes money by his poetry (the public are greater fools); and so 'the fellow says true things now and then. . .'. Keats goes home deflated. A few pages later (we are midway in the September journal-letter to his brother and sister-in-law) we read: 'You speak of Lord Byron and me' (et tu, Brute?) '—There is this great difference between us. He describes what he sees—I describe what I imagine. Mine is the hardest task.'

The hardest task—yes. And the least rewarding of tasks if, as in so much of *Endymion*, the imagination is exercised in fields where the thing seen and known is indispensable. Keats *had* to write *Endymion*, it was an excellent thing that he did write it; and everything that he says about his own immaturity, 'mawkishness', 'failure in a great object', and so on, is perfectly justified. He took the plunge, and he sounded the depths. That is not all, of course. He failed as far as the public was concerned, which did not matter very much; if he had retained his health, it would have come less and less to matter as the masterpieces of 1818 flowed from his pen. He succeeded as far as he himself was concerned. He finished his poem, and in doing so he worked out lines of thought and 'sensations' that had to be worked out before he could go on to his flowering. He also wrote a good deal of superb poetry: there are passages in *Endymion* which we would be willing to lose for no verse of Keats's outside the final Odes.

But he failed: and he failed, above all, in a field that was crucial to him as he wrote *Endymion*; that came to be more crucial to him as he went on to write the later narrative poems. It is the field

---

[1] Which came out on 28 April 1818.

that he tried, agonizingly, to escape from in the 'abstractions' of *Hyperion*, and that he could not escape from: so that, in *Isabella* and *St Agnes* and above all *Lamia*, he turns and stands at bay. He failed in the degree that his poem is a sexual poem. And that, of course, it very decidedly is. I have already suggested that Keats would have been wise to choose another vehicle for his 'vast idea' than the Endymion myth; but the hindsight is purely academic. Keats, being Keats, did not choose: he followed his daimon. And he wrote about some things he had very little experience of. In particular, about romantic love.

And here, I think, we have another reason for his resentment against Byron. *Manfred* is a sexual poem; but the sexual theme is managed with considerable skill—with, indeed, a diabolical reticence. Keats was quite incapable of this reticence. The *undercurrent* in Manfred is sexual; the surface forces are magical, intellectual, philosophical. The sexual is kept where it belongs, in the unconscious; it comes to the surface only at the crises of the poem. And comes, then, with what a wealth of meaning, with how massive an impact! The same is true of Byron's other major poems. Whatever our final judgment of them, they are triumphs of aplomb. Now Keats, I suspect, saw and resented this. He felt that his powers were greater than Byron's, his aims more serious, his intuition deeper: and yet . . . and yet . . . *There* were *Childe Harold* and *Manfred* and *Don Juan*, on the one hand; *here* was *Endymion* on the other: the assured, the complete, the successful poem, over against the 'feverish attempt'. And the cause of the fever, the spoiler of the attempt? Keats rightly put his finger on 'great inexperience'.[1] And with Byron in mind, I think he might have added to that phrase the adjective 'sexual'.

I have no direct evidence of this. Byron was known, of course, as an erotic poet; the success of his poetry was in some degree a *succès de scandale*. He stared where no one stared, and dared where no one dared, to use Keats's phrases from *Daisy's Song* (a copy of verses which would have moved Byron, if he had known them, to

---

[1] Preface to *Endymion*.

choose a direr epithet for Keats than the one he used to Murray).[1]
Keats's sexual adventures seem to have been timid, sporadic, and
uniformly disastrous. There is a schoolboy's dabbling with bawdry
in his letters and minor verse which is unpleasant; a peeping Tom
element mars the tone of even his major poems. Here we have a
source, glossed over by his commentators, of certain of his deficiencies. He 'did not know enough': the phrase is Arnold's,
turned to an un-Arnoldian purpose.

He did not know enough, and Lord Byron, perhaps, knew
too much. Keats's jealousy of Byron was more than professional
jealousy. It was the envy of the fumbling for the accomplished
amorist. What rankled most, perhaps, was that the successful
amorist was also the successful poet, and that success in the one
field had contributed so much to success in the other. 'You see
what it is', he comments bitterly in February 1819 (journal-letter
to George and Georgiana Keats) 'to be under six foot and not a
lord'. The old resentment at his diminutive stature (and we remember Byron's disdainful 'Mankin') combines with a growing
resentment at Byron's rank. The dice are loaded; Keats will come
more and more to ask himself whether it is worth while going on
with the game.

However all this may be, the autumn of 1817 is a turning-point
in Keats's life and temperament as well as in his art. A certain
serenity fades from his poetry; his letters take on a distraught, a
feverish tone. He finds a companion in Charles Armitage Brown:
hardly an improvement on Benjamin Bailey, who is dropped a little
later. Together they keep house, visit the North and Chichester,
write *Otho the Great*. It is a closer intimacy than any Keats had
known before; in many ways it is an unfortunate one. I am not
suggesting that Brown's influence went very deep. His attraction
for Keats was without doubt the attraction of plain, undemanding
good-fellowship; he gave Keats the sympathy and companionship
he needed after Tom's death; and he gave him a home. Above all,

---

[1] See footnote to p. 198, above. De Selincourt remarks (*The Poems of John
Keats*, p. 599): 'Peculiarly offensive is the word *stare* which is continually introduced in the poet's early love scenes.'

he brought no memories with him. He was a fresh start.[1] But there were no depths in him to respond to depths; Keats's inner loneliness grows and grows. We feel it in the poems, in *Lamia* and the verses from Scotland: and we feel it in the letters. It is a new Keats who speaks now: a Keats very different indeed from the eager young man who wrote home to his brothers on 16 April 1817, the first day of an earlier tour: 'I am safe at Southampton . . .'

[*Endymion*, Book IV (end of October–December 1817—the whole poem revised and completed 19 March 1818)]

---

[1] The acquaintance was 'of two years standing' in March 1819 (*Letters*, 287), but as Dilke writes to Severn in 1841 (*K.C.*, II, 104): 'it was not till long after they had met & met often, that Brown became even friendly & familiar with him'.

III

THE SWEET AND BITTER WORLD

Chapter Eleven

THE LOVE OF GOOD AND ILL

The Spirit of the Clouds when passing eastwards through the expanse
of Air happened to fall in with the Vital Principle. The latter was slapping his ribs and hopping about; whereupon the Spirit of the Clouds
said, 'Who are you, old man, and what are you doing here?'

'Strolling!' replied the Vital Principle, without stopping.

'I want to *know* something,' continued the Spirit of the Clouds.

'Ugh!' uttered the Vital Principle, in a tone of disapprobation.

'The relationship of heaven and earth is out of harmony,' said the
Spirit of the Clouds; 'the six influences do not combine, and the four
seasons are no longer regular. I desire to blend the six influences so
as to nourish all living beings. What am I to do?'

'I don't know!' cried the Vital Principle, shaking his head, while
still slapping his ribs and hopping about; 'I don't know!'

THE BOOK OF CHUANG TZǓ, chapter XI, 'On Letting Alone'.

'I AM safe at Southampton', Keats begins his 15 April 1817
letter to his brothers. It is among the earliest of his letters
that have survived to us, and one of the most precious.
Spontaneity, freshness, unawareness—all the virtues we have admired in Keats's early poetry—are in evidence. He has come down
from London by coach, a cold exhausting journey, but he is in
high spirits; little sleep during the night, but his faculty for acute
observation has been active as ever, and with it his delight in
things seen—in the kaleidoscopic show of wayside affairs visible
from the coach windows. These detached snapshots seem to have
made a sharper impression on him than anything offered by the
continuous screen-play of everyday experience. *Not to know* the
context of each sharply-etched scene was in itself a joy:

I am safe at Southampton—after having ridden three stages outside
and the rest in for it began to be very cold. I did not know the Names
of any of the Towns I passed through all I can tell you is that some-

times I saw dusty Hedges sometimes Ponds—then nothing—then a
little Wood with trees look you like Launce's Sister "as white as a Lilly
and as small as a Wand["]—then came houses which died away into a
few straggling Barns then came hedge trees aforesaid again. As the
Lamp light crept along the following things were discovered. "long
heath brown furze"—Hurdles here and there half a Mile—Park
palings when the Windows of a House were always discovered by
reflection—One Nymph of Fountain *N.B.* *Stone*—lopped Trees—
Cow ruminating—ditto Donkey—Man and Woman going gingerly
along—William seeing his Sisters over the Heath—John waiting with
a Lanthen for his Mistress—Barbers Pole—Docter's Shop—However
after having had my fill of these I popped my Head out just as it
began to Dawn—*N.B.* *this tuesday Morn saw the Sun rise*—of which
I shall say nothing at present [1]—I felt rather lonely this Morning
at breakfast so I went and unbox'd a Shakspeare—"Here's my Comfort"—

Not a very impressive collection of sights: nothing there to bring
joy, one would say. But the items don't matter: what matters is
the capturing and letting go of the discrete impression, without
selection, without curiosity, without evaluation.[2] The whole letter
is written in a tone almost of drunkenness—an intoxication brought
on by complete passivity to the stream of events.

Now that is the early Keats, the Keats of the innocent eye who is
content to stroll by himself like the Vital Principle, slapping his
ribs and confessing delightedly, 'I don't know!' He recognizes the
contraries as they pass before his eye in the continuous flow of
events; he welcomes them, even, but he cannot be said to accept
them, for they are not yet proven on his pulses. He remains detached, in the no-knowledge of ignorance. His vision is graphic,

---

[1] He says something about it in Book I of *Endymion*, which he was to begin in
the next few days:

> Man's voice was on the mountains; and the mass
> Of nature's lives and wonders puls'd tenfold,
> To feel this sunrise and its glories old   (lines 104–6)

[2] A very similar series of impressions is recorded in a letter to Fanny Keats of
8 February 1820, from his sickbed at Wentworth Place; but now it is Keats who
is immobile, and the flow of life is passing him by.

not penetrating; the human figures in his field are few, and pose ornamentally, completing a pattern, rather than vitally, participating in a process.

It is a precious thing, this detached, pure vision; it is an essential for the young artist, and there is no valid development save from it. Keats had the vision, and he foresaw, clearly enough, the development; though perhaps he couldn't see how soon and how intimately he was to know 'the agony, the strife Of human hearts'. Nor with what concentrated fury they were to invade his serenity. The poems and letters we are now to study are eloquent of his distress in the period immediately following the publication—and the failure—of *Endymion*. The fragment of a letter which I have cited above will serve us as a touchstone, by which we may evaluate the letters and poems of the Scottish tour. The 1817 letter was written in a spirit of breathless expectation—the eagerness of a young poet just about to embark on his first major work. Keats is alone—but no matter, he is happy, and he is sustained by the warmth of his brothers' affection and interest. And when he feels lonely, out comes Shakespeare: 'Here's my comfort.' It is a very different situation that confronts him in June 1818. *Endymion* is finished, but he is conscious that it is a failure. His family circle has broken up; George and Georgiana have left for an uncertain future in America. Tom is desperately ill. Sexual problems are already pressing upon him. He leaves for the Lakes and Scotland, with the amiable but coarse-grained Brown for a companion; and he carries a pocket Dante with him. The stream of letters soon begins, but the Keats who writes them is no longer the Keats of April 1817. 'Our friends say I have altered completely', he will tell George in September, '—am not the same person.' And he dates the change from George's departure. His brother, twelve years later, confirms this: 'When I returned in 1820 he was not the same being. . . .'[1]

The change imports a deepening and a coarsening. There are sillinesses and unpleasantries in the Scottish letters, and some dirty

---

[1] Letter to C. W. Dilke, 7 May 1830 (*K.C.*, I, 328).

poems; Keats's chameleon mind reflects the muddy hues of Charles Brown's. There are also passages of extraordinary perception; the chameleon mind reflects the massive integrity of mountains. 'Great things are done when men and mountains meet', and this is a portentous meeting.[1] The second of Wordsworth's 'two voices' now begins to sound authentically in Keats, as the first sounded after the Margate visit. The contrast is interesting. The sea was for Keats the symbol of unlimited potentialities in nature: the fecundity and the mystery of non-human existence. The sky, we saw earlier, was the eikon of eternity: the abstract void from which principles move into manifestation. Mountains, now—and this is anticipated in *Endymion's* 'Man's voice was on the mountains' —are cognized in Blakean terms: in intimate relationship, that is, with man. They are, in fact, *magnified men*: and this notion is given definite if farcical shape in the lines beginning 'Upon my life Sir Nevis I am piqued . . .'.

This mountain perception goes along with an ever-deepening insight into suffering. The events of the past few months have brought Keats up against life's little ironies in their keenest form: he has felt 'the hateful siege of contraries' in the antithesis of genius and neglect, aspiration and capacity, vision and incompleteness, youth and sickness, immortal longings and death. He goes to Scotland with Brown to forget: but he cannot forget. The mountains *make* him forget, he says; but in saying it he demonstrates the opposite.[2] Note how, in his first letter to Tom (from Windermere,

---

[1] 'I cannot forget the joy, the rapture of my friend when he suddenly, and for the first time, became sensible to the full effect of mountain scenery', Brown wrote 23 years later (*K.C.*, II, 61). But there was another side to the picture, stressed by Keats himself in the *Lines Written in the Highlands*:

> . . . room is there for a prayer
> That man may never lose his mind on mountains black and bare.

[2] The sonnet he 'wrote on the top of Ben Nevis' ends with these revealing lines:

> Here are the craggy Stones beneath my feet;
> Thus much I know, that a poor witless elf
> I tread on them; that all my eye doth meet
> Is mist and Crag—not only on this height
> But in the world of thought and mental might—

26 June) the sweet and bitter world is exposed in its basic anti-
nomies:

> There are many disfigurements to this Lake—not in the way of land
> or water. No; the two views we have had of it are of the most noble
> tenderness—they can never fade away—they make one forget the
> divisions of life; age, youth, poverty and riches; and refine one's
> sensual vision[1] into a sort of north star which can never cease to
> be open lidded and stedfast over the wonders of the Great Power. The
> disfigurement I mean is the miasma of London. I do suppose it
> contaminated with bucks and soldiers—and hatband ignorance. . . .
> Lord Wordsworth, instead of being in retirement, has himself and
> his house full in the thick of fashionable visitors quite convenient to
> be pointed at all the summer long.

That is far indeed from the spirit of the 1817 letters, which—
mark—did not overlook the intrusive human element ('O Isle
spoilt by the Mil*a*tary!')[2] but accepted it in a mood of toleration:
'I must in honesty however confess that I did not feel very sorry
at the idea of the Women being a little profligate. . . .' What we
find now, a year later, is savage disapproval, and resentment
(was Wordsworth's comment on the Hymn to Pan, 'A pretty
piece of Paganism', still rankling?).

We begin then, in these letters, with a *contrast* of men and
mountains. But Keats could not stop there. Resentment soon
vanished in face of sublimity; and we get a new perception:

> What astonishes me more than anything is the tone, the colouring . . .
> or, if I may say so, the intellect, the countenance of such places. The
> space, the magnitude of mountains and waterfalls are well imagined
> before one sees them; but this countenance or intellectual tone must
> surpass every imagination and defy any remembrance. I shall learn
> poetry here and shall henceforth write more than ever, for the abs-
> tract endeavour of being able to add a mite to that mass of beauty
> which is harvested from these grand materials, by the finest spirits,

---

[1] 'To enlarge my vision' was the anticipation of the 9 April letter to Reynolds:
the tour was to be a 'going wonder-ways'.

[2] Keats is quoting a complaint he found scratched on a window-pane.

and put into etherial existence for the relish of one's fellows. I cannot
think with Hazlitt that these scenes make a man appear little. I
never forgot my stature[1] so completely. I live in the eye; and my
imagination, surpassed, is at rest.

There is no division of man's life from nature's; an earlier letter[2]
declares that 'Scenery is fine—but human nature is finer. The
Sward is richer for the tread of a real, nervous english foot—the
eagle's nest is finer for the Mountaineer has look'd into it.' And the
phrase 'the Life of Man is like a great Mountain' strikes a suddenly
serious note in the nonsense of the 5 September 1817 letter to the
Reynolds sisters.

In the letters from Scotland we see his interest in form deepening: shapes inanimate and human are described, not for the sake
of description, for 'descriptions are bad at all times',[3] but for
what may be called their physiognomical appeal. And above
all for their relationships. Severn tells us[4] how on their walks
together

> nothing escaped him, the song of a bird and the undernote of res-
> ponse from covert or hedge, the rustle of some animal, the changing
> of the green and brown lights and furtive shadows, the motions of
> the wind—just how it took certain tall flowers and plants—and the
> wayfaring of the clouds: even the features and gestures of passing
> tramps, the colour of one woman's hair, the smile on one child's face,
> the furtive animalism below the deceptive humanity in many of the
> vagrants.

That is the Chaucerian or Hogarthian observation, but it is
something more; in 'the motions of the wind—just how it
took certain tall flowers and plants' we mark Keats's absorbed
interest in what we shall come to recognize, in a later analysis, as
'phase-beauty'.

---

[1] Of which he was normally so conscious.

[2] To Bailey, 13 March 1818, from Teignmouth.

[3] This sentence follows immediately upon the long passage quoted above from
the June 1818 letter.

[4] William Sharp, *Life and Letters of Joseph Severn.*

Meanwhile, the letters he wrote on his Scottish tour record, *inter alia*, his fascination by the physiognomy of 'animalism'. A flying visit to Ireland provides him with this fine specimen:

> a squalid old Woman [sitting] squat like an ape half starved from a scarcity of Biscuit in its passage from Madagascar to the cape—with a pipe in her mouth and looking out with a round-eyed skinny lidded inanity—with a sort of horizontal idiotic movement of her head—squab and lean she sat and puff'd out the smoke while two ragged tattered Girls carried her along. What a thing would be a history of her life and sensations![1]

He finds a new interest in each place he visits. 'This is what I like better than scenery. I fear our continued moving from place to place, will prevent our becoming learned in village affairs; we are mere creatures of Rivers, Lakes, and Mountains.' But he makes good use of such opportunities as he has.[2] He studies the country folk; gives a pen-portrait of one Richard Bradshaw, 'a notorious tippler', who 'stood in the shape of a 3 and ballanced himself as well as he could saying with his nose right in Mr Brown's face "Do yo-u sell Spect-ta-cles?"'; lampoons the 'mahogany faced old Jackass who knew Burns'. Over against these human caricatures, yet not divorced from them, stand the majestic shapes of lake and mountain. Ailsa Rock moves him to a sonnet, prefaced by this characteristically personal note: 'In a little time I descried in the Sea Ailsa Rock 940 feet high—it was 15 Miles distant and seemed close upon us—The effect of ailsa with the peculiar perspective of the Sea in connection with the ground we stood on, and the misty rain then falling gave me a complete Idea of a deluge. Ailsa struck me very suddenly—really I was a little alarmed. . . .'[3] Fingal's Cave is even more carefully described, and

---

[1] *Letters*, 173.

[2] 'His calling', Sir Charles Sherrington writes in *Man on his Nature*, 'has always led [the physician] to view Nature with Man as its central interest'—words which may well be applied to Keats. And not all is caricature in the Scottish letters: at Ireby 'there was as fine a row of boys and girls as you ever saw, some beautiful faces, and one exquisite mouth' (*Letters*, 162).

[3] *Letters*, 180. The sonnet is discussed below, p. 350.

we may suppose that memories of its 'solemnity and grandeur' passed into his later presentation of the Titans' valley in *Hyperion*.

The picture of Keats that emerges from his own writings concerns us here only to the extent that it illustrates the limited subject of this book. But to this extent it does concern us; for 'proof on the pulses' must be for us, as it was for Keats, the criterion of depth in understanding. How far, then, taking the Scottish tour letters as our starting-point, can we find the themes of growth and form reflected in the patterns, embodied in the processes, of his life? To what extent does the concept of space enter into his daily living in its complexity, its hopes and struggles? 'A man's life of any worth is a continual allegory,' he declares in a letter to George and Georgiana Keats of February–May 1819, 'and very few eyes can see the mystery of his life—a life like the scriptures, figurative—which such people[1] can no more make out than they can the hebrew Bible.[2] Lord Byron cuts a figure—but he is not figurative—Shakespeare led a life of allegory: his works are the comment on it.'[3]

We know quite a lot about Keats's life, but it wasn't long enough for us to trace the allegory. An allegory needs space to unfold in. But we can see that it was symbolical. The elements of his art penetrate his life, transmute it, and are transmuted by it. His attitude is receptive, non-assertive. 'The Genius of Poetry must work out its own salvation in a man: It cannot be matured by law and precept, but by sensation & watchfulness in itself', he remarks in a letter of 9 October 1818 to J. A. Hessey: 'That which is creative must create itself.' Now this is the very principle of growth. And for this principle to work itself out in Keats, whether

---

[1] As Benjamin Bailey, who he thought had behaved shabbily to Marianne Reynolds.

[2] By which he means the Old Testament. Did he, like Blake, read the Bible 'in its diabolical sense'? Traces of his Old Testament reading abound; and at least one book of the New Testament, *Revelation*, furnished him with a stock of imagery.

[3] Cf. also his remark on Burns: 'We can see horribly clear in the works of such a Man his whole life, as if we were God's spies' (*Letters*, 177).

in his personal inner life or in the manifestation of that life in
actions or poems, certain conditions were necessary. They are
the conditions which affect all untrammelled growth, in man or
beast or plant; and they were largely denied to Keats. He needed
clear space and he needed air—in his case, dry sunny air. He needed
leisure and solitude. For most of his short life these elementary
necessities were withheld from him. Now and again, for a brief
interval, he found them; and the delight in finding them breaks
through in his poems and letters. Leaving the Isle of Wight for
Winchester (where the vastness of the cathedral was a great joy
to him) he writes to Fanny Brawne (16 August 1819): 'The little
coffin of a room at Shanklin is changed for a large room, where
I can promenade at my pleasure. . . .' The dry Winchester climate
suits him admirably: 'The delightful Weather we have had for
two Months is the highest gratification I could receive—no chill'd
red noses—no shivering—but fair atmosphere to think in—*a clean
towel mark'd with the mangle*[1] and a basin of clear Water to drench
one's face with ten times a day: no need of much exercize—a
Mile a day being quite sufficient. My greatest regret is that I have
not been well enough to bathe though I have been two Months
by the sea side and live now close to delicious bathing—Still I
enjoy the Weather I adore fine Weather as the greatest blessing
I can have.' The best country to live in, he thinks, is 'a dry,
gravelly, barren, elevated country open to the currents of air and
such a place is generally furnish'd with the finest springs'.[2]

It is hard luck, we may think, if a great poet enjoying a holiday
has nothing more exciting to write home about than a clean
towel and a basin of cold water; but that was precisely Keats's
hard luck in life. His surroundings in London, and even in Shanklin,
were cramped and stuffy. We know how he felt for others in like

---

[1] My italics, emphasizing the formal visual impression.
[2] To John Taylor, 5 September 1819. Keats's personal observation, but I think
he was also remembering Hippocrates' *Airs Waters Places*. In *Letters*, 131, he
writes: 'It is impossible to live in a country which is continually under hatches.
Who would live in the Region of Mists, Game Laws, indemnity Bills &c when
there is such a place as Italy?'

condition: his letter of 21 February 1818 pictures his sick friend
Reynolds living 'in the worst place in the world for amendment,
among the strife of women's tongues, in a hot and parch'd room'.[1]
Born to be an eagle, to traverse great spaces, Keats was condemned
to live the life of an owl. Of course he fought against the sentence.
At times there came the temptation 'to build a sort of mental
Cottage of feelings quiet and pleasant—to have a sort of Philosophical Back Garden, and cheerful holiday-keeping front one—
but Alas! this never can be: for as the material Cottager knows
there are such places as france and Italy and the Andes and the
Burning Mountains—so the spiritual Cottager has knowledge of
the terra semi incognita of things unearthly; and cannot for his
Life, keep in the check rein. . . .'[2]

The letters from which I have culled these last passages belong
to a period—August 1818 to October 1819—when Keats was
writing his most consummate poetry and withstanding the most
dreadful siege of contraries that ever poet has had to withstand.
The Scottish tour was interrupted in mid-August; he came home
to find Tom dying, and the end came on December 1st. He himself is ill, and tired; but by September he is at work on *Hyperion*.
He finds an attack on the Cockney School of poets in the August
number of *Blackwood's*; the *Quarterly*'s attack on *Endymion* follows
on about the 27th. Keats is living with Brown at Wentworth
Place, next door to the Brawnes,[3] from 1 December 1818
to 20 January 1819; he spends the rest of January and the first
three days of February at Chichester and Bedhampton; on the
fourth he is back at Hampstead. He writes *The Eve of St Agnes*
while away from Hampstead; he writes *The Eve of St Mark*
between the 13th and 17th of the month after his return. *La Belle
Dame Sans Merci* belongs to April, as do *Psyche* and the *Grecian*

---

[1] Which anticipates in its turn the horror of Keats's own plight in the cabin of
the *Maria Crowther* between 17 September and 1 November 1820.

[2] Letter of 24 March 1818 to James Rice.

[3] The weight of the evidence is in favour of November, not September, as
the date of his first meeting with Fanny.

Urn. The *Ode to a Nightingale* follows in May. In July he visits the Isle of Wight with James Rice; part I of *Lamia* is written, and (when Brown comes to join them) a beginning is made on *Otho the Great*. In August he moves with Brown to Winchester; the play is finished. September finds him working on *The Fall of Hyperion*, and *Lamia* is completed early in the same month. After a short visit to London he returns to Winchester and writes the *Ode to Autumn*.

During the whole of this period Keats was living under conditions of great strain. Creating works of astonishing richness and completion, he was himself the most tortured, the most divided of beings. The roots of his anguish are clear enough. There was deepening ill-health, frustrated ambition, uneasy passion for Fanny Brawne. The cottage metaphor in our last quotation is immensely significant. We have seen Keats as the poet of freedom, of great spaces, of indolent, eagle flight. Freedom is a passion with him: for this he renounces a career, faces poverty and scorn. And suddenly he finds himself in chains. He is obsessed, but not blinded. He errs, with Adam,

> Against his better reason, not deceiv'd,
> But fondly overcome by female charm.

The letters from now on debate a master theme: freedom versus domesticity, detachment versus obsession. But the theme is there already in the earlier letters, prompted by fear, not by experience: Keats foresees his doom. He is like Blake in his horror of 'the golden cage'. Friends marked this from an early period. 'I do not think that Love was a passion to which he would have condescended', Henry Stephens declares in the reminiscences he wrote in 1847.[1] Reading the letters, we agree: there is no dearth of satire against women, marriage, love. But the acidity of the satire is an index of the underlying uneasiness, the concern. 'The man who ridicules romance is the most romantic of Men', Keats admits in a letter of February–May 1819 to his brother and sister-

---

[1] Letter to G. F. Mathew, March 1847 (*K.C.*, II, 210). Stephens had been a fellow-student of Keats at Guy's Hospital.

in-law. He moved in a more sentimental world than Blake's, and his own temperament made Blake's clear-sighted view of the sex relationship impossible for him. His own temperament, and the conventions of his age, and the realities and unrealities of his experience. The realities include the wards of Guy's and the streets of the metropolis; the unrealities, Spenser's Una, Shakespeare's Imogen, 'pure goddesses' moving through a schoolboy's dreams.

We have the right to pry into a poet's private affairs only in so far as our prying helps us to understand his poetry. The exceptionally painful features of Keats's emotional life should prove an effective deterrent to over-curiosity. But in considering a life so 'allegorical' as Keats's, so closely integrated with his art, and in studying that art in its most vital aspects of growth and form—terms which are, indeed, less 'aspects' than complementary wholes—we cannot overlook 'the sexual strife'. For it is on this plane that the complementary wholes identify themselves formidably with the Yin and the Yang, with the ultimate pairs of opposites; and Keats's 'sexual strife' was 'woven to dreams' in the group of poems which begins with *Isabella* and ends with *Lamia*, poems which we shall study in the following pages.

In considering these poems, which are narratives of human love, we shall make use of the distinction *romantic/biological*. We were close to this distinction in the course of our study of *Endymion* and the poems immediately preceding *Endymion*: and we have seen that it can be grasped, on this plane, as an opposition between our original terms of growth and form. For the romantic picture of the sexual relation is pre-eminently the formal one: it is stereotyped, and imposes a pattern on a radically chaotic situation. The biological approach, which came naturally to Keats not only as a student of medicine but also as a highly sensual man and poet, achieves no pattern but unfolds a process. It includes growth, flowering and fruition. Its beauty lies not in the surfaces, which may be unæsthetic or banal, but in the depths. There is, right to the end, a conflict in Keats between these two apprehensions. He starts off, as a schoolboy, with the romantic, the Spenserian; from that he graduates, as a medical student, to

the crudely biological; a prolonged reading of Shakespeare initiates him, I believe, to the subtly biological; his passion for Fanny
Brawne throws him back again to the romantic. That is the broad
picture. It needs, of course, a good deal of shading in. But that
it is correct enough in its outlines is clear, I think, from a letter
to Benjamin Bailey written in July 1818—during the Scottish
tour, and after the departure of brother George and his young
bride for America.

> I am certain I have not a right feeling towards Women—at this
> moment I am striving to be just to them but I cannot—Is it because
> they fall so far beneath my Boyish imagination? When I was a
> Schoolboy I thought a fair Woman a pure Goddess, my mind was a
> soft nest in which some one of them slept, though she knew it not[1]
> —I have no right to expect more than their reality. I thought them
> etherial above Men—I find them perhaps equal—great by comparison
> is very small. . . . Is it not extraordinary? When among Men I have
> no evil thoughts, no malice, no spleen—I feel free to speak or to be
> silent—I can listen and from every one I can learn—my hands are in
> my pockets I am free from all suspicion and comfortable. When I am
> among Women I have evil thoughts, malice spleen—I cannot speak
> or be silent—I am full of Suspicions and therefore listen to nothing—
> I am in a hurry to be gone. . . .

Women, in short, upset his detachment, rouse his desire and make
him feel a fool. How will he resolve his dilemma? A letter written
three months later to his brother and sister-in-law gives one answer:

> . . . I hope I shall never marry. Though the most beautiful Creature
> were waiting for me at the end of a Journey or a Walk; though the
> carpet were of Silk, the Curtains of the morning Clouds; the chairs
> and Sofa stuffed with Cygnet's down; the food Manna, the Wine
> beyond Claret, the Window opening on Winander mere, I should
> not feel—or rather my Happiness would not be so fine, as my Soli-
> tude is sublime. Then instead of what I have described, there is a
> Sublimity to welcome me home. The roaring of the wind is my wife
> and the Stars through the window pane are my Children. The mighty

---

[1] Cf. the three very early sonnets: 'Woman! when I behold thee . . .'; 'Light
feet, dark violet eyes . . .'; 'Ah! who can e'er forget so fair a being?' printed in
Poems 1817.

abstract Idea I have of Beauty in all things stifles the more divided and minute domestic happiness—an amiable wife and sweet Children I contemplate as a part of that Beauty—but I must have a thousand of those beautiful particles to fill up my heart. I feel more and more every day, as my imagination strengthens, that I do not live in this world alone but in a thousand worlds.[1]

A little after these words were written Keats met Fanny Brawne. What he felt for her (at first sight, he tells her in a letter written when he was dying) upset his resolve to remain unmarried, but not his perception that love is 'a cloying treacle'.[2] The bitterness is there in a letter he wrote to her on 1 July 1819 from Shanklin.

I do not know how elastic my spirit might be, what pleasure I might have in living here and breathing and wandering as free as a stag about this beautiful Coast if the remembrance of you did not weigh so upon me. I have never known any unalloy'd Happiness for many days together: the death or sickness of some one has always spoilt my hours—and now when none such troubles oppress me, it is you must confess very hard that another sort of pain should haunt me. Ask yourself my love whether you are not very cruel to have so entrammelled me, so destroyed my freedom.

Remarkable sentiments, these, from a young man in love whose love has not been rejected. A normal love affair, even in its earlier and more uncertain stages, brings with it a sense of wider liberty, of heightened response, of increased potentialities. Not so to Keats. For while these are good things, they depend, basically, upon an illusion—a beneficent illusion, certainly, but none the less an illusion—the belief in the extraordinary qualities and virtues of the beloved. And Keats, because he was a poet, potentially at least, of the order of Chaucer and Blake and Shakespeare, saw through the illusion while submitting to it. Keats was capable, immensely capable, of a fulfilling union with a woman on the plane of reality; but such a relationship was made very difficult for him by the circumstances of his life and indeed of his times. Nor can we ignore, here, the physiological and emotional consequences of his disease.

---

[1] *Letters*, 239–40.   [2] Letter to John Taylor, 23 August 1819.

In those wide spaces of the mind where Keats was still at liberty (for one can be emotionally chained while intellectually free) there was no confusion. He saw clearly to the end. He sweeps away Fanny's nonsense of 'pure love' with: 'Why may I not speak of your Beauty, since without that I could never have lov'd you.' Of course it is her beauty, her physical beauty, that he loves in the first place; and, as he wrote in that terrible penultimate letter to Brown, when approaching death shattered reticence: 'I should have had her when I was in health, and I should have remained well.' Nothing indeed is more probable than that Fanny Brawne was the right girl for Keats, and that possession of her might have turned the tide for him. 'For I am not', he declares in a letter to her of 5–6 August 1819, 'one of the Paladins of old who lived upon water grass and smiles for years together.' He did not have her, and a great Prince lay in prison. But even had he succeeded in winning her, there were dangers in marriage of which he was well aware. The 'cottage of the mind' so firmly rejected in his letter to John Taylor materializes as 'the love in a hut' of *Lamia*. In the letter from Shanklin quoted above, he dangles before her what may seem to us—and would certainly seem to her—the dubious inducement of undomesticated bliss:

> We might spend a pleasant year at Berne or Zurich—if it should please Venus to hear my 'Beseech thee to hear us O Goddess'. And if she should hear god forbid we should what people call, *settle*—turn into a pond, a stagnant Lethe—a vile crescent, row or buildings. Better be imprudent moveables than prudent fixtures. Open my Mouth at the Street door like the Lion's head at Venice to receive hateful cards Letters messages. Go out and wither at tea-parties; freeze at dinners; bake at dances, simmer at routs. No my love, trust yourself to me and I will find you nobler amusements, fortune favouring.

Alas poor Keats! nobler amusements can have held small appeal for Fanny in the year 1819: tea-parties, dances and routs were all her delight. This he would have had to put up with, for a year or two at least. And, in his clearer moments, Keats was well aware of this. In ignoring the facts, he was forgetting his own wise remark

about women: 'I have no right to expect more than their reality'.
He was creating what Blake would have called 'a delusive feminine
shadow', a wish-fulfilling substitute for the real Fanny; and he
got no solid satisfaction from it. Fanny's letters in reply become
increasingly unrewarding; Keats plunges deeper into despair,
seeks refuge in the 'abstractions' of *Lamia*. For the moment he
abdicates, if only for the moment, his own kingdom—the kingdom of the free, the detached, of God's birds.

In the bulk of the letters to Fanny Brawne—letters far more
emotional, more hysterical even, than any I have quoted—we
watch passion warping a sensibility. We shall not go on watching: fortunately it is not our business. But we must ask this question finally: How far, if at all, did this deformation in the passional
sphere spill over into the social sphere, the sphere of detached
awareness which held our interest at the beginning of this chapter,
and which includes the relation of friendship? What damage, if
any, was done here?

The answer is that a good deal of damage was done; and the
cynicisms of *Lamia* and *The Cap and Bells*, the 'abstractions' of
Hyperion, bear witness to its extent. The Keats of the Scottish
tour, the Chaucerian and Shakespearian observer with his gusto
for the variety of human behaviour, for the oddities of human
growth, disappears. Misanthropy breaks in. The tolerance of the
earlier Keats—the Keats who saw himself so naturally as a peace-
maker, a reconciler of parted friends—is replaced by aversion from
society. Keats was a lover of men because he asked nothing from
them, made no demands of reformation. 'There is no altering a
Man's nature', he writes in a letter of October 1817 to Bailey.
'Men should bear with each other', he remarks a few months later:

> Men should bear with each other—there lives not the Man who may
> not be cut up, aye hashed to pieces on his weakest side. The best of
> Men have but a portion of good in them—a kind of spiritual yeast
> in their frames which creates the ferment of existence—by which a
> Man is propell'd to act and strive and buffet with Circumstance.[1]

---

[1] Letter to Bailey, 23 January 1818.

If men *can* bear with each other, if they can approach each other on their strong rather than their weak sides, then there exists the possibility of fruitful growth in relationship. It is in their very differences that the possibility exists, for, as Blake had said, 'Without Contraries is no progression'. Keats puts it like this, in his finely humane, unfussed way:

> The Minds of Mortals are so different and bent on such diverse journeys that it may at first appear impossible for any common taste and fellowship to exist between two or three under these suppositions. It is however quite the contrary. Minds would leave each other in contrary directions, traverse each other in numberless points, and at last greet each other at the journey's end. An old Man and a child would talk together and the old Man be led on his path and the child left thinking. Man should not dispute or assert but whisper results to his neighbour and thus by every germ of spirit sucking the sap from mould ethereal[1] every human might become great, and Humanity instead of being a wide heath of Furze and Briars with here and there a remote Oak or Pine, would become a grand democracy of Forest Trees![2]

Now that was the healthy Keats, like Blake 'very fond of good company', delighted to do his share in keeping it good and sweet. All the letters gathered together in *The Keats Circle* (some of the most affectionate written many years after his death) testify to this Shakespearian sense of fellowship. But set against such testimony this disquieting passage from a letter to Reynolds of 24 August 1819, from Winchester:

> My own being which I know to be becomes of more consequence to me than the crowd of Shadows in the Shape of Man and women that inhabit a Kingdom. The Soul is a world of itself and has enough to do in its own home. Those whom I know already and who have grown as it were a part of myself I could not do without: but for the rest of Mankind they are as much a dream to me as Milton's Hierarchies. I think if I had a free and healthy and lasting organization of heart and Lungs—as strong as an ox's, so as to be able to bear unhurt

---

[1] 'Mould' in the gardener's sense: the vital growth metaphor is characteristic.
[2] Letter of 19 February 1818 to J. H. Reynolds.

the shock of extreme thought and sensation without weariness, I could pass my Life very nearly alone though it should last eighty years.

We hardly need the Milton reference to give us the clue: it is Satan's voice that speaks in 'The Soul is a world of itself and has enough to do in its own home'. The healthy Keats does not think in those terms. He lives in gusto, conciliating the opposites, being all things spontaneously and naturally to all men. 'I wish I knew always the humour my friends would be in at opening a letter of mine', he writes in July 1818 to Reynolds, 'to suit it to them as nearly as possible. I could always find an egg shell for Melancholy and as for Merriment a Witty humour will turn anything to Account—My head is sometimes in such a whirl in considering the million likings and antipathies of our Moments. . . .' The highly Rabelaisian episode of letter 34, the subtler farce of letter 57, show him manipulating a 'Memorable Fancy' along lines possible to none of his contemporaries except Blake. Here we have one of his high-roads to reality. Humour is superior to wit, he tells us in letter 32; and it is superior in its deeper penetration, its broader vision, its capacity for transmuting itself and becoming wisdom.

Let us then return, to complete this survey of 'Keats the man' under our peculiar terms of reference, to the unspoilt, the original Keats. In the verse letter to Reynolds of 25 March 1818 we saw him approaching the problem of evil by way of his fearful vision of the sea. In this experience he came to a knowledge of the contraries, but not to their conciliation. And their conciliation was peculiarly difficult for him as an artist. 'The web of our Life is of mingled Yarn', he quotes from *All's Well That Ends Well*.[1] He is

---

[1] In a letter of 8 October 1817 to Bailey; the full quotation (Act IV, sc. iii) is: 'The web of our life is of a mingled yarn, good and ill together: our virtues would be proud, if our faults whipped them not; and our crimes would despair, if they were not cherished by our virtues.' There is something of the same thought in the clown's riposte to Olivia in Act I, sc. v, of *Twelfth Night*: 'virtue that transgresses is but patched with sin; and sin that amends is but patched with virtue.'

ready to accept the weaving and to admire the fineness of the thread. But he claims the detachment of the artist; and it is here that his personal difficulties—the reconciling of the warp and woof within his own life pattern—really begin. The artist, who can and must identify himself with the goings-on of life around him, with the sparrow picking about the gravel, with the rock, the stream and the flower—is he also to identify himself with 'the agony, the strife of human hearts'—and if so, how can he keep his own 'identity', his detachment? This problem haunted Keats from the moment of the sea vision, and of course became increasingly acute in his last two years. He sought desperately for a solution, and found none. He thought of consulting Hazlitt about the best road he could take in philosophy (Hazlitt who, of all men, was the least capable of self-integration!); but he had the sense to know that any solution for him must lie in the realm of spontaneity and not of system.

The problem presented itself to Keats in the form of 'abstraction' versus 'affection'. 'Abstraction', or apathy (in the sense of disengagement), is the state in which, he tells Bailey, he sometimes finds himself for a whole week; in this condition he cannot feel 'the influence of a Passion or affection'. It is a state of detachment with no thought of happiness: 'I look not for it if it be not in the present hour—nothing startles me beyond the Moment. The setting Sun will always set me to rights—or if a Sparrow come before my Window I take part in its existence and pick about the Gravel', he remarks in a letter of 22 November 1817. 'Abstraction' includes, then, the element of empathy: in this state the subject-object antithesis is annihilated. But the sharing in existence does not include a sharing in affectivity: the 'existence' in question is the primordial being, non-individual and therefore non-affective, below the springs of joy and sorrow. Keats cannot understand this state, and it worries him. 'I begin to suspect myself and the genuineness of my feelings at other times.'

The problem is a problem for most artists. For Keats, vulnerable as he was in the generosity of his heart to human suffering, and in daily contact with misery in its most wretched form, the problem was acute. He was torn in two directions. His need as a creative artist was for 'abstraction', for that state of detachment from personal emotion which alone permits the maturing of the poetic idea, the perfecting of the poetic form; the demands made upon him by 'the agony, the strife of human hearts', by his duties as a brother, his needs as a lover, robbed him of his serenity and exposed him to every form of distraction. Desperately he casts round for a solution. Can it be found by relinquishing 'abstraction' (which is simple) for 'philosophy' (which is complex): by exchanging unawareness for awareness? This was the temptation to which Coleridge, for one, succumbed. In this same letter to Bailey of November 1817, Keats subtly debates the issue between 'the simple imaginative mind' (such as his own) and the 'complex mind' (such as Coleridge's):

> . . . the simple imaginative Mind may have its rewards in the repetition of its own silent Working coming continually on the Spirit with a fine Suddenness . . . sure this cannot be exactly the case with a complex Mind—one that is imaginative and at the same time careful of its fruits—who would exist partly on Sensation partly on thought —to whom it is necessary that years should bring the philosophic Mind.

The last allusion is directly to Wordsworth; of both him and Coleridge it might be said that their development displays an adulteration, a growing 'complexity': the concept superimposed on the sensation. The adulteration blunts the poetry, but it also serves to blunt the impact of experience, to provide an armour against 'the shock of extreme thought and sensation'.[1] Thus the temptation came to Keats. Should he sell the pearl of great price, he is asking himself in effect, and buy a set of more easily negotiable stones? 'I have been hovering for some time between an exquisite sense of the luxurious and a love for Philosophy' he writes to John Taylor in April 1818. 'Were I calculated for the former I should be glad—but as I am not I shall turn all my soul to the latter.' He didn't, of course. But that he should contemplate such a

---

[1] Letter of 24 August 1819 to Reynolds, quoted above, p. 222.

resolution is eloquent of his painful uncertainty at this period. He is passing through a crisis of self-doubt reminiscent of Blake's dilemma at Felpham: 'Alas! wretched, happy, ineffectual labourer of time's moments that I am! who shall deliver me from this Spirit of Abstraction & Improvidence?' And from time to time pathetic little asides in his letters (again reminding us of Blake's) express the hope that he is becoming less 'abstract', more practical. 'I think a little change has taken place in my intellect lately', we find him writing to his brothers as early as January 1818: 'I cannot bear to be uninterested or unemployed, I, who for so long a time have been addicted to passiveness.' But the last word, he was to find, was with Blake:

> No discipline will turn one Man into another, even in the least particle, & such discipline I call Presumption & Folly. I have tried it too much not to know this, & am very sorry for all such who may be led to such ostentatious Exertion against their Eternal Existence itself, because it is Mental Rebellion against the Holy Spirit, & fit only for a Soldier of Satan to perform.

Keats's next poem, after *Endymion*, was *Isabella, or the Pot of Basil*. It is the first of his poems to explore, directly and exclusively, the sexual relationship. It is the first of a series, though *St Agnes*, *St Mark*, *Lamia*, follow only at a long interval. In between comes *Hyperion*. I shall discuss *Hyperion* before *Isabella* for two reasons: first, because I want to treat the poems of the 'sexual strife' as a series; secondly, because thematically *Hyperion* is a pendent to *Endymion*, a natural sequel. It has been promised us in *Endymion*— 'Thy lute-voic'd brother will I sing ere long'—although, when it comes, the poem is far from being what Keats meant it to be when he wrote those words. The materials he will pack into it are too diverse, too explosive: the classical structure will crumble under the stress of personal, inordinate tensions.

[*Letters*, August 1818—October 1819]

Chapter Twelve

THE GOLDEN THEME

I am the eye with which the Universe
Beholds itself and knows itself divine;
All harmony of instrument or verse,
All prophecy, all medicine is mine,
All light of art or nature;—to my song
Victory and praise in its own right belong.
P. B. SHELLEY, Hymn of Apollo.

'APOLLO is once more the golden theme!' Once more—
because in *Hyperion* Keats is returning to the central
figure of his earlier poetry, to the sun-god whose complex being embraces the functions of poet, prophet, musician,
physician and magus; and with whom Keats feels himself to be
analogically identifiable.[1] The mock-crowning to which he refers
so insistently in both poems and letters was something more than
a joke; and indeed in a 'life of allegory' such as his there are few
insignificant gestures.

Hyyerion as we now have it is by no means the poem Keats
intended it to be when the epic idea first seized upon his mind.
Quite apart from its fragmentary existence in two versions, its
manifest hesitations and contradictions in detail, it strikes as a
whole an anomalous note in the symphony of Keats's verse. It
got off to a bad start. Begun in wretchedness, at poor Tom's
bedside, it served as a refuge—a retreat from immediate misery
into ideal 'abstraction'. That was not the spirit in which Keats
had conceived the poem. He had conceived it as a pæan, a song
of triumph, a celebration (in its hidden meaning) of his own

---

[1] Two Odes to Apollo are among his earliest verse, and in 1816 he looks
forward to meeting Leigh Hunt as 'the Author of the Sonnet to the Sun'
(*Letters,* 7).

achievement of full bardship. The achievement would be won, of course, by and in the poem itself: that was Keats's way of writing. And he felt himself really capable of this triumph, in spite of hard knocks from the critics: that is why, having once undertaken the poem, he had to go on with it. He stuck to his task until the final hammer-blows from without and within beat him and all his poetizing down.

Irony, despair and death are thus woven into the texture of *Hyperion* from the beginning. It lacks vitality; it is essentially a constructed poem. Keats was not able to put the whole of himself into it. This has been generally felt; what has not, perhaps, been understood is the reason for his failure. 'To put himself into a poem' is not, with Keats, another way of saying 'exert all his powers'. It does mean the actual presence of the poet within the poem, the necessity of self-identification with the chief actor, the working out within the poem of the poet's integral life-patterns.

We have seen this happening in *Endymion*; we shall see it happening again in the narrative poems and the great Odes. And if we cast our minds back to Keats's earliest volume, the 1817 *Poems*, we see it happening there too in an imagined situation precisely anticipating Keats's actual one in September 1818. In *Sleep and Poetry* we find him traversing first the realm of Flora and old Pan, resting in erotic silence in 'the bosom of a leafy world', and coming finally to face the agonies, the strife of human hearts. We read on, expecting to find ('... for lo! ...') a recital of the agonies, a self-dedication to their assuagement, a resolution paralleling Coleridge's

> I therefore go, and join head, heart, and hand,
> Active and firm, to fight the bloodless fight. . . .

or Blake's 'Till we have built Jerusalem'. Do we get anything like this? Not at all. Instead, we are treated to a vision of a charioteer:

> for lo! I see afar,
> O'er sailing the blue cragginess, a car
> And steeds with streamy manes—the charioteer
> Looks out upon the winds with glorious fear. . . .

This *non sequitur* has annoyed some of Keats's commentators, including Miss Amy Lowell: they feel the entrance of the charioteer as an intrusion and an evasion. But for Keats it was not an evasion. The charioteer is Apollo: Apollo descending into the circle of courses to regulate, to instruct, and to heal; and with Apollo, in this work, Keats would have identified himself, as Blake identifies himself with Los in his therapeutic task in *Milton*. Keats would have identified himself . . . but he does not, precisely for the reason I have suggested: he was not ready for it. The significance of the charioteer passage thus remains obscure unless we interpret it in the light of all that Apollo came to mean for Keats. When the time comes, he tries to work out his vision, in the first *Hyperion*, in straightforward epic terms, but he finds the medium resistant: there is no place for the agony, the strife of *human* hearts. He is still determined to link Apollo and his vision of human sorrow, to bring the extremes—divine glory and mortal pain—together in an all-embracing and all-healing synthesis; to settle once for all (to his own satisfaction) the question that haunts him: What is the Poet? So he sits down to write the second *Hyperion*, bringing himself in, with all his weariness, weakness and confusion.

I shall return to this point later. Let us note, meanwhile, that while the figure of Apollo never entirely disappears from Keats's verse in the work done between *Sleep and Poetry* and *Hyperion*, the god's spiritual significance is less emphasized. He is presented more in his physical aspect, as 'Charioteer Of the patient year'[1], the beneficent fosterer of life, lord of the seasons. The emphasis is on growth rather than form. He appears but seldom in *Endymion*, which is a moon-poem (in two of the four books the scene is set in the underworlds of earth and sea). Yet the hidden presence of Apollo is never in doubt, and when Keats writes 'Thy lute-voic'd brother will I sing ere long'[2] he is already looking forward to his great attempt at the epic.

---

[1] *Ode to Apollo* ('God of the golden bow').
[2] *Endymion*, IV, 774.

Hyperion is plainly meant to set the crown on Keats's cosmogony.[1] The crown, metaphorically; but also literally, for we are concerned here with 'regalities', and the theme of sovereignty in its relation to the four elements dominates the first part of the poem. The tragedy of Saturn's fall is that he has lost this relationship. Thea laments:

> 'For heaven is parted from thee, and the earth
> Knows thee not, thus afflicted, for a God;
> And ocean too, with all its solemn noise,
> Has from thy sceptre pass'd; and all the air
> Is emptied of thine hoary majesty.'   [I, 55-9]

The theme is repeated a little later in Saturn's own words:

> '. . . I am smother'd up,
> And buried from all godlike exercise
> Of influence benign on planets pale,
> Of admonitions to the winds and seas,
> Of peaceful sway above man's harvesting,
> And all those acts which Deity supreme
> Doth ease its heart of love in.'   [106-12]

The end of a cycle implies precisely this confusion, and the confusion must persist until the new system of relationships is firmly established. This is inevitable, for the cosmos is a sphere of becoming in which the gods themselves are involved, as Plato had pointed out in *Timæus*; but this inevitability is hidden from the gods themselves, and is very hard to accept. Saturn again speaks in bewilderment:

> 'Not in my own sad breast,
> Which is its own great judge and searcher out,
> Can I find reason why ye should be thus:
> Not in the legends of the first of days,

---

[1] The idea of epic is connected with Saturn and with a universal vision as early as 1816, in the verse *Epistle* to his friend Charles Cowden Clarke, who is thanked for having shown Keats

> that epic was of all the king,
> Round, vast, and spanning all like Saturn's ring.

Studied from that old spirit-leaved book
Which starry Uranus with finger bright
Sav'd from the shores of darkness, when the waves
Low-ebb'd still hid it up in shallow gloom;—
And the which book ye know I ever kept
For my firm-based footstool:—Ah, infirm!
Not there, nor in sign, symbol, or portent
Of element, earth, water, air, and fire,—
At war, at peace, or inter-quarreling
One against one, or two, or three, or all
Each several one against the other three,
As fire with air loud warring when rain-floods
Drown both, and press them both against earth's face,
Where, finding sulphur, a quadruple wrath
Unhinges the poor world; [1]—not in that strife,
Wherefrom I take strange lore, and read it deep,
Can I find reason why ye should be thus:
No, no-where can unriddle, though I search,
And pore on Nature's universal scroll
Even to swooning, why ye, Divinities,
The first-born of all shap'd and palpable Gods,
Should cower beneath what, in comparison,
Is untremendous might.'   [II, 129–55]

In describing the traditional deities as 'all shap'd and palpable Gods' Keats is closely following the *Timæus*, in which these deities are inferior to the celestial gods (the 'forms' represented by the planets) and are caught in the revolutions of Time. Time is the product of the periodic motions of the celestial gods, who have

---

[1] Cf. *Timæus*, 177 (56C): 'And first with respect to earth: when it meets with fire, becoming dissolved by its acuteness, it is borne along; and remains in this dissolved state either in fire, or in the bulk of air, or in that of water—till its parts, associating themselves together . . . produce again a body of earth'; and *Timæus*, 180 (58D): 'But through fire entering into and dissolving its composition, in consequence of losing its equability and smoothness, it [air] participates more of a moveable nature. Hence, becoming easily agile, driven about by the proximate air, and extended over the earth, it liquefies . . . and falls upon the earth, which is called a defluxion. Again, fire flying upwards from hence . . . impels the moist bulk as yet movable into the seats of fire, with which at the same time it mingles itself.'

been created by the Demiurge as expressions of the harmony-working motions of the World-soul within the World-body. World-body and World-soul together comprise the Cosmic Animal which is itself the copy of the divine Idea existing from all eternity in the mind of the Demiurge. In this scheme, the traditional or anthropomorphic gods come rather low in the hierarchy. They are not only subsequent and inferior to the Demiurge, the Cosmic Animal, Time, and the Celestial Gods, but also to the 'ethereal' forms of the four elements which are represented cosmically by the 'unwandering stars'. The planets, the fixed stars, and Earth itself, are the direct creation of the Demiurge; but the traditional gods are the offspring of Heaven and Earth. The Demiurge addresses them thus: '. . . so far as you are generated, you are not immortal, nor in every respect indissoluble: yet you shall never be dissolved, nor become subject to the fatality of death; my will being a much greater and more excellent bond than the vital connectives with which you were bound at the commencement of your generation.'[1] But they are subject, like all sublunary things, to the sway of Necessity. They do not dwell 'above the withering of old-lipp'd Fate'.

The tragedy of the Titans is, therefore, the tragedy of incomprehension. Strictly limited in their power, and caught up in the wheel of becoming, they labour under the delusion that they are unchangeable and omnipotent. Harsh necessity urges on them a revision of this conviction; and we may surmise that the poem, if it had ever been completed, would have traced the threads of reasonableness and obstinacy running through the tangled fortunes of the Titanic wars. The theme is firmly stated in Book II in the speeches of Oceanus and Enceladus.

The relevance of all this to Keats's preoccupation with form is clear enough, and I hope will become more so; but what has it to do with growth? The answer is I think that *Hyperion* expresses the end of growth, the dead period when the cycle has reached its nadir and the seeds of the future are yet ungerminating. This is

---

[1] *Timæus*, 145–6 (41A).

unmistakably conveyed in the opening scene of the epic, with its hammer-like insistence on stony quiet, absence of life, dead leaf and deadened stream. For the first time Keats is making old age the major theme, or one of the major themes, of a long poem:

> His old right hand lay nerveless, listless, dead,
> Unsceptered; and his realmless eyes were closed.

And in so doing he is working against the grain. For Keats is most emphatically the poet of youth, of Blake's 'joy in the springing day'; he has nothing of Wordsworth's meditative sympathy with old age and decay. Meg Merrilies is no exception: she is a figure transcending youth and age, or rather enjoying a perpetual youth, as the childlike irresponsibility of her behaviour suggests.

'Plump contrast' is again the core of Keats's technique. *Hyperion* is to be the pendent to *Endymion*,[1] but a pendent brilliant as a diamond is brilliant against the warmth and softness of flesh. *Endymion* is Time aspiring to Eternity. *Hyperion* is Eternity lapsing into Time. The movement in *Endymion* is upwards from Latmos to Olympus, in *Hyperion* downwards from Olympus to valley and to cave. *Endymion* shows us man achieving divinity in a loving pilgrimage through the elements; *Hyperion* shows us divinity lapsing from control over the elements into an almost subhuman condition of mental and moral chaos. Such are the rhythms as we find them in the finished and the unfinished poem. But because *Hyperion* is unfinished, our grasp of its rhythm can be no more than partial. We can be certain that the movement of despair— however integral it was to Keats's personal mood at the time— would at some point or other be reversed. Apollo would achieve and assert his full divinity. But it may well be that the necessity of this peripeteia impelled Keats to lay the poem aside: it was out of tune with his deepest feelings, with the dead march life was now playing 'on his pulses'; and of all poets he was the least capable of pretence. He could go along with the 'fable' of *Hyperion* while the facets of that fable remained dark, despairing, *negative*, and he

---

[1] I agree with Professor de Selincourt that Keats's final intention was to confine the poem to four books.

could give it a strangely intense and brilliant life; but at the point
of dramatic reversal, at the moment of release upwards and outwards into light, his grasp loosens, his creative impulse falters and
dies. This, rather than the over-Miltonism of the style, seems to
me the reason for Keats's abandonment of the poem.

But let us look at these negative rhythms as they unfold themselves in the opening paragraphs. The elemental powers richly
active in *Endymion* are here brutally restricted:

> Deep in the shady sadness of a vale
> Far sunken from the healthy breath of morn,
> Far from the fiery noon, and eve's one star,
> Sat grey-hair'd Saturn, quiet as a stone,
> Still as the silence round about his lair;
> Forest on forest hung about his head
> Like cloud on cloud. No stir of air was there,
> Not so much life as on a summer's day
> Robs not one light seed from the feather'd grass,
> But where the dead leaf fell, there did it rest.
> A stream went voiceless by, still deadened more
> By reason of his fallen divinity,
> Spreading a shade: the Naiad 'mid her reeds
> Press'd her cold finger closer to her lips.

All is negative here. The divisions of the day are, as it were, oblit-
erated; the four elements are presented in terms of silence and
inaction. There is no air. The rhythms of the verse gyrate slug-
gishly around the fallen Saturn. Keats's key word 'healthy' is
negated; we are in a world of death. This is the simple obverse of
the opening paragraphs of *Endymion*, the concluding paragraph of
'I stood Tip-toe . . .'. Yet, like an obverse, it presents an identity
of pattern. The appearance of Thea in the next paragraph recalls
the appearance of Peona in the earlier poem; in both, the woman's
function is to hearten and console. Thea's consolation is basically
sympathy, pity: she has nothing positive to offer:

> 'Saturn look up!—though wherefore, poor old King?
> I have no comfort for thee, no not one:
> I cannot say, 'O wherefore sleepest thou?'

For heaven is parted from thee, and the earth
Knows thee not, thus afflicted, for a God;
And ocean too, with all its solemn noise,
Has from thy sceptre pass'd; and all the air
Is emptied of thine hoary majesty. . .'   [I, 52–9]

Saturn's royalty, which once penetrated the elements, has withdrawn from them; yet in the recollection that things were once
otherwise (the passage is closely linked with the interpenetrating-
regalities exordium of *Endymion* III) he finds the stimulus to
'recruit his wearied virtue'. 'The frozen God' (note how *form* here
dominates *growth*) rests with Thea for 'silver seasons four' motionless

> Like natural sculpture in cathedral cavern;

but at length raises his head, and knows his doom. In words already
quoted (see above, p. 230) he laments his impotence, and his con-
sequent loss of 'identity':

> 'I am gone
> Away from my own bosom: I have left
> My strong identity, my real self,
> Somewhere between the throne, and where I sit
> Here on this spot of earth.'   [112–16]

The words are powerfully reminiscent of Endymion's 'I Have no
self-passion or identity'. Endymion found himself again in an act
of self-realization; the broken sequence of *Hyperion* forbids any
anticipation of a similar anagnorisis for Saturn, whose stubborn
incomprehension is indeed emphasized throughout the poem; it
is only in the person of Hyperion, probably, that the old order
will find an understanding with the new.

Hyperion is counterpointed, as *Endymion* is not, in heaven-earth
antitheses; the gloom of Saturn's valley is set, midway through
Book I, against the fiery splendours of Hyperion's palace. Keats
stresses the synchronicity: 'Meanwhile in other realms . . .'[1]: the
poem gains a dimension. And, by referring us back, implicitly, to

---

[1] And, a little later (line 201): 'Even now, while Saturn . . .'

the *Song of Four Fairies*,[1] a new depth: we have not forsaken Hermes in cultivating Apollo. These shifts of attention are vital in reading Keats; if we miss them, we lose half his impact. Note, moreover, that the elements are indeed elemental, that is, primal: the Hermetic 'machinery' underlies the Olympian; the latter could be jettisoned, at a pinch, but not the former. *Hyperion* is dealing, in its negative mode, with Keats's old preoccupations, with the 'vast idea', Blake's 'body of Divine Analogy'. Saturn expresses his deposition in terms of 'harvesting', 'ripe progress', 'hymns of festival': these things (Keats's constant eikons of growth and fruition) he has forfeited. Curiously, Hyperion's realm, though of fire, provides identical metaphors: his palace-door

> like a rose in vermeil tint and shape,
> In fragrance soft, and coolness to the eye

opens for his entry. He strides forward through '*bowers* of fragrant and enwreathed light'. He waits 'six *dewy* hours' for the dawn.

And Keats's preoccupation with the holiness of the natural order is not wanting, even in these remote empyreal realms. Hyperion, 'on his orbed fire', feels the pressure of his coming doom. He will fall as the other gods have fallen. No longer do the 'spicy wreaths of incense' ascend to his nostrils from 'sacred hills'. His 'eternal essence' is distraught by fears—'lank-ear'd Phantoms of black-weeded pools'. He finds no rest from his labours; and though the hour of dawn is still six hours distant, he is impatient for action. But even he cannot alter the appointed order:

> Fain would he have commanded, fain took throne
> And bid the day begin, if but for change.
> He might not:—No, though a primeval God:
> The sacred seasons might not be disturb'd.   [290–3]

---

[1] Notably, in the emphasis on Hyperion's 'irascibility' (in Hermetic lore, as we have seen, the quality of fire): 'He enter'd, but he enter'd full of wrath.' It is by virtue of this irascible quality (corresponding to the ψυχική of the three-fold human division) that Hyperion is able to mediate between the new πνευματικοί and the old σωματικοί gods.

He must wait, then; and as he waits, stretched out along the
threshold of his palace,

>   the Heaven with its stars
> Look'd down on him with pity, and the voice
> Of Cœlus, from the universal space,
> Thus whisper'd low and solemn in his ear.
> 'O brightest of my children dear, earth-born
> And sky-engendered, Son of Mysteries
> All unrevealed even to the powers
> Which met at thy creating; at whose joys
> And palpitations sweet, and pleasures soft,
> I, Cœlus, wonder how they came and whence;
> And at the fruits thereof what shapes they be,
> Distinct, and visible; symbols divine,
> Manifestations of that beauteous life
> Diffus'd unseen throughout eternal space.'[1]   [305–18]

Keats's major preoccupations are clustered here, and, as it were,
quintessentialized in fire: the sanctity of the natural order,[2] the
universal space which is the theatre of manifestation,[3] the powers
which meet in creation,[4] the vital force omnipresent in the ether.[5]
I cannot but think that the announcement of these themes, in
terms so solemn, and by actors so venerable as Saturn and Cœlus,
implies that they will be massively though dramatically treated in
the poem. *Hyperion* is to be a cosmogonic epic. It will 'unfold
through images the theory of the world'.[6] Keats's imagination,

---

[1] Cf. *Timæus*, 126 (36D): 'But soul being every way extended from the middle
to the very extremities of the universe, and investing it externally in a circle, at
the same time herself revolving within herself, gave rise to the divine commencement of an unceasing and wise life, through the whole of time.'

[2] Is Keats thinking of Genesis viii, 22, here (quoted in Davies's *Celtic Researches*,
pp. 21–2): 'While the earth remaineth, seedtime and harvest, and cold and heat,
and summer and winter, and day and night shall not cease'? His use of 'seasons'
would suggest it; and 'the LORD smelled a sweet savour' in the preceding verse,
a phrase recalling *Hyperion*, I, 188–9: 'Instead of sweets, his ample palate took
Savour of poisonous brass and metal sick.'

[3] See above, pp. 40–4.   [4] See above, p. 231 and note.

[5] See above, pp. 112–14.

[6] Thomas Taylor, Introduction to the *Timæus*

once seized by the wheeling speculations of Plato in *Timæus*, cannot rest until it gives them artistic shape; nor is this ambition abandoned, even when *Hyperion* is abandoned. The perfect, the concentrated shape is achieved in the *Grecian Urn*.

If we ask why the *Timæus* should have had such a profound appeal for Keats we shall meet with more than one answer. There is the accidental reason: he was introduced to it, probably, at a time (the Oxford sojourn) when he was peculiarly receptive to ideas, and by a person whose basic interests were his, and whose sincerity he admired. There are the intrinsic reasons: the *Timæus* expounds Keats's 'vast idea', the theme of analogy; it is concerned from beginning to end with principles and manifestations, with growth and form; it includes a long physiological section which would interest him as a medical student (and we know that he never altogether dropped his medical interest); and it discusses sensation—taste, smell, etc.—in its cognitive aspect. The *Timæus* diagram of the planetary revolutions, and its references to harmony, agree exactly with Keats's early picture of the 'noise of harmony' that poises 'its mighty self of convoluting sound Huge as a planet, and like that roll[s] round Eternally around a dizzy void'. And there are minor assimilations which I could bring out only by a detailed exposition which would be out of place here.[1]

Admonished by Cœlus, Hyperion dives into space. At precisely the same moment (again the accent falls on synchronicity) Thea leads Saturn to the conclave of fallen Titans. The stress, as in the second book of *Endymion*, is on stubborn rock-forms, darkness and agate impenetrability. But the note of hope rang through *Endymion*; here there is nothing but despair. Not all the

---

[1] I shall give some of the more striking passages in footnotes. But only extensive quotation could demonstrate the full relevance of *Timæus* not only to *Hyperion* but to such dithyrambs in the Letters as the paragraphs quoted earlier (pp. 49 and 218). For *Timæus* is a microcosmic as well as a macrocosmic dialogue; to quote Taliaferro (Foreword to Bollingen Series reprint of the Taylor translation, p. 16): 'In the *Timæus*, the world is used as the large model of the human soul, and the emphasis is on the natural structure of the soul.' This fact did not escape Keats.

Titans are assembled; some are 'straying in the world', like Mnemosyne; others Keats describes, in words which oddly recall Blake's illustration of the element Earth in *The Gates of Paradise*[1], as

> pent in regions of laborious breath;
> Dungeon'd in opaque element, to keep
> Their clenched teeth still clench'd, and all their limbs
> Lock'd up like veins of metal, crampt and screw'd.
>
> [II, 22–5]

'Plump contrast' has brought us from the lucent realms of inter-penetrating light to these dismal rock-masses: from form to formlessness. The assembled Titans themselves approximate to the chaos surrounding them:

> Scarce images of life, one here, one there,
> Lay vast and edgeways; like a dismal circque
> Of Druid stones, upon a forlorn moor,
> When the chill rain begins at shut of eve,
> In dull November, and their chancel vault,
> The Heaven itself, is blinded throughout night. [33–8]

From stubborn rock to dark air and chill rain; and heaven itself, the seat of fire, is 'blinded': we have descended to the 'gross and sluggish' earth of the *Timæus*.[2] Plainly *Hyperion*, no less than the *Timæus* itself, is a macrocosmic model of the psyche in ignorance and enlightenment. Keats is pursuing, precisely as Blake did in the symbolic books from *Tiriel* to *Jerusalem*, the imperial theme of *la condition humaine*. He is treating it, like Blake, in mythological terms; unlike his great predecessor, he is not evolving his own mythology. He finds himself, in consequence, restricted in his scope; the classical pattern, no less than the Miltonic mode,

---

[1] This drawing may be consulted in K. 754.

[2] According to the dialogue (and the point is emphasized by Taylor in his introduction) the earth that we view with our corporeal eyes and inhabit according to sense is not the true earth, but a species of cave or sink in the body of the universe. It is into this hollow that the Titans have fallen.

oppresses him. To save his own 'identity' he will turn to the 'visionary' schema of *The Fall of Hyperion*.

With all his talk of 'abstractions', Keats cannot write an abstract poem. He has to be within the action, moving, growing, participating: as in *Endymion*. In that poem he achieved full identification with the hero: for the hero's condition was precisely his. With all its faults, *Endymion* is immensely, vitally realized; even its blunders are instinct with life. It is an organism: growing, not premeditated in its details, though planned as a whole. *Hyperion* is premeditated *in toto* and *in partibus*: it is a cerebral poem. That is not to say that it is a lesser poem than *Endymion*: the cerebrum is also a function of the human totality, selecting and concentrating values dispersed in the totality. *Lear* does not supersede *Paradise Lost*. *Lear* is greater than *Paradise Lost* because its author was a better poet; but the author of *Hyperion* was a better poet than the author of *Endymion*. Keats's personal problem in the later poem was that he could not fully identify himself with the hero. He would have liked to be Apollo: shining, triumphant, 'a foreseeing God' who 'will shape his actions like one'[1]; but he wasn't, and he could not pretend to be. If he had lived, he might well have picked *Hyperion* up again and completed it. In late 1819 he was far from being Apollo: he was a sick, disappointed, frustrated young man. Being Keats, he knew this and accepted it; he dropped *Hyperion*, in which he didn't figure, and started *The Fall of Hyperion*, in which he did. *The Fall* is obviously a failure. What Keats had done in the earlier version was unsurpassable: *Hyperion* is the most extraordinary feat in the English language; and it is a feat of pure intellect. You can't escape the Miltonisms, yet the poem is not Miltonic as a whole; it is Keatsian, the work of a Keats who has decided for once to exert his purely *technical* powers, under the stimulus of Milton: and these powers were immense. Up to now he has curbed them, subordinated them to the wavering, burgeoning impulses of the creative force within

---

[1] *Letters*, 82.

him: *that* was the important, the overriding consideration—to see where that would lead him, and to be patient and receptive in face of that. And now, suddenly, he finds himself face to face with hostility, incomprehension, stupidity: the temptation to 'lay a lion-paw against them' is irresistible (as a well man he would have resisted it) and he comes out with his fantastic masterpiece. It is fantastic and it is a masterpiece; but he couldn't go on with it beyond the entry of Apollo, for Apollo meant too much to him. The Titans meant nothing. Just for that reason, Keats was able to invent them and sustain them in being, for two books, on a plane remote from his personal life; but the effort could not be continued indefinitely. With the entry of Apollo on the scene Keats is back in the reality; and the reality demanded another sort of treatment.

Hyperion was given up in its first version in April, in its second in December 1819; he had been working on it, sporadically, for over a year.[1] In the meantime he had written *The Eve of St Agnes*, *The Eve of St Mark*, *La Belle Dame Sans Merci*, *Lamia*, and all the great Odes. *Isabella* had been written in April 1818. It is a year of remarkable fruition. *Isabella* had been a 'weak-sided' poem; a gesture of frustration, and thereby a symptom of weariness, following the great but (to Keats) unsatisfactory effort of *Endymion*. The first *Hyperion* is the swing to the other extreme: an assertion of the formal against the informal, the loose, the amorphous; of the masculine against the feminine bias; of technique against intuition. I have suggested that it is Keats's personal answer to the charges brought against him as the poet of *Endymion*. But it was not the right answer. The right answer was *St Agnes* and the Odes.

Keats dropped *Hyperion* in April as a Miltonic epic; but he couldn't drop the theme altogether. It had come to mean a good deal to him; he had got to work it out. 'Give me this credit', he writes to George on 19 March 1819 ('straining at particles of light

---

[1] Between April and September Keats was tinkering with the poem, and the second version was taking shape; but he did not begin to re-write *Hyperion* (as *The Fall*) until the latter month.

in the midst of a great darkness'), '—Do you not think I strive—
to know myself?' His mind is tenacious, with the tenacity of a
natural force; the seed, once planted, has to grow to its flowering:
the process can be ended only by consummation or death. *Hy-*
perion is like a shoot that is pushing upwards, perfectly vertically,
against a great weight; the moment comes when the weight can
no longer be sustained. The shoot does not, for this reason, arrest
itself in mid-air or sink back into the soil; it moves obliquely,
shedding its weight, into a new line of growth. *Hyperion's* new
line is that of a vision, a form that came with great naturalness to
Keats. *Sleep and Poetry, Endymion, St Agnes, Isabella, La Belle*
Dame, Indolence: all are dream poetry. Through the vision pattern
Keats is able to bring himself, in person, into the action of his
poem. Blake does the same thing in *Milton*: and it is interesting
to speculate whether (had the poem been carried successfully forward) Keats might not at some point have merged with Apollo
as Blake merges with Los. This possibility suggests itself, I think,
in Moneta's remark to Keats:

> Thou hast felt
> What 'tis to die and live again. . . .

which recalls the 'Die into life . . .' of Apollo in the first *Hyperion*.
The merging, which is a discovery of the identity of the individual
'spark of divinity' with its Original, will come only through
travail. 'Intelligences are atoms of perception—they know and
they see and they are pure, in short they are God—How then are
Souls to be made? How then are these sparks which are God to
have identity given them—so as ever to possess a bliss peculiar
to each one's individual existence? How, but by the medium of a
world like this?' The 'soul-making' letter, from which this comes,
was written in April; between April and September there is every
indication that its speculations[1] were intensely present to Keats's
mind; and I believe that in the new *Hyperion* he meant to give
them dramatic form. *The Fall* is going to develop Keats's spiritual

---

[1] Which may be compared with those of Davies and his Druids (see below,
Appendix A, pp. 399–400).

progress *pari passu* with the fortunes of the Titans up to the point where the dreamer understands that inner and outer action are one.

'It may be interesting to you to pick out some lines from Hyperion and put a mark X to the false beauty proceeding from art, and one || to the true voice of feeling.' Keats is writing to Reynolds, on 21 September 1819, to announce (among other things) the abandonment of *Hyperion*.[1] He finds it impossible to make the distinction himself. Yet at some point or other before this he has brought himself to make the distinction; for the second version, as far as we have it, is made up of old and new material in the proportions of (approximately) one to two. But it is difficult to understand his principle of selection. Why, for instance, is the superb line 'Those green-robed senators of mighty woods' omitted from the famous simile? why, again, if it is Miltonisms he wants to get rid of, does he preserve such examples as 'In solemn tenor and deep organ-tone', and even add new ones like 'Me thoughtless!' He is very far from shaking off the influence of Milton; and fortunately so, for it is only by a Miltonic nexus that the old and the new material is given any sort of homogeneity. Let me explain what I mean by this.

The character of the first *Hyperion* is, it will be agreed, 'abstract', adamantine and (for Keats) massive. Its concern is with regalities, with power and with cosmogonic patterns. The character of the second *Hyperion* is to be personal, psychological, exploratory—in a word, tentative. This we feel to be so not from the evidence of the new *Hyperion* alone, but from the evidence of the whole of Keats's work at and leading up to this period. In *Isabella*, *St Agnes* and the Odes we are firmly within the world of growth: the forms are physical forms, products of growth, themselves subject to decay and death—the fruit falling back to earth to nourish the root. The regalities of *Endymion* are abandoned until we come to *Autumn*. This is Keats's steady line of development;

---

[1] Mr Gittings's assertion that Keats is here referring to 'both versions' (*John Keats: The Living Year*, p. 189) does not convince me. According to Brown—with whom Keats was living at the time—the 'remodelling' of *Hyperion* went on into December (*K.C.*, II, 72).

and in working on *Hyperion* step by step with his other poems he is working against the grain. This he came to feel; and this, I have suggested, is the real reason for his giving up *Hyperion* in its first version. But he could not give up the theme of *Hyperion* until he had worked out its possibilities; and he decided, in planning the second version, that it was appropriate to use some (we cannot tell how much) of the old material. How far he was right in his decision is another question. But once the decision was made, the problem arose of integrating the new material with the old.

Again Milton comes to his aid: not the Milton, this time, of 'the great intelligences fair', but the Milton of *Comus*, who had been by his side in the mazes of *Endymion*, and the Milton of the fifth book of *Paradise Lost*. This is the simple, sensuous and passionate poet of growth, flowering and fruition. And let us note that Keats's problem had been in a way Milton's: to connect the immediacies of the human condition with the universal law, to present a limited and ephemeral pattern against a timeless verity. Milton succeeds, so far as he does succeed, through the idyll of Eden, through the primal garden where God walks with man in the cool of the day.

Keats could not present his garden as an idyll, the setting of a love-story. The personal love-relationship is absent from *Hyperion*. That is one reason why Keats speaks of it as 'abstract'; and it is a reason for the poem's existing at all. Indeed, it is the poem's prime justification; and when we are tempted to reject *Hyperion*, to agree with Keats in dropping it, to condemn it as a splendid abortion, let us not forget that Keats wrote it as an *escape* from the unbearable pressure of his own emotions, doubts, desires, despairs. It performed for him an essential service; the service, in a context of other woe than Keats's, that mathematics performed for Wordsworth when he 'gave up moral questions in despair': its effect was cathartic and bracing. 'Cogitating on the Characters of Saturn and Ops',[1] those majestic 'abstractions', he could forget his own misery and be free.

---

[1] Letter of 27 October 1818 to Woodhouse.

And this is why the second *Hyperion* begins with a comparison of the true and the false poet, as *Endymion* III had begun with a comparison of the true and the false king. The 'sort of induction' (as Keats calls it)[1] challenges the judgment of posterity. The true poet expresses 'the giant agony of the world'; the false poet, the dreamer, luxuriates in his own emotions. This is a conviction which has long been pressing upon Keats: he writes *The Fall* because he sees, or thinks he sees, the possibility of conveying this within a framework he had originally planned for the expression of quite another conviction: the supremacy of beauty, the triumph of spirit over matter, and the reconciliation of the three worlds in art. The stream of life has carried him away from this vision: it may be true, he thinks it is true, but it is not true for him at this moment; what is true is the immediacy of anguish, proved on the pulses. This he will express, this he will weave into the gorgeous fabric of his Olympian hierarchies. And the connection between the individual dilemma and the cosmic process is effected, where Milton effects it, in the garden.

Keats's garden is not idyllic,[2] for reasons we have seen; but it is fruitful. 'Trees of every clime' shade it, give it a universal character: the senses are delighted by the sound of fountains, 'the touch of scent', the sight

> Of trellis vines, and bells, and larger blooms,
> Like floral censers swinging light in air;

and before the 'wreathed doorway' of an arbour

>   on a mound
> Of moss, was spread a feast of summer fruits,
> Which nearer seen, seem'd refuse of a meal
> By Angel tasted, or our Mother Eve.

The reference leads us straight to *Paradise Lost*, but smashes the classical framework before we are aware of it: the introduction of Proserpine in the next few lines is powerless to right the balance.

---

[1] Letter of 21 September 1819 to Woodhouse.
[2] I am using 'idyllic' here as a not too accurate and perhaps vulgar shorthand for pastoral-erotic.

> Still was more plenty than the fabled horn
> Thrice emptied could pour forth, at banqueting,
> For Proserpine return'd to her own fields,
> Where the white heifers low.   [I, 35–8]

The last five words work the miracle of adding a touch of beauty to what had seemed untouchable, the Miltonic fields of Enna.[1]

The 'fragrant husks and berries crushed' on the grass of the garden come straight from the feast prepared by Eve for Raphael in *Paradise Lost* V—linking, thus, the human and the celestial worlds. I have already pointed out that the fruit is a solary form, reproducing in shape and colour the source of its existence, and passing on to man the energies which have gone into its making. There is a ritual quality about all of Keats's many feasts, leading as they do to 'the chief intensity' of the love-encounter. But the meal which opens this new *Hyperion* carries the most precise initiation overtones; it is preparatory to the vision, the entry into the temple.

>   And appetite,
> More yearning than on earth I ever felt,
> Growing within, I ate deliciously;
> And, after not long, thirsted, for thereby
> Stood a cool vessel of transparent juice,
> Sipp'd by the wander'd bee, the which I took,
> And, pledging all the Mortals of the world,
> And all the dead whose names are in our lips,
> Drank. That full draught is parent of my theme.   [38–46]

The preparation for the vision by partaking of special food and drink is an initiation commonplace.[2] It comes to life in Keats's poem because of his peculiar feeling for sense-data, in particular for taste and smell. These most intimate of the senses are not left

---

[1] 'When I see you', he had written to Bailey from Inverary on 18 July 1818, 'the first thing I shall do will be to read that about [*i.e.* in] Milton and [*i.e.* about] Ceres and Proserpine.'

[2] As Cornford tells us (*Principium Sapientiæ*, p. 92). The theme is bardic, including the entrance to the temple and the questioning of the occupants of 'high-seats' about cosmogonic truth (*ibid.*, 92 and 93). Keats's temple may owe something to Darwin's (cf. Appendix B, II. 2, below).

behind, as we shall see, even when Keats reaches the temple's dark and adamantine centre.

> How long I slumber'd 'tis a chance to guess.
> When sense of life return'd, I started up
> As if with wings; but the fair trees were gone,
> The mossy mound and arbour were no more;
> I look'd around upon the carved sides
> Of an old sanctuary . . .   [57–62]

In moving from the garden to the temple, Keats reproduces Endymion's transit from forest to underworld: would he, one wonders, have made the complete circuit through sea and air too? I think he would, and a completer one than Endymion's, with Moneta as his guide: already in Canto II we find him in the realm of fire, which the shepherd-prince could not penetrate. The Dantean vision-pattern is serving him well, opening up (I suspect) possibilities of progressive semi-identifications with the Gods which would culminate in his final and total identification with Apollo. Moneta is at once Virgil and Beatrice: she guides, but she also admonishes: the voyage through the circles is to be, plainly, a purgation.

Keats wakes to find himself at the temple's centre, under the great dome. 'Strange vessels and large draperies' lie at his feet; above, the 'embossed roof'; ranges of columns to north and south. He looks, now,

> Eastward, where black gates
> Were shut against the sunrise evermore;
> Then to the west I look'd, and saw far off
> An Image, huge of feature as a cloud,
> At level of whose feet an altar slept,
> To be approach'd on either side by steps,
> And marble balustrade, and patient travail
> To count with toil the innumerable degrees.
> Towards the altar sober-pac'd I went,
> Repressing haste, as too unholy there;
> And, coming nearer, saw beside the shrine
> One minist'ring; and there arose a flame.   [85–96]

This is a new Keats. As we have seen (p. 208, above) he wrote to George, this September, that friends were saying he had 'altered completely' and was 'not the same person'. We feel it in *The Fall*: in its sombre, measured pace, in its pithiness and compression of language. Though he dated the change in himself from George's departure—that is, from the previous June—we may prefer to date it, more plausibly, from the September exactly a year ago when he began the first *Hyperion*. Many sorrows have beset him since that day: Tom's death, his own illness, professional disappointment, money troubles, sexual stresses. And throughout this period he is reading the great poet of sorrows; a poet whose spirit is to fight with Milton's for possession of Keats and finally, if but for a moment, to prevail. References to Dante are few in his letters; but that means little. Keats is always most reticent where his personal emotions are concerned, and Dante is coming, at this period, to be oddly associated with his minor and major worries. To stand in a queue in a bank is (as early as January 1819) 'to me worse than anything in Dante'; in April 'The fifth canto of Dante pleases me more and more' and he writes the sonnet on his own dream-visit to the circle of the lovers. 'The reading of Dante is well worth the while', he comments meiotically in September. These are scattered letter references, and may carry little weight; more decisive for Dante's growing impact is the evidence of the verse. There are traces even in the first *Hyperion* of a second current, flowing against the current of Milton[1]; and many an echo sounds in the fugitive verse.[2] The attraction stems, I believe, from two sources: Keats's own deepening seriousness—one might say, sombreness—and his trend, stylistically, to austerity and compression.

She who ministers beside the flame is Moneta. I shall not quote the famous lines in which Keats describes her unveiled face: they are well enough known, and reinforce rather than develop what

---

[1] Cf. the two passages quoted above, p. 239.

[2] I had intended to give examples: but Mr Robert Gittings's later book *The Mask of Keats* confirms my findings and makes further evidence unnecessary.

has already been said of the Dantean current in *The Fall*. They are certainly evidence of a quite new power of visual imagination in Keats: an imagination steeped in sorrow, and directed towards humanity. The passage has a dramatic quality, flexible, varied, complex; the poet who could write like this might be (what I have often doubted) capable of 'a few fine plays', and they would be plays very different from *Otho the Great* and *King Stephen*. This may explain the impersonal impact of *The Fall*. Though Keats is a major actor, it is as a *representative* figure from the human world admitted to the world of forms that he functions in the poem; we feel his personality much more intrusive in *Endymion*. Here he is, if not Everyman, at least a particular crystallization of Everyman: he is the 'poet of the human heart', *in posse* if not yet *in esse*.

Much critical ink has been spilt on this first meeting of the poet with Moneta. Keats's account is anything but perspicuous; and there is a question of how far the manuscript, as left by him, would have been revised to exclude certain lines. But one thing seems clear: Keats himself is *not* included in the class of the 'dreamers' chastised by Moneta. He does, in actual fact, reach the summit of the altar stairs; and Moneta's words are precise:

> 'None can usurp this height,' returned that shade,
> 'But those to whom the miseries of the world
> Are misery, and will not let them rest.'   [147–9]

Keats is 'encourag'd by the sooth voice' of Moneta to enquire further. Why is he alone in the temple? Are there not men who in response to 'the giant agony of the world' labour 'like slaves to poor humanity . . . for mortal good'? There are indeed such, Moneta replies, but they are men of action; they have no time to dream and, in consequence, they never enter the temple. But Keats, she suggests, *is* a dreamer.

> 'What benefit canst thou do, or all thy tribe,
> To the great world? Thou art a dreaming thing;
> A fever of thyself—think of the Earth;
> What bliss even in hope is there for thee?

What haven? every creature hath its home;
Every sole man hath days of joy and pain,
Whether his labours be sublime or low—
The pain alone; the joy alone; distinct:
Only the dreamer venoms all his days,
Bearing more woe than all his sins deserve.'   [167–76]

What is Moneta aiming at here? She is certainly contradicting her-self. She has divided men into three classes: the true poet, one of those 'to whom the miseries of the world Are misery', who enters the temple and ascends to the altar; the false poet or dreamer, who enters the temple, fails to ascend the altar steps, and dies; and the philanthropist, who is too busy to enter the temple. She now challenges Keats: 'You are not a man of action, you are a dreamer, *are you not?*' But she has already shown that he is *not* a dreamer: for he has, indisputably, gained the summit of the steps. Her challenge is, then, a *test*, corresponding to the ordeals with which (as we have seen) Endymion, in the earlier adventure, was faced at each stage of his pilgrimage. Endymion's trials were external; Keats's are more subtle, stemming from his own self-doubt; Moneta plays pitilessly on the exposed nerves of the despondent Keats of late 1819. It is a magnificent feat of double-talk, and again suggests to us the possibility of a rich dramatic development for Keats, had he survived. For here, in exploiting his personal emo-tions, he frees himself from them: Endymion's Cave of Quietude is projected, with its enantiodromia, into Moneta's temple.

The suggestion is of a danger only just escaped. The dreamers,

'If by a chance into this fane they come,
Rot on the pavement where thou rotted'st half.'   [152–3]

'Where thou rotted'st half' means, I think, 'Where you came very near to rotting'. Keats is 'a fever of himself': he 'venoms all his days' by failing to take life as it comes, 'The pain alone; the joy alone; distinct'. Is he not then of the dreamer tribe? Moneta contradicts her statements as she utters them, proffering the clue together with the conundrum. In presence of her veiled majesty (for she has not yet shown her face) Keats will surely falter. But no: his reply comes promptly, blending irony with appropriate deference:

> 'That I am favored for unworthiness,
> By such propitious parley medicin'd
> In sickness not ignoble, I rejoice,
> Aye, and could weep for love of such award.' [182–5]

The tone slides in and out of the pompous;[1] Keats's double-talk in answer to Moneta's. Deeper resonances inform the next few lines; here a truce is implicitly offered:

> 'If it please,
> Majestic shadow, tell me: sure not all
> Those melodies sung into the world's ear
> Are useless: sure a poet is a sage;
> A humanist, Physician to all men.
> That I am none I feel, as Vultures feel
> They are no birds when Eagles are abroad.
> What am I then? Thou spakest of my tribe:
> What tribe?' [186–94]

The direct challenge calls for a direct answer: but Moneta is still evasive.

> 'Art thou not of the dreamer tribe?
> The poet and the dreamer are distinct,
> Diverse, sheer opposite, antipodes.
> The one pours out a balm upon the world,
> The other vexes it.' [198–202]

She no longer, we note, advances the bald assertion: 'Thou art a dreaming thing'; she calls upon Keats to assert his own identity. That he fails, in fact, to do so should cause us no surprise; the present state of the text is chaotic, and there is every indication that Keats intended it for thorough revision. As the passage stands, he gets as far in his reply as a 'Pythian' condemnation of bad poets—'mock lyrists, large self-worshippers'[2]—prefaced by an

---

[1] Reminding us of nothing so much as the First Tempster's speeches in *Murder in the Cathedral*.

[2] With Byron in mind, perhaps.

invocation of Apollo; but the second part of his defence, which would no doubt have been a modest expression of his aspirations to the band of 'poet-sages', is lacking. Whether Keats would have supplied it verbally here, on revision, or whether (as I take it) the idea has come into his mind of *proving* his identity through later action in the poem, we cannot know. The point is of small importance.

Dropping the subject, he returns to his narrative. What is this temple, he asks Moneta; what is the giant Image; and who is she? Moneta now speaks of the long-past Titans' war, and of Saturn, whose priestess she is. The poet keeps silence, lost in wonder; at length Moneta promises to reveal to him

> '. . . the scenes
> Still swooning vivid through my globed brain.'

In preparation she unveils.

> So at the view of sad Moneta's brow,
> I ached to see what things the hollow brain
> Behind enwombed: what high tragedy
> In the dark secret Chambers of her skull
> Was acting, that could give so dread a stress
> To her cold lips, and fill with such a light
> Her planetary eyes. . . .[1]   [275–81]

And immediately we are led back into the familiar valley of the first *Hyperion*: 'Deep in the shady sadness of a vale . . .'. The original text, with slight revision, and with interpolations explanatory from Moneta and marvelling from Keats, is reproduced up to the entry of Hyperion into his palace; and there the fragment ends.

The first Canto (the change of name from 'Book' is significant) comes to a close with the departure of Saturn, led by Thea, for the

---

[1] See below, p. 330, for comment on this passage. The fourth line seems to derive from *Venus and Adonis*, line 1038, 'Into the deep dark Cabins of her head' (quoted in *Letters*, 65).

Titanic conclave. The second Canto opens with Moneta's warning
that the events she describes to Keats (and which, through her eyes,
he sees) are *humanized*: a divine process is being apprehended in
human terms. The warning is meant, of course, for the reader; it
is Raphael's warning to Adam in *Paradise Lost* V; and it stems from
the distinction of the *Timæus* between the sublunary gods and the
mighty powers which keep their state above the elements.[1] The
sublunary gods and their struggles are in fact the terms in which
we apprehend the processes in the unmanifested world (which is
also the world of the human psyche) and I believe that Keats
is preparing us here for the later development of his story in
which the three worlds will be reconciled. He has already told
us, in Canto I, that looking through the eyes of Moneta he has
gained

> A power within me of enormous ken,
> To see as a God sees, and take the depth
> Of things as nimbly as the outward eye
> Can size and shape pervade. [303–6]

He can take the depth of things like a God; but he must still perceive their superficies as the outward eye takes them: in terms of
shape and size. This is the double vision of Blake; but it is not
yet his triple and quadruple vision. In *Hyperion* there will be
no escaping the formal in either the plastic or the verbal spheres,
until the moment when the supreme identity is realized; we
must escape from the formal through the formal. Hence Moneta
says:

> 'Mortal, that thou mayest understand aright,
> I humanize my sayings to thine ear,
> Making comparisons of earthly things;
> Or thou might'st better listen to the wind,
> Whose language is to thee a barren noise,
> Though it blows legend-laden through the trees.[2]
> [II, 1–6]

---

[1] Cf. also Appendix A, pp. 389–90, below.
[2] Cf. again Appendix A, p. 403.

With this warning, she goes on to describe Hyperion and his palace in language but little altered from that of the first version. As she speaks, Keats, looking into her eyes, finds himself no longer in the dark valley, where he has watched Saturn and Thea, but in the realm of fire itself. The technique is precisely that of the cinema. Keats has achieved a skilful variant on the method of Dante; and note the complexity of his 'machinery'. The dreamer in the garden is the postulant in the temple, and the postulant in the temple is the watcher in the valley, the searcher (maybe) of the long corridors of Hyperion's palace. It is tantalizing not to know how Keats would have developed his action.

It ends, in *The Fall*, with the entrance of Hyperion. Its continuation in the earlier version we know: the god's impatience, his sorrow, his wish to hasten the coming of the dawn, Uranus' admonition, and the expedition to earth. We pick the story up from that point, though Keats's dropping of the story suggests that he might well have planned quite a different sequel. It is difficult, indeed, to see what effective contribution Hyperion could make to the debate of the Titans. We do not hear him speak in the conclave: his coming is greeted with enthusiasm, though his aspect betrays his despondency. It may well be that Keats would have cut out this episode from his revised version of the poem, to replace it by some powerful stroke of action.

'Just at the self-same beat of Time's wide wings', then, Hyperion dives 'all noiseless into the deep night' and Saturn, with Thea, enters the den of the Titans. Keats's picture of their despairing immobility, a masterpiece of plastic invention, we have already, noted.[1] In a total hundred lines of considerable virtuosity, the fallen gods are characterized through a mere distinction of attitudes: without speech, the core of each divinity is laid bare

---

[1] A Wordsworthian echo which de Selincourt seems to have missed (though he has a note on the lines) is 'the solid roar Of thunderous waterfalls and torrents hoarse', which surely comes from 'The stationary blasts of waterfalls' in *The Simplon Pass*, a fragment not published until 1845 though composed in 1799. The two passages should be compared in detail for similarities of wording and atmosphere. When did Keats get a glimpse of Wordsworth's manuscript?

to us.[1] When, finally, they do speak, it is with majesty, and the elemental words are finely prologued:

> There is a roaring in the bleak-grown pines
> When Winter lifts his voice; there is a noise
> Among immortals when a God gives sign,
> With hushing finger, how he means to load
> His tongue with the full weight of utterless thought,
> With thunder, and with music, and with pomp:
> Such noise is like the roar of bleak-grown pines;
> Which, when it ceases in this mountain'd world,
> No other sound succeeds. . . .   [II, 116–24]

The passage conveys all Keats's awe in the presence of primal sound (that first of created things, as the tradition has it) and inevitably invokes the mysterious tree-voices that haunt his verse from first to last. It is Saturn himself who will speak; and his words[2] when they come span times and eternities, from ancient chaos to present catastrophe. But they are bewildered words, with no germ of hope or strength. It is left to Oceanus, who speaks next, to offer positive counsels.

The character of Oceanus—wise, simple, generous, most reminiscent indeed of Orleans, 'generous as mountains', in Blake's *The French Revolution*—has been sketched already, in the fourth book of *Endymion*. His wisdom springs from 'cogitation in his watery shades'—from, that is, the energies of the unconscious; the tones of his voice are caught 'from the far-foamed sands'. The wisdom of the unconscious accepts the new (the ocean, as we have seen, is the sphere of creations and destroyings) which the brute will and the bewildered reason (in Enceladus and Saturn) repudiate. Oceanus will offer the comfort of truth. The truth is that the catastrophe into which they are all plunged is inevitable, and must be accepted.

> 'We fall by course of Nature's law, not force
> Of thunder, or of Jove.'

Saturn was not the first of powers, nor will he be the last. In a long cosmogonic passage, drawn largely from *Timæus*, though not

---

[1] Keats's catalogue may be compared with that of *Timæus*, 142 (41).
[2] Already quoted in part (above, pp. 230–1).

without debt to Hesiod and others, Oceanus sketches the birth of
the universe. His description is in terms of light, the 'first-fruits
of . . . That sullen ferment [in Chaos] which for wondrous ends
Was ripening in itself.' When 'the ripe hour' comes, light, 'en-
gendering Upon its own producer',

> '. . . forthwith touch'd
> The whole enormous matter into Life.'

The giant race of the gods was created at this moment, and found
itself 'ruling new and beauteous realms'. Bliss was in this empire.
But 'Now comes the pain of truth . . .'

> 'As Heaven and Earth are fairer, fairer far
> Than Chaos and blank Darkness, though once chiefs;
> And as we show beyond that Heaven and Earth
> In form and shape compact and beautiful . . .
> So on our heels a fresh perfection treads,
> A power more strong in beauty, born of us
> And fated to excel us, as we pass
> In glory that old Darkness . . .'

And a characteristic tree-metaphor follows:[1]

> 'Say, doth the dull soil
> Quarrel with the proud forests it hath fed,
> And feedeth still, more comely than itself?
> Can it deny the chiefdom of green groves?'   [181–220]

The conclusion of Oceanus' argument is famous: '. . . 'tis the
eternal law That first in beauty should be first in might'; and by
this law the new dynasty will fall in its turn before still greater
perfection.

Here, then, is an answer to my self-posed but not altogether

---

[1] Characteristic, but perhaps not uninfluenced by Taylor's long account of the
procession of Chaos and the gods from the First Cause, in the Introduction to
Parmenides, which Keats may have read in Benjamin Bailey's little 1793 edition.
Having first compared them to rays of light issuing from a centre, Taylor, quoting
Proclus, continues: 'And hence they are all established in the first cause like the
roots of trees in the earth; so that they are all as much as possible superessential, just
as trees are eminently of an earthly nature, without at the same time being earth
itself . . .' (*op. cit.*, pp. 274–5).

rhetorical question at the outset of our study of *Hyperion*: 'What is the poem's concern with growth?' It is concerned very much with growth, not in the sublunary world this time but in the empyrean. Commentators have read *Hyperion* as evolutionism, but its evolutionism is cyclic: the Great Year revolves, reaches its consummation, explodes; and there is a fresh beginning. Here we have Keats's dominant pattern. We recognize it again in the speech of Clymene which follows, in which Oceanus' broad praise of beauty is concentrated upon a pæan of Apollo. Clymene's terms are musical rather than physical: a melody-breathing shell takes the place of Oceanus' 'proud forests', and Apollo's voice stands, in Clymene's account, for his doves and 'eagles golden-feather'd'; yet the doves are there too, in his singing:

> 'I threw my shell away upon the sand,
> And a wave fill'd it, as my sense was fill'd
> With that new blissful golden melody.
> A living death was in each gush of sounds,
> Each family of rapturous hurried notes . . .
> And then another, then another strain,
> Each like a dove leaving its olive perch,
> With music wing'd instead of silent plumes,
> To hover round my head, and make me sick
> Of joy and grief at once . . .'   [278-89]

'A living death'—'joy and grief at once': Keats's favourite anti-nomies are expressed in vivid synæsthesis.

I shall omit discussion of Enceladus's speech, and the welcome given to Hyperion, which serve the interests of the dramatic action, rather than add to our understanding of Keats's 'darker purpose'. Our concern now is with Book III—with its 136 lines, which were all Keats penned, and its presentation of Apollo, as far as Keats was able to present him. So far, in the first version, we have been moving among impersonalities (where Keats had moved, and found breathing so difficult that he embarked upon his second version). Acutely conscious, I think, that the first was more assured, if not better poetry than the second, he patches and

17

conflates. He brings in this and that; but the versions are at logger-heads, will not live together. How reconcile the morbid psychology of *The Fall* with the extrovert brilliance of *Hyperion*? That *Hyperion* is not really extrovert matters little; we are considering effect. Keats mutilates his first version, and it must have been with tears of blood: but the sacrifice is in vain. Book III, however, opens with happier possibilities, from one point of view. Its theme is Apollo: and (in the original version) an Apollo bewildered, not triumphant. A 'possible sublimity' hovers over him; there are moments of self-doubt, 'aching ignorance'. This is Keats's own situation. And I think Keats felt the possibility of 'going on from here' when he dropped the first version. But events moved swiftly. The first version was abandoned in April (as it seems); the second was taken up in September. In those six months a lot of things had happened, including the Winchester visit. It was always difficult for Keats to renounce a project on which he had once set his mind: otherwise, I think, he would have abandoned *Hyperion* long before December 1819.

The poem moves, we have seen, within three worlds: the empyrean, Hyperion's 'bowers of fragrant and enwreathed light'; the infernal, where the Titans sit, 'self-hid or prison-bound', in their 'nest of woe'; and the terrestrial, to which we now turn— the isle of Delos, with its olives green,

> And poplars, and lawn-shading palms, and beech,
> In which the Zephyr breathes the loudest song,
> And hazels thick, dark-stemm'd beneath the shade:
> Apollo is once more the golden theme!   [III, 25–8]

The book opens happily: here are Keats's beloved trees, here is the sea's murmur, and here is the god of song. We feel a tremendous release from the tensions and the agonies of the first two books: and of course it is Keats's own release. On 1 December Tom had died; the long solitary watch at his bedside was over. A little earlier Keats had completed his second book. He goes to live with Brown; there is some renewal of old friendships; and he falls in love with Fanny Brawne. It is under these new stimuli that he pushes on with *Hyperion*. A third of Book III—perhaps down to Apollo's encounter with Mnemosyne—belongs in all probability to the second half of December. And then, for some reason, the impulse fails. He writes a little minor verse, 'goes everywhere', decides to read a passage of Shakespeare every Sunday at ten o' clock, is confined with a sore throat, is pestered for money by Haydon. On 20 January he sets out for Chichester: and *Hyperion* is abandoned for *St Agnes' Eve*. He returns to Wentworth Place in February, and writes *The Eve of St Mark*. The agonized sonnet 'Why did I laugh tonight . . .?' comes in the March section of the journal letter to George and Georgiana; in April we have *Psyche*. And about this time, it would seem, *Hyperion* in its first version came to a stop.

The third book begins with a farewell to poor Tom.

> Thus, in alternate uproar and sad peace,
> Amazed were those Titans utterly.
> O leave them, Muse! O leave them to their woes;
> For thou art weak to sing such tumults dire:
> A solitary sorrow best befits
> Thy lips, and antheming a lonely grief.

It is not only a farewell to Tom; it is also a forecast of his final abandonment of *Hyperion*. If Keats feels himself too weak to sing the tumults dire of the Titans while they are still immobilized in their 'nest of woe', his diffidence will be still greater when he contemplates the epic action with which he will have to grapple in the sequel. Plainly, he has lost his assurance. The third book of *Hyperion* is already moving away from epic into lyric writing. And this is not a simple matter of contrast—of the lyricism of *Paradise Lost* in its garden scenes heightening the sublimities which precede and follow. It is a fresh start, a projection of the story on to a personal plane alien to the spirit of the epic. Milton is within his poem, but he is within it impersonally, as it were, on the bardic level: associated with

> Blind *Thamyris* and blind *Mæonides*,
> And *Tiresias* and *Phineus* Prophets old

less in their blindness, their weakness, than in their representative function, doctrinal to a nation. Keats can claim no such charter. And this, I think, he felt. He had neither Milton's depth of reading and reflection, self-dedication to the supreme task, nor his adamantine firmness of character and purpose. The truth is that the epic age had passed—had passed, indeed, centuries before Milton; only his colossal seriousness and virtuosity made possible the limited success he achieved. And this too Keats must have felt. The idea of *Hyperion* had come to him in the first flush of excitement as he was writing *Endymion*; he had not realized how very different an affair the epic was from the romance; and even in the romance he had failed.

Hence the half-apology with which the third book begins. Hence, too, the change of tone. The first thirty lines return to the manner of *Endymion*; almost, here and there, to the mannerisms of 'I stood tip-toe . . .'.

> Flush every thing that hath a vermeil hue,
> Let the rose glow intense and warm the air,
> And let the clouds of even and of morn
> Float in voluptuous fleeces o'er the hills;
> Let the red wine within the goblet boil,
> Cold as a bubbling well; let faint-lipp'd shells,
> On sands, or in great deeps, vermilion turn
> Through all their labyrinths; and let the maid
> Blush keenly, as with some warm kiss surpris'd. [14–22]

The maid surprised by some warm kiss is not really at home in *Hyperion*—the clouds of even and of morn and the great deeps could have got on without her. But Keats could not get on without her: she is Fanny Brawne, or Isabella Jones, a new world of experience. And here we have the root of his strength and his weakness. He is completely sincere: he cannot say what he does not feel, and he says everything he feels. This makes for organic wholeness, for unity of the *opus* in its entirety, the whole body of Keats's work. But it makes too for weakness of texture in the individual poem, for a flaw in self-criticism. I would not be misunderstood. In one sense Keats is the most self-critical of poets, the most conscious of flaws and deficiencies. But, precisely because he is *within* and *of* the poem he is writing, he is unable to judge it effectively as he writes it; he cannot detach himself, stand aside, coldly scrutinize. He has to get on with it, finish it, and start something new. If he had lived it might have been otherwise: he might have learned to integrate his critical with his creative insight in the making of the poem; or, more likely perhaps, he would have learned, as Wordsworth and Yeats did (and maybe to better effect than them), the art of revision.

Hyperion III gives no hint of any such development. External stresses press in upon it, break the continuity of tone hitherto so admirably if artificially maintained. Tom's illness and death; Fanny's beauty; Keats's wavering ambition: these are strands woven into the lyric texture. 'Apollo is once more the golden theme': yes, but Apollo is once more John Keats.

> Where was he, when the Giant of the Sun
> Stood bright, amid the sorrow of his peers?

He was at Keats's favourite occupation: gazing on, listening to, 'nature's gentle doings'.

> Together had he left his mother fair
> And his twin-sister sleeping in their bower,
> And in the morning twilight wandered forth
> Beside the osiers of a rivulet,
> Full ankle-deep in lilies of the vale.
> The nightingale had ceas'd, and a few stars
> Were lingering in the heavens, while the thrush
> Began calm-throated. Throughout all the isle
> There was no covert, no retired cave
> Unhaunted by the murmurous noise of waves,
> Though scarcely heard in many a green recess.
> He listen'd, and he wept, and his bright tears
> Went trickling down the golden bow he held. [29–43]

It is all very well: but this is not the epic hero. We are back again in Endymion's sister-lulled, sentimental world. And we see what has happened. The release from Tom's sick-room, the new excitements of love, the new intimacy with Brown, have indeed given him the impulse to create: but not the impulse to create *Hyperion*. They have brought him release from tension; but for the epic effort tension, concentration, are imperative. Probably he should not have attempted the epic at all. Attempting it, he needed a 'crystallization'[1]: fortified, as Milton's was, by the consciousness of long preparation, of sublime powers, of a Biblical or otherwise traditional background.

Yet there were possibilities in Book III. If Keats had been able to follow them up it would have meant writing a different sort of 'epic'; Books I and II would have had to be scrapped. And of course they were scrapped: that is the meaning of *The Fall of Hyperion*. An epic without a hero—a 'vegetative', tentative, evolutionary epic—this would have been a novelty. The germ is there in Oceanus' speech in Book II. It sprouts in Book III, in Apollo's address to Mnemosyne. Keats is wobbling: he has not quite decided to abandon the conventional epic for the psychological epic. It seems to me that in December he got as far as line 43 [2]; and he felt he could not go on. What he had written was so antithetical to Books I and II that further progress was barred. When he takes the manuscript up again, in April, he tries to get back to his original manner:

> While from beneath some cumbrous boughs hard by
> With solemn step an awful Goddess came,
> And there was purport in her looks for him,
> Which he with eager guess began to read
> Perplex'd, the while melodiously he said:
> 'How cam'st thou over the unfooted sea? . . .'

These are the accents of Book I. Mnemosyne appears to Apollo as Thea had appeared to Saturn. And, of course, to much better

---

[1] As Keats himself recognized: he breaks off a letter of 16 August 1819 to Fanny Brawne with the words: '. . . a few more moments thought of you would uncrystallize and dissolve me. I must not give way to it—but turn to my writing again——'.

[2] I disagree here with Mr R. Gittings, who takes the December portion (*The Living Year*, p. 53) down to line 60.

purpose. For Apollo is youth, inspiration, growth, where Saturn
was age, despair, death. Thea could give no real comfort; she
could do no more than pity. And Apollo is, proleptically, Keats.
Mnemosyne is the incarnation of the original 'vast idea' which
had 'floated before him' as he traversed, in those early days, the
realm of Flora and old Pan, unwitting what it was. Now the
truth will be revealed to him in its fulness. It is Keats who speaks
now:

> 'How cam'st thou over the unfooted sea?
> Or hath that antique mien and robed form
> Mov'd in these vales invisible till now?
> Sure I have heard those vestments sweeping o'er
> The fallen leaves, when I have sat alone
> In cool mid-forest. Surely I have traced
> The rustle of those ample skirts about
> These grassy solitudes, and seen the flowers
> Lift up their heads, as still the whisper pass'd. . . .' [45–58]

The idea, then, *is* Mnemosyne, and Mnemosyne is identical, here,
with Anamnesis, the Platonic recollection. Through recollection,
or realization, Apollo will attain his full godhead. The truth is hid
from him only by ignorance. I pointed out, in discussing *Endymion*, that the pilgrim comes to understand, at the close of all his
wanderings, that they have been strictly unnecessary: the truth,
the realization and the glory lay under his nose all the time. In
Hyperion Apollo is in the situation attained by Endymion when
he is 'spiritualized . . . from this mortal state' by his union with
Diana. He is already conscious of his godhead in its essence but
not in its function. He is sad because he does not know how to
exercise the powers he feels burgeoning within him.

Now if this seems to us a curious conception of divinity, it is
because we do not bear in mind Keats's major source for his
cosmogony: the *Timæus*. The creation account in that treatise
teaches us, as I have already pointed out, that the 'shap'd and palpable gods' of Olympus are far from being self-sufficient: they
are the offspring of Heaven and Earth, and, as such, inferior both
to the celestial gods and the elements. They can degenerate into

sub-divine forms as man can elevate himself into superhuman form. Power resides in the correct exercise of the functions proper to each being at each particular stage of his growth. And this is the lesson which Apollo begins to learn before the fragment ends. First he remembers: the majestic figure standing before him is Mnemosyne. Next he confesses his ignorance:

> 'For me, dark, dark,
> And painful vile oblivion seals my eyes:
> I strive to search wherefore I am so sad. . . .'   [86–8]

He calls on the goddess to point out, among the many spheres of heaven, some 'one particular beauteous star' in which he may dwell

> 'And make its silvery splendour pant with bliss'.

'What is power?' he demands. But plainly he is going too fast. Before assuming the empire of the sun there is much he has to learn. The goddess remains silent, but Apollo reads

> A wondrous lesson in [her] silent face

exactly as Keats himself, in the later version, reads the war of the Titans in Moneta's eyes.

> 'Knowledge enormous makes a god of me.
> Names, deeds, gray legends, dire events, rebellions,
> Majesties, sovran voices, agonies,
> Creations and destroyings, all at once
> Pour into the wide hollows of my brain,
> And deify me, as if some blithe wine
> Or bright elixir peerless I had drunk,
> And so become immortal.'   [111–20]

The parallels in the two versions are complete; the 'wide hollows' of Apollo's brain echo, in the 'Fragment', to the 'high tragedy In the dark secret Chambers of [Moneta's] skull' in the 'Dream'.

The 'Fragment' ends with Apollo's divinization. It ends, that is, triumphantly, though for a moment it teeters on the brink of disaster, as the god, keeping his steadfast eyes on Mnemosyne's, trembles and flushes

> Into a hue more roseate than sweet pain
> Gives to a Nymph new-ravish'd . . .

The lines are suppressed in the final draft and must count for nothing in our estimate of the poem. But Keats did write them; and the mere fact that he could write them, in this place of all places, bespeaks confusions more dire than any in *Endymion*. You cannot live in two worlds at once, if you are a poet; and the world Keats is living in here is the world of *St Agnes*. For over a month now he has been writing against the grain, taking *Hyperion* up and putting it down again, subjecting his creative impulse to dictation, making a mock of his own doctrine that poetry should come like the leaves to a tree, or not at all. The rosy maid has almost wrecked the poem already, in line 21; now here she is again, disturbing the clear lake of transcendental vision, giving the lie to the whole theme of self-realization. And of course Keats could not go on. It would have been a pretence, and pretence was not in his nature. He will try once again, on a new plan: a plan which will include human weakness and self-doubt in its basic pattern: he will write *The Fall of Hyperion*.

He wrote, as we have seen, 529 lines before he gave his epic up altogether for the adventure of the narrative romances and the great Odes.

[*Hyperion*: *A Fragment* (September 1818–April 1819)—*The Fall of Hyperion*: *A Dream* (September 1819–December 1819)]

Chapter Thirteen

THE SEXUAL STRIFE

The power of your benediction is of not so weak a nature as to pass
from the ring in four and twenty hours—it is like a sacred Chalice once
consecrated and ever consecrate.

Letter of February 1820 *to Fanny Brawne.*

KEATS'S development is far from being the steady trek
from position to position—naturalism, Platonism, humanism, and so on—which some of his critics[1] have made it
out to be. It is much more of a tidal movement, ebbing and
flowing; a process of growth, expanding here, contracting there;
a systole and diastole, following a natural rhythm. Keats's world
is 'the sweet-and-bitter world', a field for the play of antinomies
in thought, feeling, will: a world in which contradictory attitudes
can be held in focus together. This is evident in the letters, where
he tosses ideas and emotions about like a juggler, squeezing the
last drop of entertainment (or wisdom) out of the mood of the
moment; it is evident too in the poems, where quite incompatible
styles as well as divergent 'philosophies' may mark the work
of the same month. He 'cogitates on . . . Saturn and Ops'
while writing *Isabella*: *St Mark* follows close upon *St Agnes*. The
jewels of the great year are strung together on no continuous
thread.

The last three-quarters of 1818 are a period of painful ferment.
He is 'all uncertain' of his direction. He is uncertain, even, of his
centre: of *what he is* in himself, of how far he can be said to *be*
anything. The adventure of self-discovery in *Endymion* has failed.
He is farther from his centre than ever. And, as if to mirror his
inner chaos, his social centre disintegrates. George and Georgiana

---

[1] Notably C. L. Finney, in *The Evolution of Keats's Poetry.*

go into exile; Tom dies; Fanny is a virtual prisoner; Hunt and Haydon are at loggerheads: Bailey acts scurvily to Marianne Reynolds; only Brown remains as a constant. The flights into Scotland and Chichester and the Isle of Wight are really flights, moves to escape from unbearable tensions.

Hyperion too, we have seen, is an escape. And what of *Isabella*, Keats's first poem after *Endymion*? It may not be a poem of escape, but it is certainly a poem of defeat. It is the backwash of *Endymion*: a distillation of the weakness of that poem. 'In Endymion', he told Hessey, 'I leaped headlong into the Sea, and thereby have become better acquainted with the Soundings, the quicksands, & the rocks, than if I had stayed upon the green shore, and piped a silly pipe, and took tea & comfortable advice.—I was never afraid of failure; for I would sooner fail than not be among the greatest.'[1] In spite of these brave words, we see that Keats is disappointed. And the proof that he is disappointed is this: when he climbs out of the sea again he does sit on the green shore and pipe a silly pipe.

Or, at least, silly sooth. *Isabella* is a charming poem and we could ill spare it: it dallies with the innocence of love like the old age. But it is no advance on *Endymion*. In a letter of January 1818 Keats writes with a touch of scorn of his long poem: 'in Endymion I think you may have many bits of the deep and sentimental cast'. That is true; but *Isabella* is altogether of the sentimental cast; and Keats came later to feel this so strongly that he took a real dislike to the poem.

This does not mean that the student of Keats can by-pass *Isabella*. It is not deep, it is sentimental, and it is enormously suggestive. It is, in miniature, the obverse of *Endymion*. Its writer, one feels, has swung consciously or unconsciously to an extreme; as though he were saying, 'I have given you an allegory, now I will tell you a tale; I have analysed love as a spiritual force, now I will show it as a motion of the blood; I have dabbled in the divine, but here I will confine myself to the human; I have traced the processes of growth

---

[1] *Letters*, 221.

and fruition, but now I will sink into the mould of decay and death'. This negative impulse is at work throughout *Isabella*. There is no attempt to idealize the characters. Lorenzo has nothing of the heroic about him; he is ludicrously timid in his love-making, and he dies without a struggle. Isabella mourns, goes mad, and dies. Even the brothers are little more than passive agents of evil.

Keats omitted the season of winter from his *Endymion* canvas. In that great picture only the vital processes were displayed. Winter threatens in the close: but the hero escapes by an act of will. In *Isabella*, on the contrary, the hero (who is no hero) dies; and dies, as he lives and loves, passively. 'They could not ... they could not ... they could not ... He might not' is the note moaning through the first two stanzas. The poem is to be a record of impotence and frustration and sterility. Lorenzo and Isabella are brought into proximity: they fall, inevitably, in love. But their love is destined to failure. Their doom is the tragedy of kinship—the old ballad theme which Keats essays again, to bring to a very different conclusion, in *The Eve of St Agnes*. They are star-crossed lovers.

The poem lives by dramatic irony. The promise of the early stanzas is never fulfilled: for this promise is of life and consummation. The progress of simple human love is integrated with the quiet courses of nature:

> With every morn their love grew tenderer,
>   With every eve deeper and tenderer still;
> He might not in house, field, or garden stir,
>   But her full shape would all his seeing fill;
> And his continual voice was pleasanter
>   To her, than noise of trees or hidden rill;
> Her lute-string gave an echo of his name,
> She spoilt her half-done broidery with the same.

We are here among the tender domesticities: the *Endymion* forest, with its glooms and grandeurs, its panthers and eagles, is far away. This is a woman's world. If Lorenzo finally declares his love, it is Isabella who brings him to the point, who directs the course

of events into the ironically defined channels of warmth and
flowering:

> 'Love! thou art leading me from wintry cold,
>   Lady! thou leadest me to summer clime,
> And I must taste the blossoms that unfold
>   In its ripe warmth this gracious morning time.'
> So said, his erewhile timid lips grew bold,
>   And poesied with hers in dewy rhyme:
> Great bliss was with them, and great happiness
> Grew, like a lusty flower in June's caress.

The initiative is Isabella's. And, running through the whole poem,
we sense a curiously biological motif (if I may so phrase it): the
suggestion of a passion between the lovers that is unindividual,
undifferentiated, unsexual almost. Or let us say the sexuality is
unwilled, passive, responding to a vegetative rather than a strictly
human or even animal drive. The lovers in their joy are

> Twin roses by the zephyr blown apart
> Only to meet again more close, and share
> The inward fragrance of each other's heart.

Chance has brought them together, as it brings the bee to the
flower; a breeze serves to separate them, like blossoms on con-
tiguous sprays. They are helpless in the grip of a biological destiny.
That is why we feel them as anonymous. They have no 'identity'.
Their love is a means to an end: and Keats makes almost painfully
plain what that end is to be. From first to last Isabella is presented
as the potential mother. When, at the outset of the story, Lorenzo
fails to declare his love, letting pass 'honeyless days and days',

> . . . sweet Isabella's untouch'd cheek
> Fell sick within the rose's just domain,
> Fell thin as a young mother's, who doth seek
> By every lull to cool her infant's pain.

Her tragedy is the tragedy of frustrated motherhood. When she
hears the truth of Lorenzo's disappearance, her only thought is to

> find the clay, so dearly prized,
> And sing to it one latest lullaby.

She unearths Lorenzo's glove, the fabric
>   whereon
>   Her silk had play'd in purple phantasies—

something of his, therefore, in whose creation she has shared—

>   And put it in her bosom, where it dries
>   And freezes utterly unto the bone
>   Those dainties made to still an infant's cries.

And when, finally, she has buried the severed head in her basil-pot she tends it with all a mother's care:

>   And when she left, she hurried back, as swift
>   As bird on wing to breast its eggs again;
>   And, patient as a hen-bird, sat her there
>   Beside her basil, weeping through her hair.

The tragedy of *Isabella*, then, is not the tragedy of romantic love, for hero and heroine are not sufficiently individualized to be capable of such a passion. It is a tragedy of destiny: of a biological destiny which is frustrated. We shall see later the importance of this for Keats's thought.[1] Let us meanwhile note that the instrument and the locus of that frustration again represent a reversal of the *Endymion* situation. The brother-sister relationship in the earlier poem is a factor of warm, simple affection making for the fruition of human love. Peona does her best to convince Endymion that earthlier-happy is the love distilled out of normal human passion than the crazy dreams he cherishes. She urges her brother to take the young Indian maid to wife. Isabella's brothers, on the contrary, want to wed their sister to 'some old noble' who in all likelihood will be impotent. They are instruments of frustration and destruction. Their lives are spent in creating and spreading misery, in shutting others up from the light of the sun. A cancelled stanza links a birth-image to a money-image: the brothers have been warped from normality as embryos:

>   their good Mother dream'd
>   In the longing time of Units in their teens

---

[1] See below, pp. 297–8.

Of proudly bas'd addition and of net—
And both their backs were mark'd with tare and tret.

They are agents of destruction; the forest is its locus. The forest, which in *Endymion* is the great theatre of vigorous growth, of heaven's light pouring through netted branches to foster vital processes, is here 'that dismal forest-hearse', a place of death and decay. The skyward thrust of plants in free growth, 'feeding a little space with ever-budding green', is now replaced by a downwards rhythm: the movement is towards the grave:

> 'Red whortle-berries droop above my head,
> And a large flint-stone weighs upon my feet,
> Around me beeches and high chestnuts shed
> Their leaves and prickly nuts; a sheep-fold bleat
> Comes from beyond the river to my bed:
> Go, shed one tear upon my heather-bloom,
> And it shall comfort me within the tomb.'

The forest-loam, in *Endymion* the generous feeder of roots upwards into green leaves and golden fruit, is in *Isabella* the defiler of human flesh, the ghastly nourisher of 'green and livid spot'. So the Druid's harp, which sang through the earlier poems and is heard by anticipation in the prologue to *Endymion* IV, is here unstrung in a palsied hand; and the wind that blew legend-laden through the trees is transmogrified to 'hoarse night-gusts sepulchral briers among'.

Winter, from which Keats shrank in *Endymion*, is now stressed with peculiar pathos.

> In the mid days of autumn, on their eves,
> The breath of Winter comes from far away,
> And the sick west continually bereaves
> Of some gold tinge, and plays a roundelay
> Of death among the bushes and the leaves
> To make all bare before he dares to stray
> From his north cavern.[1] So sweet Isabel
> By gradual decay from beauty fell.

---

[1] Keats proposes reading the poem to Bailey in Scotland 'among the Snows of next Winter' (*Letters*, 152).

Lorenzo too has died with the dying year. Endymion escaped the
doom of the vegetation god by his own power of spiritual affirmation; but Lorenzo, *l'homme moyen sensuel*, has to die. And if he
rises again, it will only be in the spring, in the immutable course
of nature, as vegetable being. The flourishing growth of the pot
of basil well expresses Lorenzo's destiny. For he has not died
utterly. 'They felt the kernel of the grave' is a precisely accurate
statement. But, because he has not transcended himself, the spiritual
in him cannot draw its nourishment from the earthly root; on
the contrary, it must now be the vegetable, the purely 'natural',
that feeds on the human in order to survive:

> And so she ever fed it with thin tears,
>   Whence thick, and green, and beautiful it grew,
> So that it smelt more balmy than its peers
>   Of basil-tufts in Florence; for it drew
> Nurture besides, and life, from human fears,
>   From the fast mouldering head there shut from view:
> So that the jewel, safely casketed,
> Came forth, and in perfumed leafits spread.

The urn is thus the locus, here, of a reversed metamorphosis.
These meanings lie, I believe, beneath the light surface of *Isabella*:
they form an eddy in the broad onward current of Keats's thought;
and we shall not meet them again until we come to the *Ode on
Melancholy*. They are the outcome of a mood of despondency and
even life-denial.[1] If we generally miss these pointers when reading
Isabella, it is because we do not expect to find them. 'There are
very few', as Keats foresaw (*Letters*, 391), who 'look to the reality'.
But they are there. I have not, I think, over-subtilized or read into
the poem more than its apparently thin texture will bear. Indeed,
in the case of Keats we cannot speak of thinness of texture. Even
his minor poems have an inexhaustible richness.

No other verse, outside Shakespeare and Blake, rewards minute

---

[1] Keats recognized the tendency in himself as early as May 1817: '—truth is I
have a horrid Morbidity of Temperament which has shown itself at intervals—it
is I have no doubt the greatest Enemy and stumbling block I have to fear—I may
even say that it is likely to be the cause of my disappointment' (*Letters*, 30).

scrutiny as does Keats's. Its texture is truly organic (including the flaws, which are there in abundance); we can put it under the microscope, and it doesn't degenerate into a blur of dots like a photographic reproduction; it opens out into new patterns like a piece of living tissue. It is 'full poetry'. More and more we understand what Keats meant when he spoke of loading every rift with ore; and if we compare his poetry with that of the man to whom he wrote those words we understand them more clearly still. For Shelley's verse, lovely and exciting as it is, lacks this organic texture—seems, somehow, unrooted. Its achievement is that of broad brush-strokes, or simple melody. Wordsworth's vision, again, may point to depths beyond depths, but the depths are not *in* the poetry, they are discussed by it. With Keats, as perhaps only with Shakespeare and Blake before him, we constantly find our thoughts going back to a phrase here, a simile there, discerning new ore in the rift, new voices in the song.

There is, then, in Keats, this richness, this complexity and depth, this 'ore'. But there is something else too: what he called 'gusto'. The ore is a matter of life's texture; the gusto is a matter of its rhythms. Keats never forgot that life is energy, that the stream flows, and that we are in and of the stream. Gusto is life's movement conscious of itself: the energy which is eternal delight. And the delight is in the complexity, in the pattern as it unfolds itself. Hence the chameleon poet lives in gusto. This zest we recognize as the source of some of Keats's most regrettable juvenile blunders. But without it we should never have had the masterpieces. He is not afraid to make mistakes, a trait he has in common with great creating nature. Like her, he moves on from form to form, from experiment to experiment. There is no lingering, no looking back. He is swept forwards. And, he finds, the surrender to impulse justifies itself in the event: 'for things which I do half at Random are afterwards confirmed by my judgment in a dozen features of Propriety'.[1]

---

[1] Letter to B. R. Haydon, 10–11 May 1817. Cf. Blake: 'Great ends never look at means, but produce them spontaneously.'

He is swept forward, in *The Eve of St Agnes*, to a new triumph of gusto—almost, one might say, of bravura. *Isabella* had ore but it lacked zest; it was a beautiful but a tired poem. Its very virtues stem from the qualities which Keats was eager to outgrow. He himself judged it 'smokable'—open, that is, to ridicule:

> There is too much inexperience of life, and simplicity of knowledge in it—which might do very well after one's death—but not while one is alive. There are very few would look to the reality. I intend to use more finesse with the Public. It is possible to write fine things which cannot be laugh'd at in any way. Isabella is what I should call were I a reviewer 'A weak-sided Poem' with an amusing sober-sadness about it. Not that I do not think Reynolds and you are quite right about it—it is enough for me. But this will not do to be public. If I may so say, in my dramatic capacity I enter fully into the feeling: but in Propria Persona I should be apt to quiz it myself—There is no objection of this kind to Lamia—A good deal to St Agnes Eve—only not so glaring. . . .

He is writing (21 September 1819) to Richard Woodhouse; the letter includes a draft of the *Ode to Autumn* and the opening paragraph of *The Fall of Hyperion*. In contrast to these he might well 'smoke' *Isabella*. But he acknowledges a 'reality' in the poem; Woodhouse and Reynolds admire it,[1] but he thinks its appeal for the public would be small. That he could think *St Agnes* 'smokable' too is a gauge of his despondency at this period. For *St Agnes* is not in the least open to ridicule; it has always been, I think, the most popular among Keats's longer poems. Its atmosphere is the very antithesis of *Isabella*'s. It glows with light, colour, movement, romantic sensibility. It is, like *Isabella*, a 'Gothic' poem; but in it the Gothic glooms and terrors are counterpointed and finally eclipsed by 'the fairy power of unreflecting love'.

---

[1] Reynolds had written as long before as October 1818: 'I am confident, Keats, that the Pot of Basil hath that simplicity and quiet pathos, which are of sure Sovereignty over all hearts' (*K.C.*, I, 43).

The Eve of St Agnes is, in a sense, Keats's own answer to *Isabella*. The earlier poem had been a tragedy of kinship; *St Agnes* is a narrative of kinship with a happy ending. *Isabella* had culminated in the frustration of a biological destiny; *St Agnes* carries to a triumphant conclusion an adventure of romantic daring. *Isabella* had diverted Keats from his main current; in *St Agnes* he returns to it.

The poem's movement is precisely antithetical to that of *Isabella*. There, the flow was from life to death, from the specious promise of 'great happiness' growing 'like a lusty flower in June's caress' to the 'wintry cold' of the forest tomb. Nature's purposes are thwarted: 'those dainties made to still an infant's cries' are 'frozen utterly unto the bone'. Wintry images, together with 'marble tombs', dying plants, decay, and mournful music, throng its concluding stanzas. In *St Agnes* the tombs are initial: we move rapidly from the 'bitter chill' of 'sculptur'd dead' seeming to freeze 'emprison'd in black, purgatorial rails' to 'the poppied warmth' of Madeline's slumber and the luxuriant pyramids of fruit and spices

> heap'd with glowing hand
> On golden dishes and in baskets bright
> Of wreathed silver.

The movement is vertical: we journey with Porphyro from the darkness and cold of the grave (which is also the place of the seed and the root) into the warmth and fragrance of the nuptial chamber (the place of flowering and fruition). All in all, we can say that *St Agnes* constitutes a new manifesto for Keats—more assured, more compact and more finished than *Endymion*—of faith in his own powers, of trust in those 'great allies' the rhythms of the seasons and the blessedly steadfast, impersonal forces of nature; and above all, perhaps, it is a pæan of rejoicing in the flowering of his love for Fanny Brawne, and the love she gave him in return.

In *Endymion* the rigours of winter, as we have seen, were omitted from the picture. The development of the poem, which Keats intended initially to integrate with the course of his own life from April to October 1817,[1] must close with autumn:

> O may no wintry season, bare and hoary,
> See it half-finish'd; but let Autumn bold,
> With universal tinge of sober gold,
> Be all about me when I make an end.

In *Isabella* the season is introduced in a simile. But at last, in the *Eve*, Keats comes to close grips with winter. It is a sign of his own development, of his growing acceptance of life's darker aspects.[2] An acceptance which is not a surrender, but involves their mastery and their transmutation. The static quality of *Isabella* has disappeared. The new poem is instinct with that energy by which principles pressed to their extreme suffer dramatic reversal. We noted this 'dialectic' in the Cave of Quietude episode of *Endymion*. It is evident again in two sonnets of early 1818: the one, *To Homer*, stresses darkness:

> Aye, on the shores of darkness there is light,
> And precipices show untrodden green;
> There is a budding morrow in midnight;
> There is a triple sight in blindness keen;

the other, untitled, stresses both darkness and winter:

> O thou whose face hath felt the Winter's wind,
> Whose eye has seen the snow-clouds hung in mist,
> And the black elm tops 'mong the freezing stars,
> To thee the spring will be a harvest-time.
> O thou, whose only book has been the light
> Of supreme darkness which thou feddest on
> Night after night when Phœbus was away,
> To thee the Spring shall be a triple morn.

---

[1] Keats was a month out in his reckoning: the poem was not finished until near the end of November. But he had already 'revoked' the promise in *Letters*, 29.

[2] And of course of life's basic rhythm too. It is in the sonnet 'Four seasons fill the measure of the year' of September 1818 that he admits of man: 'He has his Winter too of pale misfeature, Or else he would forego his mortal nature.'

Into his basic pattern of growth, flowering and fruition Keats is now learning to integrate the essential, though seemingly negative, element of immobility, darkness, and cold. The richness of *St Agnes' Eve* derives, as we shall see, from this integration.

The poem develops by dramatic contrasts. Throughout the first three stanzas we are, to all intents and purposes, in the grave. The Beadsman, crouched 'among rough ashes' in his crypt, is more dead than alive—'already had his deathbell rung'. He is encompassed by images of death.[1] Cold and darkness triumph. Then, abruptly, the silence is broken by the blare of trumpets 'up aloft'. We ascend to another level of this microcosm which is the storm-beaten castle among the moors. We move from the 'mineral' realm to the 'vegetable': to the plane of mechanical enjoyment, of noise and laughter and bustle:

> At length burst in the argent revelry,
> With plume, tiara, and all rich array,
> Numerous as shadows haunting fairily
> The brain, new stuff'd, in youth, with triumphs gay
> Of old romance.[2]

As the poem stands Keats's intention is far from clear. The revellers are shadows, yes: but how are we to think of them? In some omitted lines we find the answer:

> Ah what are they? the idle pulse scarce stirs
> The Muse should never make the spirit gay;
> Away, bright dulness, laughing fools away—

Life lived on the purely sensual level—which is also the social level, so that Keats's later anguish about Fanny Brawne is anticipated here—is unworthy of the Muse. We turn away from the

---

[1] Cf. Darwin, *The Loves of the Plants*, III, 19–30, for some odd 'Mother Radcliffe' parallels with this and other parts of *St Agnes* and *St Mark*. We find much the same locus and atmosphere in Pope's *Eloisa to Abelard* (cf. especially lines 17–24 and 303–8).

[2] Such, indeed, as had haunted Keats's own brain. *St Agnes* is the poem to which the *Specimen of an Induction* (*c.* 1816) is prefatory. *Calidore*, the second Gothic fragment in *Poems 1817*, gives us the 'trumpet's silver voice' (line 55) which will sound again in *St Agnes* and *Lamia*.

bright surface which conceals such depths of dullness, to Madeline, whose thoughts are of love. Here our progress is still upwards, to the human level, with its possibilities of transformation under 'the fairy power Of unreflecting love'. Madeline incarnates the power of a single emotion firmly conceived and held to create a new situation. She is the radiant centre of the microcosm, protected from trivial assault by the one-pointedness of her vision—

> . . . in vain
> Came many a tiptoe, amorous cavalier,
> And back retir'd

—yet attracting by the same concentration the one person necessary for her completion. Porphyro crosses the moors and enters the castle.

I have represented the process of the poem as a movement upwards through the three worlds. Rather more concretely, within the same framework, it might be represented as a plant with root, leaves and flowers. The root remains in the darkness below. It is cold and immobile. But it is not functionless. The Beadsman spends his hours in prayer for the inhabitants of the castle. He affords, that is, nourishment, and makes possible the final ripening of the golden fruit of love. Above the surface we see the leaves spreading. The 'level chambers' of the castle are 'ready with their pride'. The leaves too are essential; but they are sterile; they do not flower. From among them there rises the single blossom, Madeline.

The above interpretation is, I believe, valid; but it should not be pushed too far or stressed exclusively. It is valid in that it 'explains' the poem from one point of view, and because it helps us to integrate the poem with the corpus of Keats's growth and fruition symbolism. But there is another part of his symbolism which is just as basic: the hermetic-magical. Not that the two are radically separate. On the contrary, it is the vitalism in hermetic thought that attracted Keats. It is the sense of 'no frontiers' in magic, and the sense of growth, of power, in contrast to the empirical philosophy's sterile restriction, that held his interest.

St Agnes' Eve belongs to a group of poems, including *Isabella* and *St Mark's Eve*, that exploit the same central situation: the appearance of a ghostly lover to a waiting girl. This situation is a supernatural one; and from this point of view we can place the group within a still wider group, written between April 1818 and September 1819, which are all poems of spell-binding or transformation. The series begins with *Isabella*, and ends with *Lamia*. We can say something else about these poems; they are all love-poems, and they explore the love-relationship from various angles. The approach in *Isabella* is sentimental, and in *Lamia* cynical.

In *St Agnes' Eve* the approach is 'romantic', to use that word in the sense most commonly given it. When we talk of 'romantic love' we mean the passion of which Keats's poem is a brilliant expression. It is 'unreflecting love', but it is not 'biological' or instinctive in the sense that the love of Isabella and Lorenzo was. The young mother note is not sounded. What is sounded is the religious note: and this is perhaps what we mean when we speak of romantic love. The same note rings in *Romeo and Juliet*. The girl is a saint, and the lover is her eremite. Love is their religion, and they need no other. Their love is an end in itself.[1]

It is by virtue of this devotion to an ideal, this concentration on a relationship, that love can become a power for self-transcendence. This is what Keats implies in his poem. The action leads up to a physical consummation; and, as Keats said in answer to criticism, this was inevitable. But in Keats's dialectical scheme nothing remains fixed within its own boundaries: everything, in so far as it achieves 'intensity', is transmuted. And only at the point of maximum intensity can the possibility of transcendence be realized. This, in Donne's phrase, is love's alchemy. The idea is explicit in Keats's language:

> Beyond a mortal man impassion'd far
> At these voluptuous accents, he arose,
> Ethereal, flush'd, and like a throbbing star

---

[1] Thus Keats will write to Fanny (13 October 1819): '—I could be martyr'd for my Religion—Love is my religion—I could die for that . . .'

> Seen mid the sapphire heaven's deep repose
> Into her dream he melted, as the rose
> Blendeth its odour with the violet,—
> Solution sweet: meantime the frost-wind blows
> Like Love's alarum pattering the sharp sleet
> Against the window-panes; St Agnes' moon hath set.

These lines—to my mind the supreme exemplar of 'Romanticism' in English poetry—are precise in their statements. Porphyro is impassioned 'beyond a mortal man'; he is 'ethereal' (and we know by now what this means for Keats); he is like a star set in the deep repose of the unclouded sky (Keats's favourite eternity image). And he has attained this state, not through what Blake would call 'negation', but through 'energy' and 'an improvement of sensual enjoyment'. The stanza recognizes, moreover, life's bitter-sweet counterpoint: '. . . meantime the frost-wind blows'.

I am afraid Benjamin Bailey was right when he accused Keats of approaching, in the second book of *Endymion*, 'to that abominable principle of *Shelley's*—that *Sensual Love* is the principle of *things*'.[1] And Taylor, Keats's publisher, was right too about *The Eve of St Agnes* when he wondered if 'it was so natural a process in Keats's Mind to carry on the Train of his Story in the way he has done, that he could not write decently . . . if he had that Disease of the Mind which renders the Perceptions too dull to discover Right from Wrong in Matters of moral Taste'.[2] For Keats, like Blake, was 'a man without a mask'. He could not pretend. As he saw, so he set down. He saw sensual love as a principle, and as such he presented it. What quite escaped Woodhouse and Bailey and Taylor was the bearing of Keats's other principle of *intensity*: the dialectical process.

In bringing *Endymion* and *St Agnes' Eve* together like this I have suggested (what is indeed very obvious) the close connection between the two. Indeed, we can go farther. *Endymion*, which by any standards is Keats's major work (and as such I have treated it), contains in germ or in flower every single aspect of Keats's think-

---

[1] *K.C.*, I, 34.   [2] *K.C.*, I, 96.

ing and feeling and knowing. He put the whole of himself into it; and, what is more important, he put the whole of himself before disease and disappointment had conspired to warp, however slightly, that totality. *Endymion* is naïve, is immature, is garrulous; but it is unspoiled. If he had lived, Keats would doubtless have gone far beyond it. But he did not live. He never wrote a poem of that magnitude again. He tried, and gave up. *Endymion* remains, with all its faults, Keats's most complete and most spontaneous expression of a total vision.

As such I have regarded it, and as such I shall continue to regard it in this book. The significances of Keats's later poems reveal themselves only when related to the total structure of *Endymion*. Keats developed, of course; but he had not the time to develop very far. The marvel is that, in so many respects, he had no need to develop—only to consolidate and connect. The marvel is that on so many points he was so unhesitatingly right.

Endymion is the great expansive, the great embracing poem. In all that follows (with the partial exception of *Hyperion*) Keats simply detaches and writes variations upon the themes of his master-work. To put it in a slightly different way, the later poems are focusing points for the great themes of *Endymion* which, now from one angle and now from another, Keats examines and amplifies.

In *St Agnes' Eve* Keats examines the thesis that love, human love, is in itself a great good. When I say that he examines it I mean, of course, that he examines it as a poet. He doesn't analyse it. He doesn't rationalize the matter to himself. The word 'examines' is my rationalization, not his. He simply writes a poem because he has to write a poem. But, viewed from *our* critical standpoint, that is what *St Agnes' Eve* is: a discussion of romantic love. The suggestion of *Endymion* that human love is 'the chief intensity' is here spot-lighted.[1] *Isabella* had shown the defeat of 'vegetative' love. *St Agnes' Eve* shows the triumph of romantic love. Madeline and Porphyro are in difficulties: but they do something about it. In the

---

[1] The same principle is asserted in the 'Bright Star' sonnet.

midst of enemies they are undefeated: they go on, they achieve, they escape. 'O'er the southern moors' they build a new life.

All this is implicit in the poem, and in the way Keats develops the poem. That he develops it by contrasts is obvious enough. What is less obvious, perhaps, is that the contrasts are based on a life-death dichotomy, on a process from darkness (the root) to light (the flower), and on the religious pattern of initiation. These themes we have seen already treated in *Endymion*—indeed, in very great detail and complexity. Here they are isolated by Keats and confined to a local context.

My mention of initiation may seem pompous. But it is not unconsidered. The initiation ritual here in *St Agnes' Eve* is as clear as in *Endymion*. Clearer perhaps, since the moment is isolated. Let us watch Porphyro's progress. Attracted by the adamant of Madeline's one-pointed concentration, he is drawn over the moors to the central castle. The castle is a place of peril (danger is an element in the initiation pattern). Evil forces are ready to assail him if he shrinks from the trial.

> For him, those chambers held barbarian hordes,
> Hyena foemen, and hot-blooded lords,
> Whose very dogs would execrations howl
> Against his lineage.

But Porphyro's heart is 'on fire for Madeline'. Her chamber is the central shrine to which he must win his way through whatever difficulties. And once he has achieved his initiation and gained the prize, all doors will open to him. Accompanied by his mystical bride, he has nothing to fear, in the event, from any Cerberus:

> The wakeful bloodhound rose, and shook his hide,
> But his sagacious eye an inmate owns:
> By one, and one, the bolts full easy slide.

The initiation begins with the lesser mysteries. Porphyro stands *outside* the castle, in darkness.

> Beside the portal doors,
> Buttress'd from moonlight, stands he, and implores
> All saints to give him sight of Madeline.

Then he ventures in. Still in accordance with the initiation pattern, he puts himself in the hands of a guide. Old Angela (the name is significant) first warns him of his danger: '. . . Porphyro! Hie thee from this place!' The warning is typical and constitutes the ritual putting-to-the-proof. But Porphyro is a true hero: he boldly accepts the challenge; and he is conducted on the third stage of his journey.

> He follow'd through a lowly arched way,
> Brushing the cobwebs with his lofty plume;
> And as she mutter'd 'Well-a—well-a-day!'
> He found him in a little moonlight room,
> Pale, latticed, chill, and silent as a tomb.

Threading the needle's eye, he finds himself in the place of waiting where he must face a new trial—the testing of his faith and his patience. He asks for a glimpse of Madeline. Angela continues to express dismay at his daring:

> 'Thou must hold water in a witch's sieve,
> And be liege-lord of all the Elves and Fays,
> To venture so: it fills me with amaze
> To see thee, Porphyro!'

Angela, admittedly, is a doddering old crone (she dies before the night is out), but she is also a witch, a Sybil, a keeper of the mysteries:

> Feebly she laugheth in the languid moon,
> While Porphyro upon her face doth look,
> Like puzzled urchin on an aged crone
> Who keepeth clos'd a wond'rous riddle-book.

With all his dash and courage, the hero is reduced to the condition of a child, and it is the feeble old woman who holds the keys of his success. She tells him now of 'his lady's purpose' upon this Eve of St Agnes: of how Madeline too is seeking, is drawing her destiny towards her by the power of enchantment.

And now, once again, the initiative is taken by the hero, while the test is administered by the Sybil. He asks to be taken directly to Madeline's chamber *in accordance with the prophecy* of which he claims to be the fulfilment in person.[1] Angela charges him with evil purposes, and commands him to go: but he remains firm, attesting his purity of intention: 'I will not harm her, by all saints I swear'. Boldly he threatens to rouse the castle if his wish is denied: and thus he forces the issue.

> 'Wait here, my child, with patience; kneel in prayer
> The while . . .',

Angela instructs him, before she goes off to prepare the ritual meal in Madeline's chamber. Porphyro is now exposed to the trial of patience: 'The lover's endless minutes slowly pass'd'. The old woman returns, and leads him on the fourth and last stage of his journey.

> Safe at last,
> Through many a dusky gallery, they gain
> The maiden's chamber, silken, hush'd, and chaste;
> Where Porphyro took covert, pleas'd amain.

If the vertical pattern of the poem is one of *growth* upward through successive levels of existence—mineral, vegetative, human, spiritual—the horizontal pattern is that of concentric circles of attainment to a central peace 'at the heart Of endless agitation'. The first or outer circle is that of the storm-lashed moor; the second circle is of the castle riotous with unholy feast and merriment; the third circle is Madeline's chamber. Here a concentration is achieved, under the moon's ægis, of the three worlds in the person of Madeline.

The moon reigns throughout *St Agnes' Eve* as throughout *Endymion*. Her benign influence waxes with the progress of the action. While still outside the castle, Porphyro is 'buttress'd from moonlight'. This is the first mention of the moon. The second mention comes with the third stage of the journey: 'He found him in a little moonlight room'. The third mention comes with Madeline's entry into her chamber.

---

[1] The reference to Merlin and the 'monstrous debt' paid to his 'Demon' is noteworthy (line 171).

Out went the taper as she hurried in;
Its little smoke, in pallid moonshine, died.
She closed the door, she panted, all akin
To spirits of the air, and visions wide.

The whole succeeding action of the poem is conducted in moonlight—within, that is to say, the circle of enchantment. Torchlight and candlelight, the impure flames of *this* world, must be extinguished. Only the moon-goddess now reigns. And it is she who concentres all her powers upon 'the charmed maid' who is 'like a mission'd spirit' for Porphyro's apotheosis. The focusing of light and power is through 'a casement high and triple-arch'd', which throws upon the kneeling girl the motley images of life: the life of plants:

> Of fruits, and flowers, and bunches of knot-grass;

the life of minerals:

> And diamonded with panes of quaint device,
> Innumerable of stains and splendid dyes;

the life of animals:

> . . . the tiger-moth's deep-damask'd wings;

and of men:

> . . . in the midst, 'mong thousand heraldries,
> And twilight saints, and dim emblazonings,
> A shielded scutcheon blush'd with blood of queens and kings.

Madeline kneels at the centre of all this glory. Note that the cross, Keats's great reconciling symbol, is the inner focus which redirects, with its silver shining, a ray of the glory to Porphyro's eyes.

> Full on this casement shone the wintry moon,
> And threw warm gules on Madeline's fair breast,
> As down she knelt for heaven's grace and boon;
> Rose-bloom fell on her hands, together prest,
> And on her silver cross soft amethyst,
> And on her hair a glory, like a saint:

> She seem'd a splendid angel, newly drest,
> Save wings, for heaven:—Porphyro grew faint:
> She knelt, so pure a thing, so free from mortal taint.

At this point the vigorous and decisive action of the poem (contrasting so powerfully with the languor of *Isabella* and the meanderings of *Endymion*) is immobilized, like a stream suddenly frozen under a 'wintry moon'. There is a moment of absolute stillness. All human warmth and passion are withdrawn. But the moment cannot continue. Warmth and passion must return: for the action is working up to a climax not of abnegation, but of identification and fruition. The human and the spiritual loves must, as in *Endymion*, be reconciled.

The next two stanzas, therefore, offer us a cluster of highly sensual images, as Madeline 'unclasps her warmed jewels one by one, loosens her fragrant bodice', and lies down in her soft nest 'until the poppied warmth of sleep' finally overcomes her. The contrast with the previous stanza is powerful, but not incongruous. Similarly, we have the silence of the bedchamber suddenly broken, but not permanently, by

> The boisterous, midnight, festive clarion,
> The kettle-drum, and far-heard clarionet

as the hall-door below opens for a moment and shuts again.

Now comes the setting-out of the ritual meal. This central feature of the initiation pattern is developed with all Keats's mastery of tactile, non-visual sensory detail. The visual has been given us already in the triple-arched casement: now we must grasp the sacramental through the media of taste and smell and touch. Upon the altar-table, with its cloth 'of woven crimson, gold and jet', the non-animal, initiatory food[1] is set out in presence of the sleeping maid:

> And still she slept an azure-lidded sleep,
> In blanched linen, smooth, and lavender'd,

---

[1] A cancelled item of the window's store—'sunny corn ears parched'—recalls the final revelation to the initiate in the Eleusinian mysteries.

> While he from forth the closet brought a heap
> Of candied apple, quince, and plum, and gourd
> With jellies soother than the creamy curd,
> And lucent syrops, tinct with cinnamon;
> Manna and dates, in argosy transferr'd
> From Fez; and spiced dainties, every one,
> From silken Samarcand to cedar'd Lebanon.

And here once again we have, transposed into the key of food, of the sacramental meal, the same idea of the concentration of Nature's store: 'infinite riches in a little room'.

Porphyro wakes Madeline to share the sacrament. He wakes her with music—the 'ancient ditty' of *La Belle Dame sans Mercy*. Her dream extends—after a last trial of doubt and fear for Porphyro and herself—into the waking bliss of consummation. So the fourth circle, of physical passion which by its supreme 'intensity' is spiritual and spiritualizes, is attained: 'St Agnes' moon hath set'.

> 'Ah, silver shrine, here will I take my rest
> After so many hours of toil and quest,
> A famish'd pilgrim,—saved by miracle.'

But the pattern of initiation is conflated—as so often—with the pattern of deliverance: Persephone is not only the goddess, the final revelation of the mysteries, she is also the Kore, the imprisoned maiden who must be rescued and restored to freedom by Hermes. The story is identical in this respect with that of Orpheus and Eurydice: and Madeline's caution in embarking on her 'dream' underlines this point:

> [She] dares not look behind, or all the charm is fled.

So, with the escape past 'sleeping dragons', 'wakeful bloodhound', and armed foes, the story ends. It is a love story, as purely sensuous and passionate as *The Song of Solomon*, and as much an allegory of spiritual awakening; it is an adventure story, as brisk and straightforward as any tale of the Round Table, and as complete an expression of the age-old pattern of initiation and achievement. It is set firmly in the Gothic north of castles, storms, hermits and witches, but its meaning constantly spills over into the wider and sunnier currents of Keats's beloved Greece.

In *The Eve of St Mark*, however, the enclosure is complete. This is literally a cloistered poem. We cannot guess, of course, how it would have developed: we have only the fragment of some hundred and twenty lines. As much as *St Agnes' Eve*, which in order of composition it immediately follows, *The Eve of St Mark* draws for its 'Gothic' detail and atmosphere on Keats's impressions of Chichester,[1] where he stayed from 21 to 23 January 1819. The season has moved on now to early Spring:

> The chilly sunset faintly told
> Of unmatured green vallies cold,
> Of the green thorny bloomless hedge,
> Of rivers new with spring-tide sedge,
> Of primroses by shelter'd rills,
> And daisies on the aguish hills.

Chilly, unmatured, bloomless; yet a season of promise. Keats, as his manner is, makes his prime statement in terms of a surrounding Nature before dramatizing it in hero or heroine. He works from the outside inwards, a centripetal technique exactly opposed to Coleridge's. If we bear in mind how intricately all his verse interweaves the cosmic processes with the human ballet of seedtime, growth and fruition, decay and death, we shall not undervalue the importance of this opening paragraph. And let us remember once more the words he wrote in a letter to George in this very month of February when he was working on the poem: 'A Man's life of any worth is a continual allegory—and very few eyes can see the Mystery of his life—a life like the scriptures, figurative— . . . Shakspeare led a life of Allegory: his works are the comments on it—'. These words are our charter for as full an interpretation of Keats's poem as it can bear.

St Mark begins, as *St Agnes* had begun, with devotion, with a religious picture. In both poems religion is associated with cold.

---

[1] With some reminiscences, probably, of the churches and abbeys seen on his earlier tour with Brown to North England and Scotland.

The 'bitter chill' of the earlier poem, crystallizing in the self-denying austerities of the Beadsman, chimes in with the 'chilly sunset' of *St Mark*, with its picture of Bertha as a 'poor cheated soul'. We do not see the sunset directly: it is *reflected* from 'the western window-panes'; Bertha at her fireside does not see it at all. Again the theme is of the maiden who must be awakened and delivered. The frosty promise of spring, always prone to relapse into winter, must be matured into summer warmth.

Bertha is not even thinking of summer warmth: she is thinking of death. Now death is a dominant motif of all these poems written after *Endymion*, in what we may call Keats's third period; poems which stem from but are so different from that master poem. They, like it, are narratives; and the problem in them is whether death is to conquer or be conquered. In *Isabella* it conquers, in *St Agnes' Eve* it doesn't, in *Lamia* it does. As for the *Eve of St Mark*, we don't know, the poem is unfinished. But as far as we have it *St Mark* gives little hope of a triumph of life. It is as though the hateful siege of contraries is once more having its way with Keats. And this pendulum swing is of course the penalty Keats pays for not being a simple, a monochromatic but, as he himself phrased it, a chameleon poet.

He is chameleon in his ambivalent attitude towards religion—an attitude which it may be appropriate to consider at this point. He has been represented as anti-religious; and he was of course anti-clerical. Belonging to Hunt's circle in his early days, he took his cue from Hunt, Hazlitt and Shelley. 'The last *Examiner* was [a] Battering Ram against Christianity', he writes to Hunt on 10 May 1817. He grieves to find Christian sentiments in Shakespeare. But at Oxford, in conversation with Bailey the theological student, he is not aggressive, 'He was never a scoffer; he was guiltless of irreverence', Bailey writes in 1848 to Milnes.[1] And in a later letter (7 May 1849) the statement is repeated and amplified:

In one word his religious education seems to have been greatly or wholly neglected; and he was early thrown among men, such as his

---

[1] *K.C.*, II, 261.

friend Mr Hunt (who I have heard, & *hope*, has amended this fatal error) and of others of the literary Society of that day. Yet he was no scoffer, & in no sense was he an infidel. When he visited me at Oxford, I had much earnest conversation with him on this subject. He well knew, & always respected my feelings & principles. He promised me, & I believe he kept his promise, that he would never scoff at religion. And when he returned to London,—it was remarked to me afterwards by one of his most intimate friends,—there was a decided change in his manner regarding religion.

Bailey goes on to show by quotation from Keats's letters that he trusted in Providence and had a firm belief in immortality. 'That will be one of the grandeurs of immortality', Keats writes to George and Georgiana in December 1818, 'there will be no space and consequently the only commerce between spirits will be by their intelligence of each other—when they will completely understand each other—while we in this world merely comprehend each other in different degrees—the higher the degree of good so higher is our Love and friendship'.[1] This is genuine enough; but Bailey had missed the chameleon in Keats, who in July 1820 cannot say more than that he wants to believe in immortality—because 'I wish to live with you for ever'.[2]

Keats's hatred of the clergy prompts a hysterical attack on the Bishop of Lincoln (who had behaved shabbily to Bailey) in a letter of 3 November 1817 to his friend at Oxford. 'There is something so nauseous in self-willed yawning impudence in the shape of conscience—it sinks the Bishop of Lincoln into a smashed frog putrifying: that a rebel against common decency should escape the Pillory! That a mitre should cover a Man guilty of the most coxcombical, tyrannical and indolent impertinence! . . . Yet doth he sit in his Palace.' Keats's generous nature up in arms to defend a friend, one will say; yes, but there is a more general and ingrained antipathy here. A later outburst against parsons comes in a letter to George and Georgiana (February 1819): 'A Parson is a Lamb in a drawing room and a lion in a Vestry. The notions of Society

[1] Quoted in the same letter from Bailey to Milnes: *K.C.*, II, pp. 292–3.
[2] Letter to Fanny Brawne of July 1820.

will nót permit a Parson to give way to his temper in any shape—
so he festers in himself—his features get a peculiar diabolical self
sufficient iron stupid expression. He is continually acting. His mind
is against every Man and every Mans mind is against him. He is
an Hypocrite to the Believer and a Coward to the unbeliever—
He must be either a Knave or an Idiot. . . .'[1] Bailey is a parson; but
Bailey is now cast off.

As for Keats's belief in a Deity, Bailey thought 'his mind was
gradually working itself round to the more healthy tone of a
Disciple of Christ . . .'. Severn, who was with him at the last,
thought that 'he died a Christian'. He also tells of 'a singular
argument I had with Shell[e]y about the Christian religion in
which Keats continually to the annoyance of Shell[e]y declared
I had the advantage—I have often thought that it was an interesting example of his generosity and love of justice . . .'[2] Keats's
writings, however, give no sign of belief in the divinity of Christ
or in a revelation. He reproduces the view current in his circle
that Jesus was a great and good man whose message has been
distorted.

> What I heard a little time ago, Taylor observe with respect to Soc-
> rates may be said of Jesus—That he was so great a man that though
> he transmitted no writing of his own to posterity, we have his Mind
> and his sayings and his greatness handed to us by others. It is to be
> lamented that the history of the latter was written and revised by
> Men interested in the pious frauds of Religion. Yet through all this
> I see his splendour.[3]

He thinks that the different races of mankind shape their gods in
accordance with their several needs and limitations: 'For as one
part of the human species must have their carved Jupiter; so
another part must have the palpable and named Mediator and
Saviour, their Christ their Oromanes and their Vishnu. . . .' These

---

[1] This is very much in the spirit of Hazlitt's essay 'On the Clerical Character'
(*The Yellow Dwarf*, 24, 31 January and 7 February 1818).

[2] *K.C.*, II, 233.

[3] Letter-entry of 19 March 1819 to George and Georgiana Keats.

words do not, of course, deny the existence of a supreme being. On the contrary, they assume His existence while rejecting the idea of a personal God.

It was the exclusiveness and narrowness and hardness of institutional religion which most repelled Keats: its anti-vitalism. He learned to hate these things from his reading, from frequenting the Hunt circle, and most of all from personal experience. 'I am reading Voltaire and Gibbon', he remarks in a letter to his brothers of 21 February 1818. There is a good deal of anti-religious writing in his favourite Chatterton. Another favourite, Burns, he considered a victim of the Scottish Church. On his 1818 tour with Charles Brown, Keats received a very unfavourable impression of Presbyterianism. He speaks of 'the horrible dominion of the Scotch Kirk'. It is an instrument of repression of the instincts, of the forces of life and growth. 'A Scotch Girl stands in terrible awe of the Elders—poor little Susannas—They will scarcely laugh —they are greatly to be pitied and the Kirk is greatly to be damn'd. . . . I would sooner be a wild deer than a Girl under the dominion of the Kirk, and I would sooner be a wild hog than be the occasion of a Poor Creature's penance before those execrable elders.'[1] Keats's indignation is directed against the assault on human freedom and human dignity. Yet even here, confronted by the Juggernaut, his peculiar fairness comes into play. The Kirk teaches wariness, coldness, repression—all qualities of which he cannot approve; and yet, in face of the harsh realities of life in Scotland, may it not be that these are the price of survival? He has been across to Ireland and seen the misery there, the fruit of fecklessness. It is better to be a wild deer than a girl under the dominion of the Kirk, yes; but if you can't be a wild deer, it is better to be a clean and warmly-dressed Presbyterian girl, with a pair of good shoes on your feet. So Keats, in fairness, gives us both sides of the picture.

These Kirkmen have done Scotland good (Query?) they have made Men, Women, Old Men Young Men old Women young women boys, girls and infants all careful—so that they are formed into regu-

---

[1] Letter of 3–9 July 1818 to Tom Keats.

lar Phalanges of savers and gainers—such a thrifty army cannot fail to enrich their Country and give it a greater appearance of comfort than that of their poor irish neighbours—These Kirkmen have done Scotland harm—they have banished puns and laughing and Kissing (except in cases where the very danger and crime must make it very fine and gustful). . . . I have not sufficient reasoning faculty to settle the doctrine of thrift—as it is consistent with the dignity of human Society—with the happiness of Cottagers—All I can do is by plump contrasts—Were the fingers made to squeeze a guinea or a white hand? Were the Lips made to hold a pen or a Kiss?[1] and yet in Cities Man is shut out from his fellows if he is poor, the Cottager must be dirty and very wretched if she be not thrifty.

Keats had no such difficulty in deciding between the old and the new religion—but here, one feels, his standpoint was mainly æsthetic. From the rational point of view, he can understand Milton's Protestantism:

In his time englishmen were just emancipated from a great super-stition—and Men had got hold of certain points and resting places in reasoning which were too newly born to be doubted, and too much opposed by the Mass of Europe not to be thought etherial and authentically divine—who could gainsay his ideas on virtue, vice, and Chastity in Comus, just at the time of the dismissal of Codpieces and a hundred other disgraces?[2] who would not rest satisfied with his hintings at good and evil in the Paradise Lost, when just free from the inquisition and burning in Smithfield? The Reformation produced such immediate and great benefits, that Protestantism was considered under the immediate eye of heaven, and its own remaining Dogmas and superstitions, then, as it were, regenerated, constituted those resting places and seeming sure points of Reasoning. . . .

---

[1] Cf. T. S. Eliot, *The Hollow Men*, III:

Lips that would kiss
Form prayers to broken stone.

[2] The query implies that Milton's ideas on morality can be challenged, as can the Kirk's. The passage comes from the letter of 3 May 1818 to John Hamilton Reynolds and is immediately preceded by the Mansion of Many Apartments argument.

Well, there again we have the voice of Keats's circle and Keats's age speaking: an opinion genuinely accepted but not his own.[1] Where his voice does speak is in appreciation of the charm of old buildings and old ceremonies: of 'the carved angels, ever eager-eyed' in *St Agnes' Eve*; of cathedrals, in the letters from Winchester, and of abbeys in the Scottish letters—'one of them very fine called Crossraguel Abbey—there is a winding Staircase to the top of a little Watch Tower'. He appreciates the glories of Iona (though he speaks of Columba, churlishly, as 'a would-be Bishop-saint') and is indignant that Glasgow cathedral has been 'devilled into a "High Kirk"'. Similarly, he rejoices in a manuscript by Horace Smith called 'Nehemiah Muggs, an exposure of the Methodists', and clearly disliked living (in 1816) in a house 'nearly opposite a Meeting'. He has a sentimental affection for hermits, 'old corner oaken pews', and cathedral closes. We may say that he is tolerant and appreciative of the antiquity of churches and legends and ceremonies when these things have intertwined themselves with life in its richness and strangeness. He feels the charm of old traditions. At Winchester he will have the pleasure ('always a great one to me') of reading Fanny Brawne's letters 'during the service up and down the Aisle'.

All this we recognize, to return, in *The Eve of St Mark*. Perhaps Bailey was right in thinking that Keats had learned to be more tolerant after his Oxford visit. There is a difference between this picture of an English Sunday evening, dating from December 1816 ('Written in Disgust of Vulgar Superstition'):

> The church bells toll a melancholy round,
>   Calling the people to some other prayers,

---

[1] The passage is curiously anticipatory of a paragraph of the Preface to *Prometheus Unbound*: 'We owe the great writers of the golden age of our literature to that fervid awakening of the public mind which shook to dust the oldest and most oppressive form of the Christian religion. We owe Milton to the progress and development of the same spirit: the sacred Milton was, let it ever be remembered, a republican, and a bold inquirer into morals and religion. . . .' Was Leigh Hunt's or Hazlitt's conversation the common source? Cf. the last two paragraphs of Hazlitt's essay 'On Court-Influence' (*The Yellow Dwarf*, 10 January 1818).

> Some other gloominess, more dreadful cares,
> More hearkening to the sermon's horrid sound.
> Surely the mind of man is closely bound
>   In some black spell; seeing that each one tears
>   Himself from fireside joys, and Lydian airs,
> And converse high of those with glory crown'd.
> Still, still they toll, and I should feel a damp—
>   A chill as from a tomb, did I not know
> That they are dying like an outburnt lamp;
>   That 'tis their sighing, wailing ere they go
>   Into oblivion;—that fresh flowers will grow,
> And many glories of immortal stamp

and this from the beginning of *The Eve of St Mark*:

> Twice holy was the Sabbath-bell:
> The silent streets were crowded well
> With staid and pious companies,
> Warm from their fire-side orat'ries;
> And moving, with demurest air,
> To even-song, and vesper prayer.
> Each arched porch, and entry low,
> Was fill'd with patient folk and slow,
> With whispers hush, and shuffling feet,
> While play'd the organ loud and sweet.

The elements of the two poems are identical, but they are combined into quite different patterns. The sonnet voices dislike and the wishful thought that religion is on its last legs. The *St Mark* paragraph appreciates the flavour of cathedral-city piety.[1] 'Fireside joys' have themselves become 'fire-side oratories': religion is invited to mingle with life. Our first sight of Bertha shows her poring over a book of legends of the saints.

All this is true enough; and yet, and yet—is the difference so great after all? Hasn't the 'chill as from a tomb' crept into the

---

[1] 'Some time since I began a Poem call'd 'The Eve of St Mark' quite in the spirit of town quietude. I think it will give you the Sensation of walking about an old country Town in a coolish evening. I know not yet whether I shall ever finish it.' (*Letters*, 414).

cosy pieties of the *Eve*? And isn't this perhaps why Keats could not
finish the poem? In attempting it, he was living on his memories.
And very pleasant memories they were. The society at Chichester,
with Brown's puns and nonsense and games of cards with the old
ladies of the Close, and the quiet streets and the 'rich antiquity' of
the Cathedral—all this had been delightful and refreshing. Keats
returned to Wentworth Place restored and grateful. We can
understand that he tried to express his sense of gratitude for that
quiet retreat in a poem. But, unfortunately, that wasn't Keats's
way of writing poems. It was Wordsworth's way, but not Keats's.
For Keats it had to be 'a present joy' that made 'the matter for a
song'. And the emotion in the *Eve* isn't joy and it isn't present.
It is a slightly off-the-note nostalgia. And this nostalgia, which
was so to charm the Pre-Raphaelites that they formed an adoring
circle round the poem and acclaimed it as his masterpiece, finally
annoyed Keats. He pokes fun at the *Eve* in *The Cap and Bells*.

But let us look at the *Eve* more closely. It is clearly going to be
a bookish poem. The curtain rises on a young lady reading an
illuminated manuscript.[1] Now Keats got a lot from books but—
as we have seen—he didn't over-value them. He got more from
life. And he would never make a written record the mainspring
of a poem. The mainspring of *St Agnes' Eve* is also a saintly legend:
but we are quite sure it is not a legend that Madeline has come
across in a book—she has heard it from 'old dames', and it is itself
humanized: 'Madeline asleep in lap of legends old'. In *The Eve of
St Mark* Bertha reads, pores over, her legend in the deepening
twilight. And here is a significant point. The concentration of
colours—a device which Keats is using in all his poems of this period
to suggest the richness of nature's store, and which in *St Agnes* is
shed by the brilliant moonlight on Madeline's breast as in *Lamia*
it is revealed by brilliant sunshine in the vigorous coils of the
snake—is in *The Eve of St Mark* fitfully glimpsed by firelight

---

[1] If we accept the later *Cap and Bells* as giving us any real clue to the plot of
The Eve of St Mark, the 'old and legend-leaved book' (as it is there described) has
been brought to Bertha by a fairy prince.

within the pages of a hagiography.[1] Here is the index of this poem's remoteness from Keats's own deeper interests.

Again, the legend of St Agnes envisages life, and more abundant life; the legend of St Mark envisages death, and multiple death. Who among the 'staid and pious companies' now thronging the streets will be alive when St Mark's Eve comes round again? Bertha's book tells her that if she stands in the church porch at midnight she will see the phantoms of all those who are to die within the year. It is a gruesome thought, and we cannot tell what Keats would have made of it. In the fragment of the poem that we have, our attention is concentrated on Bertha. She is a curiously unsatisfactory heroine.

> Bertha was a maiden fair,
> Dwelling in the old Minster-square;
> From her fire-side she could see,
> Sidelong, its rich antiquity,
> Far as the Bishop's garden-wall;
> Where sycamores and elm-trees tall,
> Full-leaved, the forest had outstript,
> By no sharp north-wind ever nipt,
> So shelter'd by the mighty pile.

And Bertha too is sheltered by the cathedral—sheltered from life, it seems. Though a 'maiden fair' she has the mannerisms of an old maid. She spends the day in reading. Living alone[2] in a house where 'all was silent, all was gloom', she is a 'poor cheated soul'. There is a suggestion of dire poverty. Even the book she reads is 'a curious volume, patch'd and torn'. When light fades she doesn't

---

[1] The germ of *St Mark* can be seen sprouting, I think, in the two stanzas and odd lines which Keats contributed to Brown's Scottish tour poem, *Stanzas on some Skulls in Beauley Abbey*. He begins: 'In silent *barren* Synod met . . .', goes on to apostrophize a 'poor Skull' (VIII):

> . . . thy fingers set ablaze
> With silver Saint in golden rays
> The holy Missal; thou didst craze
> 'Mid bead and spangle . . .

and adds (X) a reference to a dead lover.

[2] Or, according to *The Cap and Bells*, 'with her old grand-dame'.

light a candle; she 'strikes a lamp from the dismal coal'. And her own shadow hovers about the room with sinister effect:

> her shadow still
> Glower'd about, as it would fill
> The room with wildest forms and shades,
> As though some ghostly queen of spades
> Had come to mock behind her back,
> And dance, and ruffle her garments black.

There we have the atmosphere—the suggestion of a helpless creature being mocked and frustrated, together with the more eery hint of worse things to come. We may, however, expect the advent of a hero, a deliverer; and it would indeed be interesting to see how Keats would handle the theme of rescue here. For we have quite a different situation from that of either *Isabella* or *St Agnes' Eve*. The Renaissance villa and the Gothic castle were closely guarded prisons, and the problem was to awaken the princess and rescue her from her ferocious warders. In *The Eve of St Mark* the suggestion seems to be that Bertha is her own prisoner. She lives in a world of shadows. She is threatened by her own imaginations, her own timorousness.

If Keats had continued the poem, we might expect to see, I think, a really valuable and original treatment of the love theme with some emphasis on the psychology of frustration. I have suggested that all these offshoots from the great forest tree of *Endymion* are luxuriant or stunted expressions of the imperial theme: *Isabella* a 'sentimental' expression, *St Agnes' Eve* a 'romantic', *The Eve of St Mark* a 'cheated', and *Lamia* a 'cynical'. These are merely labels: but there is no doubt of Keats's growing interest in the darker aspects of the love relationship. *Lamia* is a presentation of love as obsession and as degradation. It might have been written around the antinomy of Blake's *The Clod and the Pebble*, with its remorseless third verse:

> Love seeketh only Self to please,
> To bind another to Its delight,
> Joys in another's loss of ease,
> And builds a Hell in Heaven's despite.

It reproduces and explores the Circean situation of evil metamorphosis sketched in Book III of *Endymion*: lust as a prison and a devourer. It is one of 'the unhealthy and o'erdarkened ways Made for our searching' which thread the *Endymion* forest. Indeed, Keats has already begun to explore it not only in that poem but in *La Belle Dame sans Merci*, written immediately after *The Eve of St Mark* (April 1819).[1] We can have no doubt that it was the morbidity and ambiguity of his passion for Fanny Brawne—a passion he fought against the more it 'entrammelled' him[2]—which led him into this area of thought, the area of the sedgeless lake and the cold hill-side. The circular movement of the poem, that of a Delilah-betrayed Samson at the mill with slaves, is an expression of hopeless obsession.[3]

Thus the transmutation theme, normally Keats's pattern of growth in free space, narrows into a schema of imprisonment. *Lamia* repeats and develops this evil change. In it, all Keats's romantic love-values are reversed. The process is no longer of expansion, but of contraction.[4] No longer does the hero set out on the quest of understanding or the mission of deliverance; instead, he is waylaid and captured by the dark lady. Sleep is no longer a boon bringing health and quiet breathing; it is now a 'dull shade' to which men are 'betrayed' (Part II, lines 104-5). Fauns and satyrs are no longer benevolent powers but lustful

---

[1] The poem is humorously adumbrated in this sentence of a Scottish tour letter: 'Sometimes when I am rather tired, I lean rather languishingly on a Rock, and long for some famous Beauty to get down from her Palfrey in passing; approach me with—her saddle bags and give me—a dozen or two Capital roast beef Sandwiches——' (*Letters*, 209).

[2] See above, pp. 217-21.

[3] Writing to Reynolds at this time (25 August) Keats can find 'scarcely anything else to say, leading so monotonous a life, except I was to give you a history of sensations, and day-nightmares'.

[4] This is suggested even by the versification, in which the closed couplets (in contrast to the flowing enjambement of *Endymion*) would have satisfied Croker's demand (in his *Quarterly* review of that poem) for 'a complete couplet inclosing a complete idea'. Keats writes of the poem (Letter of 11 July 1819 to Reynolds): 'I have great hopes of success [with the public], because I make use of my Judgment more deliberately than I have yet done . . .'

monsters. Even Keats's beloved urns are 'dusty'[1] (II, 94); and the brilliance of many colours that had spelled holiness in Madeline has turned evilly metallic in Lamia (I, 47–56). In short, Keats is exploring the ambivalence of sexual passion and emphasizing its dangerous and negative aspect, its potentiality for irresponsible degradation and destruction.

Irresponsibility colours the opening paragraph of the poem before Lamia even makes her appearance. The first *dramatis persona* is Hermes the thief. He descends from Olympus, neither missioned to redeem Persephone from the underworld nor as Psychopomp, but as a seducer, 'bent warm on amorous theft'. He has heard the fame of a nymph's beauty and is determined to possess her. Failing to find her, he rests

> on the lonely ground,
> Pensive, and full of painful jealousies
> Of the Wood-Gods, and even the very trees. [I, 32–4]

The second episode of the poem is an episode of betrayal. When he meets the serpent Lamia, the two make a bargain.[2] She will deliver the nymph up to him if he will give her a woman's form. The morality is completely cynical. There are strong echoes here of the Miltonic temptation scene. But now the serpent is Eve, or rather, let us say, Lilith (Eve or the feminine principle in her dark aspect); it is Hermes, Milton's Raphael, who is tempted and falls[3]; and the twofold victim is the nymph (Eve in her innocent aspect) and Lycius, the philosophical Adam.

---

[1] The tendency to press his consecrated urn symbol into the service of passion at this period is noteworthy (see the epigraph to this chapter, and cf. the lines 'Squeeze as lovers should—O kiss And in thy heart inurn me . . .' from the poem 'You Say You Love', which I would judge (disagreeing with de Selincourt) to be of late date).

[2] Cf. Glaucus' recourse to Circe in *Endymion* III. Lamia's serpentine aspect—'She was a gordian shape, etc.'—is a conflation and expansion of *Endymion* II, 109–11 and *Endymion* III, 494.

[3] There are strong verbal echoes: Hermes' 'celestial heat' and ears that 'blush'd into roses 'mid his golden hair' reproduce Raphael's 'Celestial rosie red, Loves proper hue'; and Keats's 'Then thus again the brilliance feminine' out-Miltons Milton. The description of Raphael's descent and poised alighting—'like *Maia's* son he stood'—is closely paralleled (*P.L.*, V, 285–7).

It is the delight of the nymph 'to wander as she loves, in liberty':
and this is Lycius' delight too. Passion destroys this freedom.
The betrayed nymph is led away by Hermes. But she is more
fortunate than Lycius:

> Real are the dreams of Gods, and smoothly pass
> Their pleasures in a long immortal dream. . . .
> Into the green-recessed woods they flew;
> Nor grew they pale, as mortal lovers do.   [127-45]

The nymph will not wake from her dream, for the dreams of
Gods are what we call reality. 'For ever wilt thou love, and she
be fair.' The universe itself exists as a dream in the mind of the
sleeping Brahma. The notion is oriental rather than Greek; but it
serves Keats to emphasize the double-facedness of human passion,
which cheats us into a dream from which we shall certainly have
a rude awakening.

The second act of this strange morality play opens in the foot-
hills near Corinth. Lycius, a young man of action who is also a
serious student of philosophy—an authentically Greek combination—is returning home from Cenchreas:

> Over the solitary hills he fared,
> Thoughtless at first, but ere eve's star appeared
> His phantasy was lost, where reason fades,
> In the calm'd twilight of Platonic shades.   [233-6]

Lamia, now in woman's form, accosts him. He is at once ensnared
by her beauty; and at once—this is Keats's point—the cruelty of
sexual love makes its appearance. He thinks she is a goddess; and
she, when 'she [sees] his chain so sure', is willing to let him fear that
she is on the point of leaving him. The situation is repeated from
Book IV of *Endymion*.[1] There is a taunt in 'Thou art a scholar' in
what follows—a woman's taunt at intellect and all that may
challenge her dominion:

> 'If I should stay,'
> Said Lamia, 'here, upon this floor of clay,

---

[1] Cf. particularly lines 797-9.

And pain my steps upon these flowers too rough,
What canst thou say or do of charm enough
To dull the nice remembrance of my home?
Thou canst not ask me with thee here to roam
Over these hills and vales, where no joy is,—
Empty of immortality and bliss!
Thou art a scholar, Lycius, and must know
That finer spirits cannot breathe below
In human climes, and live: Alas! poor youth,
What taste of purer air hast thou to soothe
My essence? What serener palaces,
Where I may all my many senses please,
And by mysterious sleights a hundred thirsts appease?
It cannot be—Adieu!' So said, she rose
Tiptoe with white arms spread.   [271-87]

Thus this 'poor idle Thing of woman-kind, to whom he has so unaccountably attached himself',[1] exalts herself ('O woman's triumph!' as Blake exclaimed) in spirituality over the very mind she is about to degrade. But the triumph of sexual passion is double-edged, as Lamia will discover. Love on this level, with 'no tinge of sanctuary splendour', is a devouring element that destroys both sacrificer and victim; or which, more accurately, has power to reverse the relationship.

At Lamia's threat of desertion, Lycius swoons away; and

The cruel lady, without any show
Of sorrow for her tender favourite's woe,
Or rather, if her eyes could brighter be,
With brighter eyes and slow amenity,
Put her new lips to his, and gave afresh
The life she had so tangled in her mesh.   [290-5]

She sings to him, like Circe and the Belle Dame; tells him she is only a mortal woman after all; and leads him to her magic home

---

[1] John Hamilton Reynold's verdict on Fanny Brawne (*K.C.*, I, 156). One cannot help linking this aspect of *Lamia* with Fanny's coyness and Keats's frequent complaints of her 'cruelty'. The words '. . . to roam Over these hills and vales, where no joy is,—' are an ironic echo of his complaint to Fanny in the letter (written while he was working on this first part of *Lamia*) quoted above, p. 219.

in Corinth. Meeting his tutor, Apollonius, he shrinks back into his mantle; for the philosopher incarnates the power of reason and sanity that he has now abjured.

The third act of the drama opens, with Part II, in Lamia's palace. The witch and her victim are 'enthroned' on a couch 'in the even tide'. What follows takes place by lamplight; we have quitted the clear sunshine and the open air. They recline 'with eyelids closed', though they are not asleep, in the trance of sensuality. Lycius' degradation has proceeded apace in this brief interval; but with his degradation has grown his power. The rôles are now subtly reversed. In the purely sensual union to which he has committed himself, Lycius has had the opportunity of finding out Lamia's weaknesses and defects. The physical passion is still there, stronger perhaps than ever; but there has developed, inevitably, a contempt. Contempt and dissatisfaction. And now comes the thought of escape.

> When from the slope side of a suburb hill,
> Deafening the swallow's twitter, came a thrill
> Of trumpets—Lycius started—the sounds fled,
> But left a thought a buzzing in his head.
> For the first time, since first he harbour'd in
> That purple-lined palace of sweet sin,
> His spirit pass'd beyond its golden bourn
> Into the noisy world almost forsworn. [II, 26–33]

The silver-snarling trumpets which in *St Agnes* heralded love's consummation now sound for the retreat, for the aftermath of passion. The escape will not involve a rejection of Lamia. He will take her with him into that outer world. But it means that her love is no longer sufficient for him. She reproaches him with this; and his reply is eloquent of the change in him:

> 'My silver planet, both of eve and morn!
> Why will you plead yourself so sad forlorn,
> While I am striving how to fill my heart
> With deeper crimson, and a double smart?
> How to entangle, trammel up and snare

> Your soul in mine, and labyrinth you there
> Like the hid scent in an unbudded rose?[1]
> Ay, a sweet kiss—you see your mighty woes.
> My thoughts! shall I unveil them? Listen then!
> What mortal hath a prize, that other men
> May be confounded and abash'd withal,
> But lets it sometimes pace abroad majestical,
> And triumph, as in thee I should rejoice
> Amid the hoarse alarm of Corinth's voice.
> Let my foes choke, and my friends shout afar,
> While through the thronèd streets your bridal car
> Wheels round its dazzling spokes.'   [48–64]

What has happened to the Lycius who was initially pictured 'like a young Jove with calm uneager face'? He has been transmuted in Lamia's bower into a boaster, possessive, vulgar and odious. And insincere: for it is to stifle his own doubts of the value of Lamia's love that he wants to show her off to friends and foes. Finally, he is cruel. When Lamia pleads with him not to spoil their happiness in this rash way, weeping ' a rain of sorrows at his words', he delights in his power to hurt her:

> He thereat was stung,
> Perverse, with stronger fancy to reclaim
> Her wild and timid nature to his aim:
> Besides, for all his love, in self despite
> Against his better self, he took delight
> Luxurious in her sorrows, soft and new.
> His passion, cruel grown, took on a hue
> Fierce and sanguineous as 'twas possible
> In one whose brow had no dark veins to swell.   [69–77]

In this reversal of the earlier situation of the drama, we see Keats exploring the perversity of sexual love, its cruelty and its capacity for self-destruction. The debt to Milton's presentation of the relations of Adam and Eve after the Fall is obvious.[2]

---

[1] Cf. again *St Agnes*: 'As though a rose should shut, and be a bud again'.

[2] It is at about this time that Keats writes in the margin of his Burton: 'Here is the old plague spot: the pestilence, the raw scrofula. I mean that there is nothing disgraces me in my own eyes so much as being one of a race of eyes, nose and

Lamia yields to Lycius' insistence. Indeed—a further twist in this labyrinth of perversity—

> She burnt, she lov'd the tyranny,
> And, all subdued, consented to the hour
> When to the bridal he should lead his paramour. [81–3]

The bridal and the bridal feast compose the fourth act of *Lamia*. A magnificent banqueting-hall is built and furnished by the witch's magical arts. The guests arrive, and among them the sophist Apollonius, though at Lamia's instance he has not been invited. Keats's evocation of the feast outdoes all his previous and succeeding efforts in this kind; but it is a last flash of brilliance, of luxurious life and warmth in the poem before the catastrophe:

> Soon was God Bacchus at meridian height;
> Flush'd were their cheeks, and bright eyes double bright:
> Garlands of every green, and every scent
> From vales deflower'd, or forest-trees branch-rent,
> In baskets of bright osier'd gold were brought
> High as the handles heap'd, to suit the thought
> Of every guest; that each, as he did please,
> Might fancy-fit his brows, silk-pillow'd at his ease. [213–20]

And even in this brightness of life, we note, destruction is implicit. The natural order of growing trees and blossoms has been violated to provide these luxuries. A brief glimpse is given, through the incense-clouds that wreathe the orgy, of clear vales and distant forests: and the glimpse implies a condemnation. The relentless eye and voice of Apollonius will pass judgment not merely on Lamia or Lycius, but on all human folly.

Critics have questioned Keats's art in the conclusion of the poem. They want a clear-cut moral. Keats doesn't give them one,

---

mouth beings in a planet called the earth who all from Plato to Wesley have always mingled goatish, winnyish, lustful love with the abstract adoration of the deity. I don't understand Greek—is the Love of God and the Love of women expressed by the same word in Greek? I hope my little mind is wrong—if not I could—Has Plato separated these loves?' Keats concludes this Swiftian outburst by answering his own question (on the next page of the *Anatomy*): 'Ha! I see how they endeavour to divide—but there appears to be a horrid relationship.'

because he is not describing what ought to be, but what is. The situation, like the situations of life itself, is too involved for a neat solution. Apollonius is justified, from his point of view, in destroying Lamia. But in doing so he inevitably destroys Lycius too; for Lycius is now inextricably involved, by passion, in Lamia's fate. Lycius is justified in denouncing Apollonius; for he is fighting for his life. Keats is justified in denouncing Apollonius; for he is aware that the sophist's too simple solution is fatal to life in its vast complexity. Apollonius performs a surgical operation, which is perfectly successful; the tumour is removed, but unfortunately the patient dies.

> Had Lycius liv'd to hand his story down,
> He might have given the moral a fresh frown. [II, 7–8]

Lycius has behaved like a fool: but Apollonius is a fool too, and a blundering fool. Keats does not accept Burton's complacent account as it stands; he adds to it the death of Lycius, and so makes the story a mirror of life instead of an improving fairy-tale. He identifies himself with Lycius, knowing within his own being the fatality of love.

We can put the point—or one of the points—of this remarkably complex narrative in a somewhat different way. It asserts the danger of meddling in a developing situation. Apollonius is cold reason intervening in a context where reason has no right of entry. Growth and change, positive if rather messy processes, are checked by a cool negative force. The situation, if left alone, had the chance of righting itself. Already we have seen a reversal taking place. In Lamia, experience is giving way to innocence; in Lycius, innocence is retreating before experience. These are Blake's terms, but they are applicable to Keats's story. Lamia, at the outset, is presented thus:

> A virgin purest lipp'd, yet in the lore
> Of love deep learned to the red heart's core:
> Not one hour old, yet of sciential brain
> To unperplex bliss from its neighbour pain;

Define their pettish limits, and estrange
Their points of contact, and swift counterchange;
Intrigue with the specious chaos, and dispart
Its most ambiguous atoms with sure art;
As though in Cupid's college she had spent
Sweet days a lovely graduate, still unshent,
And kept his rosy terms in idle languishment. [I, 189–99]

She is skilled, that is, in knowledge of the contraries and in all the arts of love. We have seen her capacity for deceit and for cruelty. But in the course of ensnaring Lycius she builds a cage for herself. She genuinely falls in love. In the third act we find her 'pale and meek', credited by Lycius (and there is no irony here) with a maiden's 'wild and timid nature'. He, contrariwise, has passed from gentleness and unreflecting love to brutality and selfishness. In such constantly shifting relationships the dance of life is woven. And the dance is only resolved within the dance. Apollonius's intervention offers no true solution, but merely a destruction. The 'gordian shape' of the serpent at the poem's beginning is the shape of the poem: Apollonius, with the stupid complacency of an Alexander, cuts the knot.

Here, then, we have the explanation of Keats's famous and obscure outburst:

What wreath for Lamia? What for Lycius?
What for the sage, old Apollonius?
Upon her aching forehead be there hung
The leaves of willow and of adder's tongue;
And for the youth, quick, let us strip for him
The thyrsus, that his watching eyes may swim
Into forgetfulness; and, for the sage,
Let spear-grass and the spiteful thistle wage
War on his temples. Do not all charms fly
At the mere touch of cold philosophy?
There was an awful rainbow once in heaven:
We know her woof, her texture; she is given
In the dull catalogue of common things.
Philosophy will clip an Angel's wings,

Conquer all mysteries by rule and line,
Empty the haunted air, and gnomed mine—
Unweave a rainbow, as it erewhile made
The tender-person'd Lamia melt into a shade. [II, 221–38]

Yes, tender-personed. For life is never static; and Keats, confounding his commentators who want black to remain black and white white, has watched his characters grow along with his poem. Lamia, from first to last, is beautiful; and Keats worships the principle of beauty in all things. Even in an evil beauty there is the seed of good. Keats has watched the growth of his characters; and he has grown too. This is another way of expressing the complaint of the critics: 'Keats begins a poem without knowing what he is going to do with it and he allows himself to be carried on with no set plan from incident to incident.' Quite: because Keats trusted in an intelligence greater than his own to supply the plan; he had faith in 'great creating Nature'. He believes in the existence of a universal pattern which, if he remains receptive to its influence, will mirror its magnificently complex and organic unity in whatever structure of ideas and events he is at the moment engaged on.

Consciously or unconsciously, our old friend Erasmus Darwin has come back to his mind here. Keats is not attacking science; he is objecting to the presence of science, of calculating reason, at parties where it can be only a gate-crasher. Poetry is such a party; and Lamia's pathetic feast is just such a piece of poetry. Apollonius has no place here. And Darwin's science has no place in poetry. Keats is not attacking science; no one knew better than he did, with his long medical training, the value of objective thinking. But operating theatres, and not triclinia are, as Keats shows, the place for displays of surgical skill. Learned treatises, and not poems, are the place for displays of analytical erudition. The tender-personed Lamia—poetry, that is, as enchantment, as magic—melts into a shade at the mere touch of cold philosophy. Science and poetry inhabit disparate worlds: let them live amicably apart.

[*Isabella* (April 1818)—*The Eve of St Agnes* (January 1819)—
The Eve of St Mark (February 1819)—*Lamia* (July–September 1819)]

Chapter Fourteen

NOT TO THE SENSUAL EAR

The attunement of the world is of opposite tensions, as is that of the
harp or the bow.

HERACLEITUS, *On the Universe*, aph. LVI.

MUCH of the turbulence, the anguish, the questioning of
these narrative explorations of 'the sexual strife' spills
over into the intrinsically calmer lake of the great Odes.
There is little relaxation of tension in *To a Nightingale* and *On
Melancholy*. Pain is an undercurrent in the *Grecian Urn*, and lingers
as regret in the placid wheelings of *To Autumn*. But there is a
difference. Tensions remain, but are integrated in a broader pattern. It is as though what had existed in *Isabella*, *St Mark* and *Lamia*
as pure suffering, loneliness, waste—as pain seen and felt in isolation—is here transmuted through *relationship*. The Odes form a
unity, as the narratives did not. Keats is feeling his way towards
an inclusive vision. I shall advance a little later the suggestion that
we may find a useful analogy in music.

Before beginning to discuss the Odes of the great year I want to
go back to two poems of mid-1818: the fragment of an *Ode to
May*, and the ballad, *Meg Merrilies*. These are poems which achieve
a certain serenity, a crystallization out from personal stresses into
the lucid world of art; and which are thus vestibular to the later
odes. Both are poems of freedom, and both are impersonal (though
in different ways). Formally, they stand at extremes: the ballad,
simple, 'folkish', centred on a fragment of human jetsam, and the
strophe, majestic, traditional, celebrating archaic powers, are as
antipodal as Scotland and Hellas.[1]

---

[1] 'I know not how it is, the Clouds, the Sky, the Houses, all [in Scotland] seem
Anti Grecian and Anti Charlemagnish . . .' (*Letters*, 163).

The contrast is more specious than real. In both poems we are in the world of the archetypes. Meg and Maia belong to the clan of Moneta, Mnemosyne, and the English Muse (note the obsessive consonant)—maternal figures focusing remoteness and intimacy. They are remote from the world of man in its pettinesses and its strife; they are intimate with cosmic powers. Yet they bring man and the powers together under 'the dower of spanning wisdom'. Human yet inhuman, they bridge the worlds. They interpret, attune, and heal. I have already suggested, in discussing Keats's presentation of the English Muse in *Endymion*, that he found relief from personal suffering in the large maternity of these presences: and indeed it is a relief felt not only by Keats: we meet it too in De Quincey, and to a lesser degree in Shelley. The Romantic disorientation sought a refuge here.

Meg Merrilies achieves the impersonal through the personal. Keats had never read Scott's novel; Brown told him the story as they trudged along, passing Solway Firth ('We are now in Meg Merrilies county and have this morning passed through some parts exactly suited to her . . . very beautiful, very wild with craggy hills'[1]) and at once his imagination was seized. 'There was a little spot, close to our path-way—"There", he said, in an instant positively realising a creation of the novellist, "in that very spot, without a shadow of doubt, has old Meg Merrilies often boiled her kettle!" It was among pieces of rock, and brambles, and broom, ornamented with a profusion of honeysuckle, wild roses, and foxglove, all in the very blush and fullness of blossom. While we sat at breakfast, he was occupied in writing to his young sister, and, for her amusement, he composed a ballad on old Meg.'[2] At the risk of absurdity I will invite the reader to connect Meg's homely utensil in its floral setting with what I have already said, and with what I shall later say in more detail,[3] of the consecrated

---

[1] Letter of 3–9 July 1818 to Tom Keats.   [2] Brown, in *K.C.*, II, 61.

[3] See below, pp. 329–40. Another delightfully intimate example may be mentioned here—the 'handsome Globe of gold-fish' which he proposes (in a letter of 13 March 1819, to his sister) to put 'before a handsome painted window' and 'shade all round with myrtles and Japonicas . . . and, there I'd sit and read all day like the picture of somebody reading'.

urn, the supreme form, concentrating natural forces from the area surrounding it: the powers of growth. And the concentration is, inevitably, in fire.

Old Meg is the most detached of Keats's poems. It is as though the objectivity of the story-teller, Scott's objectivity, has seized him (even in Brown's paraphrase): for once he is free to present the thing-in-itself. Note the areal opening:

> Old Meg she was a Gipsey,
> And liv'd upon the Moors;
> Her bed it was the brown heath turf,
> And her house was out of doors.

Meg is firmly *placed*: large spaces frame an eikon of freedom. Link this up with what Keats has said already of free movement in space, with what he is to say of spiritual freedom[1]: a principle of continuity emerges. And then:

> Her Brothers were the craggy hills,
> Her Sisters larchen trees;
> Alone with her great family
> She liv'd as she did please.

Link this up, again, with the resolutions of the October letter to George and Georgiana[2]: we glimpse a principle of renunciation. Keats wasn't to stick to it, but its emergence is important. Detachment (what Keats calls 'abstraction') fights a running fight with commitment in his poems and in his life; the resolution came only with death. Otherwise, perhaps, it could not have come. Keats was too deeply involved.

Meg is not involved. The asexuality of her being is assumed from the outset. Keats goes farther: she is immune from ordinary human needs:

> No breakfast had she many a morn,
> No dinner many a noon,
> And, 'stead of supper, she would stare
> Full hard against the Moon.

---

[1] See below, pp. 353–4.   [2] Above, pp. 218–19.

Possessing nothing for herself, she exercises the indiscriminate bounty of Nature:

> And with her fingers, old and brown,
>   She plaited Mats o' Rushes,
> And gave them to the Cottagers
>   She met among the Bushes.

A genuine ballad impersonality, anonymity, is captured. Keats keeps himself out of the poem. No moral is offered us, but we may, if we wish, share for a moment an interchange, a human-natural nexus.

Meg Merrilies is simple enough; the *Ode to May* is simpler, because more formal. Fragmentary as it is, it has always commanded attention as one of Keats's major achievements. Lucidity stems, here, from the initial oxymoron:

> *Mother* of Hermes! and *still youthful* Maia!

Note the 'family' resonance, as in *Old Meg*: note too the antithesis within the 'family' context of the power which integrating with time yet surpasses, dominates time; the *Grecian Urn* is adumbrated. For a moment we share the integrated vision of

> bards who died content on pleasant sward,
> Leaving great verse unto a little clan.

All Keats's classical sympathies focus here: luminous areas remote from Gothic glooms and mists, objective action moving towards precise goals: the clear light-and-shadow world of *Lamia* and the *Grecian Urn*. These fourteen quiet lines would not have been out of place among the divine hymns of *Endymion*.[1]

---

[1] The 'pleasant sward' recalls Endymion's words (IV, 935–6): '. . . nor much it grieves To die, when summer dies on the cold sward'. Keats himself saw the ode as a comment on his abstraction-commitment dilemma. 'When we come to human Life and the affections it is impossible [to know] how a parallel of breast and head can be drawn. . . . With respect to the affections and Poetry you must know by a sympathy my thoughts that way; and I dare say these few lines will be but a ratification: I wrote them on May-day—and intend to finish the ode all in good time—' A sentence which comes a little later: 'I shall relish Hamlet more

With the first of the great odes to take shape—the *Ode on Indo-lence*—Keats returns (superficially) to his Greek context and to his beloved image of the urn. At first sight we are in that classical world.

> One morn before me were three figures seen,
>   With bowed necks, and joined hands, side-faced;
> And one behind the other stepp'd serene,
>   In placid sandals, and in white robes graced.

Keats has been looking at—or recollecting—the Elgin marbles. But in the sequel we are rapidly undeceived. No Attic lucidity shines here. *On Indolence* is a drowsy, uneasy, seminal poem: an experience between sleep and wake half-rejected, half-submitted to. The urn is central, attracting to itself psychic entities—love, ambition, poetry—as it later, in the *Grecian Urn*, compresses legendary, religious, human values of a more general order. The mood is of 'half-seeing'. Keats is sunk in 'indolence': not quite the indolence of the Reynolds letter,[1] but something more physical, less aware: a winter sleep. This entry in the long journal letter to George and Georgiana pin-points the ode's genesis:

> This morning I am in a sort of temper indolent and supremely care-less: I long after a stanza or two of Thomson's Castle of Indolence. My passions are all asleep from my having slumbered till nearly eleven and weakened the animal fibre all over me to a delightful sensation about three degrees on this side of faintness—if I had teeth of pearl and the breath of lillies I should call it languor—but as I am I must call it Laziness. In this state of effeminacy the fibres of the brain are relaxed in common with the rest of the body, and to such a happy degree that pleasure has no show of enticement and pain no unbearable frown. Neither Poetry, nor Ambition, nor Love have any alertness of countenance as they pass by me: they seem rather like three figures on a greek vase—a Man and two women whom no one but myself could distinguish in their disguisement. This is the

---

than I have ever done', shows Keats moving into the world of 'Man delights not me, no nor woman neither' which is to be increasingly his from now on (Letter of 3 May 1818 to J. H. Reynolds).

[1] 19 February 1818. See above, pp. 59–64.

only happiness: and is a rare instance of advantage in the body
overpowering the Mind.

The mood cannot have lasted long, for Keats moves on promptly
to a closely-argued discourse on destiny, disinterestedness, and
creative power.[1] But it left a deep and singular impression. It is
plainly a mood of *creative* indolence (we are told that it 'is the
only happiness') and indeed it may be more creative than the more
conscious and controlled mood of the Reynolds letter. Both experiences belong to the turn of the year: Keats's rhythms are, as
always, deeply integrated with the seasonal rhythms; but in 1819
we have something more. There is a feeling of spiritual and
physical exhaustion absent from the earlier entry: the disappointments, tribulations, journeyings, almost feverish creativeness of
the intervening twelvemonth have taken their toll.

The experience is half-rejected because Keats, perhaps, is not
yet ready for it: the waking is a trifle premature. He is sunk in his
winter sleep 'rotting like a grain of wheat': marshalling psychic
and physical energies he is badly in need of. It may be a heresy
to say so, but I will venture the suggestion that Keats would have
done better to have slept his winter out undisturbed by love,
ambition and poetry. The Odes are great verse, but they are not
the flawless masterpieces they are sometimes made out to be.
They are marred by technical and emotional imperfections.[2] Keats
needed a long rest after *Isabella, Hyperion, St Agnes, St Mark*—
and his other stresses, amatory and worldly. Resentment at being
woken up runs through the ode, giving it a curiously querulous
tone. Keats is *not* writing from the plenitude of his powers. He is
looking through half-closed eyes[3] at a phantasmagoria: a 'masque'

---

[1] 19 March 1819. The question of the ode's date is puzzling but not supremely
important. Colvin ascribed the poem, like the letter, to March and is followed,
more recently, by Fairchild; other scholars prefer May or even June. Contradictions within the poem are relevant here (I comment on them later): Keats assigns
his vision of the three figures to May, but we know from the letter that he saw
them in March. The point of real importance is the early date of the conception,
and not of the composition.

[2] This criticism does not, however, apply to *Autumn*.

[3] One of them very effectively closed, by a cricket ball.

(to use his own word) of the odd figures that present themselves to us in the shadow-land between sleep and wake:

> They pass'd, like figures on a marble urn,
>   When shifted round to see the other side;
> They came again; as when the urn once more
>   Is shifted round, the first seen shades return;
> And they were strange to me, as may betide
>   With vases, to one deep in Phidian lore.

A weak conclusion, and it betrays what is even clearer on analysis: an element of insincerity. The figures were not strange to him, as the letter shows. *On Indolence* is a made-up poem.

It is nonetheless a very interesting poem. It is the bridge between the world of the narrative poems and the world of the final lyrics, and in its complex uneasiness it reminds me of nothing so much as the first group of Shakespeare's *Sonnets*. The transition between *Venus and Adonis* and *Lucrece*, and the sonnet sequence, is very largely Keats's transition from *Endymion*, *St Agnes* and *St Mark* to the *Odes*. Brilliance of narrative, richness of descriptive detail, give place now to a subjective, meditative counterpoint: themes are introduced and interwoven, 'the uncertain glory of an April day' casts shadows and sun-flecks over a wide field of ideas. Shakespeare's first cluster of sonnets links up, indisputably, with the past, with *Venus and Adonis*; *On Indolence* links up with the future, with the *Nightingale* and the *Grecian Urn*: and the thread is the same—ripeness, beauty, flowering, fruition, death, immortality. We tend to soft-pedal what Keats tells us about Shakespeare 'the Presidor', but the link was serious for Keats, determining formal structures as well as themes and vocabulary.[1]

---

[1] Detailed comparisons would be misplaced here, but the reader may compare Shakespeare's and Keats's treatment of the Adonis story in terms of flowering and fruition, the antithetical relevance of *Lucrece* to *St Agnes*, and connect these lines of sonnet 15:

> that men as plants increase,
> Cheared and checkt euen by the selfe-same skie:
> Vaunt in their youthful sap, at height decrease

with the whole tenor of Keats's verse and the grim realism of the letter of April 1819 to George and Georgiana.

The plea for creativeness urged so forcibly by Shakespeare in the early sonnets moved Keats, I believe, in its double impact: in its literal application he would feel it relevant to his hopes and fears concerning love and marriage, while its insistence on the dangers of delay, on the inexorable lapse of time:

> For neuer resting time leads Summer on,
> To hidious winter and confounds him there,
> Sap checkt with frost and lustie leau's quite gon,
> Beauty ore-snow'd and barenes euerywhere,

would work (as we see it working in the 'When I have fears that I may cease to be' sonnet of January 1818) towards a renewed stirring of his ambition. It is significant that we have six sonnets in this same journal-letter of February–April 1819, and that the tenor of them all is given in the concluding lines of the first ('Why did I laugh tonight?'):

> Verse, fame and Beauty are intense indeed
> But Death intenser—Death is Life's high meed.

The expression in sonnet form thus precedes the writing of the ode, and is technically, I think, superior.

But to the ode we must now return. The silent figures of Love, Ambition and Poetry parade before the poet's half-closed eyes: they pass 'like figures on a marble urn' as the urn is slowly turned round—not, therefore, with voluntary motion, but like automata obedient to a puppet-master: Keats is stressing the element of unreality, of apathy, of uncontrol that goes with the mood of indolence. Sluggish rhythms and half-formed imagery reinforce this impression:

> Ripe was the drowsy hour;
> The blissful cloud of summer-indolence[1]
> Benumb'd my eyes; my pulse grew less and less . . .

---

[1] 'Summer-indolence' is a falsification that bespeaks Keats's peculiar honesty. The indolence belongs to late winter: the ode is written (perhaps) in early summer; Keats cannot deal with a *past* experience; as he writes about it, it becomes present to him; and so we have 'summer-indolence'.

Contradictions abound in the second strophe: the apparitions are accused first of stealing the poet's days and leaving them 'without a task', and a few lines later of disturbing his deep enjoyment of 'nothingness'. The poem proceeds by fits and starts, thoughts and second thoughts. At each entry of the figures (there are four in all) the poet is roused from his lethargy; the urn gyrates with the inevitability of a pharos, casting its passing beam across Keats's eyes; stirring him—at the third turn—to the point of enthusiasm:

> A third time pass'd they by, and, passing, turn'd
> Each one the face a moment whiles to me;
> Then faded, and to follow them I burn'd
> And ached for wings because I knew the three;

but the impulse is transitory; and on a fourth appearance they are definitely rejected:

> And once more came they by;—alas! wherefore?
> My sleep had been embroider'd with dim dreams;
> My soul had been a lawn besprinkled o'er
> With flowers, and stirring shades, and baffled beams:

an admirable expression of the creative chaos of Keats's mind in early 1819. His soul is a *lawn*: the open space of 'flowery grass' which is his constant image of natural freedom (as the open sky is his image of supernatural freedom) and in the centre of which stands, inevitably, the urn. The figures have detached themselves from the urn's rondure: but prematurely; the final strophe dismisses them:

> Fade softly from my eyes, and be once more
> In masque-like figures on the dreamy urn;
> Farewell! I yet have visions for the night,
> And for the day faint visions there is store. . . .

Keats falls back to his chaos, to the visions of sleep and of day-dreaming. Or rather, let us say, he tries to return: that he could not is witnessed by the creative frenzy of the months that follow.

Once again we see how an interpretation of Keats's work based on the categories of growth and form can lead us to the heart of his mystery, and, above all, help us to connect and relate poem to poems and 'period' to 'period'. We work towards an understanding from within. This approach is doubly significant for the Odes, which have all too often been considered in isolation (from each other, and from the rest of the poems) and accused sometimes, in consequence, of incoherence. We can best understand the Odes by returning to our initial concept of areas in space and time in which manifestations come into being through cosmic processes. (The 'nothingness' of strophe II is the void which is also the pleroma.) Keats himself suggests the areal approach in these three introductory poems. *To May* gave us the picture of a 'pleasant sward'—a lucid plateau where the 'span of heaven' overarches woods rich with 'the quiet Primrose'. *Meg Merrilies* invokes the bracing freedom of the out-of-doors. *On Indolence* presents the dappled lawn which is the land of dreams. And in the centre of this 'lawn', as we have seen, there rises the 'supreme shape' of the urn. That the urn is both a focusing point of the attention and a vortex of stored power we already know. What is of special interest to us in considering the Odes as a unity is the position of the two urns, at the beginning (in *On Indolence*) and at the close (in the *Grecian Urn*): poles around which the odic rhythms weave their elliptical patterns, resolved into circularity only in the final masterpiece, *To Autumn*, which escapes in acceptance from the wheel.

Our areal interpretation is very close to another kind of interpretation which yields positive results in the study of Keats: the analogy with music. This must not be pushed too far: there are pitfalls in conflating the arts; but the poet to whom music meant so much, and who told Bailey that 'had he studied music, he had some notions of the combinations of sounds, by which he thought he could have done something as original as his poetry',[1] inclined

---

[1] *K.C.*, II, 278. Perhaps Keats, browsing along Bailey's shelves, had just come across this remark of Socrates in the *Phædo*: '. . . in the past part of my life the same dream has often occurred to me, exhibiting at different times a different appearance, yet always advising me the same thing; for it said, Socrates, produce and exercise music . . .' (p. 148 of Taylor's 1793 translation). Severn also remarks:

naturally towards a musical structure—especially in his larger, more choral works. We note that it is *the combinations of sounds* that interest him; in his sonnet *On the Sea* he rejects 'cloying melody', the sentimental or frivolous lilt of a tune, in favour of the sea's complex harmony. We note too how frequently and characteristically music is equated with processes of growth and fruition. The 'Delicious symphonies, like airy flowers' which greet the resuscitation of the dead lovers in *Endymion* III have already been commented on.[1] And not with growth only, but with our second interpretative term: with form too. The flower-symphony passage modulates directly to the baroque magnificence of Neptune's palace. And again, with energy: in Book I (lines 115–21) of the same poem music is powerfully realized as an air-wave.

> . . . a faint breath of music, which ev'n then
> Fill'd out its voice, and died away again.
> Within a little space again it gave
> Its airy swellings, with a gentle wave,
> To light-hung leaves, in smoothest echoes breaking
> Through copse-clad vallies,—ere their death, o'ertaking
> The surgy murmurs of the lonely sea.

Here the musical phrase exists, to begin with, in isolation: it sounds, lingers a moment, and dies away. But this will not do for Keats. It is not 'rich' enough. He sounds the phrase again, and there is a relationship: the music *gives* its airy *swellings* to *light-hung leaves*, breaks through wooded valleys, and integrates finally with the ocean symphony. We are returned, thus, through music to our areal concept: Keats's sound-loop snares woods, valleys and sea.

The Odes may best be considered as a choral whole, the themes of which are firmly stated in the first movement, *On Indolence*.

'He had an ample capacity for Painting & Music & applied them largely to his Poetry, I could point out many passages taken from the one or the other—Titians picture of Bacchus & Ariadne is the original of the scene in the Endymion —There is [a] beautifull air of Glucks which furnishd the groundwork of the coming of Apollo in Hyperion—' (*K.C.*, II, 133).

[1] See above, p. 157.

They are developed in *To Psyche, To a Nightingale, On a Grecian Urn*: love, ambition, art. I am not suggesting a detached treatment in any of the Odes; that, as we know, would be far from Keats's way; but there is a predominance, I think, and in that order. *On Melancholy* brings the themes more equally together in the minor; they are restated, in the major, in the final chorus which is *To Autumn*.

Our musical analogy will hold good, I believe, in a close analysis of the Odes. But we cannot divorce it from our still deeper analogy of growth in relationship. Indeed, the first strophe of *To Psyche* presents Keats's most acutely realized vision of human love in its relation to nature—a concrete expression, that is, of the thesis long ago proffered in *Endymion*.[1] It was a major aspect of Endymion's reading of his 'pleasure thermometer' that there is a *participation mystique* between the fruition of human passion and the fruitfulness of nature's store. Here, in *To Psyche*, we find the cosmic nuptials of Eros and Psyche consummated in the lap of

> hush'd, cool-rooted flowers, fragrant-eyed,
> Blue, silver-white, and budded Tyrian,

within a forest glade. This is a spring world after the dying-into-life of *On Indolence*. (The whole sequence of Odes runs the seasonal course from winter to autumn.) It is a world of light after darkness, of germination and budding after the torpor of winter; and the pulse of Spring beats through it. *To Psyche* is the most agonizingly alive of the Odes, for it celebrates the only-just-won triumph of love over death—the reunion of Eros with his Psyche after their

---

[1] See *Endymion*, I, 832–42; and above, p. 131. More personal is the remarkably Tennysonian conclusion to the lyric 'Hush, hush! tread softly!' in which the *warmth* of human love-making acts directly on flowers and birds:

> The shut rose shall dream of our loves and awake
> Full-blown, and such warmth for the morning's take;
> The stock-dove shall hatch her soft brace and shall coo,
> While I kiss to the melody, aching all through!

Here we have a complete reciprocity. In *Lamia*, again, we find Hermes
> Breathing upon the flowers his passion new (I, 28).

long ordeal.[1] It is therefore a poem of initiation—the religious note is dominant—and for this reason Keats begins with a plea for pardon: in describing these nuptials he is violating the mysteries.

The revelation of the mysteries has come to him suddenly, while still in the apathetic trance of *On Indolence*, 'I wander'd in a forest thoughtlessly'[2]: it is the 'old oak forest' of the *Lear* sonnet with its prayer 'Let me not wander in a barren dream'; and here too, as in *To a Nightingale*, he is not sure whether he is experiencing a vision or a waking dream:

> Surely I dreamt today, or did I see
> The winged Psyche with awaken'd eyes?

This capacity for vision is an element in Keats's mythopoeia in which he surpassed all his contemporaries with the exception of Blake. The visions were not, I think, so definite as Blake's—they emerged from a natural background of which they were the formal expression and into which they blended again. We cannot imagine him interrogating the ghost of a flea in a Lambeth sitting-room. But the faculty is real enough.[3] Here, in *To Psyche*, it projects an immediate picture:

> I wander'd in a forest thoughtlessly,
>   And, on the sudden, fainting with surprise,
>   Saw two fair creatures, couched side by side

---

[1] The poem owes something to Mary Tighe's *Psyche*, an old favourite of Keats's. I have noted one or two obvious echoes. The theme is already briefly anticipated in 'I Stood Tip-toe . . . ', lines 141–9. A possible stimulus of Keats's interest is suggested by Hazlitt's account of a merry meeting at 'the S—— tavern', where 'W—— [probably C. J. Wells, Keats's early friend] . . . spoke of Lucius Apuleus and his Golden Ass, which contains the story of Cupid and Psyche, with other matter rich and rare, and went on to the romance of Heliodorus. . . . This, as he affirmed, opens with a pastoral landscape equal to Claude, and in it the presiding deities of Love and Wine appear in all their pristine strength, youth and grace, crowned and worshipped as of yore' ('On Coffee-House Politicians'). There is no suggestion that Keats was present.

[2] The forest setting is there in *Psyche*: 'Fair Psyche through untrodden forests went.'

[3] 'Shapes of epic greatness' surround him when he is alone (*Letters*, 240 and 271): 'I do not live in this world alone but in a thousand worlds.' . . . 'I value more the Privilege of seeing great things in loneliness than the fame of a Prophet.'

21

> In deepest grass,[1] beneath the whisp'ring roof
> Of leaves and trembled blossoms, where there ran
> A brooklet, scarce espied.

In *To Psyche* he achieves an apotheosis of the power of love unapproached in any previous poem. Even his long-beloved Diana is dethroned in favour of the new goddess: Psyche is hailed as 'loveliest vision far Of all Olympus' faded hierarchy' and exalted above Phoebe and Vesper.

And what does Psyche mean for Keats? The answer is, I think, that she means human love. His poem is suffused with pity and understanding. We feel a tenderness that springs from the recognition of fragility. From Mary Tighe's poem Keats would have learned to think of Psyche as essentially human, fallible, and variable. She is 'Psyche true': but the truth is Eros's rather than hers. She is human nature that has learned through Love to love. Keats's theme is again, at bottom, the theme of struggle and attainment.

Psyche could never have a temple and a priest devoted to her worship: she is too human and too vulnerable. Her temple must be the human heart. 'Thanks to the human heart by which we live'—the note of Wordsworth's concluding lines in another and greater ode, with its 'natural piety', sounds in *To Psyche*. And if her apotheosis came too late for the ancients, too late

> for the fond believing lyre,
> When holy were the haunted forest boughs,
> Holy the air, the water, and the fire,[2]

---

[1] Cf. *On Indolence*, 'cool-bedded in the flowery grass'.
[2] The thought came to Wordsworth too, in Sonnet XIII of *Itinerary Poems* of 1833:

> O Fancy, what an age was *that* for song!
> That age, when not by *laws* inanimate,
> As men believed, the waters were impelled,
> The air controlled, the stars their courses held;
> But element and orb on *acts* did wait
> Of *Powers* endued with visible form, instinct
> With will, and to their work by passion linked.

Characteristically, Wordsworth repudiates this 'fancy' in the succeeding sonnet.

what possibility of worship remains for her in these latter days 'so far retir'd From happy pieties' into the gloom and morality of Christianity? Only in the poet's heart can she find her sanctuary.

> Yes, I will be thy priest, and build a fane
>   In some untrodden region of my mind,
> Where branched thoughts, new grown with pleasant pain,
>   Instead of pines shall murmur in the wind:
> Far, far around shall those dark-cluster'd trees
>   Fledge the wild-ridged mountains steep by steep;[1]
> And there by zephyrs, streams, and birds, and bees,
>   The moss-lain Dryads shall be lull'd to sleep;
> And in the midst of this wide quietness
>   A rosy sanctuary will I dress
> With the wreath'd trellis of a working brain,
>   With buds, and bells, and stars without a name.
> With all the gardener Fancy e'er could feign,
>   Who breeding flowers, will never breed the same :[2]
> And there shall be for thee all soft delight
>   That shadowy thought can win,
> A bright torch, and a casement ope at night,
>   To let the warm Love in![3]

Again the pattern reasserts itself—the sanctuary in the midst of a wide quietness, which in *Endymion* was the altar in the forest

---

[1] De Selincourt (*op. cit.*, p. 479) has noted a debt to *The Faithful Shepherdess* here; I think Keats also has in mind some lines (155–62) from *Eloisa to Abelard*:

> The darksom pines that o'er yon' rocks reclin'd
> Wave high, and murmur to the hollow wind,
> The wand'ring streams that shine between the hills,
> The grots that eccho to the tinkling rills,
> The dying gales that pant upon the trees,
> The lakes that quiver to the curling breeze;
> No more these scenes my meditation aid,
> Or lull to rest the visionary maid . . .

The lines that follow, on Melancholy, may have contributed something to Keats's later ode.

[2] Cf. *Psyche*: 'For her they cull unknown, celestial flowers.'

[3] Cf. *On Indolence*, V: 'The open casement press'd a new-leav'd vine, Let in the budding warmth and throstle's lay'.

glade, and in *On Indolence* the urn focusing the details of a flower-strewn lawn. But now Keats has forcibly extricated himself from the world in which youth grows pale and spectre-thin and dies, into some untrodden region of his own mind. A solution through acceptance of a traditional metaphysic is hinted at. Note how the images of branching and flowering are identified with mental or 'psychic' phenomena. Like Hopkins, Keats can cry 'The mind has mountains!'—it has, too, its pine forests fledging those mountains; ' a working brain' throws out a 'trellis' of buds and star-blossoms. Note too how it is from the *contraries* that a new growth arises: 'branched thoughts, new grown with pleasant pain'. For a retreat from the outside world does not mean a retreat from the contraries: it means, as Blake would put it, a retreat from the opposites, from the frustrations and denials which are not contraries but negations. Keats has his own way of saying this, in *Bards of Passion and of Mirth*, where the great poets are shown passing through the contraries to wisdom. They taste all experience, but not all experience leads to heavenly truth; for there is one kind that 'strengthens', and another that 'maims'. The retreat in *To Psyche* is not an escape, but a means of refreshment; and it cannot be permanent. In *To a Nightingale* Keats has to return to 'the sweet and bitter world' that cripples as it teaches.[1]

He returns in seeking to escape. That is the meaning of the poem: the tension between the opposites—not the contraries; between the world and the spirit. *To Psyche* celebrated a genuine moment of freedom, fleeting but assured. *To a Nightingale* misses the moment; it is crippled from the start. Not crippled as a poem, of course; frustration is the theme, not the expression. Yet the expression too has traces of uneasiness. The dull pain in the first

---

[1] Thus the hint of serenity in *To Psyche* is soon lost. 'I have done [*To Psyche*] leisurely', he tells George (30 April 1819): 'I think it reads the more richly for it and will I hope encourage me to write other things in even a more peaceable and healthy spirit'; but only a month later (30 May) he can see no alternative to becoming a ship's surgeon than 'leading a *fevrous* life alone with Poetry. . . . I must choose between despair & Energy—I choose the latter—though the world has taken on a quakerish look with me, which I once thought was impossible.'

strophe is, to my hearing, more real than the triumphant escape
from it. Keats protests too much in the soaring

> 'Tis not through envy of thy happy lot
> But being too happy in thy happiness—

the capacity to be 'too happy' may coexist with an aching heart
but hardly with 'a drowsy numbness'.[1] Keats tries to bridge too
wide an emotional gap in his first six lines.

The contrast between what is and what ought to be is sustained in the second strophe through the imagery of wine. The
movement of the poem is a vertical one—up and down. The first
quatrain of the first strophe plunges downward: 'hemlock'[2] invites death, the 'dull opiate' drags the poet 'Lethe-wards'. The
last sextet soars upward into the 'melodious plot of beechen
green'.[3] But with the first lines of the second strophe we are
underground again:

> O for a draught of vintage, that hath been
> Cool'd a long age in the deep-delvéd earth.

The earth has its values too, which can be enjoyed on the surface:
compensations of the natural life which neither soars nor plunges:

> Tasting of Flora and the country green,
> Dance, and Provençal song, and sunburnt mirth.

But with these lines, and the remaining lines of the strophe, the
context widens. Is there an escape from the world into the world:
from personal frustration into a community of happy human
beings? A life neither in the depths nor on the heights? The last

---

[1] *To a Nightingale* also is an 'indolent' ode: cf. its 'drowsy numbness' with the
'drowsy hour' and 'benumb'd ... eyes' of *On Indolence*. We note other parallels—
the 'melt' of *On Indolence* and the 'dissolve' of *To a Nightingale*, with the latter's
'fever and fret' echoing the former's 'short fever-fit'.

[2] In *Letters*, 334, he links the themes of Socrates, 'happiness carried to an
extreme' and death, in a single sentence, written (probably) only a day or two
before the Ode.

[3] The curious 'areal' suggestion of 'plot' will be noted, corresponding to the
earlier 'sward' and 'lawn'.

couplet of the poem answers, No: for wine is an aid not to community but to forgetfulness.

Forgetfulness of the world in its sinister aspect of weariness, fever and fret. For this is the aspect that Keats has really known; Provençal song and sunburnt mirth he has only imagined. The third strophe opposes a stark realization to the lilting gaiety of the second. This, for Keats, is the real world: a world of impotence and frustration.[1] In suggesting that *To a Nightingale* treats the theme of ambition I would be understood in no restricted sense: there is an ambition of love, of friendship, as well as of fame. But the thought of fame underlies it all: the ode is a meditation on immortality, in which the deathless song of the bird is set over against all human accomplishment. Fame was much in Keats's thoughts at this time: the two sonnets on that theme belong to the last days of April, and at precisely this time he is writing *To a Nightingale*. Only in June does he note an 'abatement of my love of fame' in a letter to Miss Jeffrey. That he is thinking of mighty poets in their misery dead when he writes 'No hungry generations tread thee down' is plain from a bitter comment in the same letter: 'One of the great reasons that the English have produced the finest writers in the world is, that the English world has ill-treated them during their lives and foster'd them after their deaths. They have in general been trampled aside into the bye paths of life and seen the festerings of Society. . . .'

Life is pain; and there can be no anodyne. Keats rejects the aid of wine in his fourth strophe and relies on 'the viewless wings of Poesy'[2] to bear him aloft into the charmed world of the Nightingale. But his trust is only half justified.[3] If for a moment he catches a glimpse of the bird in an exalted, celestial setting of

---

[1] Cf. again *Letters*, 334 (the passage is quoted below, p. 368).

[2] In the *Indolence* ode too he has 'ach'd for wings' (strophe III); and 'O for a draught of vintage . . . that I might drink and leave the world unseen' is paralleled by 'O for an age so shelter'd . . . that I may never know how change the moons'.

[3] Or, on one reading, not justified at all. For if we read 'Already with thee tender is the night' (from the Egerton autograph) the 'with thee' will receive a stress which opposes it to 'But here . . .'; and the aspiration 'I will fly to thee' will remain unfulfilled. It cannot be denied that this makes perfectly good sense.

moon and stars and night sky, he is quickly back on earth again: *But here there is no light.* The illumination is a fleeting one. Yet it is effective. It has the power to order and tranquillize the poet's anguished thoughts: it brings harmony. And if we consider it, we see why. The vision of the nightingale serene in its wide expanse of sky is a new mode of Keats's perennial image: the consecrated object at the spatial and temporal centre. The nightingale epitomizes, like the urn and the altar, the whole of experience: gathers into itself and gives out again the powers of love and death.

The tortured movement of the ode broadens, now, into tranquillity. The central vision brings acceptance. Keats cannot *see*; but he can *guess*, and he is content to guess. The acceptance is in line with his doctrine of 'negative capability', of patience with half-truths. He returns to himself, and, in returning to himself, he *attends* for the first time in the poem to what exists around him. The process of the ode thus closely follows the movement of Wordsworth's *Intimations of Immortality* (a favourite of Keats's) in which the initial self-centred disquiet is replaced by a self-surrender to the spirit of the here and now—'No more shall grief of mine the season wrong'. So in *To a Nightingale*:

> I cannot see what flowers are at my feet,
>   Nor what soft incense hangs upon the boughs,
> But, in embalmed darkness, guess each sweet
>   Wherewith the seasonable month endows
> The grass, the thicket, and the fruit-tree wild. . . .

And in the last lines of the strophe the catalogue of spring flowers brings the reassurance of loved, familiar things. The roses are 'coming', the violets are 'fading'; the 'child' of line 48 introduces the tender pieties; the last line compresses Blakean intuitions of insect and floral worlds linked in amity; music flows in the epithet 'murmurous'. This is 'full poetry'.

The thought of death must return; but when it does, in the sixth strophe, it is with the richness of consummation. 'Darkling I listen': and the darkness is no longer terrible. Ignorance accepted bears within itself the possibility of its own transmutation. So death can be welcomed as an integral part of the total process, the unending three-fold rhythm of birth, growth and death, which Keats recognized in life and in the dialectic of poetry itself.[1] The nightingale, like the consecrated urn and the altar, stands above this process but is not detached from it: is, indeed, the still centre round which it all revolves:

> Thou wast not made for death, immortal Bird!
>   No hungry generations tread thee down;
> The voice I hear this passing night was heard
>   In ancient days by emperor and clown:
> Perhaps the self-same song that found a path
>   Through the sad heart of Ruth, when, sick for home,
>   She stood in tears amid the alien corn;
>   The same that oft-times hath
> Charm'd magic casements, opening on the foam
>   Of perilous seas, in faery lands forlorn.

In this, perhaps the most celebrated stanza of the ode, we watch some very interesting things happening. Once again, as in stanza two, Keats's scope has widened; but with a difference. There, the picture of sunburnt mirth was local and self-centred: Keats sought community as escape from pain. Here, he achieves a universal vision: a vision which takes in the hungry generations, the social structure, the pain of parting and exile and longing, the pangs of disprized or frustrated love; and fuses them into a synthesis. Under the spell of the nightingale's song Keats has forgotten himself for the moment, and found the release of pity. Technically the strophe stands amongst his major triumphs.

The journey homeward to habitual self is painful after this supreme vision. The nightingale flies away; the high requiem

---

[1] Cf. letter to John Taylor, 27 February 1818: 'the rise, the progress, the setting of imagery should like the Sun come natural . . .' Do we catch, in 'Now more than ever seems it rich to die', an echo from the *Phædo*: '. . . those who philosophize rightly will meditate how to *die*; and *to be dead* will be to them of all men a thing the least terrible' (Taylor's 1793 translation, p. 160)? 'Death is life's high meed' is a constant theme of the post-Oxford verse.

declines into a plaintive anthem.[1] We are not left on the heights; for Keats knew well that in the courses of this world such trans- figurations are not permitted. There must be a descent from the Mount. Keats manages his transition, it seems to me, with ex- quisite tact; and the return, in 'a waking dream', to the initial note of 'drowsy numbness' gives the poem that circular structure he so much loved.

To a Nightingale has brought Keats to the stage reached by the shepherd-prince in the Glaucus episode of *Endymion*: the achieve- ment of compassion. And this has reorganized his central image, given it a new balance and a new complexity. In the *Ode on a Grecian Urn*, to which we must now turn, the still centre is no longer poised above the smoke and stir of this dim spot, or set within the wide quietness of nature: it stands in the midst of woe, a friend to man, with power to admonish and to soothe. It main- tains its ancient dignity, but has become more approachable, more companiable. This is inevitable, of course, the moment Keats comes to identify the still centre with a work of art; for it is, as he told us in *Sleep and Poetry*, the 'great aim' of poetry (or any other art) 'To soothe the cares, and lift the thoughts of man'.

On a Grecian Urn is the *Hamlet* among Keats's odes, in more senses than one. It is the most familiar, the richest in texture, the most obscure. Puzzlement over its concluding phrases has become a critical commonplace. Of all the odes, it comes nearest to a for- mal expression of 'philosophy'. We shall need, therefore, to look at its structure and images and statements with some care. And we shall be well advised, too, to grant it what I have called a *gestalt* consideration: to bear in mind, throughout our discussion, its rela- tionship to the other odes and to the rest of Keats's work. This of course has been our guiding principle throughout this study: in reading the *Urn* we shall rely upon it more tenaciously than ever.

---

[1] I cannot agree with Bridges and Professor Garrod that 'plaintive anthem' is wrong. There is no contradiction; the poem is not static, and the fading away of the bird's song into the distance may well strike a plaintive note. The 'dying fall' of this finale is repeated from *On Indolence*: 'So, ye three Ghosts, adieu!'

For the *Urn* is, by its very theme, our central poem. It gathers to itself the resonances of all the other urns, vases, pots and jars that stud Keats's poetry. Moreover, it would be a mistake to attempt an interpretation of the urn in isolation from other concavities. Reading the ode, we must bear in mind all Keats's sea-grottoes and mountain-caves, the 'lucid wombs' of the winds which breathe 'Eolian magic' in *Endymion*, the hollow chambers of Moneta's skull within which the epic of the Titans unrolls itself for the poet's instruction in *Hyperion*. We must remember the 'sphery strains caught from the blue dome' of the first letter to George. In a note by Proclus on the *Timæus*, eternity is characterized, in a splendid image, as 'the centre of resounding light' to which the intellect must 'hasten to conjoin itself'. The urn is specifically the artefact of which the cave is the physical, and the dome of the sky the formal, analogy. Beyond these range the heavenly spheres themselves, and Time the moving image of eternity.[1] In his Hippocrates (book IV) Keats would read how 'Potters spin a wheel, which shifts neither forwards nor backwards, yet moves both ways at once, therein copying the revolution of the universe. . . .' Or again, moving back from the macrocosm to the microcosm, he would learn from the *Timæus* how the Demiurge fashioned the human skull to the model of the universe: 'He fashioned like one working with the wheel a bony sphere, and placed it round the brain; leaving a narrow passage in the sphere itself.'

The urn is a foster-child of silence and slow time because what is in essence an eternal form (the sphere) has descended into, become adopted by, the 'circle of courses'. Its perfect sphericity is now deformed to suit human requirements. And it exhibits this dual origin in every contour of its surfaces. It is an unravished bride of quietness through its Sybilline function: the Sybil is a maiden, dwelling in the darkness and silence of the tomb, perpetually 'married' to Dis yet remaining ever virgin. The authenticity of her utterances proceeds from this dual role. The image of the

---

[1] The famous phrase has its birth in the *Timæus*.

womb then is our best human analogy for the urn,[1] focusing as it does both ideas: thus we see the Attic shape as its own matrix and its own child, abiding in but not subdued by space and time.

We have already noted a remarkable phrase in *Endymion* which shows us the urn before its descent into the circle of courses. The lines occur in the exordium to Book III in which Keats is concerned with 'regalities' poised far above the fury and the mire of our mortal destiny:

> Aye, 'bove the withering of old-lipp'd Fate
> A thousand Powers keep religious state,
> In water, fiery realm, and airy bourne;
> And, silent as a consecrated urn,
> Hold sphery sessions for a season due.

The reference takes the form of a simile; but it is none the less integral. We note that these are powers, energies, which concentrate themselves in the *silence* of the sacred form. In *that* world the urn is silent, immobile: but its message is for *this* world. Descending to our circle and refashioned on the potter's wheel, it is motionless— yet, like Eliot's Chinese jar, 'moves in its stillness'; it remains silent —yet speaks, not to the sensual ear but to the spirit. The potter builds the same energies into the urn, on his scale, as the Demiurge built into the universal urn-form at its creating.[2]

This is the first thing to note about the urn: it is a centre of *power*. In this it is one with Keats's other concavities. And the power is therapeutic: a point we have noted at an early stage in this study. It is a force of healing and of wisdom. It reconciles the contraries in itself: through the turning of the wheel a form of

---

[1] To stand beside the other analogies (physical and formal) given in the preceding paragraph. The skull is a second human analogy, counterpointing memory and intellectual birth against the womb's heredity and physical generation.

[2] Cf. D'Arcy Thompson, *Growth and Form*, p. 392: '. . . the potter's art illustrates the somewhat obscurer and more complex problems (scarcely less frequent in biology) of a figure of equilibrium which is an *open* surface of revolution'; and p. 523: 'The plastic clay was first shaped upon a wheel, and *potential stress-energy so acquired is stored up even in the finished ware*. . . .' My italics.

supreme stillness is evolved; through the silent co-operation of divine powers the urn is endued with a voice. It reconciles, moreover, the dead with the living. It provides a vehicle of continuity. If it is a funerary urn (and that it is so for Keats is plain, I think, from the original draft, where instead of 'And silent as a consecrated urn' we read 'And silent as a corpse upon a pyre'[1]) it links past and present, the wisdom of the past with the needs of the present. The voice that speaks from the Grecian urn in friendship to man is no simple voice. We are not concerned solely or even principally with the beauty of the æsthetic surfaces; we are concerned with the voice of silence and slow time. It is the voice of the ancestors linked forever with their children, it is the voice of the rotating spheres and of their energy here stored up in the consecrated form, that proclaims, 'Beauty is truth, truth beauty . . .'.[2] It is the silent form, and not the brede of marble men and maidens overwrought, that teases us out of thought as doth eternity: for the urn *is* eternity here earth-bound as the foster-child of time. The forest branches and the trodden weed are indeed the formal opposites of what the attic shape is essentially in itself: their asymmetrical ramifications contradict or counterpoint the urn's self-poised security.[3] And yet, because the urn is fashioned from earth and is a storehouse of energy, it is also the creative

---

[1] Keats thus transfers the emphasis from the ashes to the vessel which contains them. But the idea of the ashes persists.

[2] The Voodoo ceremonies of Haiti present curious affinities. 'The ceremony of reclamation [of the soul of the dead ancestor from the waters of the abyss] is as the third and final birth of a man. He emerged into the world, for the first time, as an animal. Initiation was his second birth, as a proper man. And this soul which, with death and the perishing of the flesh, was lost to the visible world, is brought back into it once more. The clay jar . . . in which it is placed at this ceremony is a substitute for the vessel of flesh which once contained it. Out of the mouth of that jar issue the counsels and wisdoms by which the deceased continues to aid and advance his descendants' (Maya Deren, *Divine Horsemen*).

[3] So Taylor, illustrating (Introduction to *Timæus*) Plato's theme of the cosmos as the product principally of eternity, but in manifestation of time: 'Nor is it more difficult to conceive matter after this manner invested with form and distributed into order, than to conceive a potter making clay with his own hands, giving it a shape when made, through the assistance of a wheel, and, when fashioned, adorning it through another instrument with figures. . . .'

womb of all manifestations: the branches are not alien to the sphere.

The urn is the womb from which all manifestation proceeds. It is also the tomb into which all manifestations descend. The Jacobean moralists delighted to confront the noisy, vigorous, angry, sinewy animal called man with the pinch of quiet dust that is all that remains of him after death. Yet the urn does not cease to be womb on becoming tomb. There is a new birth in the spirit. The mortal body purified through fire is recreated through fire and becomes a new thing: it now partakes of the sphericity or eternity of the vehicle in which it is enclosed, and by that very fact is no longer *enclosed* in any kind of limits. By the removal of the limitations of the body, we may say, the man's potential energies are actualized and he is able to function with a new freedom. When Keats talks of acting under the guidance of some high power, when he 'speculates' on the possibility that this power may be Spenser or Shakespeare, we can be sure that these considerations are at the back of his mind. Or, maybe, at the forefront.

These are generalizations, preparatory to an analysis of the ode itself: but they may help us to its closer understanding. They have helped me, at least, to understand how the urn can be at one and the same time a *bride* of quietness and a *foster-child* of silence and slow time, a difficulty that had long puzzled me and in comparison with which the celebrated truth-beauty equation seemed clarity itself. These were points that the commentators disdained to raise, much less answer. I think I understand, now, why the urn is an 'unravished' bride of quietness, and why Keats could write the phrase (an odd phrase, if you come to think of it, for him) with approbation. The Sybilline function of the urn gives us the key. Resonant hollows remain virginal, however 'glutted' they may be day after day by the sea's incursions or those of quietness: for they are under the sway of Hecate.[1] And Hecate is Diana, the ever-virgin.

---

[1] See the sonnet *On the Sea*.

The first two lines of the *Ode on a Grecian Urn* are, then, elucidated.

> Thou still unravish'd bride of quietness!
> Thou foster-child of Silence and slow Time.

We have an apostrophe, and an antithesis.[1] Keats looks at the urn,
and cognizes it, at first glance, in its double character: as the
eternal form, and as the human artefact. He concentrates upon it,
unawares, the whole complex of associations, half-seeings, hypotheses glimpsed in Bailey's rooms at Magdalen, bitter-sweetnesses
digested in later months of watchings with Tom, meetings with
Fanny, disappointments with *Endymion* and *Hyperion*: it shines
suddenly, in its stillness poised within the cold walls of the
Museum (as the charioteer shines in his chamber at Delphi),
complete, remote, uncaring, yet also, through the energies and
weaknesses built into it in those ancient days, flawed, human,
sympathetic. For such is the permanent antithesis of art. Between
the conception and the achievement falls the shadow; and the
shadow is what makes the conception and the achievement live
for us.[2]

> Sylvan historian, who canst thus express
> A flowery tale more sweetly than our rhyme:

the concluding lines of the quatrain arrest us. They break the
continuity, they constitute the shadow. Woods and flowers: what
have these to do with the intellectual beauty? At once we find
ourselves in the world of nature, not of art; within the circle of
courses, not 'the circle of space, which none but God alone can
pervade'.[3] This is another kind of beauty, belonging to growth
more than to form. It is linked as decoration to the formal beauty
of the urn. It is linked to, but is not organically connected with it.

We are dealing, once again, with the distinction between

---

[1] Catching up the initial mother/maiden oxymoron of the *Ode to May*.

[2] In *Fragment of the 'Castle Builder'* Keats avers his preference for 'cinque-
coloured potter's clay' over 'the marble fairness of old Greece': here he isolates
one term of the oxymoron. Cf. the 'baked earth' of Appendix C, 4.

[3] See Appendix A, p. 399, below.

growth and form, the constant antithesis of Keats's verse; and the interest of the ode is that in it Keats comes out into the open. He sets the one against the other, and he probes their relationship. The antithesis arises, of course, even before he sets pen to paper to write the ode. It arises when he first looks at the urn. In that moment, growth and form, the temporal and the eternal, the suffering and the impassible, are face to face. And with the moment Keats's perennial problem arises: the dilemma that presented itself when he took up his pen to write *Hyperion*. But there is a difference. *Then* he felt he had to do something about it—to work it out, to solve it within the structure of his poem. As we know, he failed. *Now* he contemplates the antithesis; he embodies it in verse, but he does nothing about it. He has learned a new wisdom.

He accepts the antithesis now on its own terms, impersonally. If he is within the poem he is within it not as John Keats, with his particular load of worries, but simply as a human being caught up, momentarily, in the vortex of energy vibrant in the urn's poised being. This is a great advance not only on *Hyperion* and the odes which precede the *Grecian Urn*, but also on the sonnet, *Bright Star*, a poem which poses the oxymoron in all too personal terms. Let us glance at the sonnet before proceeding with our analysis of the *Urn*. We shall find it yields effective contrasts.

> Bright star! would I were steadfast as thou art—
>   Not in lone splendour hung aloft the night
> And watching, with eternal lids apart,
>   Like nature's patient, sleepless Eremite,
> The moving waters at their priestlike task
>   Of pure ablution round earth's human shores,
> Or gazing on the new soft fallen mask
>   Of snow upon the mountains and the moors—
> No—yet still steadfast, still unchangeable,
>   Pillow'd upon my fair love's ripening breast,
> To feel for ever its soft fall and swell,
>   Awake for ever in a sweet unrest,
> Still, still to hear her tender-taken breath,
> And so live ever—or else swoon to death.

'Half-passionless, and so swoon on to death', as an earlier version reads. But Keats is not half-passionless in the poem—he is not passionless at all. And for this reason the poem is, to my mind, a failure. It attempts to reconcile two species of beauty—the formal and the vital—but without success. Steadfastness belongs to the formal, the intellectual beauty: to the star or the urn; but not to the vital beauty, the beauty of phases. To the beauty of phases, which includes Fanny Brawne's and all human and organic beauty, belong change and decay, sweat and warmth and flowering and birth and death. The lover calls for the eternity of the phase-beauty which is by definition transitory.[1] He is disappointed, and turns, in his grief, to the only realm which seems to him to combine the two terms: the world of art.

In the sonnet the formal is set apart from the vital: the star remains aloft, the poet and his love below. The poet's aspiration to share the star's impassibility is at once negated by his desire for another kind of beauty. Both desires are frustrated: the poem ends with death. It does so because it has left the body of divine analogy: it has proposed a set of contraries which are unreconcilable. In the ode this is not so. The star has come down to earth, has taken upon itself the form of the urn, has submitted itself to the wheel of the potter, has held mortal ashes, has sunk into the ground and lain there in death like a seed, and risen again to the light of day. It has undergone, in fact, the cycle of mortal destiny: it is human by its fate, if divine by its form. What is more, it is adorned, on its surface, with figures parabolic of human life.

Nowhere is the doctrine of divine analogy more persuasively conveyed than in a comparison of the forms of living nature with human artefacts. Coleridge, with little or no scientific training, felt this keenly. Keats, endowed by temperament with a faculty of sense-perception far richer than Coleridge's and by fortune with a medical education which certainly included more than the elements of physiology and morphology, felt it more keenly still.

---

[1] In the letter of 25 July 1819 to Fanny she is herself the star.

Even the common reader today, glancing through the illustrations to *Growth and Form*, catches his breath in admiration at the strangeness and complexity of these structures of cells and shells and fruits, in whose making a plastic intelligence has worked through the medium of physical law to produce miracles of inhuman handiwork. Keats was fascinated by these natural structures. From his earliest *vers de société* in which he acknowledges the receipt of a 'curious shell', to the last poignant lines in which he gazes with agonized detachment at the configuration of 'This living hand, now warm and capable Of earnest grasping', the fascination persisted. The forms and functions of things, the production of these forms and the unfolding of these functions through the processes of growth and through mechanical forces, pervade his poetry.

It is worth remarking that the only English writers with whom we can compare him in this respect were both of them doctors: Browne and Darwin. I have not found that he read Browne, but there is no doubt that he read Darwin. Indeed, his life's work is in one sense a correction of Darwin. Darwin gave him clues to his 'vast idea'; and the fact that Darwin himself read the clues in the wrong way gave Keats the impulse to construe them in the right way. The beautiful plant figures in Darwin's books remind us of *Growth and Form* and I believe they meant a lot to Keats. The journey we go from the calixes of 'small buds unfolding' in the early *Sleep and Poetry* to the ultimate *Grecian Urn* is the same journey we go from the opening plates of urn-like seed-cases and flowers in *The Loves of the Plants* to the concluding engravings of the Portland Vase in *The Economy of Vegetation*.[1] The road between traverses, for both poets, the realm of Flora and old Pan. It is adorned with flowers and fruits and corn and branching trees, haunted by spirits of the four elements; it passes over caves bright with crystals and veins of gold and silver ore.

The analogy holds, then, even in the *Grecian Urn*, between the human and the divine artefact. The fruit carries solary virtue in

---

[1] The two Parts of *The Botanic Garden* were published in this order.

vegetable shape; the urn carries 'ethereal' power in its walls of clay. These recognitions are imperative if we are to gauge the full significance of Keats's opening quatrain and lines that follow. For the quatrain already states the double theme. As the still unravished bride of quietness the urn's Sybilline function is asserted: its participation in the eternal order of truth and beauty. As the sylvan historian its presentation of human and natural action is stressed: its participation in the circle of courses. The poem continues:

> What leaf-fring'd legend haunts about thy shape
>   Of deities or mortals, or of both,
>   In Tempe or the dales of Arcady?
> What men or gods are these? What maidens loth?
>   What mad pursuit? What struggle to escape?
>   What pipes and timbrels? What wild ecstasy?

Keats's wording is important. The legend 'haunts about' the shape of the urn: is, therefore, in a sense detached from it. Here is the shape, the form; and there is the legend. The form has attracted the legend to itself by the power stored up within it. The power is from eternity: the legend is within time, and functions in the world of the contraries. For note: there are two legends, the one expressing passionate desire, violent movement, 'wild ecstasy'; the other expressing piety, sacrifice, ritual death. These polar elements of the phantasmagoria which is life play about the sphericity of the urn. But for its surfaces they could not exist, but it could very well exist without them.

But Keats is anxious to present the total picture. The 'coarse-bred son of a livery-stable keeper', he will deal in no domes, moon-lit or star-lit, that disdain all that man is: his verse is warm with compassion and understanding. In his opening strophe he has questioned the urn not on its message but on its story: the strophe expresses a simple human curiosity. There is nothing metaphysical here. What is it all about, he asks: what is all this complexity of frenzied or dignified movement? The answer comes in the second strophe: here we pass from eye-perception to ear-perception, though the ear is not the 'sensual ear'. The answer comes from time, but from time arrested. The lovers enjoy a species of false eternity on the margin of the urn's austere, impassible being. The pipe-player's temporal music has suffered a transposition into the toneless ditties of eternity; the lover enjoys the delight of loving, though not its fruition (which might prove 'the worst torment of love satisfied'). The lament of an earlier ode for beauty which 'cannot keep her lustrous eyes' and new love which 'cannot pine at them beyond tomorrow' is here appeased. 'To think is to be full of sorrow'; but the Urn teases us 'out of thought As doth eternity'. Nature, inevitably for Keats, enters the picture as sharing in this glad suspension:

> Ah, happy, happy boughs! that cannot shed
> Your leaves, nor ever bid the Spring adieu. . . .

But then, inevitably too, we return to Keats's perennial contrast: the anguish of human passion set against the tranquillity of nature and (in this case) of art. The third strophe ends with 'A burning forehead and a parching tongue'.

The poem unfolds, we see, in no simple rhythm. There are antitheses within antitheses: the evolution is by question and answer. The first antithesis is situational: the man confronts the urn, human longing and anguish come up against the finished form of art. But in the urn itself we discern two movements: first the *shape*, which moves in its stillness; and second, the *legend*, arrested action which enjoys a momentary life only in the spectator's imagination. The poet is linked to the legend by his weakness, by the exactitude with which these ghosts of lovers and priests enact his own all-too-human hopes and desires. He is linked to the supreme shape of the urn by his strength, by his participation, beneath the flux of emotion, in the eternal being. His route—and we have seen that this is Keats's inevitable track—is through the realm of Flora and old Pan, then through the agony, the strife of human hearts, to the goal of realization. The 'vast idea' moulds the Ode as it moulded *Endymion*.

The track leads, again, through myth, and through the 'old pieties' of Greek religion. The sacrifice anticipated in the fourth

strophe links the human, the animal and the divine. The little town
is deserted: at this moment concentration on ritual is complete.
We remember once more Keats's reverence for tradition, for
'sacred custom': for a religion that *connects* the three worlds (and
not, as Christianity seemed to him to do, divides). It was inevitable, therefore, that the urn, the all-inclusive symbol, should
present this facet of human life side by side with the passion of the
lovers and the ecstasy of the musicians.[1]

But at its close the ode comes full circle to its initial paradox.

> O Attic shape! fair attitude! with brede
>   Of marble men and maidens overwrought,
> With forest branches and the trodden weed,
>   Thou, silent form, dost tease us out of thought
> As doth eternity. . . .

We return to the shape. It is overwrought with brede human and
vegetative: brede which invites us to think, to speculate, to imagine; but the form teases us *out of thought* 'as doth eternity'. For,
as we know, the form of the urn *is* eternity in a plastic analogy:
and, like the consecrated urn which is its prototype in the empyrean, it acts as a focus for a thousand powers. It has drawn the
multifariousness of natural life to its surfaces as adornment; it
draws ethereal power into its void: power which admonishes and
comforts.

'Beauty is truth, truth beauty.' The equation remains mysterious,
partly through lack of definition. Which truth, what kind of
beauty? I shall not linger over the famous phrase, which seems to
me nowhere near so cryptic as its commentators have made it
out to be. It is to be interpreted in the light of Keats's whole work,
of such statements in the Letters, for instance, as 'What the Imagination seizes as beauty must be truth'. Hegel, we may remember,
distinguished two kinds of truth: what he called *Richtigheit*, or
statistical truth, the congruence of a statement with brute fact;
and *Wahrheit*, living truth, the congruence of a part with its whole.

---

[1] Keats's urn is known to have been a composite of several he had seen.

A thing or a thought is true if it finds its place and is able to develop itself—to *grow*—within wider and wider contexts. And this is precisely Keats's kind of truth. The verity proved on the pulses is the verity that moves and grows with the rhythm of the blood. And that rhythm may vary from day to day, from hour to hour, from moment to moment.

> And in that moment the poet's task is done,
> In a moment, a pulsation of the artery.

There are, then, two kinds of truth; with one of which Keats, as a poet, is hardly concerned. There are also two kinds of beauty, with both of which Keats is very much concerned indeed. He is concerned with the relations between them and with their relationship to the truth which is *Wahrheit*. We have noted these two kinds of beauty before. We have seen that the one is the intellectual beauty, the beauty of form; and that the other is the temporal beauty, the beauty of phases. Before going on to consider the ode —*On Melancholy*—which seems to me to treat peculiarly of phase-beauty, it may be as well if I make some attempt to define or at least illustrate the term.

Pulchrum est quod visu placet: Aquinas's definition will serve as a starting point. Phase-beauty is grasped immediately, by the eye or the ear. It is an earthly beauty, a *datum* of the processes of growth, change and decay. It holds the pathos of the impermanent. We hear it in a musical cadence; we see it in the barest branch which, as it breaks, is beautiful. It is not the beauty of the mountain, whose rate of change is imperceptibly slow; it is the beauty of the sea in breaking wave and withdrawing tide, of the billow

> Down whose green back the short-liv'd foam, all hoar,
> Bursts gradual, with a wayward indolence.

In short, it is the beauty which not only holds the seeds of its own destruction, but also exhibits those seeds and the process of decay in its very form and pressure.

Now human artefacts cannot display this beauty. The germ of their decay is not in themselves, but in the external forces which

forever menace them.[1] For it is not the *result* of impermanence
that we are considering—if it were, we should be able to include

<blockquote>
what I have seen
Of grey cathedrals, buttress'd walls, rent towers,
The superannuations of sunk realms,
</blockquote>

objects which have a peculiar pathos of their own, 'the unimagin-
able touch of time'. The beauty of phases is the graph of change
in progress—the *display* of mutability. The change occurs as we
watch, as in the breaking wave; or else we compass with our eyes
the varying stages of mutation displayed at the same moment.
But I cannot do better than bring forward in explanation a paragraph of D'Arcy Thompson's *Growth and Form* which provided
me, originally, with my term:

> A flowering spray of Montbretia or lily-of-the-valley exemplifies a
> growth-gradient, after a simple fashion of its own. Along the stalk
> the growth-rate falls away; the florets are of descending age, from
> flower to bud: their graded differences of age lead to an exquisite
> gradation of size and form; the time-interval between one and an-
> other or the 'space-time relation' between them all, gives a peculiar
> quality—we may call it phase-beauty—to the whole. A clump of
> reeds or rushes shews this same phase-beauty, and so do the waves on
> a cornfield or on the sea. A jet of water is not much, but a fountain
> becomes a beautiful thing, and the play of many fountains is an
> enchantment at Versailles.

In writing that paragraph the author might well have had Keats[2]
in mind. Every example that he gives is of a manifestation of
phase-beauty that interested Keats.

The flowering or budding sprays are everywhere. We meet
them on the first page of his 1817 volume, in lines which ring the
changes on the theme of phase beauty—

<blockquote>
I stood *tip-toe* upon a little hill,
The air was cooling, and so very still,
</blockquote>

---

[1] The urn, as we have seen (note from *Growth and Form* at p. 331 above), is an
exception: *i.e.* it reconciles formal and phase beauty.

[2] It is noteworthy that his index shows more references to Keats than to any
other poet.

That the sweet *buds* which with a *modest pride*
Pull droopingly, *in slanting curve* aside,
Their *scantly leaved*, and *finely tapering* stems,
Had *not yet lost* those *starry diadems*
Caught from the early sobbing of the morn.

My italicizing points the phasic quality of the passage: it is a
sustained oxymoron, running through the fields of human ex-
pectancy, plant growth (with the metaphor in *modest pride* linking
the two fields), plant form (depending on principles of growth in
finely tapering and of mechanics in *slanting curve*), and meteorology
(dew formation and evaporation). My analysis is perhaps heavy-
handed, but I have found in discussion of Keats that these points
are missed, and they seem to me to be constant, and integral to a
general effect gained by his poetry and no other that I know.[1]
Such precise observation stems from a deep-rooted attitude. Indeed, to call it an attitude is not enough: what is at work here is a
kind of perception which is unique. I will call it 'total attention'.
Keats is alive, in the moment of perception, to the whole of what
is going on within his field of awareness; he throws round the
event, whatever it may be, a multi-sensual net; he grasps it in its
spatial relations (its references between components of the field of
experience); he grasps it in its temporal relations (in its coming-
to-be and its passing-away); he grasps it, when he is writing at his
best, in its eternal relations, as the moment in and out of time.

D'Arcy Thompson, in the passage quoted, points to a 'space-
time relation' at the heart of phase beauty. This is what I have
called the awareness of coming-to-be and passing away. I will not
quote more examples from Keats of the flowering-spray type;
they are innumerable, and a reader once put on the scent will not
fail to find them in the course of his reading. It is interesting,
however, to see the same awareness in action in other fields than

---

[1] Though I think there is a real possibility for criticism to examine other verse
along these lines and to find other attitudes and effects equally rewarding for their
contribution to an understanding of the poetry. The results will at least be concrete; and it was dissatisfaction with the abstract character of much contemporary
criticism which led me to my own findings in this field.

'the realm of Flora'. Who but Keats, observing the sand at the bottom of a clear pool, would envisage its gradual silting from distant deserts:

> my grotto-sands
> Tawny and gold, ooz'd slowly from far lands
> By my diligent springs [1]

and in the *slow-diligent* oxymoron pinpoint the present immobility, catch the flow at its moment of stasis? 'The curly foam' of Endymion's deep-sea vision [2] is no more than decorative, perhaps; but when we read in *Hyperion* of Saturn's locks, which

> Shone like the bubbling foam about a keel
> When the prow sweeps into a midnight cove [3]

we are again at the space-time crossroads. And let us glance at Keats's illustration of D'Arcy-Thompson's 'play of many fountains'. Here it is in *Endymion* II (lines 601–26):

> Enormous chasms, where, all foam and roar,
> Streams subterranean tease their granite beds;
> Then heighten'd just above the silvery heads
> Of a thousand fountains, so that he could dash
> The waters with his spear; but at the splash,
> Done heedlessly, those spouting columns arose
> Sudden a poplar's height. . . .

This is an experiment; done heedlessly, certainly, but the result is interesting:

> . . . and 'gan to enclose
> His diamond path with fretwork, streaming round
> Alive, and dazzling cool, and with a sound,
> Haply, like dolphin tumults, when sweet shells
> Welcome the float of Thetis. Long he dwells
> On this delight; for, every minute's space,

---

[1] *Endymion*, II, 113–15. The elements of the total picture here (lines 98–130), with its spring (with margin 'pebbly' or 'mossy' and with 'shining sands below'), its naiad arising to console a lover, are found in Pope's *Sappho to Phaon* (lines 179–200); but the phase-beauty is missing.

[2] *Ibid.*, III, 85.   [3] II, 354, 355.

The streams with changed magic interlace:
Sometimes like delicatest lattices,
Covered with crystal vines; then weeping trees,
Moving about as in a gentle wind,
Which, in a wink, to watery gauze refin'd,
Pour'd into shapes of curtain'd canopies,
Spangled, and rich with liquid broideries
Of flowers, peacocks, swans, and naiads fair.
Swifter than lightning went these wonders rare;
And then the water, into stubborn streams
Collecting, mimick'd the wrought oaken beams,
Pillars, and frieze, and high fantastic roof,
Of those dusk places in times far aloof
Cathedrals call'd.[1]

And so he modulates from the most liquid to the solidest of patterns. This is virtuoso description, and we may not care for it; but
it shows an extraordinary concern with variations of matter and
form. And with the *forces* governing form. One would like to
know a good deal more than one does know about Keats's schoolboy and later education: how much he would be expected to read
in natural and physical science, for instance; what elements of
physics, natural history, meteorology were included in his syllabus;
where he got his knowledge of morphology, his interest in the

---

[1] Schopenhauer, who misses the element of phase-beauty in plant-form (*The World as Will and Idea*, III, para. 45), has a good comment on the 'Idea' of water (*ibid.* 51): '. . . in order to comprehend fully the Ideas of water it is not sufficient to see it in the quiet pond or in the evenly-flowing stream; but these ideas disclose themselves fully only when the water appears under all circumstances and exposed to all kinds of obstacles. The effects of the varied circumstances and obstacles give it the opportunity of fully exhibiting all its qualities. This is why we find it beautiful when it tumbles, rushes and foams, or leaps into the air, or falls in a cataract of spray; or, lastly, if artificially confined it springs up in a fountain. . . . Now, what the engineer achieves with the fluid matter of water, the architect achieves with the rigid matter of stone, and just this the epic or dramatic poet achieves with the Idea of man.' All this elucidates precisely Keats's interest in form as the display of his 'vast idea'; and Schopenhauer's last phrase might be a gloss on Keats's 'chief attempt in the Drama—the playing of different Natures with Joy and Sorrow' (*Letters*, 90). The two passages may belong to the same year: Keats's Preface is dated April, and Schopenhauer's August, 1818.

connectedness of plant form with human form. The little sketches of flowers in the margins of his Guy's Hospital notebook have been seen as 'escapist'—the young poet indulging his daydreams —but is it altogether impossible that he is illustrating Sir Astley Cooper's remarks on the relations between plant and human tissue? Or even some connection which has occurred to him spontaneously?

His vision of the human form divine is within the field of phase beauty. Cynthia, in *Endymion*, is 'that completed form of all completeness',[1] but she later 'dies at the thinnest cloud'[2] and again 'rises crescented' in Book IV[3]; so too (in the purely human world now) of Isabella and Lorenzo: 'her full shape would all his seeing fill' at the outset of the idyll, but soon her cheek 'fell thin as a young mother's' for love-sickness, and in the end she 'pines' and dies. These expressions seem inevitable in the poems as we read them; what is interesting is to see Keats choosing, over and over again, this sequence for treatment: it is there in *Lamia*, *Hyperion*, *La Belle Dame*, *The Eve of St Mark* (probably) and a number of shorter poems.

A slant of this kind must produce, in the poetry and in the poet's life, situations rich in contrast. The basic oxymoron is that of completeness/incompleteness. A form is achieved, and passes. The stream of life is forever flowing into and out of the moment of consummation. And it is the phase leading up to the moment, not the phase leading away from it, that interested Keats. Wordsworth's prime interest seems to have been the other way. His concern is with the deep, tranquil things of old age, Keats's with the exciting possibilities of youth: beauty is youth, youth beauty. He can admire a 'Charmian'[4] for her rich maturity, he can have an affair with Mrs Isabella Jones ; but he does not fall in love with either, he falls in love with Fanny Brawne, 'the just new-budded flower'[5] (not yet seventeen, he thinks, but she was well over eighteen), as he had previously fallen in love with the still younger

---

[1] I, 606.   [2] III, 81.   [3] IV, 430.
[4] *Letters*, 231, 232. See R. Gittings, *Keats: The Living Year*.
[5] *Ode to Fanny*, VIII.

Georgiana Wylie. And what does he admire in Fanny and Georgiana? Let him answer for himself:

> Why may I not speak of your Beauty, since without that I could never have lov'd you. I cannot conceive any beginning of such love as I have for you but Beauty. There may be a sort of love for which, without the least sneer at it, I have the highest respect and can admire it in others: but it has not the richness, the bloom, the full form, the enchantment of love after my own heart.[1]

We are not called upon to psychoanalyse that, only to understand it. It is straightforward and honest, with the honesty of that delightful New Year resolution of 1818: 'I never intend hereafter to spend any time with Ladies unless they are handsome—you lose time to no purpose.'[2] Let us write that down as jocular or immature—it is both, but it is also very sensible for a young man of twenty-two: Keats *would* have been losing his time to no purpose.

Keats wrote very little about Fanny to anybody. In his private verse he thinks of her as 'the flower and all its budded charms'[3]; pictures himself at rest on her breast's 'soft fall and swell'; remembers (for 'Touch has a memory') how he felt

> that warm breath here and there
> To spread a rapture in my very hair.[4]

All is phasic: here lies the delight and the agony. There is warmth here too; a Scottish tour poem, which has not received the attention it merits, captures only the bleakness of transience. It is merely an imagination, an imitation of Burns, but all the regret of Keats's life is in it. He has not yet met Fanny. He is at a cross-roads of his life.

> As I stood where a rocky brig
> A torrent crosses
> I spied upon a misty rig
> A troup o' Horses—

---

[1] *Letters*, 356.

[2] Journal-letter of December–January 1818 to George and Georgiana Keats (the letter in which he first mentions Fanny Brawne to them).

[3] Sonnet, 'The day is gone, and all its sweets are gone!'

[4] 'What can I do to drive away . . .?'

What follows is 'past expressing'—the emotion is beyond words, but he will set down, in barest terms, the occasion:

> And as they trotted down the glen
> I sped to meet them
> To see if I might know the Men
> To stop and greet them.

The move is towards communication. Note the situation. Keats is at a cross-roads: a pathway and a torrent; the pathway is the road of prudent, painstaking endeavour towards achievement of which he speaks so often in his letters of this period; the torrent is the abandonment to desire. But what is the desire? This he hardly knows. He leaves his point of vantage on the bridge, and 'speeds' towards the group on the 'misty rig'.

It is a wedding party. First come the men-folk, then the bride:

> I saw her wrappit in her hood
> Fra wind and raining—
> Her cheek was flush wi timid blood
> Twixt growth and waning—

caught phasically at the cross-roads of *her* life (the expression is one of Keats's triumphs of insight). She is 'dazed', she does not see Keats; no one speaks to him, the cavalcade passes joyfully:

> An every heart is full on flame
> An light as feather
> Ah! Marie they are all gone hame
> Fra happy wedding,
> Whilst I—Ah is it not a shame?
> Sad tears am shedding.

The poem has been judged too trivial for inclusion in E. de Selincourt's edition, and no one, as far as I know, has had anything good to say about it except Buxton Forman (in a footnote to the letter of 17 July 1818 to Tom Keats in which it is included); to me it marks a cross-roads indeed, a point of decision, broken only by the coming of Fanny Brawne. That is opinion merely [1]: what is not a matter of opinion is its phasic quality, its impact established in the breaking of impact, which is one species of integrity. It is the integrity of the reed before the wind, more beautiful perhaps than the oak's, and more lasting if less dramatic; the reed bends not merely in homage, but in sympathy too, and what results is a formal music. But the word 'form' here slips in and out of meaning.

Now in this connection we can draw an interesting contrast with Wordsworth. Keats's is a poetry of impermanence, of growth and flowering and decay, before it is a poetry of form. And when it is a poetry of form, the form is Platonic: it exists above the circle of courses. Keats moves through impermanence to permanence. But Wordsworth's is a poetry of permanence within the circle of courses. As Whitehead remarks in *Science and the Modern World*, he 'was haunted by the enormous permanences of nature. For him change is an incident which shoots across a background of endurance. . . .' Where Keats, with his old master Spenser, sees mutability as the principle, Wordsworth sees persistence. Even mountains impress Keats not by their bulk and *thereness* but by what he calls their intellect; and he reads their intellect in the 'light shade slaty Rock, Moss and Rock weed', which are all transient things.[2] For Keats, even mountains and rocks exhibit phase-beauty: they undulate, they are alive, even if their life is a sleep. We have seen how he senses 'inanimate' nature as a 'giant, pulsing underground'. Wordsworth's universe, on the other hand, is of a strange rigidity. He is interested in the completed shape; his clouds, even, 'move altogether if they move at all'. Mountains, in their austere immobility, dominate his landscapes; rivers flow, but still 'the form abides'. His preferred season is winter,

---

[1] Though one should not let the Burnsisms blind one to the excellent writing of the ballad. This is the peak of Keats's colloquial style. The poem comes from his heart: it is both nostalgic (he had George's wedding in mind) and oddly prophetic.

[2] Note too his habit of measuring time and space by units of impermanence: 'ere the hot sun count His dewy rosary'; 'about a young bird's flutter from a wood'.

with the beauteous forms of things locked in the paralysis of frost. Following the Ullswater episode, he is haunted by 'huge and mighty forms, that do not live Like living men': automata, as it were, mechanical monsters or robots. Living creatures, when they appear in his verses, are assimilated to natural forces or move slowly, with a tendency to petrifaction. In the sonnet 'Those words were uttered as in pensive mood' (1802) he writes in deprecation of the gilt-edged insecurities of sunset beauty, 'The immortal Mind craves objects that endure'.

The difference comes out clearly in a comparison of the two sonnets written by Keats and Wordsworth on Ailsa Rock. Keats's poem intuits the rock's phase-existence; it can do this because the rock rises out of the sea, is moulded by the sea, partakes then of the sea's mutability. He presents Ailsa immediately as a composite:

> Hearken, thou craggy ocean pyramid!

and proceeds to telescope the geological eras the rock has lived through as though they are present to his eye. Ailsa sinks, rises, unfolds itself in sun, rain, mist and thunder like a plant growing, budding and flowering under the cine-camera's quick-motion lens. 'Really I was a little alarmed', he tells Tom in the letter (10 July 1818) that describes his first glimpse of Ailsa. The alarm is not evoked, as is Wordsworth's alarm in the boat-stealing episode, by the crag's massive eternity. No, it is the prophetic vision (for prophecy casts its glance backwards as well as forwards) of the rock in all its cataclysmic fortunes that moves him; he sees it as indeed a brother of the ever-changing ocean from which it emerges. 'The effect of Ailsa with the peculiar perspective of the Sea in connection with the ground we stood on, and the misty rain then falling gave me a complete Idea of a Deluge.'

Wordsworth's is a minor sonnet in comparison with Keats's, and so hardly representative. He too begins with a vision of Ailsa 'risen from ocean' but it is 'ocean to defy': he rejects the amity of the elements. Or rather, he fails to see it. The mountain lords it over the surrounding sea; we are in a monarchy, not a democracy.

> Still is he seen, in lone sublimity,
> Towering above the sea and little ships.

Human 'Care, Pleasure, or Grief, and Toil' are dwarfed by the 'fixed Form' of the crag. So too in his lines on Staffa 'After the Crowd had departed' (lines which should also be compared with Keats's) he tells us that

> The pillared vestibule,
> Expanding yet precise, the roof embowed,
> Might seem designed to humble man. . . .

Wordsworth is concerned to discriminate; and, generally, to discriminate in favour of nature's 'fixed forms' against the fury and the mire of human veins. His stand is at the polar opposite from Keats's conciliating vision.

Phase-beauty, enantiodromia, the transmutation of the contraries—here we have the themes of *On Melancholy*. There is a concentration in this piece—a musical *stretto*—unparalleled in the other movements of the symphony. There is, moreover, an element of the macabre, recognizable even if we take no account of the cancelled first stanza with its dead men's bones and phantom gibbet. This ode is decidedly in a minor key—and it is of course a minor ode, very much more the expression of a mood than any of the other five except *On Indolence* (with which it has strong affinities). It has curious anticipations, too, of the matter and the manner of a later writer—Edgar Allan Poe. Here are wolfsbane, nightshade and yew-berries, beetles, death-moths and owls: all Poesque macabre properties. And Poe's capacity for extracting the quintessence of evil, of negation, out of situations which to a normal mind offer the maximum possibilities of good, of fruitfulness—out of human love, out of natural beauty, out of the affection of animals, for instance—is much in evidence in this poem.[1]

Set as it is between two great movements of affirmation, the

---

[1] I think something of the same morbidity is detectable in *The Eve of St Mark*.

Ode on a Grecian Urn and *To Autumn*, it has its legitimate place in the sequence; but I have never been able to bring myself to admire it greatly. I do not feel, with Professor Garrod, that 'perhaps there is more of Keats in this perverse ingenuity of the *Ode on Melancholy* than in the rather formal philosophy (if philosophy it be) of the *Ode on a Grecian Urn*'.[1] Perverse ingenuity (though I would not go so far as to call it that) has no real place in the life-affirming gospel of Keats. When Garrod goes on: '*Melancholy* remains fixed courageously, almost defiantly, in the gospel of the senses, ready to die for, and in, it', I would reply that Keats's gospel of the senses does not demand that sort of death—the tomb-like imprisonment in some inner shrine or suspension among cloudy (and no doubt dusty) trophies; it demands the death of the seed which is a 'dying into life', into freedom. *Melancholy* is the most shut-in of the Odes; there is a smell of the tomb about it. Even the green hill in the middle strophe is wrapt in a shroud. Technically, it is highly competent but rhetorical; the personifications of the last strophe are a return to Keats's earlier manner.

But 'perverse ingenuity'—no, there is no question of that. *On Melancholy* is the isolation of a real perception of Keats's: a perception he normally treated contrapuntally. 'Aching Pleasure nigh, Turning to poison while the bee-mouth sips': here we have life's paradox in a nutshell; but it is the same paradox as that of the poet in *The Fall of Hyperion* who 'venoms all his days'. This third strophe has a weightiness of movement quite distinct from the weirdness of the first or the extravagance of the second.

The poem is a plea for 'intensity'. Just as Keats had rejected the anodyne of wine in *To a Nightingale*, and was to reject it again in the lines to Fanny 'What can I do to drive away...?'[2] as 'a vulgarism, A heresy and schism, Foisted into the canon law of love': so here he counsels the man afflicted with love-melancholy to

---

[1] Garrod takes the *Melancholy* to have been written first and the *Grecian Urn* to have been 'written in a mood of strong revulsion' from its thesis. My own impression is that the contrary was the case.

[2] In complete contrast to the sense of the early (1814) 'Fill for me a brimming bowl', with its plea for 'as deep a draught As e'er from Lethe's wave was quaff'd'.

savour his disease to the full, to 'glut his sorrow' on the lovely things that present so agonizing a contrast to his own mood. Don't go to Lethe (as suggested in *To a Nightingale*), don't seek forgetfulness in slow or rapid suicide; don't (like the knight-at-arms) haunt sombre and silent places. Instead, 'in the destructive element immerse': gaze deep into your mistress's eyes, and find there, in the very temple of delight, the same fatal antithesis on which you are yourself racked. Such is Keats's advice. Whether it is good advice or not is, for us, beside the point. What is important for us is to notice this further stage in Keats's analytical treatment of love in its more morbid aspects: a treatment which, as we have seen, he embarked upon with *Isabella*. But *Isabella* was impersonal; now, with *On Melancholy*, Keats's personal dilemma has reached such intensity that it is bursting the frame of art, and the remaining love-poems that he was to write are human documents rather than literature. We cannot read them with detachment or without discomfort.

To Autumn is the product of Keats's own bid for detachment. He wrote it at Winchester, where he was trying to forget Fanny Brawne and all the anguish and confusion that his love for her had brought him. Now he wants only peace, fair weather, and solitude. He rejoices in a large room that looks out on a 'beautiful blank side of a house'. 'It is strange I should like it better than the view of the sea from our window at Shanklin.' Strange, yes; but after all, not so strange. One can bear just so much, and no more: the doctrine of 'intensity' may be all very well for a healthy man, but a sick mind and body cannot stand up to the strain. There has to be a retraction from the 'sweet and bitter world'.[1] In Keats's state the blank side of a house could be more than a symbol—it could be a medicine, a tonic. He goes neither to Lethe nor to laudanum, but to the elements which he had declared in an

---

[1] 'Some think I have lost that poetic ardour and fire 'tis said I once had', he writes on 21 September to George and Georgiana Keats: '—the fact is perhaps I have: but instead of that I hope I shall substitute a more thoughtful and quiet power.' This hope was unfulfilled.

23

early letter to be such 'great comforters'. In this case he goes to the simple voidness of space itself. And from that, to the simple, untarnished beauty of free motion in space which had been the ground of all his early love of nature. The wheel of his thought has come full circle to this water-colour of the yachts racing at Cowes: 'circuiting and tacking . . . in every direction—I never beheld any thing so silent, light and graceful'. This is the very accent of his youthful lake, sea and river poems, with their delight in the gliding movements of swans and seagulls. It is a release from the compulsive throbbings of his own brain—'You see how I go on, like so many strokes of a Hammer', he writes despairingly in the same letter—into these free circuitings.

'I equally dislike the favour of the public with the love of a woman—they are both a cloying treacle to the wings of independence', he writes a week later to John Taylor. This is the voice of a sick Keats and a tired Keats—but not a Keats altogether unknown to us. He is reverting in his attitude towards women to that earlier period before the meeting with Fanny Brawne. What was then premonition is now reality—proved on the pulses. And such a reversion, or retreat, was (I should judge) absolutely necessary for him. It brought with it a certain degeneration,[1] but it brought respite too. And in that respite Keats was able to compose his most perfect work of art.

It is noteworthy that *To Autumn* is the only major poem of Keats that is completely unsexual. Woman as erotic object has been banished from this placid landscape. And with, all in all, what enormous relief—both for the poet and for us! For once we are absolved from peerless eyes and slippery blisses. The poem is one great sigh of relief. Thank God I'm rid of that obsession, the expanding rhythm seems to say, and can look around me again and see and enjoy the seeing! This is the real, beloved, warm world again; no longer the nightmare of wolfsbane and nightshade and death-moths. No longer, even, the pathetic fallacy of 'for ever

---

[1] See above, p. 222, for a further passage from the same letter expressing a morbid self-sufficiency.

shalt thou love, and she be fair'. For now we are back in the real
world, which fades, and dies, and grows and lives again, in the
undisturbable free courses of its seasons. The note is placid:

> Season of mists and mellow fruitfulness. . . .

It is written without an exclamation mark—nor do we find one
throughout the whole poem. The tone chimes with the occasion
of its composition, as described in the 21 September letter to John
Hamilton Reynolds: 'How beautiful the season is now—How fine
the air. A temperate sharpness about it. Really, without joking,
chaste weather—Dian skies—I never lik'd stubble-fields so much
as now—Aye better than the chilly green of the Spring. Somehow
a stubble-plain looks warm—in the same way that some pictures
look warm—This struck me so much in my Sunday's walk that
I composed upon it.' 'A temperate sharpness' in the air; but the
stubble-field 'looks warm': the objective and the subjective impressions side by side. The objective, mediating the dry bracing
quality of the chalkland air that Keats so much loved; the subjective, welcoming the suddenly apprehended friendliness of sun-
drenched spaces. It is like an emergence at the end of a long
tunnel.

And all this is built not only into what I have called the expanding rhythms of *To Autumn* but into its spreading landscape, its
branching and fructifying images as well. The symphonic movement of the Odes has now passed the narrows of *On Melancholy*
to widen into the placid lake of this great choric song. For choric
the ode is, not only in its clear insistence, in the final strophe, on
the variety of natural sounds, but in its range of 'beauty's silent
music' in the foison of the completed year.

The movement proceeds in Keats's now familiar pattern[1] from
the outer to the inner, from the broader 'manifestations of that
beauteous life' in the field of space to the minuter organisms. The
bold onward sweep of the verse catches a Handelian splendour.
We are in the immediate presence of Autumn, the fourth in the

---

[1] See above, p. 288.

sisterhood of 'sacred seasons' watched over by the maturing sun; from her and from him we descend into a lower circle, in which human and vegetable meet in the vines that run round the thatch-eaves; lower still is the circle of the orchard trees; whence we descend to the ripe gourd creeping on the ground; and finally, at the centre of this little cosmos, the clammy cell of the honey-bee. Schematic as this 'development' may seem, it is not in the least artificial, it has certainly not been thought out—and its end result forfeits nothing in immediacy, depth, or warmth. Autumn exists throughout the strophe as a *presence*, a spirit of generosity and prodigal luxuriance.

There is further devel¡pment in the second strophe. Autumn herself descends into the circle of courses, into this world; now she is more or less than a presence, she is a person. To those with eyes to see, she is visible, like the goddesses of the ancient world; and with what majestic intimacy Keats presents her !

> Who hath not seen thee oft amid thy store?
>   Sometimes whoever seeks abroad may find
> Thee sitting careless on a granary floor,
>   Thy hair soft-lifted by the winnowing wind;[1]
> Or on a half-reap'd furrow sound asleep,
>   Drows'd with the fume of poppies, while thy hook
>   Spares the next swath and all its twined flowers:
> And sometimes like a gleaner thou dost keep
>   Steady thy laden head across a brook;
>   Or by a cyder-press, with patient look,
>   Thou watchest the last oozings hours by hours.

That to my mind is the greatest personification in English poetry. It counterpoints an unbroken dignity against a delicate pathos. Hesiod and Moschus meet here. The pathos is not simply that of 'spares the next swath and all its twined flowers'—not, that is, the Miltonic regret. It is inherent in the mother-figure herself: in her

---

[1] Cf. Darwin, *The Economy of Vegetation*, Canto I, lines 75, 76:
  Gay SYLPHS attendant beat the fragrant air
  On winnowing wings, and waft her golden hair.

loneliness, in her patience and laboriousness and great strength and her occasional weariness. It is inherent in our knowledge that she too, with the flowers and the corn she reaps, and with the dying year, must vanish. It is for this reason, I think, that the note of tenderness here penetrates Keats's verse.

All the other odes, to a greater or lesser degree, protest and exclaim. At one point or another the note becomes a little shrill. Only *To Autumn* simply accepts. It accepts the inevitability of the cycle. And in the acceptance there is joy. Keats rejoices, first in the *relationship* of season, sun, and earth, and then in the *fruition* that stems from that relationship. Let us look back at the first strophe:

> Season of mists and mellow fruitfulness,
> Close bosom-friend of the maturing sun;
> Conspiring with him how to load and bless
> With fruit the vines that round the thatch-eaves run;
> To bend with apples the moss'd cottage-trees,
> And fill all fruit with ripeness to the core;
> To swell the gourd, and plump the hazel shells
> With a sweet kernel; to set budding more
> And still more, later flowers for the bees,
> Until they think warm days will never cease,
> For Summer has o'er-brimm'd their clammy cells.

Here all is ripeness, tumescence, fruition. The cottage-trees bend, in Keats's beloved 'springy' curve, under their load of fruit, the vines hang tensely under their weight of grapes. Operative verbs are 'load', 'bend', 'swell', 'plump', 'o'er-brim': the verse itself strains under the packed sweetness and nourishment. Yet 'strain' is the wrong word—we need another expression which will convey the shining tension of the gourd and the rich geometrizing of the honey-cell, growth and form in dynamic harmony. In the budding of the later flowers and the swelling of the fruit the extremes of a cycle meet: and here too are the bees, those 'little almsmen of Spring flowers', linking the four seasons and the three kingdoms, vegetative, animal and human. *Endymion* had presented the 'far majesties' that dwell in the ethereal realm as remote and unattainable; few there are, we were told,

> who with gorgeous pageantry enrobe
> Our piece of heaven—whose benevolence
> Shakes hands with our own Ceres; every sense
> Filling with spiritual sweets to plenitude,
> As bees gorge full their cells.[1]

The moon is one of these benevolent deities, he says; and he mentions no other. But here the sun and the autumnal season are gathered into the same fellowship of gracious conspiracy for earthly happiness.[2] The lines are so familiar to us from our childhood that we hardly stop to apprehend their extraordinary cosmic sweep, or to visualize, however mistily, the two great figures bending from the sky over our globe and touching with hands that bless the slowly maturing forms of life.

To Autumn presents the consummation of the process of which the Hymn to Pan in *Endymion* presented the initiation. The Hymn was concerned with seedtime, with roots, with young flowers: but it looked forward to the season of fruition. To Pan,

> Broad-leaved fig-trees even now foredoom
> Their ripen'd fruitage; yellow-girted bees
> Their golden honeycombs . . .
> . . . yea, the fresh-budding year
> All its completions.

It is a 'note' of the Keatsian vision that nothing is seen in isolation; Spring is not enjoyed purely in and for itself, but as part of the annual cycle. The whole is apprehended in the part, and the

---

[1] The connection of these lines with the first strophe of the ode is evident. Keats may have got his bees from *Georgics*, IV, 163, 164, or from the almost identical idea in *Æneid* I, 432, 433:

> cum liquentia mella
> stipant et dulci distendunt nectare cellas.

See too Appendix C.

[2] A reference here to *Celtic Researches*, with its celebration of the sun who 'deals in bounty', and is 'Father of beauty—and principle of the seasons' (see Appendix A, p. 398) may not be out of place.

consummation in the inauguration. Everything has a use, a rôle to play in the total process; when, in the ode, 'more, And still more, later flowers' are set budding, it is 'for the bees', for the replenishment of cells which in their turn become the centres of new life. The sweet kernel of the hazel nut is for human nourishment.

The first strophe of *To Autumn* celebrates the effortless fruitfulness of nature; only in the last four lines are the bees brought in to make the link with human labour which is the theme of the second strophe. This middle section of corn and wine releases us from the cottage garden into a broad landscape of cornfields traversed by little brooks, of farms with their granaries and ciderpresses. Are we in England or Italy? It doesn't matter: what matters is the 'weaving together'. The initial movement of the poem, now, is being reversed: no longer from outward inward, from the cosmic spaces to the bee's cell, but centrifugally from the human environment to the void of the sky. This is quite clear in the third and last strophe, and the poem ends with the skies in which it began:

> Where are the songs of Spring? Ay, where are they?
>   Think not of them, thou hast thy music too,—
> While barred clouds bloom the soft-dying day,
>   And touch the stubble-plains with rosy hue;
> Then in a wailful choir the small gnats mourn
>   Among the river sallows, borne aloft
>   Or sinking as the light wind lives or dies;
> And full-grown lambs loud bleat from hilly bourn;
>   Hedge-crickets sing; and now with treble soft
> The red-breast whistles from a garden-croft;
>   And gathering swallows twitter in the skies.

The movement is undulating, in broad contrast to the strong earthward thrust of the laden trees and swollen gourds of strophe one, and to the wide horizontal sweep of the blown hair and the steady gleaner of strophe two. Here we are borne like the gnats themselves, in a wavering rhythm, resolved only in the last line which plumps for departure; and the poem achieves its final acceptance, which is the acceptance of Winter, of seasonal death. The strophe makes no attempt to escape the note of sadness. There is nostalgia in 'Where are the songs of Spring? Ay, where are they?', though it is a gentle nostalgia. And note that Autumn has now to be *comforted*: the regret that we detected in the second strophe (where the season had given up her majestic remoteness to be incarnated as a simple peasant-woman) has reached its climax, and it is the human voice that proffers comfort: 'Think not of them, thou hast thy music too'. The touch is masterly, focusing a final pathos.

[*Ode to May* (1 May 1818)—*Old Meg* (2 July 1818)—*Ode on Indolence* (March–May 1819)—*To Psyche* (April 1819)—*Ode on a Grecian Urn* (May 1819)—*Ode to a Nightingale* (May 1819)—*Ode to Autumn* (September 1819)]

Chapter Fifteen

RIPENESS IS ALL

And calmest thoughts come round us—as of leaves
　　Budding—fruit ripening in stillness—autumn suns
Smiling at eve upon the quiet sheaves—
Sweet Sappho's cheek—a sleeping infant's breath—
　　The gradual sand that through an hour-glass runs—
A woodland rivulet—a Poet's death.

Sonnet: 'After dark vapours . . .', January 1817.

W E have been probing structure, and the growth of
structure. First and foremost, the pattern of Keats's
verse itself, and the way it came into being. We have
examined it from the viewpoint of the morphologist, not of the
anatomist: our concern has been not with the minutiæ of technical criticism, with variant readings or successive draughts, but
with moulding and warping forces from without, creative and
inhibiting forces from within, which have given it its final shape
and texture. In short, we have considered Keats's verse as though
it were a plant: our justification for this being that Keats himself
evidently so regarded it, consciously or unconsciously. 'Poetry
should be great and unobtrusive', he writes to Reynolds on
3 February 1818: 'a thing which enters into one's soul, and does
not startle it or amaze it with itself, but with its subject.—How
beautiful are the retired flowers! how would they lose their
beauty were they to throng into the highway crying out, "admire
me I am a violet!—dote upon me I am a primrose!"' And again,
and even better known: the 'axiom' that 'if Poetry comes not as
naturally as the Leaves to a tree it had better not come at all'.[1]

I have treated Keats's poetry as a plant. 'Each way of contemplating the plant—provided that it is a genuine and logical attempt

---

[1] *Letters*, 107. In *Sleep and Poetry* the revival of English poetry is seen as a
myrtle tree growing up from among 'bitter weeds' (lines 248-64).

to interpret well-attested facts—may have something of its own to offer, and what we need is a synthetic standpoint, combining the advantages of methods of analysis, which are usually treated as antagonistic.'[1] I began this book with an apology from an earlier morphologist, appropriating it to myself; I will end with this plea for eclecticism from a modern exponent of the same point of view. In my interpretation of Keats I have been eclectic indeed. Growth-and-form has been my synthetic standpoint: but in probing into the vital processes of the Keatsian plant I have used methods of analysis—historical, psychological, 'metaphysical', occul ist, 'practical' (as the criticism of my Cambridge days used to be called), biological—which are commonly regarded as antagonistic. They are so regarded today; but not in Keats's own day. I began my exposition with a long chapter on Erasmus Darwin, because his poetry combines the elements of my theme as none other does, outside Keats's own. But it was not long before I was with Coleridge in the depths of speculation, with Taylor on the heights of metaphysics. I dared, even, to make forays into that academically most suspect of fields, the oriental. Now this is precisely what Darwin himself does. Read *The Botanic Garden*, or *The Temple of Nature*, or even the prose treatises, and you will find him in text and notes passing with quiet unconcern from the corollas of flowers and the strata of coal-mines to the Eleusinian Mysteries and Egyptian hieroglyphics. The late eighteenth and early nineteenth century mind was still flexible enough to make these transitions easily, unselfconsciously. Here is a sentence from Edward Moor's *The Hindu Pantheon* (London, Joseph Johnson, 1810) which illustrates my point admirably: 'As the oak exists in the acorn, or rather, as the *Hindu* would express it, as the fruit is in the seed, awaiting development and expansion, so all material forms existed in BRAHMA, and their germs were at once produced by him.

> Grain within grain, successive harvests dwell,
> And boundless forests slumber in a shell.
>   DARWIN.'

---

[1] Agnes Arber, *The Natural Philosophy of Plant Form* (Cambridge, 1950).

That one sentence sums up my first two chapters, and Darwin shakes hands with the forest-sages of the Upanishads.

More than a sentence will be required to sum up the fourteen chapters which have preceded this, the last. And more than a mere summing up is called for. In these final pages I want to draw together the threads of my argument in so far as they weave, this time without antagonism or complexity, the woof of growth and form. In a sense, we have been looking up to now at the back of the tapestry: and in the medley of cross-threads and botches and end-pieces the total pattern has been hard to see. Let us look once again, simply, but with all that has gone before in mind, at the processes of growth and the exhibitions of form as they present themselves in this great unfinished web of Keats's verse.

And although form is metaphysically prior, let us begin with growth, reversing our initial approach.[1] Let us start from the roots. Or, better still, from the seed. Starting from the root, we are skirting form: the existence of the plant as an entity in space. Starting from the seed, we are probing growth: the plant as a process in time. It is well that both these concepts should be simultaneously present in our minds: for purposes of discussion, however, we have to separate them. And while, in eternity, the form may be prior, the process precedes the form in time: and it is in time that our discussion must unroll itself. The finished form—the fruit or the sonnet—is the end-product of a process; the product, which itself finally breaks down into seeds or thoughts to initiate a further process. This is the cyclic pattern identical with the evolution of the Great Year or of a single day or of the life of man, beast or plant: it is precisely and lucidly expressed in the sentence from *The Hindu Pantheon* cited above.

The fruit or the universe bursts: its seeds fall into the soil, into chaos, and to all appearance die. Keats liked to watch, first, the slow drifting down of the seed to the ground; as his 'thousand Powers'

> . . . poise about in cloudy thunder-tents
> To watch the abysm-birth of elements,

---

[1] See Preface, p. xiii, above.

so he delights to mark the 'uncertain speed' of 'blow-ball from the mead'.[1] And more than this: he sinks down with the 'light seed' into the dark earth, sharing its chthonic 'dying into life': 'I lay awake last night listening to the Rain with a sense of being drown'd and rotted like a grain of wheat.'[2] The New Testament resonance points the solemnity of Keats's 'sensation'; the dying into life is the self-naughting of the artist, and its meaning is resurrection: the creative act.[3] Few poets admit us, as Keats does, to the dark chambers of germination, rooting and growth; or pass on to us the 'feel' of the artist's integration with natural energies. The experience is more than personal: in this empathy we are initiated into a universal wisdom:

'Listen. I will tell thee what is done in the caverns of the grave. . . .
As the seed waits Eagerly watching for its flower & fruit,
Anxious its little soul looks out into the clear expanse
To see if hungry winds are abroad with their invisible array,
So Man looks out in tree & herb & fish & bird & beast
Collecting up the scatter'd portions of his immortal body
Into the Elemental forms of every thing that grows. . . .
And in the cries of birth & in the groans of death his voice
Is heard throughout the Universe: wherever a grass grows
Or a leaf buds, The Eternal Man is seen, is heard, is felt,
And all his sorrows, till he reassumes his ancient bliss.'[4]

The seed lies buried in the mineral kingdom, the dead, formless realm. The earth-element encloses it. In the second book of *Endymion* the hero (who is not much of a hero, because besides being Endymion he is also very modestly Keats) explores this kingdom. He penetrates its rocky masses, experiences its darkness and soli-

---

[1] And in the mock-Spenserian lines on Brown, 'He was to weet a melancholy Carle . . .':

. . . the seeded thistle when in parle
It holds the Zephyr ere it sendeth fair
Its light balloons into the summer air . . .

[2] Letter of 27 April 1818 to J. H. Reynolds.
[3] 'For from the dead come nourishment, growth and seed . . .' (Hippocrates, *Regimen*, IV, xcii.)
[4] Blake, *The Four Zoas* (K. 420–21).

tude. This is necessary for his growth: we noted in the first book how he had mistakenly come to despise the earth-element; now he must appreciate its power and its possibilities. It is while he is in the underworld that his love for Diana is consummated; and he begins to feel himself a new being. The terms in which this realization are couched are most significant:

> 'Now I have tasted her sweet soul to the core
> All other depths are shallow: essences,
> Once spiritual, are like muddy lees,
> Meant but to fertilize my earthly root,
> And make my branches lift a golden fruit
> Into the bloom of heaven. . . .'

I have already commented on this passage in its place, but it is a key passage and we cannot afford to lose sight of it. It is part of the lesson taught Endymion by the earth-element that 'essences' which to the once-born man seem 'spiritual' are not, in fact, superior to the 'muddy lees' of unpretentious physical sensation. He is learning not to discriminate, not to choose: but to accept, as the seed accepts, every fostering influence, every contribution to its growth. He understands that the vigour of the *earthly root* (adequate adaptation to ordinary living) is indispensable to the lifting up of the *golden fruit* (total realization). This is a very great step forward.

The seed, now, has begun to sprout. It has put forth an 'earthly root'. The root remains in the underworld, penetrating ever deeper into the earth element. For, as Keats knows,

> The flower must drink the nature of the soil
> Before it can put forth its blossoming.[1]

Most poets forget the root: Keats seems to regard it with peculiar affection. Wolf's-bane, in *On Melancholy*, is 'tight-rooted'; the flowers of *To Psyche* are 'cool-rooted'. 'Young buds sleep in the root's white core' is the most beautiful line in his *Fairy's Song*, spanning processes and seasons. The concern for the unmanifested,

---

[1] Sonnet, 'Spenser! a jealous honourer of thine!' (1818).

the embryonic, is characteristic. Ever sensitive to his own inner workings, Keats feels for this tap-root into the unconscious: the solicitude runs like a refrain through the letters to his schoolgirl sister Fanny, who *because* she was a child could share intimacies inaccessible to his adult friends. 'I shall be going to town to-morrow', he begins a letter of 31 March 1819, 'and will call at the Nursery on the road for those roots and seeds you want, which I will send by the Walthamstow stage'; and again, on the 12th of April: 'I ordered some bulbous roots for you at the Gardeners, and they sent me some, but they were all in bud—and could not be sent; so I put them in our Garden. . . .'[1] He will not risk injuring them. Instead, he proposes to send her 'some seasonable plants . . . perhaps some that are not yet in bloom that you may see them come out'. And the root interest is peculiarly a family affair. It spills over into the long journal letters to George and Georgiana in America, mingling with the richer interest which is wine. 'I like Claret,' he writes in February 1819, 'whenever I can have Claret I must drink it—'tis the only palate affair that I am at all sensual in. Would it not be a good Speck to send you some vine roots—could It be done? I'll enquire. . . .' We shall come back later to the significance of wine for Keats: what is of present moment for us is the integration of his feeling for the root and his feeling for the family. Through the sending of roots, obviously, he is forging a kind of subterranean link, a relationship symbolizing in the most vital terms the blood-relationship he prized so highly.

The seed sprouts, expands, sending its root downwards into earth, its shoot upwards into air. The seed is the expansive nucleus of the plant, as the diamond is the concentrated nucleus of the earth; or, we can say, the seed is expansive growth, the diamond is concentrated form: both dwell together in the depths. So, on the contrary, in the heights, the fruit is concentrated growth, the sky is expansive form. The diamond is the product of intense compression; the growing seed is the product of ingestion. The plant

---

[1] *Fairy's Song* is undated; perhaps this letter suggests a date.

absorbs, takes in; its growth is dependent on food. Now this theme of nutrition is central in Keats. In the lines from *Endymion*, 'fertilize' is identical with 'manure', 'nourish': the root draws its sustenance from the muddy lees, and is thus empowered to lift its branches upwards into the atmosphere until they culminate in the golden fruit. So man, 'sucking the sap from mould ethereal . . . might become great, and Humanity instead of being a wide heath of Furze and Briars with here and there a remote Oak or Pine, would become a grand democracy of Forest Trees!' The passage (already quoted, from the 19 February 1818 letter to Reynolds) develops its nutrition theme: 'let us open our leaves like a flower and be passive and receptive—budding patiently under the eye of Apollo and taking hints from every noble insect that favours us with a visit—sap will be given us for meat and dew for drink'. The picture holds, as Keats's incidental images so often do, the totality of a process: nourishment comes from above, around, beneath, energizing the structure, which passes on its bounties to the visiting insect, which in its turn fertilizes other flowers . . . and so on, expanding into the whole cycle of relationships.

Not all growth is beneficent, of course. There are weeds as well as wheat, poison trees as well as olives and vines. 'Circumstances are like Clouds continually gathering and bursting', he writes on 19 March 1819 to his brother and sister-in-law; 'While we are laughing the seed of some trouble is put into the wide arable land of events—while we are laughing it sprouts it grows and suddenly bears a poison fruit which we must pluck.' (The image is extraordinarily like Blake's.[1]) Even roots can be, if not exactly poisonous, at least stupefying: the Belle Dame gives her victim 'roots of relish sweet, And honey wild, and manna dew'. The good grain is often surrounded, strangled by tares; or there are 'menslugs and human serpentry'[2] to blight it. Pan is acclaimed, in *Endymion*, as protector against 'snouted wild-boars routing tender corn', and

> Breather round our farms,
> To keep off mildews, and all weather harms.

---

[1] Cf. *The Human Image* and *A Poison Tree.*   [2] *Endymion*, I, 821.

The good life is consistently presented as the unimpeded growth, flowering and fruiting of the plant, and in particular of corn; evil is that which blights and warps the natural process. And against this evil a man can do little or nothing, in so far as it affects himself. He can do something for others, for the young plant; he can clear a little space of weeds so that it may grow in freedom;[1] but against his own fate he is powerless. 'For instance suppose a rose to have sensation, it blooms on a beautiful morning it enjoys itself—but there comes a cold wind, a hot sun—it cannot escape it, it cannot destroy its annoyances—they are as native to the world as itself: no more can man be happy in spite, the worldly elements will prey upon his nature.'[2] The forces of destruction are as native to the world as the forces of creation; and the last sentence gives us the obverse of 'sucking the sap from mould ethereal'. This is Keats's inclusive vision.

The vision depends, as we have seen again and again, upon analogy. The considerations which occupied us at the beginning of this inquiry, when we traced something of the thought of Erasmus Darwin, have been pervasively with us through the succeeding chapters, and must again be brought into focus. The macrocosm-microcosm parallel is dominant in Keats. *Ut supra, sic et infra*. Man has his seasons, as have the sun and the plant. Sun, man, and plant are linked in this poetry of mystical correspondences. And they are linked through *rhythm*. Note how in his judgment on poetry he relies on both sun-imagery and plant-imagery to make his point. Poetry should come as naturally as the leaves to a tree, or it had better not come at all; moreover, 'the rise, the progress, the setting of imagery should like the Sun come natural to him'.[3] The rhythm displays three stages; the poet's task is that of integration with this three-fold process. In the plant, we find metabolism occurring in and through the

---

[1] Cf. 'I stood tip-toe . . .' (lines 29–34).
[2] Letter to George and Georgiana Keats, April 1819.
[3] In the verse *Epistle to Charles Cowden Clarke* he envisages (lines 60, 61):
the sonnet swelling loudly
Up to its climax and then dying proudly.

rhythm. From the downward-shooting root and the upward-shooting stem a new thing comes into being: the horizontal world of leaves, flowers and fruit.

Or we can regard the rhythm in this way. There is an absorption in the seed, a dilation in the shoot, a concentration in the fruit. This is the systole and diastole of nature, the in-coming and out-going breath, separated by that *tertium quid* which is the pause, the moment out of time in which all things bud and flower. It is a movement explicit or implicit in all Keats has to say about natural processes. Take the minnows of 'I stood tip-toe . . .' (to leave the vegetable kingdom for a moment). They move in the same rhythm; they tense themselves against the flowing stream, they suddenly let go, they are carried downstream, and in a moment they are back again. But the acme of 'their own sweet delight' is in the letting go. The stream itself follows the pattern, presented by Keats in reverse: it flows from quietness (lines 65–8) to agitation (69–80) and back to quietness again (81–86).

So with the grain of wheat which is 'drown'd and rotted'. Drowning is death: the retraction of the vital forces; rotting is expansion: the opening of the entity to forces outside itself. The third term is left unexpressed by Keats: we must seek it in the New Testament: 'if it die, it bringeth forth much fruit'. This is life's oxymoron—given dramatic expression by Darwin as 'The embryon panting in the arms of Death'.[1] We are here at the heart of Keats's poetry, which is also the heart of the Mystery religions and of the alchemical Great Work. We are also, by the principle of rhythm, modulating out of growth into form: and form which is not a product of growth—I mean the momentary diagram plotted by the tension between vital and mechanical forces and its relaxation. Keats's keen eye noted the 'raft branch down sweeping from a tall ash top'[2] and the sea-bird 'winging along where the great water throes'.[3] In the second book of *Endymion* we saw him

---

[1] See above, p. 19.   [2] *Endymion*, I, 334 and 335.
[3] 'What can I do to drive away . . .', line 17. 'The albatross uses the upward current on the lee-side of a great ocean wave . . .' (D'Arcy Thompson, *Growth and Form*, p. 49).

24

delighting in the fountain-patterns which stem from the stress
of purely mechanical forces.

In an earlier chapter I remarked on the *Ode to a Nightingale* as
exhibiting the three-fold rhythm. But we can trace it in almost every
major poem of Keats's. There is first the consciousness of the self,
its problems, its agonies, its expectations; then the letting go, the
going out and release from the self; finally, the reconcentration at
a higher level. It is the master-theme of *Endymion*, and it would no
doubt have been, more triumphantly, the theme of *Hyperion*.
We can express it as the antinomy of life and death: of the mechanical life which in its blindness, its insensitiveness, is veritable death;
of the spiritual death which, in its discovery of the Self, is veritable
and more abundant life. The basic antinomy of 'death is life's high
meed' runs through the whole work of Keats and helps to give it
a special richness and depth. The process of life is the process of
death. The moment of birth of the organism is the moment when
metabolism begins to slow down and ageing begins. Living is thus
a continual tension between growth and decay—a physical tension up to the middle point of life, when it transmutes itself (if the
individual has realized his capacities) into a psychic tension which
has to be resolved before the moment of death. These ideas are
peculiarly explicit and implicit in the art of Keats because for him
the process had to be so incredibly foreshortened. His premonition
of an early death—so often expressed—causes a kind of crystallization of thought at key moments in his poems and letters. He is
intensely conscious of life in its double aspect: as evolution and
devolution, as growth and running-down. Even in his earliest,
most lyrical work, the conviction of transience seizes upon him:

> Stop and consider! life is but a day;
> A fragile dewdrop on its perilous way
> From a tree's summit; a poor Indian's sleep
> While his boat hastens to the monstrous steep
> Of Montmorenci.

The conviction is, of course, immediately counterpointed:

> Why so sad a moan?
> Life is the rose's hope while yet unblown;

The reading of an everchanging tale;
The light uplifting of a maiden's veil;
A pigeon tumbling in clear summer air;
A laughing schoolboy, without grief or care,
Riding the springy branches of an elm.

The two down-flowing death-images (the falling dew-drop, the gliding boat) are counterpoised by the two rising life-images (the growing rose, the uplifted veil): the two final images graph the tension of forces (the pigeon playing air-currents against gravity, the schoolboy playing gravity against elasticity).

Every seven years comes the 'little death' of the body. 'Our bodies every seven years are completely fresh-materiald—seven years ago it was not this hand that clench'd itself against Hammond.[1] We are like the relict garments of a Saint; the same and not the same: for the careful Monks patch it and patch it: till there's not a thread of the original garment left, and still they show it for St Anthony's shirt.' The mind too changes. The illusion of an ego sustains us, but in truth there is no permanent 'I' or 'you'. 'This is the reason why men who had been bosom friends, on being separated for any number of years, afterwards meet coldly, neither of them knowing why. The fact is they are both altered.' But if contact is maintained the change goes unnoticed, for the illusory individualities flow into each other. 'Men who live

---

[1] 'This hand' will remind us of the moving 'This living hand, now warm and capable . . .' and 'When this warm scribe, my hand, is in the grave'. Keats looks at his hand with the detached scrutiny of the surgeon. And again, on his deathbed, 'these ghastly hands' (*K.C.*, I, 267). Perhaps the most striking phrase of all is 'This mortal body of a thousand days': the physical structure seen as *occupying a space* in Burns's cottage (in the sonnet on this theme). Since 1911 this perception has been known technically to psychologists as the 'body schema'. We may ascribe it, in the present case, to the effects of fatigue. Compare Hamlet's 'this machine'. This kind of perception involves an apprehension of a part by the whole; its obverse is found in the remarkable 'new to the feet' of the July 1818 *Lines Written in the Highlands*. D'Arcy Thompson notes (*op. cit.*, p. 949), in a discussion of 'hydrodynamical' problems 'in connection with the flow of blood through the blood-vessels', that 'the subject greatly interested Keats', and refers to p. 7 of the poet's Notebook (ed. M. B. Forman). Keats, Coleridge and Milton are the only English poets alluded to in *Growth and Form*.

together have a silent moulding, and influencing power over each other. They interassimilate.'[1]

Change continues; but growth comes to an end with the ripening of the organism and the maturing of the seed. It is with the life of man as with that of plants. Keats's intense interest in the union of George and Georgiana is biological: the note is unmistakable in his earliest letters and in the poems addressed to his sister-in-law. The maternal element is stressed. In the breast references of these verses to Georgiana critics have sensed an indelicacy; but they miss the point, as they miss it in the imagined pillowing 'on my fair love's ripening breast' in the 'Bright Star' sonnet, where Keats is writing as always within his organic context of growth and fruition, of systole and diastole: 'To feel, for ever, its soft fall and swell'. So too, with the numerous images from suckling which illustrate his most 'abstract' conceptions: many readers have found them distasteful, but to minds with the training of Keats's and Darwin's they suggested themselves with the utmost naturalness.[2]

From the moment of George's marriage John's letters look forward to the birth of a child to the young couple. The acrostic verses 'Give me your patience Sister . . .' (enclosed in the letter of 27–28 June 1818) end with the wish that the new name 'Keats' may prove a blessing to Georgiana:

> Ah! may it taste to you like good old wine—
> Take you to real happiness and give
> Sons, daughters and a Home like honied hive.[3]

The intense solidarity of the Keats family, the close bonds between John and George and Tom and Fanny revealed by the extant

---

[1] These passages are continuous and are taken from the September 1819 journal-letter to George and Georgiana Keats.

[2] I am thinking of images like the following from the 'soul-making' passage in Letter 123: 'Not merely is the Heart a Hornbook, It is the Minds Bible, it is the Minds experience, it is the teat from which the Mind or intelligence sucks its identity.' See Appendix B, I, 2, and II, 1 (pp. 404–6).

[3] The marriage was in fact happy and fruitful. There were eight children, who all survived—the fifth, John Henry, until 1917.

correspondence and the verse, linked with John's premonition that he would never marry,[1] made it inevitable that a man with Keats's temperament should read his own physical immortality into the fruitfulness of George and Georgiana. In the acrostic poem it is the family name (described as 'entranced' in the 1818 version and 'enchanted' in the 1819 version) which is to taste to Georgiana like good old wine. 'Your content in each other is a delight to me which I cannot express', he writes in his first letter to America (14–31 October 1818). He loves Georgiana: her identity 'presses upon him' more even than that of his sister Fanny. If he is to be 'ruined' by the rich femininity of a woman like 'Charmian', he would wish to be 'saved' by the chaste maternity of Georgiana. 'As a Man in the world I love the rich talk of a Charmian; as an eternal Being I love the thought of you.' What wonder then if he projects his own 'eternal' identity—the identity of the poet—into the hoped-for offspring of George and Georgiana?

> If I had a prayer to make for any great good, next to Tom's recovery, it should be that one of your Children should be the first American Poet. I have a great mind to make a prophecy and they say prophecies work out their own fulfilment—

and he goes on to write the ecstatic verses, "'Tis the witching time of night'. The verses are not negligible; couched in his favourite mantic form of the Miltonic tetrameter, they achieve a notable effect of anticipation and awe. The orbed moon and the stars are listening 'for a song and for a charm'. The spheres and the 'eternal sky' hearken to the cradle song:[2]

> Child! I see thee! Child I've found thee
> Midst the quiet all around thee!
> Child I see thee! Child I spy thee
> And thy mother sweet is nigh thee!—

---

[1] Expressed in this same letter.
[2] A fulfilment of the 1816 prediction:

> To sweet rest
> Shall the dear babe, upon its mother's breast
> Be lull'd with songs of mine.

(*Epistle: To My Brother George*, 101–2).

Child I know thee! Child no more
But a Poet evermore!
See, see, the Lyre, the Lyre,
In a flame of fire
Upon the little cradle's top
Flaring, flaring, flaring
Past the eyesight's bearing—
Awake it from its sleep
And see if it can keep
Its eyes upon the blaze—
Amaze, amaze!
It stares, it stares, it stares. . . .

The Virgilian parallel of the flame-crowned child comes to mind here; we remember too the Hermetic creation in fire. More than this: Keats is carrying into the frame of his family relationships the final 'shewing' of the Eleusinian mysteries, the fiery birth of the divine child Zagreus to the mother-goddess. Psychologically considered, this is the last of the great archetypes, 'the magic image of the Magic Child'.[1]

And now let us return from these considerations on human fruitfulness to the process of the plant and its culmination in the bright consummate flower and the perfection of the fruit. Fostered by warmth and moisture, the green shoot has put forth its leaves, the 'tiny rings' of its tendrils, and its butterfly-mimicking corolla. Bees 'hum about globes of clover'. The marigold discloses its 'round of starry folds'. Energy is drawn from sun and air: oxygen is returned to the atmosphere:

a myrtle fairer far than
E'er grew in Paphos, from the bitter weeds
Lifts its sweet head into the air, and feeds
A silent space with ever sprouting green.[2]

---

[1] The phrase is Coleridge's from *The Pang More Sharp Than All*.

[2] Hermetic and scientific observation. Erasmus Darwin writes (in *Phytologia*, p. 299): '. . . the vital air, liberated from the surface of plants by the sunshine, must much exceed the quantity of it absorbed by their respiration; and hence they improve the air, in which they live, during the light part of the day. . . .'

We are witnessing the courteous interchange between the elements on which life itself depends; we are watching the transition from mineral kingdom to vegetable kingdom. And, since we know that Keats's myrtle is an image for the new poetry of England, we are witnessing an integration with the human and the celestial kingdoms as well.

What flowers meant for Keats has already become apparent in the course of this study. They do not give him thoughts too deep for tears: indeed, they do not give him thoughts at all. He watches, and he feels. He feels the life of the flower, is the flower. As he watches, he half creates: a process is concentrated. He may begin with musing:

> A tuft of evening primroses,
> O'er which the mind may hover till it dozes. . . .

observation leading to sleep, the trance state; but in the trance state there is a gathering of energy, culminating in an electric discharge; the mind is suddenly

> startled by the leap
> Of buds into ripe flowers.

However we may explain it, the sensation is of a dynamic relation between the mind and the flower: the flower is 'forced', as it were, into growth under the poet's eye—just as the marigold is compelled to open by command from the sun. Indeed, it is crystal clear even in this very early poem 'I stood tip-toe . . .' that Keats's mind already functions within spontaneously hermetic contexts— Blake's 'body of Divine Analogy'. The bud bursts into flower under the poet's eye;[1] the marigold, the solary flower, opens its Ptolemaic circles of *starry* folds at the sun's bidding. We might be looking at a woodcut from some Renaissance astro-botanical treatise.

We are also, of course, enjoying a moment of reality caught in

---

[1] As, again, in *Endymion*, II, 59: 'It swells, it buds, it flowers beneath his sight'. And in his last illness he writes: 'I muse with the greatest affection on every flower I have known from my infancy—their shapes and colours are as new to me *as if I had just created them with a superhuman fancy*. . . . The simple flowers of our spring are what I want to see again' (Letter to James Rice, 14 February 1820). My italics.

all its power and freshness. The one way of looking does not preclude the other. Here again, in his double vision, and in the multiple viewpoints of his poetry, Keats is with Blake. They humanize, but not in the fabular way of Wordsworth or Tennyson. They humanize because for them there is nothing that is not human *sub specie æternitatis*; nevertheless the essential queerness of the spider and the tapeworm and the minnow *sub specie temporis* is never lost sight of. Blake's great dance of flowers in *Milton* is a rejoicing within the mind of the Cosmic Man: they are his thoughts but then he *is* thought: what he thinks composes him. There is no separation of thought and thinker.

'Watching the growth of a little flower . . . the silent growth of Flowers', Severn tells us in that most pathetic of his last letters from Rome, seemed to Keats as he lay dying 'perhaps the only happiness I have had in the world'.[1] But there *had* been other happinesses. Keats spoke these words in his agony, when his palate had lost its gust for life, when even the memory of how life could be lived in its fullness was leaving him; but he had known his moments of fruition. The flower had brought him happiness and peace and insight; the fruit brought him fulfilment, ecstasy, and power. With the flower he went out: contemplation; with the fruit he took in: absorption. Taking in, and giving out: and going out. It is notable how consistently he sees his own work—especially his future achievements—under the image of corn.

> When I have fears that I may cease to be
> Before my pen has glean'd my teeming brain,
> Before high piled Books in charactery
> Hold like rich garners the full ripen'd grain. . . .[2]

'The Spring will be a harvest-time' to the poet who has borne contentedly the rigours of winter and 'fed on' the 'light of supreme darkness'.[3] 'To see high golden corn wave in the light'[4]

---

[1] *K.C.*, I, 267.

[2] Cf. letter of 23 January 1818: 'Nothing is finer for the purposes of great productions than a very gradual ripening of the intellectual powers.'

[3] Sonnet, 'O thou whose face hath felt the Winter's wind', in the letter of 19 February 1818 to J. H. Reynolds.

[4] *Epistle to Charles Cowden Clarke.*

is from the beginning a great joy to him; the dedication of his *Poems 1817* to Leigh Hunt pictures nymphs 'In woven baskets bringing ears of corn', and Severn's description of Keats's delight in the wind sweeping over a cornfield is vivid. The sun, and the colour gold, are of course constantly associated with the harvest-field:

> autumn suns
> Smiling at eve upon the quiet sheaves;[1]

and the phrase 'the gold Autumn's whole kingdom of corn' may remind us of Blake's Autumn in the *Poetical Sketches* with his 'golden load'. The climax of all Keats's garnering is of course the famous Ode, in which the patient figure at watch over the cider-press and the mossed cottage trees links the abundances of grain and fruit with human necessities.

Images of nutrition are integral to Keats's poetry. Some of them we have noted in passing; but the subject demands more than a cursory treatment. The fruit is not there merely to be looked at and admired for its beauty: it is there to be eaten. 'Come, let us go for a walk, O mind, to Kali, the wish-fulfilling Tree, and there beneath It gather the four fruits of life': these words from the Rāmprasād are a fitting epigraph for Keats's poetry. Among all the nonsense that has been written about Keats none is more nonsensical than the strictures that have their root in squeamishness, in aversion from his naïve delight in the enjoyment of food and drink. The mind that reads the following with distaste reads it in isolation, not in relationship: and relationship is the nexus of understanding:

> Talking of Pleasure, this moment I was writing with one hand, and with the other holding to my Mouth a Nectarine—good god how fine. It went down soft pulpy, slushy, oozy—all its delicious embon-point melted down my throat like a large beatified Strawberry.[2]

The tone of the passage (established by the simile) should disarm criticism; but if Keats were being as solemn as a judge, we should still have to accept his report. The nectarine or curious peach does

---

[1] *Apollo to the Graces.*   [2] Letter to C. W. Dilke, 22 September 1819.

in fact go down like that—and if we shrink from Keats's slushery and ooziness it is because we have shrunk, in the first instance, from the experience; we have had our mind elsewhere, we have been thinking of something else, we have seen the ooziness of the fruit as a bother (while desiring its delicacies of taste), and thus our eating has been a rape, not a communion. We are among those spoken of by the Zen master who fail to 'discipline themselves in their daily life', because 'when they eat, they dare not eat, their minds are filled with all kinds of contrivances'. When Keats ate, he ate. There were no distractions.[1] That, on this occasion, he writes and eats at the same time does not spell distraction, but an extraordinary act of synthesis: the tone of the letter is a 'follow-through' of the flavour of the fruit.

The enjoyment of the fruit, or the claret,[2] is the culmination of enjoyment of the whole process of growth from seed to seed. It is the practical affirmation of the wholeness of the human four-fold, of the holiness of all the senses (sight, hearing, taste-smell, touch) and not merely of the favoured two.[3] The gates of perception are cleansed, as with Blake, by an 'improvement of sensual enjoyment'. Openness to the physical qualities of the ripe peach in the act of eating is the equivalent on the nutritional plane of openness, on the intellectual plane, to the heights and depths of 'spiritual' experience. 'Quest for food is one attribute of the zest-for-life', as Sherrington tells us in *Man on his Nature*: by 'life' we may understand more than the 'natural' life.[4]

---

[1] The principle is capable of unlimited application. Thus Keats writes of Kean's acting (in one of his *Champion* critiques): 'Kean delivers himself up to the instant feeling, without a shadow of a thought about anything else.' That is the actor's 'holiness', as the nectarine rhapsody was the eater's.

[2] See below, pp. 381–3.

[3] Cf. the 'double peach' of *Endymion* I (see above, p. 126) as an image of wholeness.

[4] And from Zimmer (*op. cit.*, p. 345) we learn how the idea of *food* as 'the source and substance of all things, Brahman, the divine essence', persisted in the Hindu sacred writings from the Vedas to the Upanishads: 'The divine material out of which the living universe and its creatures are composed is revealed here as food, which is matter and force combined. This life-sap builds up and constitutes all the forms of life . . .'

If I seem to be making a fuss about a very simple matter, it is because I believe that Keats's mind was of a curious all-of-a-pieceness and that we cannot interpret any facet of him in isolation. There is a connectedness in his experience which made even the eating of a nectarine a link in the total pattern. For all eating is in its nature representative, sacramental, the 'incarnation' or making flesh of that which was not flesh, a receiving into the self of that which was other. Thus it presents the very image of that destruction which becomes identity: the only solution in this world to the problem posed by the 'eternal fierce destruction' of Keats's deep-sea vision.[1] And more than that. As the sacrificial victim is here a fruit (*i.e.* that form in which the vegetative process has completed its cycle[2]) the destruction is only a seeming destruction, or rather we may say that the destruction of the husk (of the fruit form as an individual, and a very beautiful individual) is absolutely necessary for the release of the seed and the beginning of a new cycle of growth. None of this, of course, is explicit in Keats's sentence. If it were, we should know the experience was false as assuredly as, in fact, we know it to be true.

'Life feeds on life.' The sentence is Blake's; the truth of the sentence is universal, and universally recognized.

> For know, whatever was created, needs
> To be sustained and fed; of Elements
> The grosser feeds the purer, Earth the Sea,
> Earth and the Sea feed Air, the Air those Fires
> Ethereal, and as lowest first the Moon. . .[3]

But no poet, I believe, has *felt* this as profoundly, as instinctively, as Keats. In this realization lies nine-tenths of the solid impact of his verse. When we read, at the outset of *Endymion*,

---

[1] See above, p. 52. And compare the gruesome 'true story' of the December 1819 letter to James Rice. 'The creatures thrive', Zimmer continues (*op. cit.*, p. 345), 'by feeding on each other—feeding on each other, devouring, and begetting—but the divine substance itself lives on . . .'

[2] The fruit metaphor is ubiquitous: cf. letter of 3 October 1819 to Haydon: 'I shall expect to see your Picture plumped out like a ripe Peach—you would not be very willing to give me a slice of it.'

[3] *Paradise Lost*, V, 414–18. See above, p. 102.

the moist earth *fed*
So plenteously *all* weed-hidden *roots*
Into o'erhanging *boughs* and previous *fruits*

we are at once prepared to accept the poem in all its multi-dimen-
sional quality, for we are placed in these lines at a focus of creation: if we understand them, we understand the poem. You, or I,
can approach the poem (as the *Quarterly* reviewer did) along lines
alien to its structure, and condemn it, rightly, for infelicities: but
if we have seen the structure we can only marvel at a boy's insight and proceed, as he invites us, to connect our experiences in
a variety of worlds, without giving exclusive stress to the aspect
of feeder or of fed.

Experience of every possible kind presents itself in Keats as
eating. We have already glanced at some of his love-feasts, where
the shared meal is sacramental; the actual biting of the beloved by
the lover is a recurrent feature of the early verse; in *Endymion* love
is an 'unsating food', and in its enjoyment 'Life's self is nourish'd
by its proper pith'.[1] Circe is 'the banquet of my arms'[2] for
Glaucus; Endymion swoons 'drunken from Pleasure's nipple'.[3]
Jealousy is conveyed in the same terms: 'Who now, with greedy
looks, eats up my feast?'; and later, in a fusion of devotional,
growth and nutrition imagery:

Let none profane my Holy See of love,
   Or with a rude hand break
   The sacramental cake:
Let none else touch the just new-budded flower.[4]

There is no need to multiply instances. The same image is used for
intellectual and spiritual experience. *Lear* is a 'Shakespearian fruit'
whose 'bitter-sweet' he will assay[5]; the phrase 'the sweet and
bitter world' suggests that he thought of the globe too as a fruit.[6]
The early Greeks 'cull Time's sweet first-fruits'.[7] 'I find that I can

---

[1] *Endymion*, I, 813-16.　　　　　　　[2] *Ibid.*, III, 498.
[3] *Ibid.*, II, 869.　　　　　　　　　　[4] *Ode To Fanny.*
[5] Sonnet, *On Sitting Down To Read King Lear Once Again.*
[6] *Lines Written in the Highlands* . . . (line 30).　　[7] *Endymion*, I, 321.

have no enjoyment in the World but continual drinking of Knowledge', he writes to John Taylor on 24 April 1818. Blind Orion is *hungry* for the morn in a famous simile.[1] The theme is sometimes given humorous expression, as in the 3 February 1818 letter to John Hamilton Reynolds: 'Would we were a sort of ethereal Pigs, and turn'd loose to feed upon spiritual Mast and Acorns—which would be merely being a squirrel and feeding upon filberts, for what is a squirrel but an airy pig, or a filbert but a sort of archangelical acorn.'[2] The same correspondent is urged in a latter letter (22 September 1818?) to 'Gorge the honey of life'. Milton 'gormandizes on intellect' (letter to James Rice, 24 March 1818), and Keats 'feasts upon Milton' (letter to Reynolds, 27 April 1818). Examples might again be multiplied.

Corn is the sacramental food; wine is the sacramental drink. Corn is the consummation of the ripening process, but wine goes beyond the consummation: the fermentation of the grape quint-essentializes powers unsuspected in the simple fruit. Corn is for the body; wine for the soul. The magical and mystical aspects of wine were not hidden from Keats: he knew its power to stimulate thought beyond thought, to open a third eye (for however brief a moment) into the life of things. There is some evidence that he used it in this way, as De Quincey and Coleridge used opium, though more tentatively.[3] 'O there is nothing like fine weather, and health, and Books, and a fine country, and a contented Mind, and Diligent habit of reading and thinking, and an amulet against the ennui—and please heaven, a little claret-wine cool out of a cellar a mile deep . . .' he writes to his sister on 17 April 1819. An earlier letter (18 February 1819, to George and Georgiana Keats) tells of the effect claret had upon him:

I like Claret—whenever I can have Claret I must drink it—'tis the only palate affair that I am at all sensual in. Would it not be a good

---

[1] *Ibid.*, II, 198.
[2] The 'filberts' are two Robin Hood sonnets sent by Reynolds.
[3] According to Brown he began taking laudanum in late 1819 but was dissuaded from continuing.

Speck to send you some vine roots—could It be done? I'll enquire
—If you could make some wine like Claret to drink on Summer
evenings in an arbour! For really 'tis so fine—it fills the mouth one's
mouth with a gushing freshness—then goes down cool and feverless
—then you do not feel it quar[r]elling with your liver—no it is
rather a Peace maker and lies as quiet as it did in the grape—then it is
as fragrant as the Queen Bee; and the more ethereal Part of it mounts
into the brain, not assaulting the cerebral apartments like a bully
in a bad-house looking for his trul[l] and hurrying from door to door
bouncing against the waistcoat [*for* wainscot]; but rather walks like
Aladdin about his own enchanted palace so gently that you do not
feel his step. Other wines of a heavy and spirituous nature transform a
Man to a Silenus; this makes him a Hermes. . . .[1]

I have already quoted part of this passage (in its reference to roots)
and pointed out that such references (and, we must now add,
those to wine) are confined, or nearly so, to family letters:[2] roots
and fruits are sacred, sacramental, and belong to Keats's innermost
world of the affections.

They are ubiquitous, of course, in his poetry. An odd allusion
in *Endymion*, II, 511–12, presents an experiment in form which
might have come straight from D'Arcy Thompson's book:

> For, as delicious wine doth, sparkling, dive
> In nectar'd clouds and curls through water fair,
> So from the arbour roof down swell'd an air
> Odorous and enlivening . . .[3]

---

[1] Cf. *Timæus*, 190 (67), on odours: 'the pleasant and the disagreeable: the latter
of which disturbs and violently assaults all that cavity which lies between the top
of the head and the navel; but the former allures this part of the body, and by its
amicable ingress preserves it in a condition accommodated to its nature'.

[2] The prophetic blessing which concludes his 'Mansion of many Apartments'
letter is an index of the special regard he had for J. H. Reynolds: 'Your third
Chamber of Life shall be a lucky and a gentle one—stored with the wine of love—
and the Bread of Friendship' (*Letters*, 144).

[3] Blake notes the same phenomenon in *The Four Zoas* (K. 308):

> they separate the furious particles
> Into mild currents as the water mingles with the wine.

That is Keats's recollection of some moment in a Hampstead 'arbour' (perhaps the occasion when he took wine with Hunt and received the laurel crown) when he added a little water to his claret to make it more 'ethereal' or to observe the changes in colour: his keen eye has noted the exfoliations—and they are well worth watching—produced as the coloured liquid sinks down through the transparent. Other allusions are less technical. The 'beaded bubbles winking at the brim' in *To a Nightingale* suggests the wine's sparkling freshness;[1] this and the 'deep-delved earth' take us back to the letter to Fanny. Elsewhere we read of 'three fit wines in a cup' as a symbol of the mingled pleasures of the three smiling seasons. The emphasis is consistently on concentration, distillation, transmutation: the alchemical Great Work. The 22 November letter of 1817 to Benjamin Bailey, which puts Keats's 'favorite Speculation' that 'all our Passions . . . are in their sublime, creative of essential Beauty', and 'another favorite Speculation . . . that we shall enjoy ourselves here after by having what we called happiness on Earth repeated in a finer tone and so repeated'—distilled, that is, and re-distilled—acknowledges finally that such concentration has, for most minds (and Bailey's is one of them), to be tempered: 'it is necessary to your eternal Happiness that you not only drink this old Wine of Heaven, which I shall call the redigestion of our most ethereal Musings on Earth; but also increase in knowledge and know all things.' In a later letter (21–25 May 1818) he makes a disarming apology for his laziness in letter-writing by presenting *himself* as wine: 'I will be to you wine in the cellar and the more modestly or rather indolently I retire into the backward Bin, the more falerne will I be at the drinking.'

I should like to end our survey of Keats on this note of the old wine of heaven. It was not necessary for him to increase in knowledge: his strength lay in a divine intoxication, an 'unknowing' not in a cloud but in full sunlight. We began this survey with what I called 'the receptacle', the inverted bowl of the sky; we end it

---

[1] Suggest, too, *eyes*, and with the 'purple-stained mouth' transform the beaker and its contents into a personification of Bacchus.

with wine, the uplifted urn of the fruit, the 'beaker cool'd a long age in the deep-delved earth'. The madness of the grape is the madness of the poetic frenzy; it is also, as many religions have seen, the madness of noesis and participation in the divine nature. It is fitting that, on 31 January 1818, in the letter to J. H. Reynolds which presents 'Eve's sweet pippin' as the image of amorous consummation, and 'the full ripen'd grain' stored in 'rich garners' as the image of artistic fruition, he should bring wine and unclouded sky together as the perfect synthesis to portray that enjoyment of supreme delight which is else beyond portrayal:

> My bowl is the sky
> And I drink at my eye
> Till I feel in the brain
> A delphian pain—
> Then follow my Caius then follow
> On the Green of the Hill
> We will drink our fill
> Of golden sunshine
> Till our brains intertwine
> With the glory and grace of Apollo!

The unwearied form prevails. 'When we look at the Heavens we cannot be proud'; we cannot be proud because there is no longer any *We*. The individual is lost in the Identity. That is the climax of Keats's vision.

APPENDICES

Appendix A

EDWARD DAVIES'S
'CELTIC RESEARCHES'

CELTIC RESEARCHES (1804)

I

The 'vast idea' of cosmic analogy which possessed Keats around 1816 with a wonderful sense of revelation—the revelation of power as well as wisdom—was moulding the thought of other writers in a variety of ways. It moved Blake to prophesy, to denounce, and to instruct through the twin media of poetry and painting. It evoked the best writing of Wordsworth and Coleridge, though in their case the revelation was what Keats called 'a vision in the form of youth' and vanished in shades of the prison-house. We catch smoky glimpses of it in Byron. Shelley clothed his understanding of it in the forms of myth; and in this respect he is with Keats and Blake.

These names head the Romantic roll of fame. There were lesser poets, too, who caught a glimpse of the vast idea: Landor, and Clare, and Christopher Smart. There were painters: Fuseli and Palmer and Linnell. Above all there were, behind these creative artists, the 'speculative mythologists': Jacob Bryant, author of *A New System: or, An Analysis of Ancient Mythology: Wherein an Attempt is Made to Divest Tradition of Fable; and to Reduce the Truth to Its Original Purity*;[1] Francis Wilford, who in a number of papers in *Asiatic Researches, or, Transactions of the Society . . . for Inquiry into the History and Antiquities, the Arts, Sciences, and Literature of Asia*,[2] tried to prove that Britain was the seat of the Garden of Eden; Edward Davies, whose *Celtic Researches*[3] upheld the culture of the patriarchs and the existence of a Golden Age; and a host of others.

---

[1] London, 3 vols., 1774–6.
[2] Calcutta, vols. I–XX, 1788–1839
[3] London, 1804.

The value of these historians of myth for the Romantic poets cannot be exaggerated.[1] Not only did their works supply Blake, Keats and Shelley with material apt for poetic treatment, but their unorthodox attitude towards the accepted tenets of history chimed admirably with Romantic rebelliousness. Most important of all, they offered the new literature a tradition, a link with the past. The new vitalism saluted, across the centuries, the old vitalism. History, it seemed, was not after all a dead catalogue of events: it was a thrilling pattern of eternal truths translated into terms of human action. The continuity of human life came to be a real and a felt thing. And not the continuity of life only, but the continuity and the identity of thought. Those forms and patterns which rose spontaneously in the creative mind in face of the forms and patterns of Nature were found to be identical with the ancient myths of the race. The Romantics were not alone, after all. Voices in a spiritual wilderness they might be; but the wilderness was coterminous only with *their* age, not with history. A Golden Age had existed—and was it, perhaps, their business to help restore it? The idea was new, exhilarating and revealing. Blake made it the mainspring of his work. Shelley, cramped though he was by early Godwinian and Holbachian fetters, fluttered round it like a moth round a candle. Keats came slowly but surely to accept it.

His main 'source' (after Thomas Taylor) was the Rev. Edward Davies's *Celtic Researches, on the Origin, Traditions & Language of the Ancient Britons; with some Introductory Sketches on Primitive Society*. This book was on his shelves; and there is evidence that he read it carefully. For this reason, and because it is less accessible than *The Anatomy of Melancholy* and the *Timæus*, I shall give a fairly detailed account of those parts of the book which influenced Keats and which therefore help us to understand him.

Davies's treatise falls into three parts. The first, *Sketches, on the State and Attainments of Primitive Society*, extends from page 1 to page 116 and comprises eight sections. The second, *Essay, on the Origin of the Celtæ: their Institution of Druidism: and their Pretensions to the Knowledge of Letters*, occupies pages 117 to 343 and is in nine sections. The third part, *Essay on the Celtic Language: in which Its Radical Principles, are Appreciated and Compared with Primitives, and Simple Terms, in Hebrew,*

---

[1] *Shores of Darkness*, by Edward B. Hungerford (Columbia University Press, 1941), is an excellent survey.

Greek, and Latin, makes up the rest of the book, from page 347 to page 561; it has six sections.[1]

The most interesting parts of the work from our point of view are the first and second. These I shall summarize in some detail. I shall not tackle the third part, which merely supports the argument of the second with etymological evidence.

2

In his first part, Davies is concerned to refute evolutionary views of man's origin (he may have had Erasmus Darwin in mind) and to uphold the tradition of a Golden Age. Section I, *The importance of distinctly marking fundamental principles,* gives us his authority: the Old Testament. It is true, he says, that the poetry and mythology of Greece and Rome 'have transmitted some interesting tales, respecting the most early times: but these, are delivered in language highly figurative, and are mixed with so much allegory, or fable, that it seems hardly possible to reduce them into fact'. This obscurity caused the chief philosophers of Greece and Rome to reject myth 'and frame new theories of their own, upon the original state of mankind'. This was dangerous, a prolific source of error. The Epicureans, for instance, rejected the idea of a first cause, 'ascribed the formation of all things to a fortuitous concourse of atoms, and consigned the government of the world into the hands of chance'.

The Epicureans believed in the slow advance of mankind from a state of savagery to civilization. They were deceived into this belief by observing the condition of modern savages in the countries subdued by the Roman arms. 'The condition of a few ancient hunters, who, as is usual in all newly inhabited countries, wandered amongst the woods, and were driven occasionally to extreme difficulties in procuring food, and lodging, was brought forwards, and was obtruded, as the general picture of original society.' This hypothesis became very popular and has been adopted and developed by modern thinkers. 'We have consequently been amused with strange, and monstrous tales of that mute, as well as ill-contrived quadruped, *Man,*—a being, who, for a series of ages, crawled upon the earth, before he began, occasionally, to assume

---

[1] Davies does not give any name (I have called them 'parts') to his three major divisions. As the third division has a title-page to itself, it may be considered a separate work. Nor does Davies give any name to his numbered subdivisions in 'Part I'. The subdivisions of the other two parts he calls 'sections'. For the sake of uniformity I have called the subdivisions of Part I sections too.

an erect posture, and walk upon his hinder feet; who afterwards made slow progress through the monkey, and the savage, *accidentally* acquired *speech* and reason; till at length, forming himself into a kind of terrestrial God, he established a dominion over his brethren of the forest.' While few people in Britain would give full support to these notions, there is no doubt, Davies says, that a great many are taken in by them to some degree. This is inexcusable: for the evolutionary theory is not only derogatory to the dignity of human nature, but also contrary to the facts about the origin of mankind as they are recorded for us in the Old Testament. Even philosophers who reject the Scriptures as the oracles of God, admit their authenticity in matters of early history. From now on Davies will take the books of Moses as his prime authority.

In the next few sections Davies seeks to prove that the antediluvians were in possession of the arts and crafts of civilization. Adam was created a rational being endowed with the faculty of speech. His two elder sons were respectively a tiller of the ground and a keeper of sheep: this shows that the principle of the division of labour was already known and applied. In the fourth chapter of Genesis we learn of the discovery of several arts. 'Thus, the first inventor of stringed instruments kept sight of the general principles of music, and the scale of harmonious sounds, till, by analogy, he had found out the nature of wind-instruments: and, by repeated efforts of genius, he became *the father* of all such as handle the HARP and the ORGAN. The first artificer in brass pursued the same course, till he had likewise developed the nature and proper management of iron ore.' We have to remember too that these men lived to an age of six or seven hundred years, and thus had ample time to carry out prolonged experiments and improve their inventions. Hence, we see, '*the state of nature*, or the original state of man, was not that of brutes and savages, but a state of immediate mental exertion, and of rapid progress in civilization, and the acquisition of useful arts'.

What of the theological notions of primitive man? Davies is emphatic here. The antediluvians were not polytheists. 'They regarded One Being as supreme over all the world of spirits, acknowledging at the same time that there were other spirits, endowed with many of his attributes, though under his controul, and employed in the execution of his commands. But in their forms of expression, at least, they were seldom careful to discriminate between the One, Eternal, Universal

Spirit, and his created ministers.' There were prophets and holy men long before the flood, Davies tells us. These mediated the Divine revelation. In doing so they had to speak the language of men; and in the sacred writings we read of God 'walking in the garden in the cool of the day', or of 'going down' to the earth 'to see' what was going on. But this merely 'affords a proof, that in all ages the Almighty revealed himself in a manner which might be level to the capacities and comprehensions of men. A more spiritual and adequate revelation of his nature might, at this period, have been totally unintelligible, and consequently useless.'[1]

Davies thus holds the view of a progressive revelation, which is itself a kind of modified evolutionism. He is bound to do this, of course, on the evidence of the Old Testament which is his prime authority. But the necessity is plainly an embarrassment to him. One may suggest that if he could have used the scriptures of some less anthropomorphic religion than Judaism his argument would have been considerably strengthened. For every admission that the capacity of primitive man was in any respect lower than that of modern man is a blow, though not a serious one, to his original thesis.

The divine revelation, which Davies believes to have been much fuller than is expressly stated in the Pentateuch, extended to the smallest details of moral and ritual law as well as to the subtleties of theology. The institutions of Moses were merely a 'renewal of a primitive and universal law'. Traces of such a *dharma* are to be found among many widely dispersed nations in China, Africa, Mexico and the South Seas. 'They are part of the stores of the antediluvian world transmitted by the patriarchs to their posterity.'

The antediluvians were skilled in natural science. In the Book of Job, which Davies considers one of the most ancient in the Old Testament, 'we have observations upon the characters, dispositions and habits of several animals, such as the wild goat, the hind, the wild ass, the unicorn, the peacock, the stork, the ostrich, the horse, the hawk, the eagle, &c. and these observations are closely connected and intimately blended with those religious and moral sentiments which had constituted the wisdom of *the former age*. They must have descended together. And this may induce a belief that the study of nature had, in a peculiar degree, attracted the attention of the early generations'.

---

[1] Keats's point of view in the opening paragraph of *The Fall of Hyperion* II and *Letters*, 336. See above, p. 253.

Astronomy, too, had reached a high state of perfection. The patriarchs were acquainted with the solar period, and they 'had the use of cycles, by which their defective years were adjusted to the course of nature'. The later Egyptians ascribed these inventions to their own ancestors—which claim can be admitted, says Davies, if we realize that the antediluvians were the common forefathers of mankind.

The Egyptians claim the Epagones, and the accurate computation of time, as inventions of their own ancestors. .... The first Thoth [identified with Hermes Trismegistus], amongst other things, calculated the annual period. We learn from Manetho, the celebrated Egyptian historian, who relates the genuine traditions of his nation, that this Thoth lived *before the flood*. For he left his discoveries engraved upon certain columns, in the *sacred Dialect*, and in Hieroglyphick Letters (where we may observe by the way that hieroglyphicks, in *any particular dialect*, were Hieroglyphicks representing elementary sounds) and, *after the deluge* (another) Thoth (or philosopher) the son of Agathodemon (Osiris or Mizraim) *transcribed* these inscriptions into books, and placed them in the sanctuaries of the Egyptian temples. ... What discoveries do the Egyptians boast of, which were not originally derived from the Great Thoth? Those ancestors of the Egyptians, who so eminently distinguished themselves, were then antediluvians, and consequently the common parents of all other nations.[1]

The Egyptians had '*years*', Davies goes on, of six, four or three months. 'They may have divided the annual *Circle* into seasons, by inscribing some of their geometrical figures, as the *line* or the *triangle*, or else the square, touching at the 4 cardinal points. Still the complete circle remained the same.' The antiquity of this computation is confirmed by evidence from the Old Testament which Davies brings forward in detail.

In his fourth section, *On the Antiquity of Writing*, Davies argues for a primitive possession of the alphabet. The Book of Job refers to writing as an art long established. If it should be asked why in that case we have no mention of its inventor in Moses' catalogue of 'antediluvian instructors', the answer is that the Mosaic account is 'a mere epitome'. Davies is not uniformly credulous. He notes the different stylistic strata in Genesis, and concludes that that book is a compilation from more ancient documents.

---

[1] I have given this extract at some length because I think that Keats read it and was impressed by it. See above, pp. 153, 237.

Section V, *Conditions of men in primitive society*, returns to a general consideration of primitive man but along an important new slant. It discusses, among other things, the question of hierarchy. Was antediluvian society a genuine democracy? Were the Rights of Man known and insisted upon? Some 'late theorists' have put forward this notion. But Davies can find nothing to support it. Even in the most savage nations of the present day, authority and subordination are recognized. The family is a hierarchy; and the family was instituted in Eden. The structure was patriarchal. But when great kingdoms and states began to be formed among the antediluvians, a monarchical system was evolved. In subsequent chapters Davies traces the dispersion of the various communities—at first a mixture of patriarchal and monarchical—over the face of the earth. The disaster at Babel was (following the flood) the starting point of this dispersion, and the wicked Nimrod its instigator. Not all the families of the earth joined with Nimrod, however, and Davies is careful to point out that the Egyptians kept aloof. They stood firm in the patriarchal tradition.

A discussion of the Hyksos or Shepherd-kings of Egypt follows. 'Egypt was governed by a Shepherd about 430 years before the Exode. The king entreated Abraham well, and gave him *Sheep*, and *Oxen*, and *He asses*, and *She asses* and *Camels*. Kings display their munificence by bestowing *estimable* things, such as constitute the riches of their country.' Unfortunately Davies's subsequent paragraphs, which attempt to link the Bible account of the Egyptians with the ancient books of the Hindus are based on the 'learned tract *On Egypt*, by Lieut. Wilford' which is itself based on false translations palmed off on Wilford by his Hindu 'pandits'.

A general feature of ancient tradition, Davies now tells us, is the existence in all lands of a race of giants, who are not related to the ordinary inhabitants but are considered 'detested strangers'. 'Universal tradition must be referred to some universal circumstance or event.' These giants lurk in caves, in forests, among rocks and desolate places, practising sorcery and diabolical arts. Davies thinks they are the descendants of the original companions of Nimrod, who were men of great strength and stature and married only with women of similar physique. 'Sanchoniathon, speaking of those people who were dispersed from Babel, says, "These are the people who are described as *Exiles* and *Wanderers*, and at the same time are called the Titans".' They are, Davies says, the same who are spoken of in the Book of Job as driven forth 'to dwell in CLIFFS of the VALLIES, in CAVES of the earth and in the ROCKS. Among the bushes they BRAYED, under the nettles they were gathered together.' Here, Davies thinks, we have a picture of savage life; and he concludes that our present-day savages descend from these degenerate though muscular creatures. The speculation is a daring one; but to our minds the quotation from Job may have a more immediate interest in recalling the first and some later paragraphs from *Hyperion*.

Section VII need concern us little: it is a lengthy discussion of the question, Is Hebrew the Primitive Language? The conclusion of the matter is that Hebrew is not the primitive language but a dialect of it. In his eighth and last section Davies returns to the theme of the dispersion after Babel. The unrebellious families no doubt began to move outwards towards those portions of the earth's surface which had been allotted to them after the flood. 'So that in an age or two after the first partition, every region of the known world, which was adapted to the support and comfort of human society, must have received that germe which gradually expanded into its primitive nation: and thus Spain, and even Britain were probably colonized by those who were born within a century of the deluge.' Societies thus planted, whether in Britain or in Japan, must have carried with them the primitive tradition. Memories of the punishment of the rebellious 'Titans' would dispose 'the fathers of the more regular societies, to preserve the sacred institutions of their ancestors, with the utmost care, and to fix the grand arcana of primitive wisdom upon a firm base. And to these ends, what could have been more conducive, than to constitute such regular Hierarchies, as ancient history describes in various parts of the earth—To make the wisest and most approved men, in every society, the instructors of the people, and the depositories of primitive tradition?'

Such traditions are coeval with the nation itself: it is useless for the antiquary or historian to enquire *by whom* a primitive institution was initiated. Local accounts will provide nothing worthy of credence. There is a nationalism in legends as well as in politics. The Greeks claim the Flood for Deucalion and Pyrrha and assert that the Ark came to rest on Parnassus. In Phoenician history the Almighty 'is represented as dwelling in the neighbourhood of Byblos, a city of Phoenicia, even before he had produced Heaven and Earth'. As for the Egyptians:

In the age immediately succeeding the Creation, The first Cronus (or husbandman) is attended by his Secretary Hermes Trismegistus, Thoth or Τααυτος. The author seems to use these terms as appellations for an inventor and recorder of arts and sciences; for from henceforth we find Thoth ready upon all occasions, in all places and in successive ages, delivering his advice, making inventions and committing them to writing.

He imitated [made a drawing of]¹ the Heavens [distinguished and described the constellations]. He drew the portraits of the Gods [a series of mystical symbols] of which he formed the sacred characters of the letters. And all this happened before the second Cronus (Noah) came into the Southern regions (Shinar) and bestowed the kingdom of Egypt upon Thoth.

It is amusing to note that Davies, while recording the fact that the 'theology, philosophy and traditional doctrines of all nations' are conveyed in terms of 'allegory, figurative titles and mystical symbols', also records his violent disapproval. Here of course he has something in common with Blake; but he does not distinguish, as Blake does, between *allegory*, which materializes and distorts noetic truth, and *myth* and *symbol*, which are necessary modes of its expression. Davies is a whole-hogger:

Long before the division of the nations, before Chna settled in Phœnicia or Thoth in Egypt, plain matter of fact had been converted into mysterious *Allegory, and sacred and historical truth blended with the symbols of seasons, revolutions of the heavenly bodies, and the like. This mystical doctrine was delivered to the priests who kept the key of knowledge, and who most criminally encouraged popular delusion (τόν τύφον αὔξειν ἐκ παντός ἐπινοοῦντες) studying above all things to promote astonishment and admiration. The introduction or the revival of such ænigmatical lore was, perhaps that evil IMAGINATION of man's heart which was reproved immediately after the deluge.

Davies agrees with Blake, again, in thinking that the Greeks and Romans 'had broken the chain of ancient lore'.

3

The second part of Davies's treatise discusses the origin of the Celts and the institution of Druidism. The Celts were the 'original possessors of the British Islands'—a simple people, but highly cultivated and acquainted with certain branches of knowledge not common to 'more

---

¹ All bracketed phrases are Davies's. The passage he is quoting is from Sanchoniathon, who 'is supposed to have lived 300 years before Homer' and is thus a very early authority.

polished neighbours'. The aristocracy had all the power in their hands, and the order of the Druids was recruited from men of high rank.

They were educated, with incredible vigilance and care, for the *most sacred offices*. . . . Their studies embraced those elevated objects which had engaged the attention of the world in its primitive age—The nature of the Deity—of the human soul—of the future State—of the heavenly bodies—of the terrestrial globe, and of its various productions. Their conceptions were great and sublime, their speculations comprehensive in their sphere, pervading most of the arts and sciences which had interested the earliest periods. Perhaps there was no order of men amongst the heathens, who preserved the history and the opinions of mankind, in its early state, with more simplicity, and with more integrity.

The Druids had 'a marked resemblance to . . . other sacred orders, in the most remote ages and countries'. Their 'general and close analogy to the *Magi* of *Persia* . . . almost constituted identity. . . . Pliny calls the Druids the *Magi of the Gauls and Britons*'. Affinities have also been noted between the Druids and the Brachmans of India,[1] the Chaldeans, and the Orphic priesthood of Thrace. Since all this cannot be coincidental, the question arises: How were the institutions and customs of the Eastern world imported into the West of Europe?

In fact, says Davies, they were not. The inhabitants of Britain had these characteristic institutions from the first—that is, from the patriarchal age. In the tenth chapter of Genesis, 'that fountain-head of universal geography', we read how the Earth was divided up, after the Flood, among the descendants of Noah. The grandsons of Japhet[2] received the Isles of the Gentiles, or in other words 'Europe and its adjacent Islands'. The sons of Gomer were the ancestors of the Celts, as the name demonstrates: Gomeri or Cymri. Davies goes into this question in great detail, and we need not attempt to follow him in his historical and etymological 'proofs'. It is of interest, however, to note

[1] Davies is supported here by more modern authority. Mrs N. Kershaw Chadwick, in her *Poetry and Prophecy* (Cambridge, 1942), writes: 'The nearest affinities of the Gaulish intellectual classes are with the Brahmins of India, to whom in many respects they bear a close resemblance, notably in their educational system, the nature of their speculations, their forest life (doubtless for the sake of seclusion), their attention to traditional oral literature. The resemblances are so close that they can hardly have been fortuitous' (*op. cit.*, 1952 edn., p. 12).

[2] T. D. Kendrick, *British Antiquities* (1950), wittily styles him 'the first proprietor of Europe after the Flood'. Camden's derivation of *Cymry* from *Gomer* is given on p. 109 of Mr Kendrick's book.

that one of the sons of Gomer, Ashkenaz, who is perhaps the Askanios of the Greeks, settled with his tribe on the conjunction of the Euxine Sea and the Bosphorus. But this territory was never intended to be his permanent inheritance. 'It was a mere halting place upon the road.' In due course—Davies is very vague here—the sons of Ashkenaz or as they are now called 'the Conian or Kynetian family' arrived in the West of Europe and some of them settled in Britain.

But a considerable body of this people did not leave their Eastern possessions in peace [*i.e.* peaceably]. After the removal of the Centimani [another name for the Kynetian family], these remains of the Celtæ were distinguished by the name of Titans. They had perhaps been joined by the real *Titanian Celtæ, Celto-Scythæ*, or those branches of the Celtic family who had assisted in building the tower of Babel, and had been compelled, at the dispersion, to follow their brethren.

The tales told by ancient poets of the wars of the Gods and the Titans really refer to the struggles of the Celts remaining in the east of Europe against neighbouring nations. A footnote tells us that 'It was in the character of a Titan that *Japetus* "married *Asia*", or that, in other words, a branch of his family *took possession* of the small district, anciently known by that name, which comprehended little more than *Phrygia*, and a part of *Lydia*. The *first-born son* of this marriage was *Atlas*, or the eldest branch of the family were *Atlantes*. Atlas was the General of the Titan army against *Jupiter*.'

A predecessor of Davies in Celtic studies, Mr Granville Penn, is now called in to lend the weight of his authority. Penn has demonstrated that Celtic terms are preserved in the Orphic Hymns, 'and quotes the following authorities, in which the Titans are acknowledged as the old Inhabitants, and which prove, that, in them, we find the parents of the Celtæ'. These authorities are excerpts from the Hymns, in the original Greek and in translation:

> TITANS, illustrious sons of Earth and Heav'n,
> Our *Sires' Progenitors*—

> Against the Greeks, then shall a future race
> Of TITANS, pouring from the utmost *West*,
> Raise the barbaric sword and CELTIC war.

These Titans, it seems, were driven out from Asia Minor into the West of Europe. 'Apollodorus, correcting authors who had written before

him, concerning the *Hesperides*, directs us to look for Atlas, not in
Lybia, but amongst the Hyperboreans', who were identified with the
Celtæ.

Section II deals with the 'Antiquity of the Druidical order, amongst
the Celtæ'. The name Druid is not known outside Gaul and the British
Isles. Britain was the centre of Druidism, and 'many sons of the nobles
in Gaul were sent hither to finish their Education'. But irruptions of
the Belgæ and later the Roman invasion drove the Druids 'from their
ancient, magnificent seat at Abury, and from their *Circular, Uncovered*
Temple on Salisbury Plain, in which the *Hyperborean* sages had once
chaunted their hymns to Apollo, or *Plenyz*', into the recesses of Mona.

'A mysticism similar to that of the Druids' was prevalent in Western
Europe among other branches of the Celtic family. The sixth book of
the *Æneid* shows that Virgil was well acquainted with certain 'doctrines of pure Druidism'. A branch of mistletoe is carried by his hero
as a talisman in his descent into Hades. Again, 'all the accounts of
Orpheus agree with Druidism: and we could expect no less; for the
Celtæ or Cimmerii were the first inhabitants of the country in which
Orpheus flourished, and some of them continued their abode, in the
same region, till this renowned character was no more'.

It would be tedious and unprofitable for our present purposes to
go into all Davies's arguments for the antiquity of Druidism and the
identity of the Welsh with the descendants of the 'Noachidæ'. His
discussion of the primitive character of the remaining monuments of
Druidism—'their Cromlechs, their Logans, the rough pillars that are
still found, as well in Britain, as upon those parts of the Continent which
the Celtæ once occupied'—and of the Druidical custom of measuring
time by nights instead of days, is not without interest, but is perhaps
more relevant to an understanding of Blake than of Keats. Davies is
an extremely diffuse and repetitive writer; his book is totally lacking
in structure, and appears to have been put together from a mass of notes
with no conception of order and development. He rarely repeats,
however, without adding something that is new, and it will be necessary for us to follow his exposition a little farther.

The Druids, Davies tells us, were not inventors. Their business was
to preserve and to expound the traditions of the past. 'Their method
of instruction was by *symbols* and by enigmas, or dark allegories, by
ancient songs, and maxims orally delivered, and in private; but which
they deemed it unlawful to reduce into writing, or communicate out of

their own pale.' Some examples of these maxims are given from the Welsh Triads, which tell, among other things, of 'The three awful events of the Island of Britain', including 'the consternation of the tempestuous fire, when the Earth was split asunder, to Annwn (the lower region) and the greatest part of all living was consumed'; and of 'The three chief master works of the Island of Britain', the last of which is 'the stones of Gwyddon Ganhebon, on which were read the arts and sciences of the world'. These triads 'consist of such allegories, or *ænigmata*, as *Druids* are known to have employed, in teaching their disciples. Thus the three primary *bards*, or *Druids*, *Plennydd*, *Alawn* and *Gwron* . . . are, in their literal import, *light*, *harmony*, and *energy*.' The triads tell us too of a God of the Druids whose worship extended well into Christian times. 'He is thus described by *Rhys Brydydd*, in the fifteenth century.

> The smallest, if compared with small,
> Is the *Mighty Hu*, in the world's judgment,
> And he is the greatest, and Lord over us,
> And our God of mystery:
> Light is his course, and swift:
> *A particle of lucid sunshine is his car*[1]:
> He is great on land and seas,
> The *greatest* whom I shall behold—
> Greater than the worlds—Let us beware
> Of mean indignity, to him who deals in bounty.'

Davies goes on to stress the links between British Druidism and the mythologies of Greece and eastern Europe.

The names of the early British princes, under whose rule Druidism was regularly established, are themselves connected with mythology. '*Prydain*, from *Pryd*, which is *Time*, *Season*, *Due time—Beauty*, *Comeliness*, and from *Ain*, a *source* or *principle*—seems to have been primarily designed as an epithet of the *sun—Father of beauty*—and *principle of the seasons*.' Druidism was a religion of sun-worship. Astronomers flourished in early Britain. 'Of those great astronomers, the first named is *Idris the giant*, whose memory is perpetuated by one of the highest and most pointed mountains in *North Wales*, called *Cader Idris*, the *chair*, or *keep*, *of Idris*. It may, perhaps, have been an observatory, in ancient periods. On the very summit, we are told there is an excavation in the

---

[1] Davies's italics. The line would seem to identify him with Apollo.

solid rock, resembling a couch, and it is pretended that, whoever should rest a night in that seat, will be found in the morning, either dead, raving-mad, or endued with supernatural genius.' The passage may remind us of Keats's plea to be allowed to spend his solitude on 'the steep—Nature's observatory'[1] and of his quite frequent references to moments of inspiration caught on cliff or mountain summits.[2] Davies goes on to identify Idris with the prophet Enoch, with the Titan Atlas, and with Hermes Trismegistus.

A long discussion now follows on the Hyperboreans. This mysterious race, which 'revered the sacred places, the Gods, and the religious rites of ancient *Greece*', and to which 'in return, *Greece* confessed her obligation for some objects of her own worship', was reputed to dwell in the North of Europe, as the name suggests. The land of the Hyperboreans was, according to ancient writers, 'a large and fruitful island, in the ocean, lying to the *North*, off the coast of *Gallia Celtica*'. This island could be no other than Britain. Thus the Druids were the Hyperboreans, who 'brought their gifts to *Apollo*, in the *Vale* of *Tempe*, down to the last ages of *Paganism*'. Davies proves all this by a comparison of the historical references and of the characters of the Druids and the Hyperboreans. Both held 'piety, inoffensive as well as peaceable conduct, and fortitude', as their chief moral maxims. More than this, it was from Britain that the worship of Apollo was carried to Delos, as Herodotus tells us. 'The legitimate *Apollo* of *Grecian* worship is, therefore, an accredited *Hyperborean*.' It comes as almost an anticlimax, after this, to learn that Davies agrees with Milton that Pythagoras derived his wisdom from Britain and that 'the philosophy of *Greece*, originated in the *Celtæ*'.

The Druids were, according to Davies, a contemplative order. Their teachings related to the spheres of existence or being and to man's journeyings through these spheres. To make these points clear a somewhat lengthy excerpt will be necessary.

Druids divided the whole of existence into three *circles*, or *spheres*. 1. *Cylch y Ceugant*, The *circle of space*, which none but God alone can pervade. 2. *Cylch yr*

---

[1] Sonnet, *O Solitude! if I must with thee dwell.*
[2] Cf. *Sleep and Poetry*, 49–52:

> Should I rather kneel
> Upon some mountain-top until I feel
> A glowing splendour round about me hung,
> And echo back the voice of thine own tongue?

Abred . . . " *The circle of courses* ", which comprehended the material creation, and the condition or state of humanity. 3. *Cylch y Gwynfyd*, the *circle of happiness*, which man would ultimately attain.

But most of their philosophy respected the *Abred*, or the changes and revolutions to which nature and man were exposed. That *circle of existence* embraced their famous doctrine of the *Metempsychosis*, which they reconciled with apparently ingenuous efforts, to the immortality, and the ultimate felicity of the soul. The circle of *Abred* was that, in which man, with all the works of nature, began in the *Great Deep*, or in the *lower* state of existence.—It contained a mixture of good and evil.

But man, endued with a power of choice, between the evil and the good, by the exercise of his religion—of the relative duties—of pure virtue and fortitude, could bring all the passions or propensities of his nature, to a *just balance*. This condition of man was termed, the *point of liberty*—he passed from thence, through the gate of mortality, into the circle of happiness: no more the victim of adversity, want, or death.

But if he permitted evil affections to govern and predominate, such as pride, falsehood, or cruelty; that bias would sink him down from the *circle of happiness*. Death would return him to the *circle of courses*, allotting him a punishment, in due proportion to his moral turpitude. Here the soul was to do penance in a *beast*, or in a *reptile*, or in several of them successively. From this degradation it rose, at length, and reassumed the human form. Repeated probations and corrections would, ultimately, subdue all evil propensities. The point of liberty would be attained, and the divine particle would be introduced, by death, to infinite happiness.

From Diodorus Siculus, as now quoted by Davies, we learn that according to tradition Latona was born in the land of the Hyperboreans, 'and for that reason, the inhabitants venerate *Apollo*, more than any other God. They are, in a manner, *his* priests, for they daily celebrate him with continual songs of praise, and pay him abundant honours.' The island contains a magnificent grove and a circular temple, both dedicated to Apollo. 'There is also a city sacred to the same God, most of the inhabitants of which are *harpers*, who continually play upon their harps *in the temple*, and *sing hymns* to the God, extolling his actions.' From this island the moon appears very near to the earth. The island, finally, has a peculiar name: *ynys prydain*, the island of *the regulator of seasons*.

Astronomy has reached a high point of perfection in Britain. Davies believes that a reference in the triads to '*Drych ab Cibddar*, or *Cilidawr*, the *speculum* of the *son of pervading glance*, or of the *searcher of mystery*' suggests the invention of the telescope, and along these lines he interprets also the reference in Diodorus to the apparent nearness of the moon and the visibility of certain eminences, 'of a terrestrial form', in her globe. The Hyperboreans also believed in the Magnus Annus of Plato, or cyclic theory of the cosmos. 'The music, and the nightly dance of *Apollo*, were, perhaps, pageants of *Druidical* device, to celebrate the completion of this period.'

In section III we return to the theme of the Titans. Davies repeats his assertion that when the first immigration of the Cymry into the western parts of Europe occurred, a certain number of the tribe remained behind in Asia Minor. Long before the Trojan war, the descendants of Iapetus fought with the Greeks. This struggle passed into mythology as the war of the Gods and the Titans. 'Such of them as became partizans for the cause of *Jupiter*, were led by *Cottus, Briareus*, and *Gyges*[1]—names which are evidently connected with a *Cimmerian*, or *Celtic* race, whether considered as designations of individual sovereigns, or of tribes: in which last view of them, we may describe the Titans in the terms *Cotti, Briarei*, and *Gygii*.' The defeated Titans were banished to the West, 'into the *regions* of *Pluto*, the acknowledged progenitor of the *Gauls*. Thither they were attended by *Cottus, Briareus*, and *Gyges*, to whose charge they were committed: that is, their chiefs, or their tribes, retained their names.' Davies follows their route westwards with some care; all that concerns us is that he finally supposes this second wave of Cymry to have settled in Britain. The first inhabitants had been peaceloving, and correspond to the Hyperboreans. The new colonists, a race 'who had less of scruple in their principles', were warlike, and 'forced their way into many possessions of their unresisting brethren'.

4

The rest of Davies's treatise (*i.e.* the remainder of section III, and sections IV to IX, in Part II, and the whole of Part III) is devoted to linguistic and etymological discussion. This might seem to concern us very little in our study of Keats; but in fact we shall find that some of the things Davies has to say, and in particular his exposition of the Druidical tree-alphabet, have a close relation to Keats's thought. This

---

[1] This collocation is repeated by Keats in *Hyperion*: 'Cœus, and Gyges, and Briareüs' (II, 19). Davies's reiterated triad obviously stuck in his mind.

26

relation springs from the interest Keats had in the general question of sound and speech and their rôle in the primordial tradition.

The sixth-century Bards of Wales preserved many of the traditions of ancient Druidism.

> *Taliesin*, who is called *the chief of the Bards*, expressly declares himself to have been received into the order of *Druids*, and professes to inculcate several of their genuine doctrines. Many of his remaining poems treat largely on the *metempsychosis*,—the *formation of the world*, and *of man*,—the *nature*, and *first principles of things*,—or other mysterious subjects, which have been ascribed, eminently, to the order of *Druids*.

From the bards we learn that the Druids possessed a symbolic alphabet based on the characters of different trees. They had noted the strength of the oak and the trembling of the poplar leaf, and come to apply these features to men by analogy. They would say of a hero, 'He is an oak', and of a coward, 'He is an aspen leaf'. From this it was but a short step to the use of leaves or sprigs of trees in conveying general ideas. A conventional alphabet was thus formed, in which the angle of branching and the degree of ramification of the various leaves or twigs formed the principle of differentiation. This alphabet was confined to the order of the Druids and was one of their most closely guarded secrets. Taliesin boasts of having learned it:

> "I am *Taliesin*,
> Chief of the *Bards* of the *west*;—
> I am acquainted with every sprig
> In the cave of the *Arch-diviner*."

Though these lines may seem to refer to *divination* by trees only, Davies brings forward much evidence to support his theory of the tree-alphabet.[1]

In his famous poem *The Battle of the Trees*, Taliesin gives an allegorical account 'of the ripening progress of art, science, or invention.[2] We may, therefore, consider him, as personifying science, or the inventive, and contemplative principle, when he says[3]—

> "I was in a multitude of shapes,
> Before I assumed a consistent form."

---

[1] A more modern treatment of the same theme will be found in Robert Graves's *The White Goddess* (1948).

[2] Keats's 'grand march of intellect' in *Letters*, 143.

[3] I omit, here and subsequently, the original Welsh and give only Davies's translation.

Having enumerated about sixteen of these forms, he says, in the twenty-third line,

"At last, I became *trees*,"—or—"A sage."

The word *Gwydd*, when plural, signifies *trees*; if singular, *a sage*, or *philosopher*.' Taliesin proceeds to 'arm' the trees, to distinguish between their several magical properties: 'and he occasionally hints that this invention, or device [the symbolizing of the trees] was of the highest antiquity.

"I was *marked* by the Sage
Of Sages, in the primitive world."

In another poem of Taliesin's, quoted by Davies, we have this remarkable passage:

"Or the points of the counterfeited trees,
What is it they whisper so forcibly;
Or what various breathings
Are in their trunks?
These are READ by the Sages
Who were versed in science,
Or who delivered books."

The whole argument is summed up by Davies as follows:

The passages I have already adduced, may be deemed sufficient, I should hope, to explain the sentiments of the oldest *British Bards*, now extant, upon this topic; namely *that our Druids possessed a kind of alphabet, which according to their tradition, and their doctrine, was formed upon the system of their symbolical sprigs or hieroglyphics, cut, or delineated, in simple figures, so as to represent the first principles, or the elementary sounds, of their language.*

I believe that Keats read all this with interest and that some of it remained with him. He was not, of course, concerned with the pseudo-etymologies, but he was fascinated by the suggestion of magic about it all, by the mention of the sages, by the ideas of metamorphosis and hieroglyphics, and above all, by the lines of verse which speak of the whispering trees.[1]

---

[1] Peacock makes use of prophetic trees in his 'Welsh novel', *The Misfortunes of Elphin*; and compare Blake, *Milton* (K. 514):

... thou seest the Trees on the mountains,
The wind blows heavy, loud they thunder thro' the darksom sky,
Uttering prophecies & speaking with instructive words to the sons
Of men: These are the sons of Los: These are the Visions of Eternity.

EXTRACTS FROM ERASMUS DARWIN'S 'ZOONOMIA' AND 'TEMPLE OF NATURE'

I attempt no summary of *Zoonomia* or of *The Temple of Nature*: the task would be formidable, and Darwin's main ideas (so far as they are relevant) have been sufficiently expounded in my chapter on *The Botanic Garden*. The following extracts, too long to be given as footnotes, will illustrate some connections between Darwin's attitude and Keats's on the subjects of love, matter and spirit, beauty, form, and nutrition.

I. ZOONOMIA

1. I beg to be understood, that I do not wish to dispute about words, and am ready to allow, that the powers of gravity, specific attraction, electricity, magnetism, and even the spirit of animation, may consist of matter of a finer kind; and to believe, with St Paul and Malbranch, that the ultimate cause only of all motion is immaterial, that is God. St Paul says, "in him we live and move, and have our being"; and, in the 15th chapter to the Corinthians, distinguishes between the psyche or living spirit, and the pneuma or reviving spirit. By the words spirit of animation or sensorial power, I mean only that animal life, which mankind possesses in common with brutes, and in some degree even with vegetables, and leave the consideration of the immortal part of us, which is the object of religion, to those who treat of revelation.

[Section XIV, i]

2. Sentimental love, as distinguished from the animal passion of that name, with which it is frequently accompanied, consists in the desire or sensation of beholding, embracing, and saluting a beautiful object.

The characteristic of beauty therefore is that it is the object of love; and though many other objects are in common language called beautiful, yet they are only called so metaphorically, and ought to be termed agreeable. A Grecian temple may give us the pleasurable idea of sublimity, a Gothic temple may give us the pleasurable idea of variety, and a modern house the pleasurable idea of utility; music and poetry may inspire our love by association of ideas; but none of these, except metaphorically, can be termed beautiful, as we have no wish to embrace or salute them.

Our perception of beauty consists in our recognition by the sense of vision of those objects, first, which have before inspired our love by the pleasure, which they have afforded to many of our senses; as to our sense of warmth, of touch [cf. Keats's 'Touch has a memory . . .'], of smell, of taste, hunger and thirst; and, secondly, which bear any analogy of form to such objects.

When the babe, soon after it is born into this cold world, is applied to its mother's bosom; its sense of perceiving warmth is first agreeably affected; next its sense of smell is delighted with the odour of her milk; then its taste is gratified by the flavour of it; afterwards the appetites of hunger and thirst afford pleasure by the possession of their objects, and by the subsequent digestion of the aliment; and, lastly, the sense of touch is delighted by the softness and smoothness of the milky fountain, the source of so much variety of happiness.

All these various kinds of pleasure at length become associated with the form of the mother's breast; which the infant embraces with its hands, presses with its lips, and watches with its eyes; and thus acquires more accurate ideas of the form of its mother's bosom, than of the odour and flavour or warmth, which it perceives by its other senses. And hence in our maturer years, when any object of vision is presented to us, which by its waving or spiral lines bears any similitude to the form of the female bosom, whether it be found in a landscape with soft gradations of rising and descending surface, or in the forms of some antique vases, or in other works of the pencil or the chissel, we feel a general glow of delight, which seems to influence all our senses; and, if the object be not too large, we experience an attraction to embrace it with our arms, and to salute it with our lips, as we did in our early infancy the bosom of our mother. And thus we find, according to the ingenious idea of Hogarth, that the waving lines of beauty were originally taken from the temple of Venus.   [Section XVI, vi]

II. THE TEMPLE OF NATURE

 1. If the wide eye the wavy lawns explores,
  The bending woodlands, or the winding shores,
  Hills, whose green sides with soft protuberance rise,
  Or the blue concave of the vaulted skies;—

Or scans with nicer gaze the pearly swell
Of spiral volutes round the twisted shell;
Or undulating sweep, whose graceful turns
Bound the smooth surface of Etrurian urns,
When on fine forms the waving lines impress'd
Give the nice curves, which swell the female breast;
The countless joys the tender Mother pours
Round the soft cradle of our infant hours,
In lively trains of unextinct delight
Rise in our bosoms *recognized by sight*;
Fond Fancy's eye recalls the form divine,
And TASTE sits smiling upon Beauty's shrine.

[Canto III, lines 207–22]

2. Here, high in air, unconscious of the storm,
Thy temple, NATURE, rears it's mystic form;
From earth to heav'n, unwrought by mortal toil,
Towers the vast fabric on the desert soil;
O'er many a league the ponderous domes extend,
And deep in earth the ribbed vaults descend;
A thousand jasper steps with circling sweep
Lead the slow votary up the winding steep;
Then thousand piers, now join'd and now aloof,
Bear on their branching arms the fretted roof.

[Canto I, lines 65–74]

3. From this first altar fam'd ELEUSIS stole[1]
Her secret symbols and her mystic scroll;
With pious fraud in after ages rear'd
Her gorgeous temple, and the gods rever'd.
—First in dim pomp before the astonish'd throng,
Silence, and Night, and Chaos, stalk'd along;

---

[1] The Eleusinian mysteries were invented in Egypt, and afterwards transferred into Greece along with most of the other early arts and religions of Europe. They seem to have consisted of scenical representations of the philosophy and religion of those times, which had previously been painted in hieroglyphic figures to perpetuate them before the discovery of letters ; and are well explained in Dr Warburton's divine legation of Moses; who believes with great probability, that Virgil in the sixth book of the Aeneid has described a part of these mysteries in his account of the Elysian fields. . . .

Dread scenes of Death, in nodding sable dress'd,
Froze the broad eye, and thrill'd the unbreathing breast.
Then the young Spring, with winged Zephyr, leads
The queen of Beauty to the blossom'd meads;
Charm'd in her train admiring Hymen moves,
And tiptoe Graces hand in hand with Loves.
Next, while on pausing step the masked mimes
Enact the triumphs of forgotten times,
Conceal from vulgar throngs the mystic truth,
Or charm with Wisdom's lore the initiate youth;
Each shifted scene, some patriot hero trod,
Some sainted beauty, or some saviour god.

[Canto I, lines 137–54]

Appendix C
EXTRACTS FROM
PLOTINUS AND PORPHYRY

The epigraph to my eighth chapter (p. 133) is taken from Thomas Taylor's translation of Porphyry's *Cave of the Nymphs*: the lines are from Homer, apparently in a modification of Pope's version, and Porphyry's charming and profound little work is a commentary on them. *The Cave of the Nymphs* is embedded in Taylor's 'History of the Restoration of the Platonic Philosophy', itself a long digression in Vol. II of his *Philosophical and Mathematical Commentaries of Proclus* (London, 1788-9). My attention was drawn to the possibility that Keats's urns, caves and honey-storing bees might owe something to Porphyry by Miss Kathleen Raine, who has long been engaged on a study of the neo-Platonic elements in the poetry of Blake. I have not been able to make up my mind decisively whether the influence is there or not, but it is quite possible that Keats came across the *Cave*, as he came across the *Timæus*, during his stay with Bailey at Oxford— or he may have been introduced to it earlier, by Coleridge. The urns and grottos of *Endymion*, the clammy cells of *To Autumn*, the imageries from a sombre loom of *The Fall of Hyperion*, may owe nothing to Porphyry's treatise in general or to Homer's lines in particular, though it is striking to note them there in so close a cluster; but when we find the stages of Endymion's descent from the heavens, through the Zodiac, with a halt in a cave of purgation in which he drinks from a cup or urn, also paralleled in *The Cave*, the coincidence may give us pause. I print these extracts without further comment. The first section of the 'Restoration of the Platonic Philosophy' contains translations of Plotinus 'On the Intelligible Beauty' and *Ennead* V, book 5. My first extract may be compared with Bailey's remark quoted above, p. 165.

1. .... Aristotle, it is well known, however he might retain some essential doctrines of his master, altered others of the highest importance, and confining himself chiefly to natural disquisitions, ascended but rarely and feebly to theological contemplations. .... (p. 216.)

2. And that which is above being, does not say I am this, nor does it determine any thing concerning its nature, nor does it tell its name, but it alone pronounces, *I am not this*, i.e. *I am nothing comprehensible and definite*. But it is impossible by this means, to comprehend its nature: since it is ridiculous to attempt to comprehend immensity itself. . . . On which account the Pythagoreans denominated him Apollo, according to a more secret signification, which also implies a negation of many. . . . (p. 244, from Plotinus, *Ennead* V, 5.)

3. Thus let us ascend higher from our intellect now purified, to intellect itself; and let us begin with the gods themselves, contemplating the intellect which they possess. For all the gods are venerable and beautiful, and endued with an inestimable gracefulness. But what is the cause of such beauty? It is intellect, energising in the most exalted manner, which produces their divinely beautiful appearance. . . . But those who are stationed in this higher world, contemplate its inhabitants possessing the whole of this divine heaven. For all things there are heaven. There the sea, animals, plants, and men are heaven. . . . (p. 255.)

Intellect itself, therefore, is the first beauty; it is total, and is every where total, without suffering a defect of beauty in any part. . . . (p. 259.) On this account being itself is desirable, because being, and beauty are the same: and the beautiful is lovely, because it is being. (p. 261.)

For beauty there, is not like that which flourishes in the superficies of bodies: but among those who do not perceive the whole, that alone which is resplendent in the superficies is considered as beauty. But those who are totally filled with the intoxicating nectar of divine contemplation, since beauty diffuses itself through every part of their souls do not become spectators alone. . . . For he who beholds any thing as external, beholds it as something visible, and because he wishes to perceive it attended with distance. But whatever is beheld as *perceptible*, is beheld externally: but it is requisite we should transfer the divine spectacle into ourselves, and behold it as one, and as the same with our essence: just as if any one hurried away by the vigorous impulse of some god, whether Apollo or one of the Muses, should procure in himself the intuition of the god; since in the secret recesses of his own essence, he will behold the divinity himself. . . . (p. 262.)

The above excerpts are from Plotinus *On the Intelligible Beauty*. Those which follow are from Porphyry's *Cave of the Nymphs*.

4. For almost all temples have their entrance and statues towards the east: but those who enter them look towards the west, when standing

with their faces turned to the statues they honour and worship the gods. (p. 279.)

After the same manner the Persians mystically signifying the descent of the soul into an inferior nature, and its ascent into the intelligible world, initiate the priest or mystic in a place which they denominate a cave. . . . But the things contained in the cavern, being disposed by certain intervals, according to symmetry and order, were symbols of the elements and climates of the world. We find too that after Zoroaster it was usual with others to perform initiatory rites in caves and dens, whether natural or artificial. . . . (p. 281.)

What then are the different symbols, some of which correspond to souls, and others to the divinities of waters, by which it may be manifest that this cave is at the same time dedicated and consecrated to both? We reply that the stony bowls and urns are symbols of the aquatic nymphs. For vessels of the same form are symbols of Bacchus; but their composition is testaceous, that is, from baked earth. And indeed such as these are correspondent to the gift of the god; since the fruit of the vine is brought to a proper maturity by the celestial fire of the sun. But the stony bowls and urns, are most admirably accommodated to nymphs presiding over waters which flow from rocks. And what symbol is more proper to souls descending into generation, and the tenacious vestment of body, than as the poet says, 'Nymphs weaving on stony beams purple garments wonderful to behold'? . . . (p. 283.)

A footnote to p. 287 of *The Cave*:

5. . . . those who are about to descend, are yet in *Cancer*, and have not left the milky way, they rank in the order of gods. But when by falling they arrive at the *Lion*; in this constellation, they enter on the exordium of their future condition. And, because in the *Lion*, the rudiments of birth, and certain primary exercizes of human nature commence; but *Aquarius* is opposite to the lion (*sic*), and presently sets, after the lion rises: hence, when the sun is in Aquarius, funeral rites are performed to departed souls; because he is then carried in a sign, which is contrary, or adverse to human life. From the confine, therefore, in which the zodiac, and galaxy touch each other, the soul descending from a round figure, which is the only divine form, is produced into a cone by its defluxion. . . .

As soon, therefore, as the soul gravitates towards body, in this first production of herself, she begins to experience a material tumult, that is, matter flowing into her essence. . . . But the starry *cup*, placed between Cancer and the Lion, is a symbol of this mystic truth, signifying that descending souls first experience intoxication in that part of the heavens, through the influx of matter. Hence, oblivion the companion of intoxication, there begins silently to creep into the recesses of the soul.

In the text we read (pp. 289, 290, 294):

6. When the star (Cancer, the Dog-star) rises they celebrate the calends of the month, which begins their year, because this is the place of the heavens where generation commences, by which the world subsists. On this account the doors of the Homeric cavern, are not dedicated to the east and west, nor to the equinoctial signs, Aries and Libra, but to the north and south . . . and this because the present cave is sacred to souls, and to nymphs the divinities of waters. But these places are particularly adapted either to souls descending into generation, or to such as are separating from it.

Again, according to Pythagoras, *the people of dreams* are souls, which are reported to be collected in the milky way; the appellation of which is derived from souls, nourished with milk after their lapse into the whirls of generation.

In this cave therefore, says Homer, all external possessions must be deposited; here, naked and assuming a suppliant habit, afflicted in body, and casting aside everything superfluous, sense too being averse from needless possessions, it is requisite to sit at the foot of the olive, and consult with Minerva, by what means we may most effectually amputate and destroy that hostile rout of passions, which lurk in the secret recesses of the soul.

INDEX